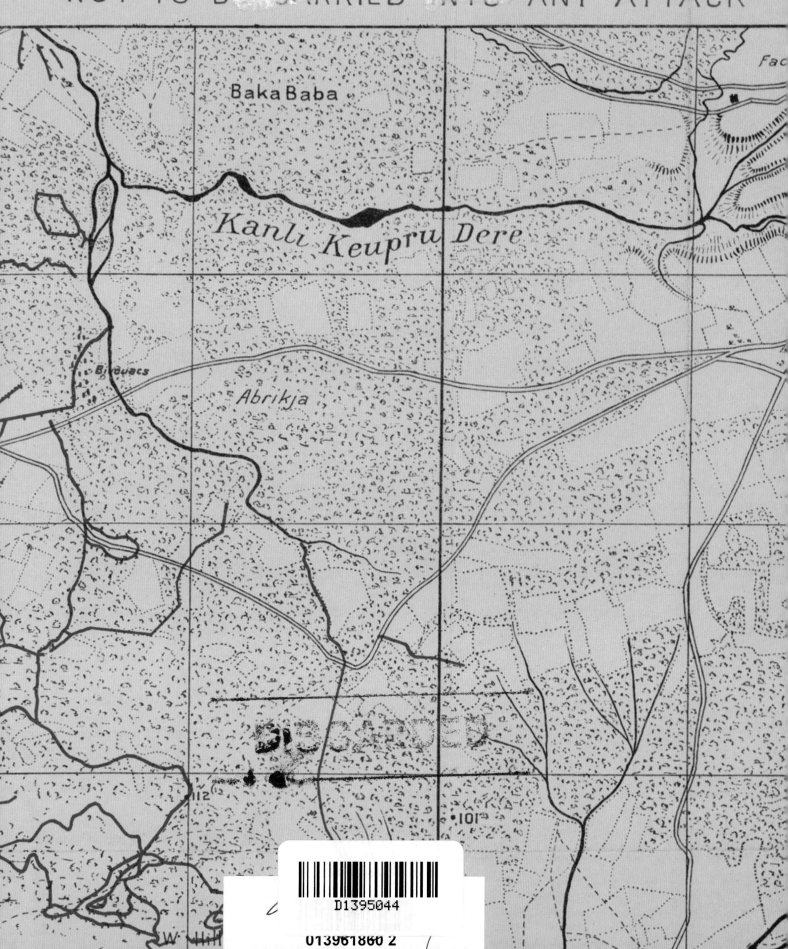

BakaBaba

Fac

Kanli Keupru Dere

Bivouacs

Abrikja

DISCARDED

112

101

MAPPING
THE FIRST WORLD WAR

MAPPING THE FIRST WORLD WAR

Published by Collins
An imprint of HarperCollins Publishers
Westerhill Road
Bishopbriggs
Glasgow G64 2QT

In association with
Imperial War Museums
Lambeth Road
London SE1 6HZ
www.iwm.org.uk

First edition 2013

British Library Cataloguing in Publication Data
A catalogue record for this book is available from the British Library

ISBN 978-0-00-752220-0
Imp 001

If you would like to comment on any aspect of this publication, please write to:
Collins Maps, HarperCollins Publishers, Westerhill Road, Bishopbriggs, Glasgow G64 2QT
e-mail: **collinsmaps@harpercollins.co.uk**

Visit our website at: **www.collinsmaps.com**

Search Facebook for 'Collins Maps'

Follow us **@collinsmaps**

With special thanks to

FRONT COVER IMAGE: Australian officers and men on a duckboard track through the shell-blasted remains of
Chateau Wood, Hooge, east of Ypres, on 29 October 1917. This had once been a picturesque area of sundappled
greenery, close to the chateau and its decorative gardens, ponds and lake. © Imperial War Museums E(AUS) 1220
BACK COVER IMAGE: See page 233 © Imperial War Museums

MAPPING
THE FIRST WORLD WAR

Peter Chasseaud

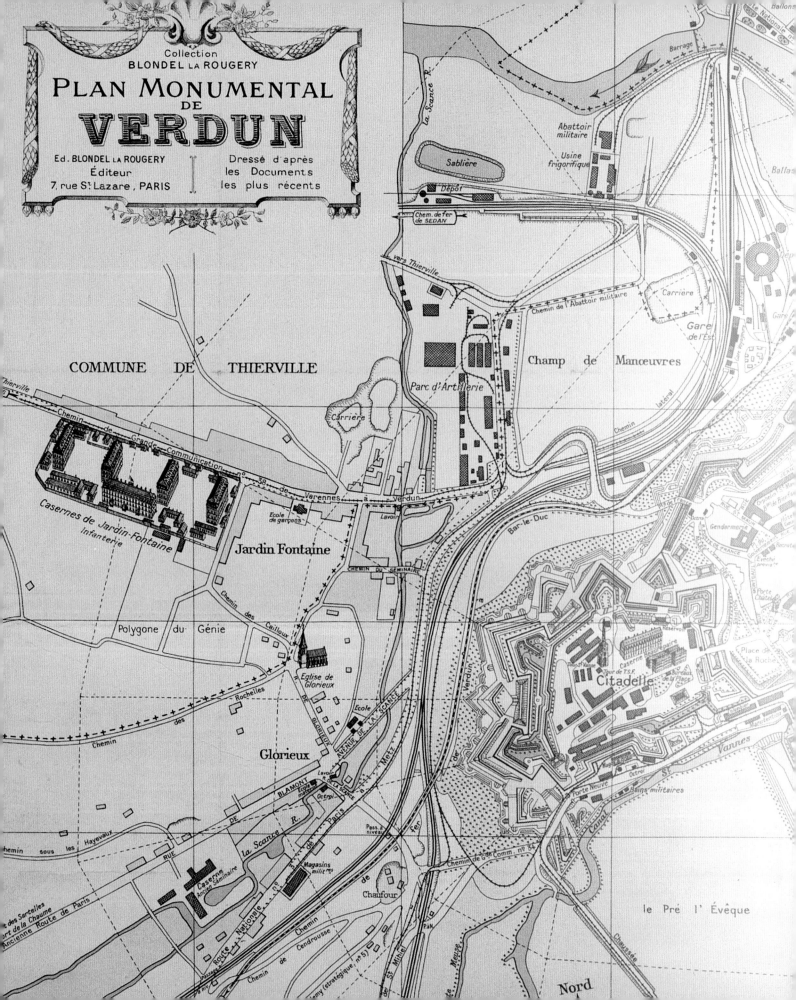

Contents

The Map Collection of the Imperial War Museums

The Imperial War Museum, or National War Museum, as it was originally named, began to acquire maps and charts as soon as it was founded on 5 March 1917 to record the events still taking place during the Great War. The intention was to collect and display material as a record of civilian and military experiences during that war, and to commemorate the sacrifices of all sections of society.

Maps and charts were acquired by direct contact with the appropriate military and civil departments of government, and also by private donation, both during and after the war. In addition, maps produced and used by the Allies, and also captured maps and other enemy maps, found their way into the archive.

Many of the maps and charts had been used in military, naval and air headquarters in London and in the various active theatres of war. Their condition naturally varies a great deal: some are stained with mud and blood, and scarred by shell-splinter or bullet. None such is shown here, but several bear evidence of their field use in the form of manuscript annotations for enemy positions, intelligence notes, tank routes, etc. One of the most tragic reminders of the human cost of the conflict is the 'body count' map of the Ypres Salient by the Imperial War Graves Commission at the end of the war, which appears at the end of the book.

Mapping in the First World War

There is a compelling view of the Western world in the years immediately before the outbreak of war in 1914 that, rather than a sunlit Edwardian (and Georgian) earthly paradise of prosperity and stability, it was an increasingly hysterical vortex of accelerating tensions and violence. God was dead or dying; man was becoming superman. Neo-Darwinist philosophies of action and doctrines of the necessity of the violent cleansing action of war vied with those extolling the new technologies of motor cars, aeroplanes and speed. In philosophy, politics and the arts, Nietzsche and nihilism, anarchism and syndicalism, modernism, imagism, cubism, futurism and vorticism all aimed to shatter bourgeois complacency and proclaimed the need to destroy in order to build a new society. The Newtonian equilibrium was destroyed; Einstein had promulgated his special theory of relativity. Like Nijinsky's dancers in Stravinsky's *Le Sacre du printemps* (*The Rite of Spring*), the jerky motion of the cinematograph contributed to the sense of fracturing. Yeats, in the aftermath of the next few years, was to write: 'Things fall apart; the centre cannot hold; Mere anarchy is loosed upon the world . . .', and Eliot his elegy for civilization, *The Waste Land*.

The neurotic envy and militarism of Germany's Kaiser Wilhelm led to the naval race with Britain, while the scramble for Africa aggravated imperial rivalries and took them to the brink of war. In France, Georges Sorel was creating a violent, anti-democratic, proto-fascist movement, and Henri Bergson was promoting anti-rationalism. In Britain women were clamouring for the vote, the workers for higher wages, the Irish nationalists for home-rule and the Ulstermen for no-surrender. In 1914, as Sinn Féin, Irish Republican Brotherhood and other nationalists, and the Ulster Volunteers drilled and armed, British army officers at the Curragh barracks, outside Dublin, prepared to mutiny in support of Ulster. The prospect of war in Ireland loomed larger in people's minds than the assassination of some obscure personage in the Balkans. Germany supported Austria–Hungary in her desire to crush Serbia, despite Russia's known support for Serbia, and France's for Russia. Europe rushed headlong towards catastrophe.

Yet on other levels, peace and prosperity seemed assured. Populations, particularly urban populations, were growing, and cities were expanding. Electric trams and buses, as well as suburban railways, were serving the growing suburbs. The middle classes were thriving, playing tennis, mowing lawns and trimming hedges. National and international tourism had extended from the traditional 'grand tour' of the aristocracy and gentry to the professional and even lower-middle classes, and this phenomenon was accompanied by the necessary maps and guidebooks – Murray's, Baedeker's, and others. Railway and road maps were used for getting about, for work and for recreation activities – including fox-hunting for the wealthy and leisured classes – while amateur yachtsmen learned to read charts.

In the late nineteenth and early twentieth centuries, mass literacy had become common in Europe and other developed parts of the world, through state-sponsored elementary, and sometimes secondary and higher, education. In these areas, more people could read and could also, having studied geography, 'read' maps, which they were exposed to in many forms – particularly the newspaper map. They learned to locate themselves on the map, to orientate it, to understand the meaning of scale and conventional signs, and to recognize ground forms from hachures and spot-heights. Urban inhabitants became walkers, ramblers, climbers and *Wandervögel*, and contributed to the demand for maps of rural areas. The late nineteenth century had seen a cycling boom and, while car ownership was extremely restricted, the early twentieth century was the start of the motor (and flying) age, and special map editions were produced for all of these. In Britain, map-reading of a sort was taught in the Boy Scouts and Girl Guides, public school cadet units (the Junior Branch of the Officers' Training Corps), the Territorial Army and other organizations.

The great expansion of map use was aided by new map-printing technology. In the eighteenth century and earlier, maps were engraved onto copper plates and laboriously printed by hand on a 'rolling press'. The invention of lithography by Senefelder at

RIGHT: A simplified British *Diagram of the Systems of Triangulation in Northern France and Belgium* used by the British on the Western Front. *Report on Survey on the Western Front*, 1920.

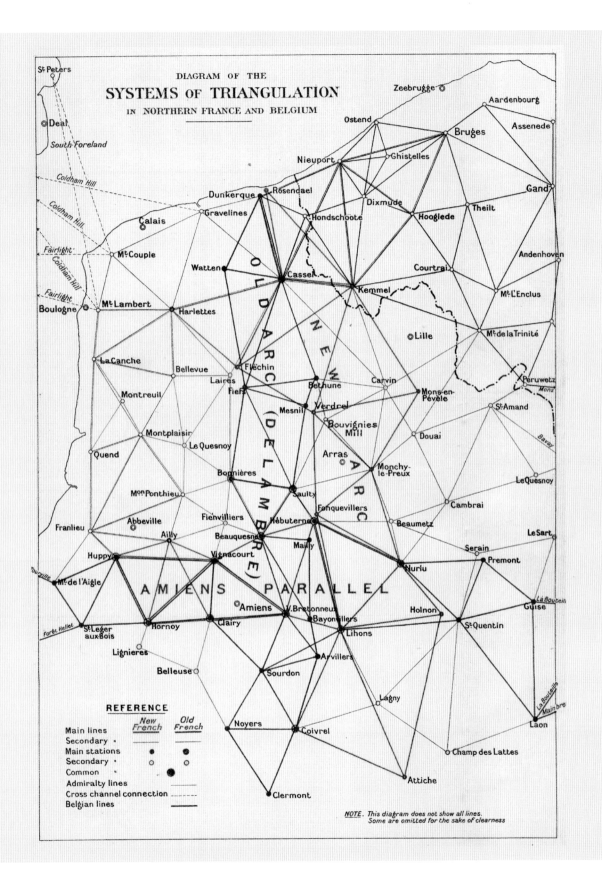

DIAGRAM OF THE
SYSTEMS OF TRIANGULATION
IN NORTHERN FRANCE AND BELGIUM

REFERENCE

	New French	Old French
Main lines		
Secondary		
Main stations	•	◉
Secondary	∘	⊙
Common	●	
Admiralty lines		
Cross channel connection		
Belgian lines		

NOTE. This diagram does not show all lines.
Some are omitted for the sake of clearness

the end of the eighteenth century led in the nineteenth century to the mass production of cheap maps. Instead of painstaking engraving on copper, lithographic draughtsmen now drew the map directly onto the printing stone, or onto transfer paper from which it was laid down onto the stone. Sheets could be printed rapidly by hand, so productivity increased and prices fell. The process was speeded up even more by the introduction of powered presses, and also by photo-mechanical processes for plate-making, and rubber blankets for 'offset' printing, which resulted in larger print-runs. Maps were no longer only for polite society; they were now popular maps, for everyman (and woman). Commercial map printing had really taken off. In Britain, among the principal publishers were G. W. Bacon & Co., W. & A. K. Johnston, Edward Stanford, George Philip & Son and John Bartholomew & Co.; in France, Taride and Michelin; in Germany, Justus Perthes, Karl Baedeker, Paasche & Luz and Dietrich Reimer.

The First World War was an industrial war, a war of material. Not for nothing did the Germans call the Somme battle the *Materialschlacht*. Mass production extended to maps. Millions of military maps were produced during the war, augmented by huge numbers of commercial maps, for politicians, statesmen and diplomats, for military, naval and air commanders and their staffs, for junior officers and NCOs (and occasionally every man in a sub-unit), for administrators and planners, industrialists and businessmen, newspapers and the general public. These totals represented an amazing variety of different types of maps – world, national, topographical, naval and air charts, military maps (artillery, trench, traffic, going, etc.), propaganda, newspaper and commercial maps showing the war situation, and so on.

The newspaper map, usually simple and crudely drawn, particularly in wartime, had much in common with the propaganda map, which was subject to various conscious and unconscious distortions, just as the newspapers themselves acted (and still act) as vehicles for the political and ideological views and prejudices of their proprietors and their political associates. Maps were published before and during the war which were overt exercises in propaganda. Governments set up their own departments to control and manipulate information, and propaganda maps were issued to newspapers and also published as posters which could be stuck up

LEFT: A manuscript 1:20,000 plane-table sheet of a back area near British GHQ in France, surveyed by a corporal of the Royal Engineers in 1918. These sheets were compiled together, on a framework of trigonometrical control points, to create map sheets of the regular series. This one carries the French Lambert grid adopted by the Allies in 1918.

where they would be seen by large numbers of people – even in the trenches! Propaganda extended to maintaining the morale of the armed forces, as well as blackening the reputation of the enemy. Both sides printed maps claiming to represent the war aims of their opponents, and their own 'legitimate' claims and successes. Particular emphasis was placed on aiming propaganda at neutral states – for example at the USA before she entered the war in 1917.

The war, in every country, saw the mobilization of civil and quasi-governmental organizations like the Royal Geographical Society (RGS) in Britain, many of which had in any case enjoyed close relationships with government before the war. In Britain there were close links between government, military and naval intelligence, the Ordnance Survey, the RGS, the Palestine Exploration Fund and other bodies. There were significant overlaps of personnel and, when it came to the need to expand wartime recruitment, the 'old boy network' came into its own. Public schools, London clubs and 'society' ensured that the right people slotted into the survey and mapping jobs. The situation was similar in other countries.

All the Great Powers had their official survey and mapping institutions serving the needs of the state and the army. In Paris the *Service Géographique de l'Armée*, in Berlin the *Königlich Preußische Landesaufnahme*, in Vienna the *k.u.k. Militärgeographische Institut*, in St Petersburg the Military Topographical Section of the General Staff. The image of generals conferring in rooms whose walls were papered with maps, poring over map-covered tables, expressing their plans with confident sweeps of the hand across the map, drawing bold arrows to push their cavalry 'through the G in Gap', long pre-dated the First World War but remains emblematic of that conflict.

Map printing had enormously speeded up during the nineteenth century with new printing methods and technology, and the application of power to presses (*The Times* newspaper was first printed by steam power in 1814, a century before the outbreak of the First World War). These changes had increased print-runs from the hundreds produced using hand processes to many thousands using powered direct and offset lithographic presses. All the Great Powers had their national military and civil mapping organizations, their general and admiralty staffs, and their famous civilian map-publishers, all of which were equipped with the capability to originate and print millions of maps. While armies at first only took hand lithographic presses with them into the field, they soon realized the need for mass-production equipment, sometimes, in the case of the Germans and French, in printing trains. Towards the end of the war the Americans were printing maps using lorry-mounted rotary litho presses.

Novel methods of distribution were deployed in some cases. In the latter part of 1918, over a million British 'propaganda' maps showing the position of the advancing Allied front line, together with messages promising good treatment to surrendering German soldiers, were printed at GHQ in France and dropped by balloon or from aeroplanes over enemy-held territory in France and Belgium.

The Military Map

'A map is a weapon . . .'
Lieut.-Col. E. M. Jack RE ('Maps' GHQ, 1914–18)

Before the days of balloons, airships, aeroplanes and aerial photography, let alone satellites, drones, electronic intelligence and remote sensing, the topographical map enabled the commander to form a mental picture of the terrain and, to some extent, to see to 'the other side of the hill'. The ability to read the map was crucial, as was some system of intelligence to provide him with information about the enemy's order-of-battle, defences, location, movements, intentions, etc. In the absence of good, existing mapping, Wellington, in Spain, sent out his scouting officers to make the maps (topographical and terrain intelligence) and to gather operational intelligence on the enemy. This intelligence was transferred to the map, as was similar information about one's own forces, and the plans for battle were made on the basis of this map. This was the case during the First World War, and also the Second. While modern operations planning is a lot more sophisticated, and can call on hitherto unknown technologies, the essence is the same. Such knowledge may be power, if the information is correctly processed, distributed and acted on.

The fundamental framework of the topographical map was the triangulation network, built up from a carefully measured and orientated base-line. For example, the first trigonometrical survey (which became the Ordnance Survey) of Britain began in the late eighteenth century with a base-line laid out on Hounslow Heath west of London near the present site of Heathrow Airport. Precision angle-measuring instruments – theodolites – were used to measure the angles from each end of the base to a series of distant, but easily identifiable, points, such as church spires. This process, known as intersection, fixed the position of these points. Theodolites would then be set up on these points (a hair-raising business) and the angles to yet more points measured. In this way a network of triangulation would extend to cover the whole country, supplemented by astronomical observations to check position and azimuth (bearing from true north) and levelling data from benchmarks to provide spot-heights and contours.

ABOVE: British 8-inch howitzers of 39th Siege battery RGA in Caterpillar Valley on the Somme, summer 1916. Indirect fire required careful survey, to fix the positions of the battery and its targets, and to provide an accurate line-of-fire.

RIGHT: A graphic depiction of battlefield geometry for the artillery; a French *canevas d'ensemble*, showing trigonometrical points and *directions repères* (bearings marked on terrain features and used by the artillery for picking up an accurate line-of-fire).

Once this network of triangulated points was created, the large triangles were broken down in to smaller ones and the detail within each triangle filled in by chain survey (measuring at right angles from the side of a triangle) or plane-table survey (angular observations plotted directly onto a field sheet on a horizontal board which was mounted on a tripod). These methods were all used during the First World War, but the great leap forward was the use of aerial photographs to provide some of the control points and much of the detail. The process of plotting or 'restituting' detail from the air photograph to the map was known as aerial photogrammetry (measuring from photographs), and was used for all trench maps, artillery maps and, indeed, any large-scale map of the enemy's (and sometimes one's own) territory which required tactical and operational detail to be added.

Battlefield Geometry: Guns, Grids and a 'Revolution in Military Affairs'

In dry and technical terms, a topographical map may be described as a two-dimensional representation of a three-dimensional part of the Earth's surface, which implies a projection of some sort. However, it is perhaps better considered as a picture or model of the landscape or terrain which enables the user to grasp its features and land-forms, and their relationship to the user and to each other. The spatial relationships between points are formalized through their underlying relative coordinate positions in a three-dimensional matrix, comprising, for example, latitude, longitude and height above datum, or, to put it another way, x, y and z coordinates. For surveying and military purposes before and during the First World War, Descartes' x and y coordinates, with a specified origin and orientation, together with height data (z), based on a chosen datum, were generally used by all participants.

Geographical coordinates are a way of defining positions on the Earth's surface. Claudius Ptolemy (AD 90–168), the Graeco-Roman mathematician, philosopher, geographer, astronomer (he used Babylonian astronomical data) and astrologer of Alexandria in Egypt, was the first person known to have used the concepts of latitude and longitude to do this. Map projections are systems of converting the spheroidal surface of the Earth to a flat plan, and projections vary according to the intended use. For example, Mercator's projection, being orthomorphic, does not distort angles, so is adopted for sea and air navigation. Courses can be

ruled as straight lines on the chart and then set on the compass for the helmsman or pilot to follow.

Topographical maps have proved vital in war, particularly, in the twentieth century, for artillery work. The First World War has often been described as an artillery war, and for scientific gunnery maps had to be as accurate as possible. Their underlying and invisible spherical trigonometry and triangulation were made visible in the form of a grid and a dense network of fixed points. For laying out lines of fire, grid north supplanted magnetic north, as the vagaries of compass bearing were replaced by the certainties of bearing pickets (or the French *directions repères*, lines of measured bearings actually marked on terrain features) and astronomical observations, and orthomorphic projections were introduced which maintained shape or bearing. All these techniques facilitated the widespread adoption of the gunnery technique of 'predicted fire', which enabled a barrage to be opened with a crash without previous registration of targets. This is why

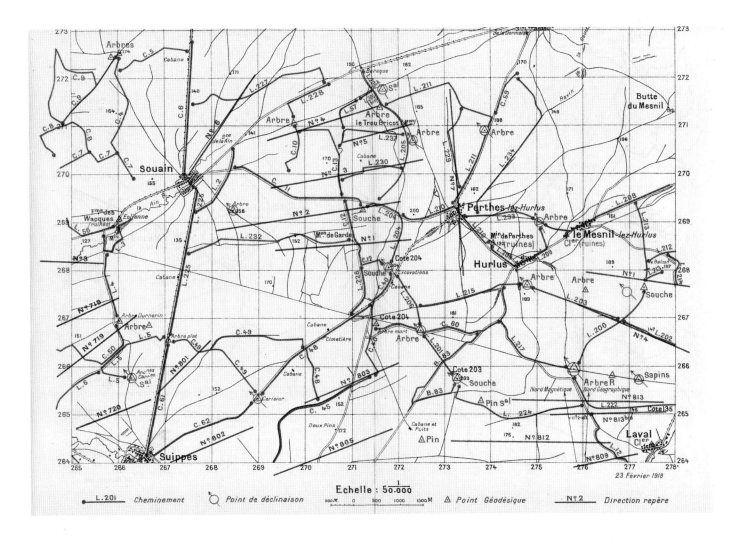

L.201 _Cheminement_   Q _Point de déclinaison_   Echelle : 1/50.000   △ _Point Géodésique_   N°2 _Direction repère_

COORDONNÉES RECTANGULAIRES DES POINTS TRIGONOMÉTRIQUES
(Système Lambert)

DÉSIGNATION DES POINTS	COORDONNÉES		ALTITUDES		OBSERVATIONS
	X	Y	SOMMET	SOL	

Feuille Chemin-des-Dames (1/20.000ᵉ)
Points Géodésiques.

DÉSIGNATION DES POINTS	X	Y	SOMMET	SOL	OBSERVATIONS
Monthenault, Clocher	205.399,3	306.683,3	193,8		
Chamouille, Moulin	205.037,5	305.475,7	172,7		
Bouconville, Château de la Bôve	211.448,0	305.150,6	206,5		
Craonnelle, Moulin de Vauclerc	212.345,7	300.940,0	211,0		
Verneuil, Tilleul	202.579,1	299.504,9	159,7		
Pont-Arcy, Clocher	202.372,3	296.500,0	68,8		
Beaurieux, Clocher	210.165,0	295.960,5	133,4		
Maizy, Clocher	210.083,2	293.705,0	105,2		
Perles, Clocher (sommet)	203.697,2	288.732,8	178,5		
Baslieux, Clocher	207.890,9	288.563,1	127,1		

Points déterminés par le G. C. T. A.

DÉSIGNATION DES POINTS	X	Y	SOMMET	SOL	OBSERVATIONS
Oulches, Clocher, coq	210.897,0	299.834,0			
Paissy, Clocher	207.398,1	299.606,2			
Moulins, Clocher	206.523,9	299.157,5			
Vassogne, Tourelle	209.430,9	299.040,8			
Verneuil-et-Courtonne, Clocher	203.017,5	298.935,8			
Blanc-Sablon, Bouleau-repère (pancarte)	212.492,7	298.933,8			E. du plateau triangulaire.
Cote 100, Cerisier (pancarte)	209.985,1	298.800,3			N.-E. de Jumigny.
Blanc-Sablon, Sapin-repère (pancarte)	212.019,6	298.650,6			S. du Plateau triangulaire.
Vassogne (S. de), Piquet nº 23	209.094,5	298.629,6			
Paissy, Tour	208.244,6	298.581,5			Dent de la tour ruinée.
Cote 175, Sapin-repère	204.237,6	298.196,8			Près de l'observatoire d'artillerie.
Jumigny, Axe du Clocher	208.695,3	297.967,7			

the surveyors were called by the gunners 'the astrologers'. A new battlefield geometry was thus created, in which the trigonometrical framework was amplified by new control points, hachures were replaced by surveyed contours, all batteries and targets were fixed to the survey grid, and surprise restored as a principle of war. Maps and survey became part of an integrated modern weapons system, which in turn constituted a revolution in military affairs.

The First World War was, more than any previous conflict, a war of maps. Millions were printed during the war, as is shown at the end of this introduction. Every country was equipped with appropriate maps for a war of movement, but the rapid emergence of trench warfare changed the nature of the conflict and therefore of the nature of the required survey and mapping; position warfare implied precision shooting on pinpoint targets, and artillery survey became paramount, particularly for

the predicted fire which reinstated surprise as a key factor in successful operations. Paradoxically, the shock effect of a 'crash' concentration required less accuracy. Most survey work was done, directly or indirectly, for the artillery, and as a leading British survey officer (M. N. McLeod) noted, 'In the battles of 1918 the gun was king and the theodolite and plane-table its unadvertised but indispensable ministers.'

In August 1914 all participants entered the conflict with stocks of small- and medium-scale maps with small staffs for distribution but, as the nature of the impending war had only partially been divined, practically no survey support during operations. While France and Germany had envisaged the need for large-scale maps and survey operations for the capture of enemy frontier fortresses, they were not prepared for the semi-siege operations that became the norm. Britain had not prepared in any serious way for siege

ABOVE: Order of the Day issued by Lt.-Col. B. F. E. Keeling RE, commanding 3rd Field Survey Company RE, after the Cambrai battle, communicating the thanks of General Byng, Third Army's Commander. The Company carried out artillery survey and enemy-battery-location work, as well as map production, printing and distribution.

RIGHT: From the pamphlet *Director Stations* prepared, printed and issued by 4th Field Survey Company RE, on 20 June 1918, to help the artillery to set a precise line-of-fire onto their dial sights.

LEFT: Battlefield geometry in numerical form. List of coordinates of trigonometrical points issued for the use of the artillery. This list was produced by the *Groupe de canevas de tir* of the French Sixth Army, in the Chemin-des-Dames sector, 1917.

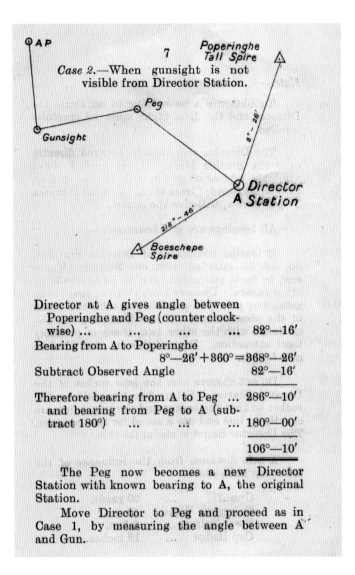

Case 2.—When gunsight is not visible from Director Station.

Director at A gives angle between Poperinghe and Peg (counter clockwise) ... ... 82°—16'

Bearing from A to Poperinghe
8°—26'+360° = 368°—26'

Subtract Observed Angle   82°—16'

Therefore bearing from A to Peg ... 286°—10'
and bearing from Peg to A (subtract 180°) ... ... 180°—00'

106°—10'

The Peg now becomes a new Director Station with known bearing to A, the original Station.

Move Director to Peg and proceed as in Case 1, by measuring the angle between A and Gun.

---

warfare, and had to adjust more to the new situation. The crucial need for such operational support – particularly artillery survey and air survey – immediately became apparent, and each country began to build up a field survey organization commensurate with the operational requirements.

A key aspect of the survey revolution was aerial photogrammetry – plotting detail from air photographs. This was realized by both sides as soon as the war changed from movement to static conditions in the late summer and autumn of 1914. From the moment the Germans dug their first trenches on the Aisne heights in mid-September, the Allies had to acquire photographic cover of the concealed zone behind the German front trench, where artillery batteries, trench mortars, rear defences and transport and reserves were located. As defence systems proliferated, this need became more intense, for intelligence,

artillery survey and mapping purposes. Both sides rapidly developed aerial photography and struggled to devise or adapt methods and technologies for rapid and accurate plotting from air photographs.

The geographical products of the survey organizations included line maps, photo-maps, plans, sketch maps, trigonometrical lists, air photographs (vertical and oblique), horizontal (terrestrial) stereo photos, panorama photographs, drawn panoramas, hostile battery position and target lists, artillery (battery) boards, etc.

Taking British military maps as an example, the basic large-scale topographical map was used as a background for the overprinting of tactical and administrative information. The most obvious tactical overprint was that of the trenches themselves, both British and German. For the years 1915–17 most British maps, for security reasons, only showed German trenches. British trenches only appeared on 'secret' editions, of which tiny editions were printed, mostly for staff use; front line troops rarely saw them. Other significant overprints were 'hostile battery positions', 'barrage', 'situation', 'target' and 'enemy organization' maps. It was important to show all aspects of the enemy defensive and offensive preparations, so that operations schemes could be worked out, barrages and neutralizing fire planned, and tanks and infantry would know the exact position and nature of the enemy dispositions. On a scale as large as 1:10,000, which was the most common for infantry and field artillery, these tactical features, down to individual machine gun and trench mortar emplacements, could be indicated with precision.

Techniques were developed for plotting topographical and tactical detail onto the map, with great accuracy, from aerial photographs. The map was itself the result of the refinement of survey techniques over four years of war, the most important parts of the process being the harmonization (not seriously undertaken until 1918) of the pre-war trigonometrical systems of France and Belgium by the British survey staff, the compilation of cadastral and other large-scale plans onto this trigonometrical framework, the plotting of additional detail from aerial photographs, and the coordination of existing levelling systems and ways of depicting ground forms.

Many parts of Europe, however, and most of the rest of the world, were not covered by accurate, large-scale mapping. In these areas, including the Ottoman Empire and Africa, the enlargement of small-scale maps, or painstaking compilation of new maps from a multitude of sources, had to be undertaken. These sources included map archives, boundary commission reports, Admiralty charts, explorers' and travellers' route surveys and notes, and official but clandestine surveys such as those by the 'pundits' of the Survey of India across the frontiers into Afghanistan and other neighbouring territories. There were parts of Arabia (the 'empty quarter') and Africa which were barely mapped.

In this context, military surveys during the First World War made a useful contribution to the mapping of certain areas, and some of those maps, particularly those compiled from aerial photographs by the British 7th Field Survey Company in Egypt and Palestine, and by the Tigris Corps mapping organization in Mesopotamia (Iraq), represented a notable advance in the mapping of those territories. For example, Map TC4, issued to troops with Tigris Corps Operation Order No. 26 dated 6 March 1916, was compiled from old pre-war small-scale maps of the river, Royal Engineers reconnaissances, air reports and sketches of the ground inland.

Survey, map compilation and printing organizations were created and expanded on all fronts as the war continued. Again

ABOVE: German aerial photograph of Fort Moulainville taken on 13 March 1916, during the early stages of the Verdun battle, showing the quality and clarity of photographs used for tactical mapping and intelligence.

TOP RIGHT: Aerial photograph of Bois-en-Hache sector, Vimy Ridge, taken while snow was lying on the ground in early 1917, showing how clearly trenches and other detail show up. Snow also made it easy to identify barbed wire entanglements, distinguish used from unused trenches, and showed blast-marks from active batteries.

BOTTOM RIGHT: A sector-shaped German *Batterieplan*, or artillery board, adopted by the German gunners at least nine years before the war. On it the pivot gun at the battery position was plotted at the narrow end, and a zero line drawn from this through a zero point (e.g. a church spire) in the centre of the battery's arc of fire. Range and bearing to any target was read off the board, using a pivoted rule and a graduated arc. The French adopted a similar method, and the British picked it up from the French. The trench map was often pasted onto the board's grid in squares (to avoid distortion), providing more detail.

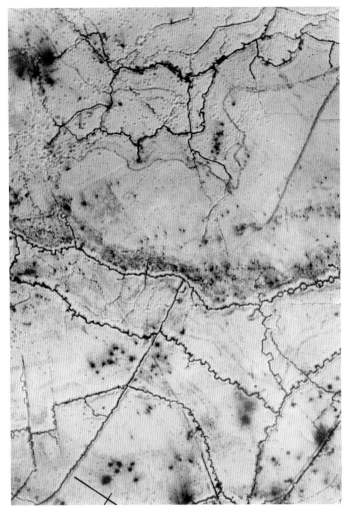

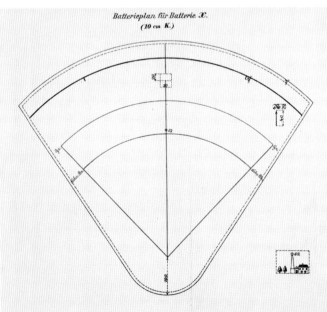

Batterieplan für Batterie X.
(10 cm K.)

taking Mesopotamia as an example, as air cooperation improved, and in order to provide the army with maps of the completely unsurveyed enemy-occupied areas, a Map Compilation Section was provided by the Survey of India in June 1916 to support the attempt to relieve General Townshend's force at Kut. As the work of the Section rapidly increased in its technical aspects and operational value, it was more closely linked with GHQ and the RFC, and a Survey Directorate was created in early 1917 to bring all aspects of mapping under one control. Between June 1916 and November 1918 the Map Compilation Section printed 931,441 maps, covering between 103,840 and 143,983 square miles (the sources disagree) at various scales. Of this area, 2,263 square miles, and 120 map sheets, were mapped from air photographs. At the larger artillery and tactical operations scales of three-, six- and twelve-inches to the mile, 180,211 copies were printed in up to three colours.

As with munitions and other forms of war work in a time of manpower shortage, women were brought in to assist with map production, particularly in the Ordnance Survey at Southampton and its out-station, the Overseas Branch (OBOS), in France. They were mainly employed in feeding paper from the high 'feedboards' of the lithographic printing machines into the grippers which took the sheets around the cylinder and onto the inked stone or zinc plate carried on the reciprocating bed of the press.

Some Military Survey and Mapping Organizations

All belligerents entered the war supplied with small-scale, ungridded, topographical maps of the expected area of operations. Soon, as trench warfare and artillery fire predominated, it was realized that accurate, large-scale, gridded maps (1:20,000–1:25,000), with tactical intelligence plotted from air photographs, were essential for the planning and control of indirect artillery fire. These had previously only been prepared for the attack and defence of fortresses. Although their pre-war general staffs had sections responsible for maps and survey, all belligerents now had to improvise field survey organizations to create and print large-scale maps, to conduct the necessary surveys and to provide the essential firing data for the artillery. Meanwhile the existing national survey departments rapidly responded to the new requirements by producing enlargements of existing maps.

France

French military survey and mapping came under General Bourgeois, *Chef du Service Géographique de l'Armée* in Paris. At the end of October and in November 1914 he ordered the creation of Artillery Board Detachments (*Groupes de canevas de tir des Armées*, or *GCTA*) from the '*brigades géodésiques*', which were created

before the war for the heavy batteries used when besieging German frontier fortresses. They began the production of gridded war *plans directeurs* from compilations of all available large-scale map material augmented by detail plotted from air photographs. They also carried out artillery survey, fixing the positions of their own and enemy batteries and providing accurate line-of-fire data. A GCTA was provided for each army in the field, and these were soon supplemented by *Sections topographiques des corps d'armées*, and similar mapping units for infantry divisions. The GCTAs made rapid progress in flash-spotting, sound-ranging and aerial-photo interpretation. At the end of 1915 they introduced the Lambert orthomorphic projection and grid, and by the end of 1916 this was in use on all their maps. Ideal for survey and artillery work, this preserved bearing, while the theatre grid ensured that all batteries, observation posts, sound-ranging microphones and targets were fixed relative to each other, enabling range and bearing to be rapidly calculated.

Britain

British field survey and mapping was coordinated from the start by Major E. M. Jack RE ('Maps' GHQ), in collaboration with Colonel W. C. Hedley RE at GSGS, War Office and Colonel Sir Charles Close RE at the Ordnance Survey. The British sent their first Royal Engineers survey unit, the 1st Ranging Section, to France in November 1914 to locate German batteries by theodolite intersection of smoke signals dropped by aircraft over the target. This Section started large-scale mapping in January 1915, and was renamed the 1st Ranging and Survey Section in April 1915. In mid-1915 it was divided into three Army Topographical Sections, which also absorbed the Army Printing Sections which had been created between March and May by the 1st Printing Company of the Royal Engineers which had accompanied the BEF to France in August 1914. These Topographical Sections became Field Survey Companies (FSCs) in February 1916 when flash-spotting and sound-ranging sections (previously under the artillery) were added.

From mid-1916 there were five FSCs, one for each army, and from early 1917 they were equipped with powered lithographic presses for map printing, to supplement their hand presses. In early 1917, Corps Topographical Sections were formed, and also a Depot Field Survey Company. In 1918 the FSCs were officially enlarged into Field Survey Battalions, although in practice this had

LEFT: Reproduction of Secret German Map. Hill 60 and Observatory Ridge. 1:5,000. German trenches red, British blue. A very elegant map, packed with intelligence, of a critical sector of the Ypres Salient, July 1916.

occurred in 1917. At the end of the war, total BEF survey personnel numbered nearly 5,000.

In late 1917, when U-boats still threatened to disrupt map supply, an Overseas Branch of the Ordnance Survey was set up in northern France, and in 1918, as the German offensives began, this began to print large quantities of maps. The Ordnance Survey at Southampton had previously printed topographical and trench maps for the BEF and for other fronts. The Belgian Bonne Projection and sheet-lines were used, but a most unfortunate reference grid was superimposed which did not fit the sheets and was unrelated to the trigonometrical grid. Towards the end of the war, however, the British were preparing to adopt the French projection and sheet-lines. Topographical Sections and Printing Sections were created for other fronts, and in most cases were merged to form Field Survey Companies (Battalions in 1918) which, as in France, were also responsible for flash-spotting and sound-ranging. The 6th FSC was in Italy, the 7th in Egypt and Palestine, and the 8th in Macedonia. The Survey of India had the main responsibility for Mesopotamia (Iraq).

Germany

The Germans initially sent detachments from their Fortress Survey Companies (*Festungsvermessungsabteilungen*) into the field to make artillery surveys and provide artillery boards (*Batteriepläne*), and these were soon supplemented by Photogrammetric and Survey Sections. Throughout the war the Germans were ahead of the Allies in photogrammetry, taking excellent terrestrial and aerial photographs and accurately plotting from these. In August 1915, following the appointment of a coordinating Director of War Survey (*Kriegsvermessungschef*), Major Siegfried Boelcke, all these units were reorganized into Field Survey Companies (*Vermessungsabteilungen*). On the Eastern and Western Fronts, Directors of Survey were appointed to army groups and armies, and survey and mapping units (*Kartenstellen*) were also created for corps and divisions. A survey weakness was the use of different trigonometrical and reference (report) grids by each army; the Germans used some twenty different trigonometrical and reference grids in the West until 1918, and never completely standardized them.

German artillery intelligence and counter-battery organization was very efficient, a plotting board section (*Messplanabteilung*) being with every artillery corps to compile all information on hostile battery positions, including the results from flash-spotting sections (*Lichtmesstrupps*) and sound-ranging sections (*Schallmesstrupps*), though these last were held back by a shortage of oscillographs.

Austria–Hungary

Austro-Hungarian military survey and mapping, under the Army High Command in Baden, was initially organized in two separate functions – War Survey and War Mapping. Both came under one head, *Kommandant Oberst des Generalstabes* Hubert Ginzl, from 16 September 1915, when a new War Survey Organization (*Kriegsvermessungswesen*) was created, growing from seven to thirteen *Kriegsvermessungsabteilungen* with armies at the end of the war, and nine independent *Kriegsmappierungsabteilungen* in the pool for work on new surveys in the Balkans and Russia. Each corps and division was later given a topographical section (*Korpsvermessungsstellen* and *Divisionsvermessungsstellen*). By 1918, military survey personnel had reached 729 officers and officials and about 4,500 men.

The main task of the field survey units was overprinting enemy defences and new topographical detail, particularly road systems, ground conditions, and the results of reconnaissance surveys. On the Italian front the Austrians used the good 1:25,000 Italian maps as a topographical base and, as with the Germans, this was their standard scale for artillery maps. Austria–Hungary, like the other belligerents, expected a short war, and had decided not to send survey personnel from the General Staff mapping department into the field, nor to make new surveys. As a result in the winter of 1914–15 the Carpathian Expeditionary Force encountered serious inadequacies in the maps of occupied enemy territory. In April 1915, therefore, they introduced photogrammetry for map revision and tactical mapping at the front. Before the war the Austrian, Theodor Scheimpflug, had pioneered air survey, using multi-lens cameras, and ground and aerial photogrammetry was widely used. In 1908 Eduard von Orel, an Austrian General Staff officer, (independently of the British Royal Engineers officer Vivian Thompson whose stereo-plotter dated from the same year), invented an automatic plotter, the Von-Orel Stereoautograph, which was later adapted for aerial photographs.

Austrian technical capability in survey and mapping was good, and modern offset lithographic printing was used for map printing.

Russia

Before the war, the Russian Military Topographical Department, with a Lieut.-General as Director, had a GHQ Staff of ten highly technically-trained officers, six officials and 156 others, and performed all astronomical, trigonometrical and topographical map production and printing for the army. There was a separate organization of skilled surveyors for field work. This was the Corps of Military Topographers, which in 1900 comprised about 300 officers and officials, plus volunteer army officers trained at the Military Topographical School. In war, Military Topographers were attached to staffs of field formations.

On the Eastern Front, the Russians used their standard topographical maps, scales and unit of length, the verst, which was about two-thirds of a mile (0.6629 miles, 3,500 feet, or 1.0668 kilometres). One (1:42,000), two (1:84,000) and three verst (1:126,000) maps were used. Half-verst (1:21,000) sheets were used for artillery work. These covered Russian Poland, a theatre of operations until the summer of 1915, after which the front moved further eastwards. They were also used by the Germans. Foreign maps were enlarged for operational use, for example 1:21,000 sheets from photographic enlargement of the Austrian 1:75,000 sheets of Galicia, on which tactical detail from aerial photographs, such as trenches, battery positions, etc., were overprinted.

Given the existence of good, large-scale surveys of Russia, and the quality of the Russian artillery, there seems every reason to reassess the dismissive British view of Russian conduct of operations in 1914–17. However, a distinction must be made between technical capability and leadership, organization and morale. In some fields the Russians were innovators. Lieut.-Colonel K. G. Guk's book, *Indirect Fire for Field Artillery*, appeared in Russia in 1882, and the Russians used and developed this technique in the war with Japan in 1904.

United States of America

Having studied operations since the beginning of the war, the American Expeditionary Force in 1917–18 selected the best elements of British and French organization and methods. The GHQ Topographical Section at Chaumont, under Colonel Roger Alexander, was a branch of General Staff (Intelligence), though under the command and administration of the Chief Engineer. Under the survey director was a technical assistant for flash-spotting and sound-ranging, the Princeton professor, Major Augustus Trowbridge. The GHQ staff comprised nine officers, including four from the Base Survey and Printing Battalion at the Advanced Base at Langres, about twenty-five miles from GHQ, where there was also a Training School. This Base Battalion provided the Base Printing Plant, Computing, Drawing and Relief Map Departments, and Stores. In each army there was a survey and printing battalion (nominally 22 officers and 750 other ranks) of three companies, and a sound-ranging and flash-spotting battalion (94 officers and 1,250 other ranks) of five companies, one for each corps.

On 1 August 1918, the First US Army relieved the Second French Army in the Verdun sector, and in the months that followed, as the Americans attacked at St Mihiel and in the Argonne, Second Army's *Groupe de canevas de tir* worked closely with the American Survey and Printing Battalion under the command of Lt.-Col. Hall. The Groupe supplied map and survey support for French troops with the First US Army and to the Americans who reciprocated with a supply of air photographs and other intelligence material. The French *Section de topographie* stayed in place, providing the Americans with trigonometrical and topographical data. Each US corps had a topographical section for mapping, while each division had four map draughtsmen. All trench and artillery maps were supplied by the French (Marne, St Mihiel and Meuse–Argonne) or the British (Hamel, Hindenburg Line, etc). American map reproduction plant, using British and American direct rotary machines, was far in advance of British and French field practice, and included mobile lorry-mounted process apparatus and rotary printing plant, some of which was lent to the British (4th Field Survey Battalion) and the French (*GCT de la VI Armée*) during the final operations.

In his post-war report, General Pershing glossed over the fact that the American forces were dependent on French and British tactical maps, and emphasized the production of intelligence maps showing the disposition and movement of enemy troops on the American front, and the truck-mounted mobile printing plants, with corps and army headquarters, which supplied fighting troops, down to company and platoon commanders, with maps just before, and during, an attack. While he noted that over five million maps were used between 1 July and 11 November 1918, he did not distinguish between French, British and American productions.

Comparative Map Production Figures

There are conflicting estimates of war map production, so the figures given here include, particularly in the Austrian case, significant variations. The UK printed 34 million war maps, France over 30 million, Germany a staggering 775 million (including the Eastern Front) of which 275 million were printed by the Prussian *Landesaufnahme* in Berlin or its outstations and about 500 million in the field by the *Vermessungsabteilungen*, Austria–Hungary between 65 and 310 million, Russia (1914–17) some 320 million, and Italy about 20 million. In operations the US army relied on British and French map production; between 1 July and 11 November 1918, the American army used over 5 million maps, mostly in the Marne, St Mihiel, Hindenburg Line and Meuse–Argonne battles.

Many of the war maps produced were topographical maps printed in the home country, with field survey unit printings (e.g. trench maps) a relatively small proportion of the total. Taking the British case as an example, the figures given by Lieut-Col. Jack ('Maps GHQ', 1914–18), and MI4 (GSGS) War Office, were:

Ordnance Survey, Southampton	21,703,798
Overseas Branch of the Ordnance Survey (OBOS)	3,111,132
War Office, London	2,149,450
Field Survey units (estimate)	7,000,000
Total (approx):	34,000,000

However, the Ordnance Survey stated that, during the war, it (including OBOS) and the War Office together printed something like 22 million maps for the armies in France and Belgium (plus maps for other theatres), while the Field Survey Battalions printed another 10 million. British production was also augmented by the Surveys of Egypt and India. And then there are printings of Admiralty charts to be considered.

These unprecedented totals of military map production, and not civilian maps, give some idea of the requirements of mass armies. They were vastly surpassed in the Second World War.

Orthography

I have retained the spelling of national and place names according to the usage during the First World War and in the various official and other histories produced in the aftermath. In general I have adopted the practice of the British, French and German official histories. To use a phrase such as 'the Ieper Salient' is clearly not just an anachronism but incorrect. It was never referred to as such; it was always, to the British, the Ypres Salient or, simply, the Salient, while to the Germans, it was *der Ypern Bogen*, to the French, *le Saillant d'Ypres*, and to the Belgians, *de Ieperboog*.

Map Scales

Large-scale (tactical) maps are those which show a small area of ground in a lot of detail on a relatively small sheet. They have a low 'representative fraction', e.g. 1:5,000, 1:10,000 or 1:20,000. Very large-scale maps (e.g. 1:500) are called plans.

Small-scale (strategic or overview) maps show a large area of ground in less detail. They have a high 'representative fraction', e.g. 1:100,000, 1:250,000, 1:500,000.

Medium-scale (operational) maps are at scales between the two extremes given above, e.g. 1:50,000.

Chapter 1

The Causes of the War

Although the First World War was triggered by a local dispute between Austria–Hungary and Serbia, its origin was an existential struggle between empires. These empires were the German Second Reich, under Kaiser Wilhelm II; the Russian, ruled by Tsar Nicholas II; the Austro-Hungarian Dual Monarchy, held together by Emperor and King (*Kaiser und König*) Franz Joseph II; and the Ottoman (Turkish), under Sultan Abdul Hamid II but with power increasingly in the hands of the 'Young Turks' of the Committee of Union and Progress. On the fringes at the outset, but drawn in by the system of alliances, were the Republican French and monarchical-democratic British Empires. While these two had been traditional enemies for reasons of proximity, religion, maritime and imperial rivalry, this enmity had faded in the face of the growing industrial, military, naval and manpower strength of Germany, which under Wilhelm II demanded its imperial 'place in the sun'. France and Britain in any case both had their own quarrels with Germany. France burned for la revanche – revenge against Germany for the loss of the provinces of Alsace and Lorraine following the disastrous Franco-Prussian War of 1870–71. Britain resented the deliberate challenge to the Royal Navy, her empire and her trade represented by Wilhelm's building up of the Kriegsmarine, and also the vain posturing of this upstart grandson of Queen Victoria.

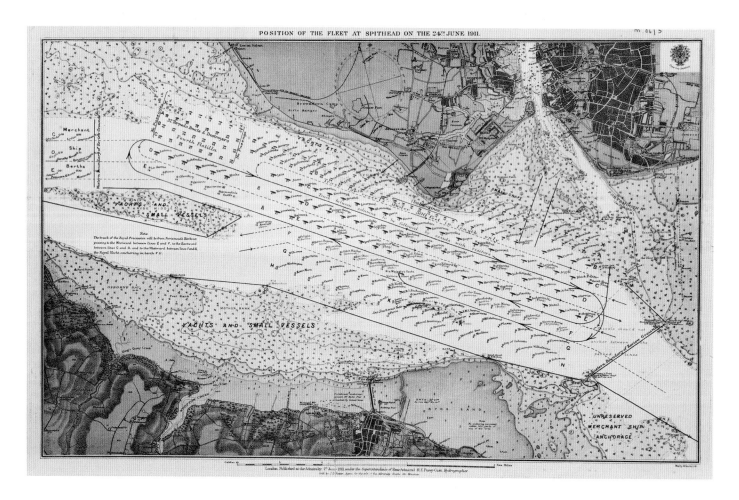

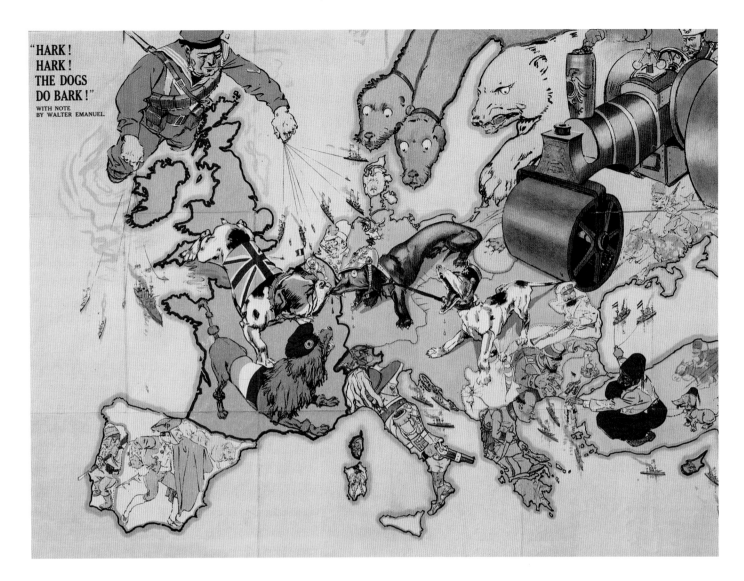

"HARK! HARK! THE DOGS DO BARK!"

WITH NOTE BY WALTER EMANUEL

The oppositional alliances had grown out of the fact that the German Reich's increasingly aggressive stance in the late nineteenth century caused corresponding insecurity in France. When William I came to the throne of Prussia in 1860, he soon began to expand the army, which had hardly changed in size since the defeat of Napoleon. Prussia had become leader of the North German Confederation following her defeat of Austria in

ABOVE: 'Hark, Hark! The Dogs do Bark.' Poster-map showing Jack Tar, Russian Steamroller, French Cock, German Dachshund, etc.

LEFT: *Position of the Fleet at Spithead on 24 June 1911.* The British fleet during a Naval review at Portsmouth, shown on a special Admiralty Chart sold to the public for a shilling. It was after such a review, in July 1914, that the Fleet was dispersed by Winston Churchill to war stations.

1866, and the states of Hesse-Darmstadt, Württemberg, Bavaria and Baden were now obliged to support Prussia if called. In the 1870–71 war with France Prussia gained Alsace-Lorraine, and with the forces of these states she was able to field some 950,000 men. On the formation of the German Empire (in which Prussia and the Hohenzollerns were dominant) in 1871, it was written into the constitution that one per cent of the population could be in military training, and by 1914 Germany's mobilization strength was about five million, with another five million untrained men.

In 1877 Germany brought Austria–Hungary and Italy into a Triple Alliance, and in 1890 France retaliated by creating an 'Entente' or defensive military understanding with Russia. Germany thereupon renewed, the following year, the Triple Alliance, and in 1899 rebuffed a mutual restriction of armaments

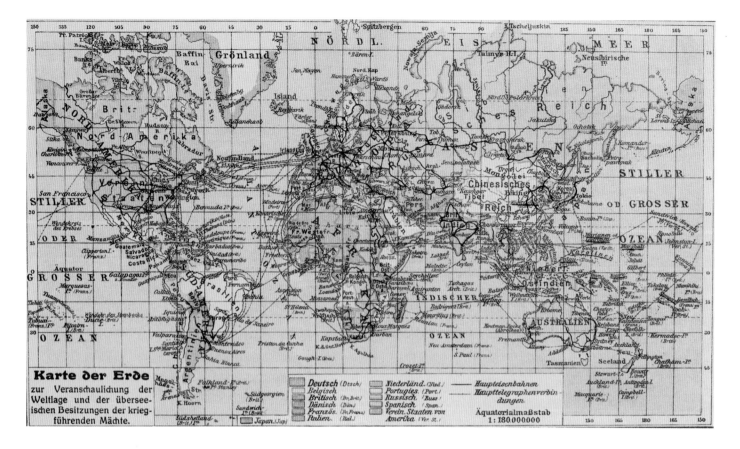

The map bears the title **Karte der Erde** with the subtitle *zur Veranschaulichung der Weltlage und der übersee-ischen Besitzungen der krieg-führenden Mächte.* The legend includes the categories **Deutsch** (Dtsch.), **Belgisch**, **Britisch** (Br.Brit.), **Dänisch** (Dän.), **Französ.** (Fr.Franz.), **Italien.** (Ital.), **Japan.** (Jap.), **Niederländ.** (Nied.), **Portugies.** (Port.), **Russisch** (Russ.), **Spanisch** (Span.), **Verein.Staaten von Amerika** (Ver.St.), — *Haupteisenbahnen*, — *Haupttelegraphenverbin-dungen*. *Äquatorialmaßstab 1:180.000000*

proposed by the Tsar. The Franco-Russian Entente was augmented, in April 1904, by a new agreement between France and Britain, which ended centuries of mutual hostility and distrust. The memory of her unpopular war in South Africa against the Boers was fading, and Britain could no longer afford her splendid isolation in Europe. King Edward VII ('Edward the Peacemaker') had broken the ice in Paris, paving the way for an *Entente Cordiale*. Russia was no longer seen as a serious threat to the Indian Empire, indeed, having just been defeated by Japan, she was temporarily a broken reed, while Germany was now viewed as Britain's major rival and threat. France, needing to look elsewhere for support, turned to Britain. The *Entente Cordiale* developed into the Triple Entente, incorporating the Franco-Russian and a new Anglo-Russian Entente.

While Belgium was not part of the system of alliances, her neutrality was guaranteed by the Treaty of London of 1839 and she was a significant imperial power. King Leopold II's greed for the acquisition and brutal exploitation of economic resources (notably ivory and rubber) and territorial expansion (notably his close involvement in the murderous 'Congo Free State') was instrumental as a catalyst in the great European 'scramble for Africa' in the late nineteenth century. The Berlin or Congo Conference of 1884–5

formalized and regulated the 'new imperialism' process of trade and colonization in Africa, and marked an acceleration of European colonial activity.

The pressures and tensions of political and economic competition and rivalries among the European powers after 1870 were reflected and contained by their transfer to a new site of conflict – Africa. The powers saw an orderly partition of Africa as a means of avoiding war with each other over African territory and resources. The old methods by which the European powers maintained hegemony through 'informal imperialism' – missionaries, military expeditions and economic penetration – gave way to outright colonization involving military occupation, annexation, administration and an enforced new economic and trading paradigm.

ABOVE: A detail from *Karte des Weltkrieges* [Map of the World War]
RIGHT: *The World, Showing German's Peaceful Penetration* (German Empire, green; *What Germany Wanted*, yellow), c.1920. An example of post-war anti-German propaganda, showing Germany's economic, trading, financial, trading, missionary and other activities.

Origins of the War

Historians sometimes attempt to disentangle the many proximate and more distant causes of the First World War by categorizing them as structural 'grand causes' on the one hand, and contingent causes on the other. In the first 'grand' category they place familiar and inter-related features of the pre-war world such as its nationalism, imperialism (attempts to maintain hegemony, competition and the scramble for colonies and empire) and economic rivalry (the struggle for markets) and the arms race, the networks of alliances which strove to maintain a balance of power, the nature of elite groups within nations (and also international elites), the structures of diplomacy, and the primacy of domestic policies which meant that international issues came to be used for internal purposes. In the second, or 'contingent' group they might include a country's or region's political history, focusing on the importance of individual agency and psychology (for example the character of the German Kaiser), the nature of the decision-making process by tiny coteries of statesmen, dominant ideology and mass psychology, and cultural traits and habits. To these two main categories could also be added 'events', or immediate causes. This is all to say that the causes were, as usual, multifarious and complex, and, whether they are theorized in terms of group conflict, games theory (rational strategies) or something else, have to be reduced here to something easier to grasp and apply.

The First World War, or Great War as it was known until twenty years later when the second such conflict grew out of the peace treaties intended to resolve the first, was initiated by the explosion of the Balkan 'powder keg of Europe'. The long and complex

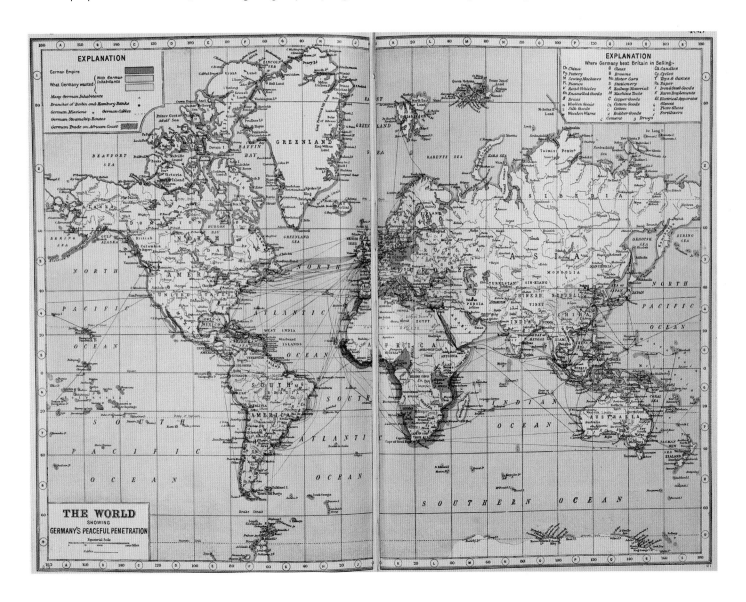

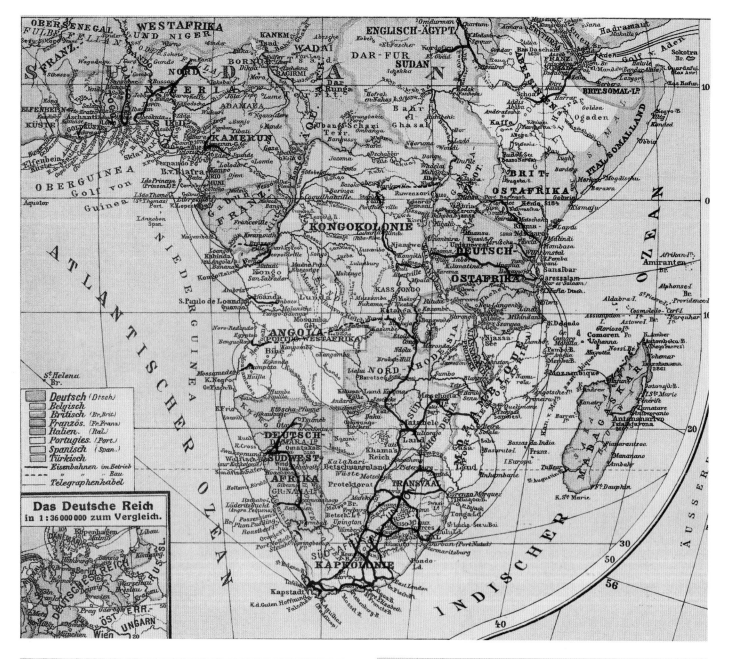

ABOVE: A detail from *Karte des Weltkrieges* [Map of the World War], showing German and other colonies in Africa. The inset shows Germany drawn to the same scale.

RIGHT: A hand-written annotation on the reverse of the map shown on the right to the effect that this was one of several maps relating to the 'nationalities' question, used by British Military Intelligence, while preparing for the peace conference at Versailles: 'used in determining Propaganda campaign and the redistribution of territory after the War on the principle of self-determination.'

OPPOSITE: *Ethnographical Map of Central and South Eastern Europe*, prepared by the War Office in 1916.

Map showing Ethnological distribution of Europe in 1918. Drawn up by M.I. War office & used in determining Propaganda campaign & the redistribution of territories after the War on the principle of self determination.

E.C.B.
M.I.3.b

ETHNOGRAPHICAL MAP OF
CENTRAL & SOUTH EASTERN EUROPE.

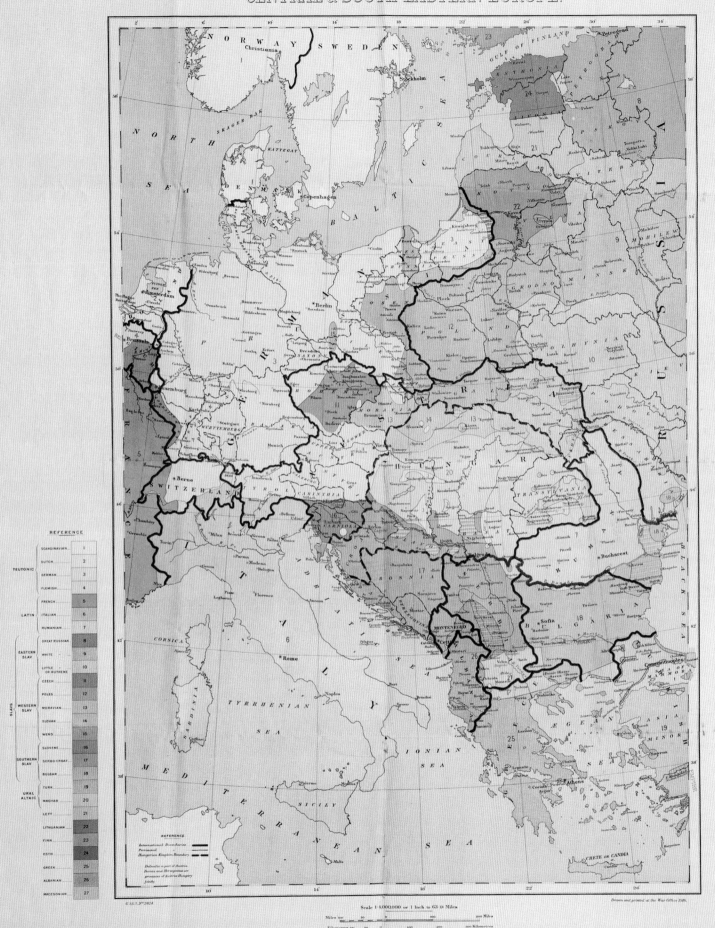

REFERENCE

TEUTONIC	SCANDINAVIAN	1
	DUTCH	2
	GERMAN	3
	FLEMISH	4
LATIN	FRENCH	5
	ITALIAN	6
	RUMANIAN	7
EASTERN SLAV	GREAT RUSSIAN	8
	WHITE	9
	LITTLE OR RUTHENE	10
WESTERN SLAV	CZECH	11
	POLES	12
	MORAVIAN	13
	SLOVAK	14
	WEND	15
SOUTHERN SLAV	SLOVENE	16
	SERBO-CROAT	17
	BULGAR	18
URAL ALTAIC	TURK	19
	MAGYAR	20
	LETT	21
	LITHUANIAN	22
	FINN	23
	ESTH	24
	GREEK	25
	ALBANIAN	26
	MACEDONIAN	27

REFERENCE

International Boundaries
Provincial
Hungarian Kingdom Boundary.

Dalmatia is part of Austria. Bosnia and Herzegovina are provinces of Austria-Hungary jointly.

Scale 1:4,000,000 or 1 Inch to 63⅓ Miles

Drawn and printed at the War Office 1916.

intertwining of national liberation struggles against Ottoman (Turkish) imperial overlords in the Balkan peninsula with the interference and intrigue of European nation states provided the slow-burning fuse which eventually blew this mine and tore apart the map of Europe and its empires.

The danger, the great 'what if?', had long been recognized, to the extent that it had been given a specific name – the Eastern Question. This question was: how could the European powers, including Russia, control the volatile and unpredictable business of national insurgence and emergence in the Balkans, in the context of a weakening Ottoman empire, without the whole process spinning out of control? How to manage the evolving situation so as to maintain national interests, without disturbing European stability and precipitating serious conflict? Perhaps, in games-theory terms, there were ultimately too many variables at work, too many fragile egos, too much emotion, too many sensibilities, perhaps too much autocracy and too little democracy, for stability to be maintained. And conflict management can only work with the consent of the parties concerned.

But other questions remain to be asked: if the Great Powers were able to 'manage' the First and Second Balkan Wars, which took place in the years immediately prior to the outbreak of war in 1914, why were they unable to control the Third? And why did this new conflict grow not just into a European War but into one of global reach? Of course, there were other factors at work in the decades before 1914 which were calculated to increase international tension, not least the three related ones of escalating industrial, imperial and naval rivalry, and also modernization, demographic and resource stresses.

Starting as a Third Balkan War, it exploded into a pan-European conflict that, because of the global imperial expansion of several European states before the war, soon spread across the world. For various reasons, the conflict brought in certain European states that were not initially involved. Some, like vultures, hovered on the sidelines waiting to pick over the corpse of empires and defeated nations, while others just waited to join the winning side. Yet more, like Switzerland, Spain, Norway and Sweden, remained neutral throughout.

During the nineteenth century, the Ottoman Empire slowly crumbled. Turkey was known as the 'sick man of Europe', and indeed at the start of that century still held large territories on the European side of the Bosphorus. Assisted by the Great European Powers, independent states were created on the principle of nationality, replacing the rule of the Ottoman sultan. Greece was the first. The Turks had dominated the Balkan peninsula since they had overrun the Christian Byzantine Empire in the second Islamic

campaign (or *jihad*) between the eleventh and seventeenth centuries. The capital of Byzantium, Constantinople (Istanbul), had fallen to them in 1453, and their armies had unsuccessfully besieged Vienna in 1529 and 1683. Ever since the fall of Constantinople, foreign powers had proposed schemes to end Turkish domination of the Balkans, but it was only when waxing Christian states began to put the Ottoman Empire on the defensive that these plans became at all significant.

Two predatory European states were the initial players in this game – Austria and Russia. After 1699, Austria conquered Hungary and Croatia, while Russia expanded southwards towards the Black Sea. By 1774, Russia had gained control of the Black Sea by destroying the Turkish navy in a long-drawn-out war. She insisted on treaty rights to intervene in Ottoman affairs to ensure 'orderly government' in the Danubian Principalities of Moldavia and Wallachia, and to act as 'protector' of Turkey's Christian subjects.

It was, however, Poland, always a prime contested area in eastern Europe, rather than Turkey, that was the ultimate victim of the aggression of Austria and Russia. In their conquest and partitions of Poland at the end of the eighteenth century, they were assisted by Prussia, another militaristic and autocratic state whose star was in the ascendant. Joseph II of Austria and Catherine the Great of Russia now planned to partition the Balkans. In this scheme, Austria would have Bosnia and Herzegovina, and part of Serbia, Dalmatia and Montenegro, while Russia would take the rest, which included Greece. Catherine's overarching idea was to make her grandson – the deliberately named Constantine – the ruler of a reconstituted Byzantine Empire in Constantinople. Catherine was prevented in this 'Greek Project' by the other Great Powers. Britain in particular, having gained an important foothold in India, was becoming concerned about Russian expansion and her possible domination of the Bosphorus, the Straits separating Europe from Asia, and the Mediterranean. Stymied in her advance on Byzantium, Catherine gobbled up the Crimea instead.

Austria and Russia, ruled by 'enlightened despots', had no interest in fostering national independence movements in the Balkans. Rather, they sought to replace the rule of the Islamic sultan by their own Christian imperial rule. The sprawling, polyglot and ethnically diverse Habsburg and Russian Empires were, as they became increasingly aware during the nineteenth century,

RIGHT: *Turkey in Europe and Greece*, from *The Advanced Atlas*, engraved by John Bartholomew, FRGS, William Collins, Sons, & Company, 1869, showing the extent of the Ottoman Empire in the Balkans at this date.

vulnerable to the doctrines of romantic nationalism and self-determination. Following the Napoleonic Wars, the Habsburgs were intensely suspicious of and hostile towards the Slav liberation struggles on their Balkan doorstep, which they perceived to be threatening the cohesion of their empire. Their role was, rather, to keep their subject peoples *Kaisertreu* – loyal to the emperor. The Russians, however, fostering pan-Slavism, saw themselves as supporters of Orthodox Christianity against the Islamic Turks.

The 'age of enlightenment', the American War of Independence, and the French Revolution with its *Declaration of the Rights of Man and of the Citizen*, and the example of Napoleon, changed not only the intellectual but also the political map of Europe and the world. Rights and nationalism proved a potent brew. Article III of the *Declaration of the Rights of Man* (1789) stated unequivocally: 'The nation is essentially the source of all sovereignty; nor can any individual, or any body of men, be

entitled to any authority which is not expressly derived from it.' In one of history's many ironies, Napoleon saw himself as embodying the will of the people, of the nation, thus creating a prototype for the great dictators, the totalitarian demagogues of the twentieth century.

For Britain and France during the nineteenth century it was a knife-edge balance between supporting Christians against Muslim despotism on the one hand, and preserving the decaying Ottoman Empire against Russian expansionism on the other. Already, therefore, in the early nineteenth century, the aspirations of any Balkan people for self-rule were constrained by the competing and conflicting interests of the Great Powers – 'a labyrinth of difficulty and complications', as the Russian Foreign Minister, Nessebode, described it in 1829.

Balkan Christians were too weak to win freedom without foreign support. Ironically, the greatest threat to Ottoman rule came initially from powerful Muslim elites in Bosnia, Herzegovina, Albania and Vidin; a set of quasi-independent beys, kapetans, pashas (provincial governors), warlords and jannisaries. In the Ottoman Empire, janissaries ('new soldiers') were selected as children from the Anatolian and Balkan Christian communities to be forcibly converted to Islam and train as the elite fighting force. While some, considered more talented, were educated to become the ruling class of viziers, as well as engineers, architects, doctors and scientists.

In the eighteenth century, Bosnian rebellions caused the Sultan serious problems. In 1803 the area seemed to a British observer to present 'a dreadful picture of anarchy, rebellion and barbarism'. As early as 1806, Christian notables in the Belgrade area (Serbia) appealed to the Russians for help against renegade jannisaries. But Russia, being preoccupied with Napoleon and fearful that any weakening of the Ottoman Empire would let it fall under Napoleon's control, did not intervene and the first Serb uprising was put down after a nine-year war. However, the second uprising, in 1815, was more successful. Napoleon being defeated at Waterloo, the Russians could put pressure on the Turks to recognize some of the Serbian demands. Miloš Obrenović, leader of the second uprising, became the *de facto* ruler. More serious uprisings were occurring at the time in Epirus (a region overlapping Greece and Albania) and Bosnia. From 1829, Serbia was effectively a separate state, but it was not accorded formal independence until the Congress of Berlin in 1878, after yet another Russo-Turkish war.

In 1821 the Greeks began their war for independence from the Ottoman Empire, which was finally achieved by the intervention of the European powers. These, favouring an autonomous Greek

state, offered mediation in 1826, and again in 1827. Refusal by the Turks initiated a classic case of gunboat diplomacy: Britain, France and Russia sent their fleets and, at the Battle of Navarino, destroyed the Ottoman Egyptian fleet. This badly crippled the Ottoman forces, but the war continued, complicated by a Russo-Turkish War in 1828–9, until a settlement was finally imposed at a London conference. In 1830 the London Protocol, signed by Britain, France and Russia, declared Greece an independent monarchical state under the protection of the European powers. Prince Otto of Bavaria, a seventeen-year-old Catholic, accepted the crown and, under the Treaty of Constantinople of 1832, the Sultan formally recognized Greek independence.

The Balkan nation states were able to emerge partly because of the inherent military and administrative weaknesses, particularly at the periphery, of the Ottoman Empire, and partly because it was in the interests of the European powers that they do so. Despite the Serbs and Greeks being defeated in bloody conflicts by Turkey by 1810 and 1827 respectively, they won independence through the support of the major powers. But the Ottomans remained the dominant power in the Balkans, centralizing its authority, modernizing its army and undertaking reforms. The rebellious Albanian, Ali Pacha, was killed, and the Bosnian beys defeated in 1831. The 'sick man of Europe' was taking a long time to die. As late as 1897, Turkish troops defeated the Greek army in battle.

The new states of Serbia and Greece suffered from savage internal divisions, embittered politics and economic weakness, and were acutely sensitive to their inferiority to the great powers. In other parts of the Balkans national movements were slow to emerge; the very concepts of Rumania, Bulgaria, Albania and Macedonia appealed to mere handfuls of activists and intellectuals. In the Danube Provinces of Moldavia and Wallachia, the failure of the Greek revolt there in 1821 led to the indigenous Rumanian boyars, or nobility, stepping into Greek shoes as elected princes, forming a potential new governing elite. In 1826 pressure from Russia forced Turkey to accept this, and in 1829 a Russian advance, almost to Constantinople, imposed military rule. Like Serbia, the provinces remained only nominally under the Sultan and they were promised 'an independent national government' in the Treaty

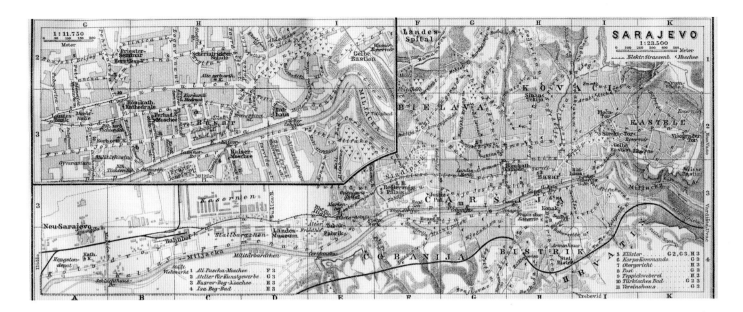

of Adrianople of 1830. But the reality of Russian military occupation caused resentment. In 1848, the year of pan-European revolt and revolution, this led to liberal nationalist uprisings; these were suppressed in joint operations by Russian and Turkish troops.

Following Russia's defeat in the Crimean War (1854–6), in which Britain, France, Turkey and Sardinia invaded Russian territory to defend Turkish interests, the French worked towards a union of Moldavia and Wallachia to create a buffer zone between Russia and Turkey and prevent a Russian expansion towards Constantinople and the Straits. In 1859 this unification was brought about, though it was not ratified until 1878 (Treaties of San Stefano and Berlin) following the Russian invasion of Ottoman Europe in 1877.

In the Treaty of Berlin, Bulgaria was granted autonomy while Serbia, Montenegro and Rumania were recognized as independent states. At the same time, Austria–Hungary occupied Bosnia–Herzegovina. In Rumania, as earlier in Greece, conflicting local elites would not accept a native head of state, and Prince Charles of Hohenzollern-Sigmaringen, cousin of the King of Prussia, was imported to found a new monarchy.

The Bulgarian Slavs, despite having developed an intelligentsia and a national cultural and economic revival during the nineteenth century, emerged as a nation state only slowly, as its closeness to Constantinople had made it easy for the Turks and the Orthodox Patriarchate to combat. Acting for the Sultan, in 1841 Albanian irregulars had ruthlessly crushed a peasant uprising. A sense of Bulgarian national identity was slow to develop, and in 1876 the Sultan suppressed one in a series of Bulgarian revolts – the 'April Uprising'. Though a failure as a revolution, the savage Turkish response – the 'Bulgarian Horrors' or 'Atrocities' – in which up to 15,000 Christians were massacred, aroused public and governmental opinion in Europe, and in Britain became the focus of an election campaign. Gladstone, after suffering an election defeat in 1874, was so angered by Disraeli's refusal to take the matter seriously that he re-entered the arena to savage both the Turks and Disraeli's government, publishing in 1876 his landmark booklet of political invective, *Bulgarian Horrors and the Question of the East*.

The Sultan rejecting international calls for internal reform, Russia invaded the Balkans in 1877 and advanced on Constantinople. Among the other clauses of the peace terms imposed on Turkey was that creating a huge, new, autonomous Bulgarian principality, still nominally paying tribute to the Sultan, extending westward to Skopje and the Vardar valley, and south to Salonika and the Aegean, thus giving Bulgaria easy access to the Mediterranean. This 'San Stefano Bulgaria', or 'Big Bulgaria', only lasted a few months as the other powers – notably Britain – perceived in it an unacceptable extension of Russian power into the Balkans, Bulgaria being in this view a Russian client state. Disraeli, at the 1878 Congress of Berlin, insisted on reducing Bulgaria's territory to less than half of that awarded at San Stefano. Turkey, as a result, regained Macedonia, including Salonika, and the new buffer state of Eastern Rumelia was created between Bulgaria and Constantinople. This, however, was soon annexed to Bulgaria, and within thirty years Bulgaria had gained full independence. But the Bulgarians never forgot the 'Big Bulgaria' promised to them by the Russians, and Macedonia in particular; the 'lost lands' became the object of their dreams of expansion.

The Bosnian crisis of 1908–9 was triggered by Austria–Hungary, with its Roman Catholic Habsburg court, which in 1908 annexed the territories of Bosnia and Herzegovina, formerly part of the Ottoman Empire, which it had already been occupying since 1878. This move antagonized Serbia, and by association Serbia's pan-Slavic and Orthodox protector, the Russian Empire. The intense Russian interest in the area led to her making political and diplomatic moves that had a destabilizing affect and weakened the will towards conciliation and peace. A key problem in Bosnia was that of conflicting models of agrarian structure. While under the feudal Ottoman system in Bosnia, most peasants were effectively serfs; they were free in the neighbouring territories of Croatia, Serbia and Hungary. Serbian nationalism was predicated on maintaining this freedom.

Gavrilo Princip, the southern Slav nationalist, was one of the anti-Austrian conspirators in the plot that resulted in the assassination of Archduke Franz Ferdinand in June 1914. He has to be seen in this context: he wanted revenge on the Habsburg Empire which he saw as having kept his fellow Bosnians in a condition of slavery. He was connected with the Young Bosnia movement, made up of Serbs, Croats and Bosnians, and his goal was to unify the southern Slavs ('Yugoslavs') in their own state

ABOVE: The arrest of the Bosnian Serb Gavrilo Princip on 28 June 1914 after his assassination of the Archduke Franz Ferdinand of Austria and his wife, Sophie, Duchess of Hohenberg, in Sarajevo.

absolutely independent of Austria. But Serbia was alarmed at the possibility that, following the imminent death of the old Emperor Franz Joseph (who had been on the throne since 1848), Austria–Hungary would grant quasi-autonomous status to the southern Slav territory. Princip and his group were totally opposed to such an Austrian creation, insisting on the need for a complete break from Austria. At the same time, while there was great tension within the Empire between Austria and Hungary over their rival social and economic visions for Bosnia's development, they were both horrified by the possibility that a 'Habsburg Yugoslavia' might develop within the Empire.

At the time of the First Balkan War in 1912, when the Serbian army was being mobilized, Princip planned to join a Serbian irregular group, or *komite*, of the secret Black Hand society (also known as Unification or Death). But, being rejected because of his lack of physique, he perhaps felt that he had something to prove. One story has it that Princip, with two others, was detailed by the head of Serbian Army Intelligence (Dragutin Dimitrijević, who was also reputed to be leader of the Black Hand) to carry out the assassination of Archduke Franz Ferdinand in June 1914. Whatever the motivations and machinations, it was the fact of the assassination which led to the international crisis of the summer of 1914, and to the war. Another story is that the Serbian prime minister was told in advance about the plot. While he was a Black Hand sympathizer, he wanted to avoid war with Austria and ordered the arrest of the three, but this order was not carried out. The changing map of the Balkans in the decades preceding 1914 may seem complicated enough, but the underlying groupings and tensions were far more complex.

The Balkan League and the Young Turks

In 1912, an anti-Ottoman alliance known as the Balkan League was concluded in the form of bilateral treaties between Serbia, Montenegro, Bulgaria and Greece. At this time, much of the Balkans was still under the control of the Ottoman Empire, which had been increasingly under pressure for the past decade from nascent national independence movements. In Macedonia there had been prolonged guerrilla warfare, culminating in the revolution of the 'Young Turks', and then came the 1908–9 Bosnian annexation crisis and, in 1911, the outbreak of war between Italy and the Ottoman Empire. This Italo-Turkish War not only weakened the Ottoman regime but encouraged the Balkan states to join together in a territorial land-grab from the Ottomans. On 13 March 1912, the Russians were instrumental in bringing Bulgaria and Serbia together, temporarily subduing their enmity,

in an alliance initially against Austria–Hungary but, secretly, against Turkey. Following this, Serbia allied with Montenegro, and Bulgaria with Greece.

In the First Balkan War, starting in October 1912, these four 'Balkan League' nations invaded and occupied most of remaining European Turkey. Salonika and its Macedonian hinterland, for example, became part of Greece in the Treaty of London, which ended the war by forcing the Ottomans to recognize the loss of their territory and dividing it between the League members. The Treaty also created an independent Albania. But the victors immediately fell out among themselves over the division of conquered territory, notably over Macedonia, and the League disintegrated. A disgruntled Bulgaria started the Second Balkan War, which lasted just over a month, by attacking her former allies Serbia and Greece on 16 June 1913, but in the subsequent peace treaty lost vast tracts of territory: Serbia and Greece gained parts of Macedonia, Rumania was awarded Southern Dobrudja, and Turkey regained Adrianople. This war led to further resentments, particularly on the part of Bulgaria.

Within the Ottoman Empire, the most significant development of the early twentieth century was the creation of the nationalist and secular Committee of Union and Progress, popularly known as the Young Turks. This reform party was influenced by European liberal principles and opposed to the absolutist monarchy of the Sultan, Abdul Hamid II. Their rebellion of 1908 was successful in establishing a new constitution, or rather re-establishing a short-lived one of 1876, which had the Sultan become little more than a figurehead (although as Caliph he remained the notional leader of the Islamic world). In 1913, at a bad time for Turkey, during the Second Balkan War, the Young Turks staged a successful coup. Their new government was led by Mehmed Talaat Bey (Minister of the Interior and Grand Vizier), Ismail Enver Pasha (Minister of War) and Ahmed Djemal Pasha (Minister of the Navy). But its policy was in fact made by the many, often dissenting, members of the Central Committee. This was the government, under increasing German influence in the immediate pre-war years, which would take Turkey into war in November 1914 on the side of the Central Powers.

Mobilization and War

On 30 June, Austria–Hungary and Germany pressed Serbia to investigate the assassination of Franz Ferdinand, but the Serbs refused. Austria–Hungary, assured of German support, on 23 July issued the 'July Ultimatum', insisting that Serbia suppress hostile propaganda, act against those responsible, arrest the conspirators and prevent arms shipments to Austria–Hungary.

Vienna would sever diplomatic relations if Serbia refused to accept within forty-eight hours. Serbia, affronted by this threat to her sovereignty, mobilized, with Russian support, on 25 July, while accepting that she should end arms smuggling, punish those who had helped the assassins and inform Vienna when measures had been taken. She refuted some of Vienna's accusations, and rejected other demands; Austria–Hungary responded by withdrawing her ambassador.

The Habsburg Emperor, Franz Joseph, now mobilized his army against Serbia and, on 28 July, declared war on Serbia. While Austria hoped to avoid war with Russia, a secret treaty between Russia and France, dating from 1892, obliged those countries to mobilize if any member of the Triple Alliance mobilized. Russia's mobilization in turn initiated full Austro-Hungarian and German mobilizations. Italy, the third member of the Triple Alliance, decided to remain neutral for the time being. Austrian guns and gunboats fired across the Danube into Belgrade and the war had begun. But was it to be a contained Third Balkan War, or a general European conflagration?

Just as Austria sought to avoid conflict with Russia, the Russian foreign minister, Sazonov, was anxious not to antagonize Germany, which he believed was seeking to use the crisis to launch a pre-emptive strike before Russia's expanding population, economy and army swamped the Reich. Germany was therefore the real danger, while Austria–Hungary was Germany's puppet. Sazonov favoured merely threatening Austria by mobilizing only the South-West Army Group facing Galicia, and this was done on 28 July. As Russia had responded similarly in earlier Balkan crises, this did not imply an escalation of the crisis into general war. But the context was now different. Despite factionalism in her officer corps and a dysfunctional wartime command and staff structure, Russia was now stronger militarily, and was determined not to lose face as she had done in the 1908–9 Bosnian Crisis. The Russian high command rejected partial mobilization as it would upset their timetables, while Sazonov's views on Germany's aggressive intentions convinced the Tsar that, despite reciprocation of soothing 'cousinly' telegrams between him and Wilhelm, he had to act. He ordered general mobilization on 30 July, news of which, reaching Berlin, tipped the balance towards war. The critical matter of a day lost or gained in mobilization and war – 'stealing a march' on the enemy – overrode more prudent considerations.

Bethmann Hollweg, who still believed the conflict could be localized, was now getting cold feet. Germany could still prevent a major war, and most European states hoped it could be avoided, but there was no mechanism for applying the brakes. The

ABOVE: The proclamation of Germany's mobilization is read to crowds gathered on the streets of a German city.

RIGHT: Invasion Scare 1914. *Confidential, Map of East Anglia*, 2½ inches to 1 mile. Probably initially prepared for the War Office c.1911 as a manoeuvre map, this series was printed by the Ordnance Survey as a defence map in 1914–15, extended south of the Thames and renamed *Map of the Eastern Counties*

British Foreign Secretary, Sir Edward Grey, suggested to Berlin an international conference, unrealistic given the slow and hidebound diplomatic routines (including ciphering and deciphering), the difficulties of routing international calls through many manual switchboards and the impatient general staffs and their remorselessly unrolling mobilization schedules. Grey addressed Germany rather than Austria–Hungary because he believed, like the Russians, that Germany held the key. On 29 July, he warned Germany that Britain would not stand aside in the event of general war, which would be 'the greatest catastrophe that the world has ever seen'. This shook the Kaiser and Bethmann

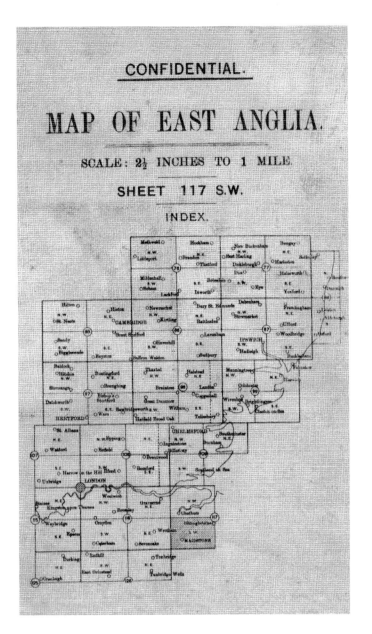

that, by 29 July, military imperatives, notably the deadly question of rigid mobilization timetables, should override political considerations. Germany was faced with the danger of war on two fronts – a situation which Wilhelm I and Bismarck had worked hard to avoid – and timing was crucial. While Moltke and Falkenhayn certainly understood the inevitability of war following German mobilization, Falkenhayn wanted to initiate the 'preliminary stages'. While other countries separated the two, Germany's survival of a two-front war depended on their integration into a rapid and seamless response. Germany could not mobilize as a precaution, sit back and await developments. Moltke refrained, therefore, from issuing the order, agreeing with Bethmann Hollweg that they should await Russia's response to Austria's attack on Serbia. Moltke feared that the Austro-Hungarian army, committed to attacking Serbia, consequently exposed East Prussia to a greater danger as she could not simultaneously hold Russian forces in Galicia; the logistics were implacable. While, therefore, Bethmann Hollweg was urging the Austrians to stand fast in Belgrade, Moltke was, on the same day, pushing Conrad to mobilize against Russia rather than Serbia. Conrad's railway staff told him he could start mobilizing his First, Third and Fourth Armies against Russia, while continuing the Second Army's rail movement to Serbia, if mobilization against Russia was delayed until 4 August – a loss of five days. On 31 July, Conrad ordered the re-routing of the Second Army to Galicia, but was informed that, to avoid chaos, the movement would have to run its course. Having reached the southern frontier, it could then be switched north.

On 30 July, Berlin, hearing of Russia's mobilization, counter-mobilized and declared war on Russia when she failed to stand-down her troops. The Schlieffen–Moltke plan was thrown into gear. On 3 August, Germany declared war on France. Seven German armies were to march on France, while one, Prittwitz's Eighth Army in East Prussia, was to hold the eastern frontier against any Russian incursion. Anticipating a slow Russian mobilization, the Germans were surprised by the speed of the 'Russian steamroller' moving rapidly to take pressure off her French ally in the west. When German forces crossed into neutral Belgium on 4 August, Britain demanded that she withdraw her troops by midnight and, when this was ignored, declared war. In this, Britain was, as she had done in the French Revolutionary and Napoleonic Wars, and was to do again in Hitler's war, enacting her long-standing axiom of foreign policy and national security that she would not tolerate a militaristic hegemony of that continental mainland which stood, in clear sight, only twenty miles away across the Straits of Dover.

Hollweg sufficiently for the latter to telegraph Vienna early on 30 July proposing that the Austrians stand fast in Belgrade while the conflict was 'mediated'. However Austria, the loser in earlier Balkan settlements, feared another diplomatic defeat, while the aggressive Conrad urged the necessity of a final crushing blow against Serbia.

Meanwhile Moltke, the German Chief-of-Staff, and Falkenhayn, the Minister of War, both now returned from summer leave, were repositioning German policy. Falkenhayn was the key player. Disturbed by Moltke's indecisiveness, and aware that some powers were preparing or undertaking mobilization, he considered

Chapter 2

The 1914 Campaign in the West and the East

At the beginning of August 1914, operations began more-or-less simultaneously on the Eastern and Western Fronts. While Austria–Hungary had to deal with the difficulty of invading Serbia as well as facing Russia, Germany had to cope with the long-feared nightmare of a major war on two fronts. The Schlieffen Plan, and its subsequent modification by Moltke, had been drawn up specifically to deal with this eventuality. It envisaged a holding operation against Russia in the east, assisted by Austro-Hungarian forces in Galicia, while assaulting the Belgian and French frontier fortresses and sweeping remorselessly down through northern France to envelop Paris and force the French armies back eastward against their own eastern frontier and the German positions there. Meanwhile Germany's

BELOW: The original German plan for the Campaign in the West. Sketch map of the Schlieffen Plan as originally conceived, showing the sweep west of Paris of the German First Army (von Kluck), from the British Official History: *Military Operations, France and Belgium, 1914, Vol. 1.*

RIGHT: The Western Front from the *'Land and Water' Map of the War*, by Hilaire Belloc. This was a very good map for showing the significance of fortresses and natural features – particularly ground-forms such as mountain ranges.

colonies, naval bases and coaling stations in Africa and the Pacific were gradually mopped up by the Allies. These operations are dealt with in Chapters 3 and 4, as are those involving the Ottoman Empire.

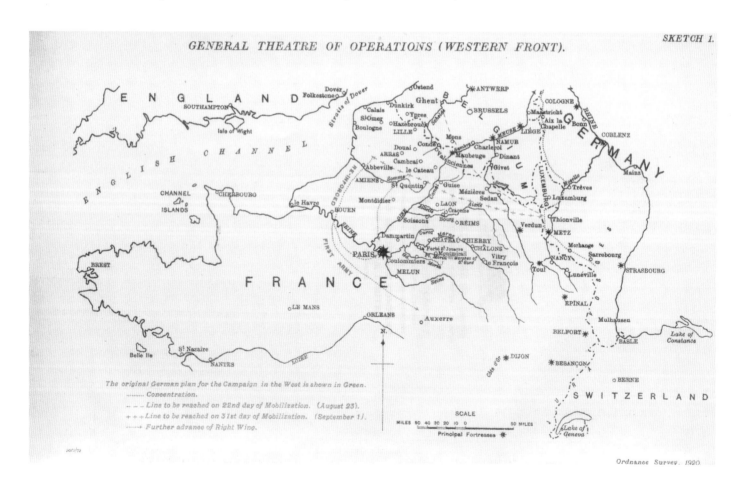

GENERAL THEATRE OF OPERATIONS (WESTERN FRONT).

SKETCH 1.

The original German plan for the Campaign in the West is shown in Green.
.... Concentration.
_ . _ . _ Line to be reached on 22nd day of Mobilization. (August 23).
+ + + + Line to be reached on 31st day of Mobilization. (September 1).
—————→ Further advance of Right Wing.

SCALE
MILES 50 40 30 20 10 0   50 MILES
Principal Fortresses ✱

Ordnance Survey. 1920.

THE WESTERN FRONT

Germany declared war on France on 3 August. When German armies crossed the Belgian frontier on 4 August, Britain issued an immediate ultimatum to Germany, requiring her assurances that she would respect Belgian neutrality and, when that expired at midnight, was at war with Germany. Late in the evening on the fourth, Sir Edward Grey marked the end of an epoch by stating portentously: 'The lamps are going out all over Europe; we shall not see them lit again in our lifetime.'

The British mobilization scheme had been prepared in 1910, the year that General Henry Wilson became Director of Military Operations, by the Committee of Imperial Defence. Staff discussions between the British and French (the Wilson–Foch scheme) had agreed that a small British Expeditionary Force (BEF) of six divisions would fight alongside the French. This possible British involvement had been acknowledged by Schlieffen, and it was accepted by the Germans that their right wing would have to deal with British as well as French and Belgian troops. However the BEF eventually sent to France in August 1914 initially comprised only four divisions and a cavalry division, but these were soon augmented by two further infantry divisions.

The first, crucial, action was the attack on the Belgian fortress of Liège, which barred the passage to the two German right wing armies. This assault started on 4 August and the fortress was finally taken on 16 August, using the secret weapons of ultra-heavy Krupp (German) and Skoda (Austrian) howitzers. The Liège forts destroyed and the citadel captured, the main advance began. Sordet's French cavalry corps had reconnoitred the river Meuse into Belgium, starting on 6 August and approaching as close to nine miles of Liège. No trace of the German Army was found west of the Meuse, and this confirmed Joffre's misguided view that Moltke would keep his armies east of the Meuse and, having only the limited strength of his first-line corps, would not extend his right wing west of the river. Joffre reckoned without the ability of the German reserve corps to march and fight with the active corps, which effectively doubled Moltke's striking power.

RIGHT: *'Land and Water' Map of the War, by Hilaire Belloc. Land and Water* was a weekly publication, running from 1914 to 1920, edited by Belloc and focusing on the war and post-war developments.

The Battles of the Frontiers – August 1914

The French war plan – Plan 17 – had been to deploy five armies, numbered from the right or south, on the frontier with Germany, to advance east into the 'lost provinces' of Alsace-Lorraine. France's First Army (Dubail) faced Alsace, her Second Army (Castelnau) was arrayed against Lorraine, and Third Army (Ruffey) fronted the great fortress of Metz. The Fourth Army (de Langle de Cary) was echeloned back from the others, to form a strategic force that could be sent east or north as required. The Fifth Army (Lanrezac), on the extreme left, was in a position to watch the difficult rugged and forested terrain of the Ardennes and the Belgian frontier, in case a German threat developed from that quarter. To the left, or northwest, of the Fifth Army, guarding the large expanse of northern France running along the Belgian frontier to the sea north of Dunkirk, there was only a thin scattering of territorial

divisions, made up of elderly and ill-equipped men, supported by little artillery.

Two weaknesses were to undermine any French prospects of success. The first was that the Commander-in-Chief, General Joffre, consistently underestimated the intentions of the German war plan, and the strength of the German right, or northern, group of armies arrayed, just south of the 'Dutch appendix' at

ABOVE: *Karte des Weltkrieges – Europaischer Kriegsschauplatz* [Map of the World War – European Theatre]. The scale of the original is 1:4 million.
RIGHT: British Index Map GSGS 2621, showing the maps prepared before the war for the use of the BEF in a limited area of northern France and Belgium: 'tactical' sheets at the scales of 1:80,000 (France) and 1:100,000 (Belgium), and the 'strategical' 1:380,160 sheet.

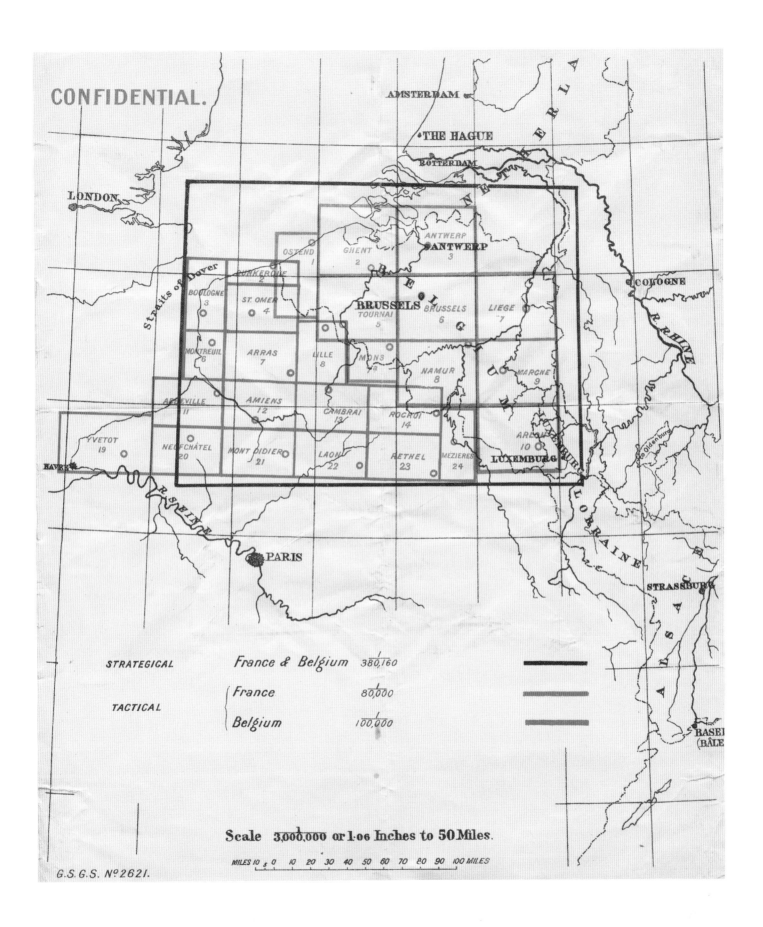

CONFIDENTIAL.

London

AMSTERDAM

·THE HAGUE

ROTTERDAM

N E T H E R L A

Straits of Dover

OSTEND
1

GHENT
2

ANTWERP
3

ANTWERP

COLOGNE

DUNKERQUE
2

BOULOGNE
3

ST. OMER
4

BRUSSELS
TOURNAI
5

BRUSSELS
6

LIEGE
7

B E L G I Q

R. RHINE

MONTREUIL
6

ARRAS
7

LILLE
8

MONS
8

NAMUR
8

MARCHE
9

ABBEVILLE
11

AMIENS
12

CAMBRAI
13

ROCROI
14

ARLON
10

LUXEMBURG

B E L G I U M

Oldenburg

YVETOT
19

NEUFCHÂTEL
20

MONT DIDIER
21

LAON
22

RETHEL
23

MEZIERES
24

HAVRE

R. SEINE

PARIS

L O R R A I N E

STRASSBURG

A L S A S

BASEL
(BÂLE)

STRATEGICAL

France & Belgium $\frac{1}{380,160}$

TACTICAL

France $\frac{1}{80,000}$

Belgium $\frac{1}{100,000}$

Scale $\frac{1}{3,000,000}$ or 1·06 Inches to 50 Miles.

MILES 10 5 0   10 20 30 40 50 60 70 80 90 100 MILES

G.S.G.S. Nº 2621.

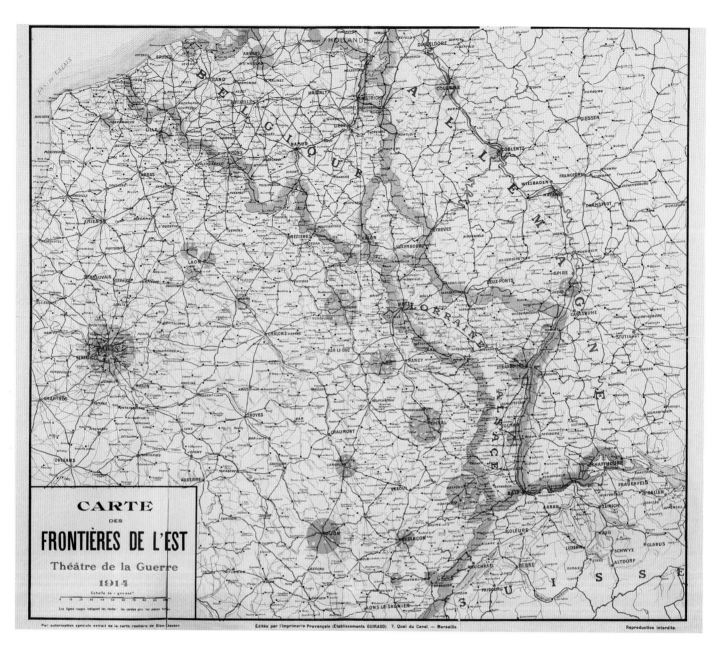

CARTE
DES
FRONTIÈRES DE L'EST
Théâtre de la Guerre
1914
Echelle de 1:925,000°

Par autorisation spéciale extrait de la carte routière de Dion-Bouton   Éditée par l'Imprimerie Provençale (Établissements GUIRAUD) 7, Quai du Canal. — Marseille.   Reproduction interdite.

Maastricht, facing west against the Meuse and the Liège fortress. Joffre's view was that the main German force was concentrated around Metz, not further north. The second was the pre-war doctrine of the extreme offensive, whatever the enemy's strength and intentions might be. Combined, these resulted in a massacre of the French infantry, and might well have led to strategic disaster, had the German Schlieffen–Moltke plan been capable of developing according to schedule. But Joffre was made of sturdy stuff, and was flexible enough to adapt to a changing situation. His staff also had a firm enough grip to be able to switch forces to the endangered left flank when required.

The original French plan had been to retain the Fourth Army in a position from which it could manoeuvre. But on hearing of the German ultimatum to Belgium on 2 August, Joffre decided to switch to pre-determined 'alternative concentration areas' for his Fourth and Fifth Armies to enable the Fourth Army to come into the line between the Third and Fifth and make it possible for the Fifth Army to extend further to the north. Thus Joffre, recognizing a possible German threat from the direction of Belgium, still clung to the modified Plan 17 – an offensive to regain Alsace-Lorraine.

The German invasion of Luxemburg began on 3 August, and Joffre's immediate response was to send Sordet's Cavalry Corps

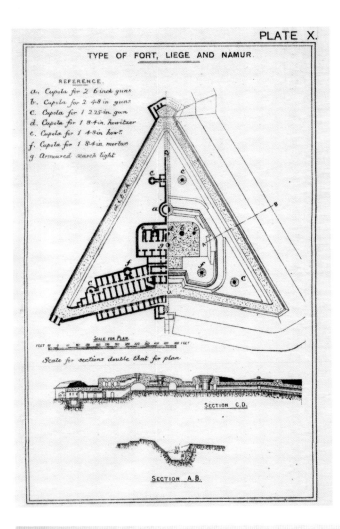

PLATE X.

TYPE OF FORT, LIEGE AND NAMUR.

REFERENCE.
a. Cupola for 2 6 inch guns
b. Cupola for 2 4·8 in guns
c. Cupola for 1 2·25 in. gun
d. Cupola for 1 8·4 in. howitzer
e. Cupola for 1 4·8 in howt.
f. Cupola for 1 8·4 in. mortar
g. Armoured search light

SCALE FOR PLAN.
FEET

Scale for sections double that for plan

SECTION C.D.

SECTION A.B.

ABOVE: Seemingly of great strength, the forts at Liège and Namur were key elements of the Belgian frontier fortresses, but proved vulnerable to German and Austrian 420 mm and 305 mm siege howitzers.

TOP LEFT: Fortresses on France's eastern frontier are shown by pink circles. The loss of Alsace-Lorraine in the Franco-Prussian War left France with a vulnerable frontier, defended by a line of new fortresses, including Verdun and Nancy.

forward to reconnoitre east of Mézières, and to warn his commanders not to cross the frontier and to avoid any provocative action. The French appreciation was that the German armies were unlikely to attempt to move through the difficult country of the Ardennes. German cavalry advanced into Belgium on the morning of the fourth, the attack on the Liège fortress beginning the same day. That evening, twenty-four hours after the German declaration of war, King Albert of Belgium gave permission for French forces to enter Belgian territory to locate the position and direction of German columns and, if possible, to delay their

advance. As a result, on 6 August, Sordet took his cavalry into Belgium in the direction of Neufchateau, thirty-six miles east of Mézières, swinging north towards Liège. For nine days they searched the Ardennes forest region and a swathe of territory westward to Charleroi. Nine miles from Liège, which was still under siege, and within sound of the German heavy howitzers still pounding the forts, he found that the Belgian field forces, though not the garrison, had withdrawn.

On the same day that Sordet's cavalry advanced, on the extreme right of the French front, in Alsace, a small diversionary offensive was started by a detachment (7th Corps and 8th Cavalry Division) of First Army, as outlined in the original plan, 'to facilitate the attack of the main armies'. This force crossed the frontier, but withdrew after encountering stronger German forces at Mülhausen (Mulhouse).

Between 6 and 8 August, Belgian Intelligence had identified units belonging to five different German corps operating against Liège, and this potentially alarming information was passed to French Intelligence. Despite this news, Joffre's staff still felt that the main group of German armies was concentrated around Metz, west of Thionville (Diedenhofen), and in Luxemburg, positioned so as to advance west if Liège was captured or, if Liège continued to resist, to wheel south pivoting on Metz. There was still, therefore, an underestimation of the strength of the German right wing. As a result, on 8 August Joffre informed his commanders that his intention was to make a hammer-blow attack on the Germans with all his armies simultaneously, as in the original plan, with his right wing (First and Second Armies) extended to the Rhine. His instructions gave directions and zones for the armies. Fifth Army was to remain concentrated facing east, in a position either to prevent a German passage of the Meuse on the twenty-mile stretch between Mouzon and Mézières, or to cross the river in the same area. If necessary his left (Fourth and Fifth Armies) would be held back to avoid a premature engagement of one of the armies before the others could assist it. However, if Liège delayed the German right wing, or if that wing turned south, the French left would be advanced to meet it. Joffre's instruction ended with an order for all armies to be ready to advance on receipt of a telegram – and to deliver a furious, crushing offensive.

To fill the gap between the French Fifth Army and the Belgian garrison at their Namur fortress, a French infantry regiment was sent on 8 August to hold all the Meuse bridges north of Dinant and to make contact with the Belgians. The French 1st Corps at the same time extended its screen northward along the Meuse from Mézières to Givet. On 9 August, Sordet's cavalry captured a German officer who gave important information about German

Daily Mail General War Map

GEORGE PHILIP & SON, LTD.

COPYRIGHT.

of Europe

WAR STRENGTH OF THE GREAT POWERS

ARMIES

TRIPLE ENTENTE			TRIPLE ALLIANCE		
RUSSIA 5,000,000	FRANCE 4,000,000	GREAT BRITAIN 750,000	GERMANY 5,000,000	AUSTRIA 2,500,000	ITALY 2,000,000 (ITALY'S NEUTRALITY DECLARED)

NAVIES

	DREADNOUGHTS	OTHER BATTLESHIPS	CRUISERS	TORPEDO-BOAT DESTROYERS	SUBMARINES	MEN (Peace Strength)
GREAT BRITAIN	31	38	111	203	69	151,000 (28,000 mobilised)
FRANCE	4	17	32	80	50	70,000
RUSSIA	NONE COMPLETED	8	14	95	25	55,000
GERMANY	20	19	52	132	29	73,000
AUSTRIA	3	11	11	15	6	20,000
ITALY	4	5	23	30	18	37,000

AIRCRAFT

AIRSHIPS

FRANCE 11 · GREAT BRITAIN 8 · GERMANY · RUSSIA 4 · AUSTRIA · ITALY 9 · 20 · 3

AEROPLANES AND SEAPLANES

500 · 500 · 500 · 100 · 150

BRITISH FORCES OVERSEAS (GRAND TOTAL 617,000)

NOTE.—These figures are drawn on a larger scale than those of the other series.

INDIA (Native) 200,000 (British) 76,000	AUSTRALIA 150,000	CANADA 76,000	S. AFRICA 32,000	NEW ZEALAND 20,000	EGYPT 23,250 (6,000 English)	MALTA GIBRALTAR & CYPRUS 11,500	TROOPS IN TROPICAL DEPENDENCIES 19,400

PEACE STRENGTH OF THE GREAT POWERS

RUSSIA	Infantry, Artillery & other Details … 1,250,000 — Cavalry 100,000 — Total, 1,350,000
FRANCE	361,549 · 92,571 · 53,568 · 113,356 · Total, 645,644
GREAT BRITAIN	98,799 · Artillery, 32,549 · Cavalry, 14,709 · Others, 26,443 · Total, 169,500 (Regulars only and exclusive of Colonial and Native Indian corps.)
GERMANY	504,126 · 128,596 · 85,708 · Others, 72,556 · Total, 790,985
AUSTRIA	265,644 · Artillery, 53,196 · Cavalry, 52,174 · Others, 49,244 · Total, 424,258
ITALY	169,527 · Artillery, 51,615 · Cavalry, 28,422 · Others, 55,008 · Total, 304,672 — Infantry coloured thus— Artillery — Cavalry — Other Details —

ARMIES OF OTHER EUROPEAN STATES

ON A WAR FOOTING

RUMANIA 700,000	SPAIN 600,000	BULGARIA 550,000	TURKEY 500,000	SERVIA 300,000	BELGIUM 300,000	HOLLAND 175,000	MONTENEGRO 90,000

THE LONDON GEOGRAPHICAL INSTITUTE.

Daily Mail WAR MAP

6D. NET.

TRIPLE ENTENTE 9,380,000 MEN

TRIPLE ALLIANCE 9,500,000 MEN

GEORGE PHILIP & SON, LTD. LONDON: 32 FLEET STREET, E.C. LIVERPOOL: 60 CHURCH STREET.

ABOVE: The cover of the *Daily Mail General War Map of Europe*, produced by George Philip & Son, Ltd at the London Geographical Institute. Note the statement of the size of the competing forces: Triple Entente, 9,380,000 men; Triple Alliance, 9,500,000 men.

LEFT: *The Daily Mail General War Map of Europe*. Insets show *War Strengths of the Great Powers*, covering armies, navies and aircraft, *Peace [pre-war] Strengths of the Great Powers* and *Armies of Other European States*, while a key shows alliances, fortresses, forts, airship depots, wireless telegraphy stations and railways, etc. Scale of original approx ½ inch to 50 miles.

movements, and the next day Sordet brought his Corps back towards the Meuse, having established that the German northern armies, held up by Belgian resistance at Liège, had not yet advanced.

Joffre's appreciation of the situation on 13 August was that the Germans were wheeling south, towards his Third, Fourth and Fifth Armies on the upper Meuse, not heading west, and that it was now too late for his armies to engage favourably beyond the Meuse. He therefore ordered them to be ready to counter-attack. Although he ignored Lanrezac's (Fifth Army) view that the Germans were about to make a much wider wheel, he now felt concerned enough to send north the whole of the 1st Corps to oppose any German attempt to cross the Meuse between Givet and Namur. Two days later, when Richthofen's Cavalry Corps attempted to cross the river near Dinant, the 1st Corps and Mangin's 8th Brigade (which was specially tasked to support Sordet's Corps) forced it to retire.

After Liège had fallen on 16 August, the full force of the German right wing was unleashed two days later into the

area previously declared clear by Sordet. On the extreme right – or northern – flank, Kluck's First Army stepped out on its gruelling 300-mile march, starting on an axis due west through Belgium, before swinging south into France. The schedule was to march for three weeks, averaging nearly fifteen miles a day, along roads that might be blocked by refugees, and this included any actions that might have to be fought on the way. Marching in the heat and dust along their allotted parallel roads, Kluck's First and Bülow's Second Armies pounded remorselessly to the west towards Brussels, forcing the Belgian field army to withdraw northwest into the entrenched protective ring of forts of the Antwerp defences.

On 20 August Kluck's Army, the extreme tip of the German wheel through Belgium, tramped into Brussels. The next day Bülow's Army started to besiege the Namur fortress, with the great siege train of Krupp and Skoda howitzers now brought up from their success at Liège. The German army was thorough in its intimidation of Belgian civilians, pursuing its doctrine of

Schrecklichkeit (frightfulness) in taking and shooting hostages, and burning towns and villages to intimidate and deter.

Meanwhile, on the extreme left, or west, wing of the French armies the four infantry divisions and one cavalry division of the BEF, under Sir John French, were completing their concentration around Maubeuge. On 20 August they prepared to advance towards Mons.

The French armies had embarked on their great offensive operations, putting their Plan 17 into action. They were imbued with Grandmaison's quasi-mystical doctrine of the offensive *à l'outrance* (to excess), and fired by the vision of *la revanche* (revenge) to regain their lost provinces of Alsace-Lorraine. While not unaware of the German threat to his left flank and rear, Joffre relied on his main offensive to unbalance the German forces. But the Battles of the Frontiers, in which four of the five French armies were to attack eastward, proved a disaster for French arms.

The vital task of acting as left flank guard on the Belgian frontier was left to Lanrezac's Fifth Army. On the right, towards the Swiss frontier, Joffre's main attack was due to begin on 18 August, when Castelnau's Second Army would be launched against Morhange. Events, however, were forcing Joffre to adapt his dispositions. The German sweep through Belgium forced him to strengthen and extend his left flank and to push Langle de Cary's Fourth Army, his only strategic reserve force, into the gap.

By 18 August, however, Joffre's complacency about his left wing had been shattered, as he had become aware that the forces of the German right wing, now free to advance beyond the shattered Liège forts, were moving north and west of the Meuse on a westerly axis between Brussels and Namur. Joffre judged that Lanrezac's Fifth Army was strong enough to hold them off, and he knew, as the Germans did not, that the four divisions of the BEF were moving up on Lanrezac's left. Joffre concluded from the German strength on his right, pressing against his First (Dubail) and Second (Castelnau) Armies in Alsace-Lorraine, and on his left coming through Belgium, that they had weakened their centre accordingly, so he planned to thrust into this vulnerable zone, as he saw it. He guessed wrongly, not realizing the full implications of the presence of German reserve corps in their order-of-battle. So he ordered his Third (Ruffey) and

Fourth (Langle de Cary) Armies forward into the difficult terrain of the Ardennes to catch the southern, or left, flank of the German right wing, formed by Bülow's Second Army, effectively sticking his head out and inviting a decapitating German pincer-movement. What happened now was not, luckily for the French, an envelopment but the bloody shock of two colliding forces as his armies, on 21–22 August, ran into the advancing German Fourth (Duke Albrecht of Württemberg) and Fifth (Crown Prince Wilhelm) Armies and suffered another disaster. The German reserve corps, as effective as their active corps, enabled them to attack with full strength all along their line, and this applied equally to the Ardennes front. The French attack, as rapid as it could be in this difficult terrain of woods and ravines, but made in blind country without proper reconnaissance, was destroyed by German fire.

On Joffre's extreme right in Alsace-Lorraine, Dubail's First and Castelnau's Second Armies, rushing forward impetuously, collided with the advancing German left, or southerly, wing. The élan of the French attack – the officers wearing while gloves and carrying swords, the men in their blue coats and red trousers and kepis – contributed to its collapse. These easy targets were blasted by the withering fire of German artillery, machine guns and rifles. The French armies were comprehensively defeated in the Battles of Sarrebourg and Morhange, east of Nancy, the remnants retreating in some disorder. Castelnau's army had run into strong German defences and he had pulled it back to the hills encircling Nancy, known as the Grand Couronné, which formed a strong defensive position, firmly held by Foch's 20th Corps. In the south, on 21 August, Castelnau told Joffre that he considered the situation very serious, and there was even a danger of Nancy being abandoned, opening the way for a German invasion of eastern France and a possible double-envelopment. This was actually in Moltke's mind for a while. Foch's spirited defence of the Grand Couronné at Nancy relieved Joffre of concern for this sector. It was also on 21 August that Moltke, alarmed at developments in East Prussia, first considered transferring formations from the Western Front.

A serious crisis was building on the Allied left; Lanrezac's army was forced to retire from the Sambre, and German columns were crowding down the roads out of Brussels. While the French Third Army held its ground along the Meuse Heights and around the anchor-position of the fortress of Verdun, to the west of this strong position the French armies were falling back under German pressure. Lanrezac, his Fifth Army facing the weight of the German advance through Belgium, expressed alarm at the situation, but Joffre's headquarters dismissed his fears. Lanrezac and Sir John French did not get on well, and soon accused each other of lack of mutual support.

On 23 August, while Hindenburg and Ludendorff got a grip on the situation in East Prussia in the period leading to the Battle of Tannenberg, the situation in the west looked dire for the Allies. In the three days of the battles of the Frontiers, the French lost 40,000 dead. By 29 August, total French casualties (killed, wounded and missing) exceeded a quarter of a million. All along the line of contact, armies on both sides were shocked by the firepower of magazine rifles, machine guns and shrapnel-firing field guns and howitzers. These experiences were repeated in the encounter battles on the Eastern Front.

The encounter battles merged to the northwest into those of Charleroi–Mons when Lanrezac's Fifth Army and then, on his left, the BEF, were hit by Bülow's Second and Kluck's First Armies. The French armies were in retreat all along their line, and Lanrezac was pulling back after being defeated in the Battle of Charleroi. Sir John French, egged on by Wilson, his Deputy Chief of Staff, had a somewhat rosy view of the situation and envisaged a further advance. On the morning of 23 August the BEF was entrenched along the Mons–Condé Canal and extended to its east, in a position with a good field of fire against the centre of Kluck's advancing First Army. The 'fifteen rounds rapid' of the British

infantry, backed by two machine guns per battalion and their divisional artilleries, stunned the Germans. But the British position was very exposed, with both flanks effectively in the air. Sir John French therefore, ordered a withdrawal that night. The scales had fallen from French's eyes when Joffre convinced him of the real peril he was in. Hausen's Third Army was driving a wedge between Lanrezac's right and Langle de Cary's left, and Lanrezac had to pull back, thus exposing the BEF's right. Joffre had full and alarming information about the German strength facing the BEF and threatening its flanks.

The German advance continued, though on 25 August Moltke finally decided to order two corps, released from the siege of Namur, which had fallen on the twenty-third, to East Prussia; they entrained the following day. Happily for the Allies they were therefore taken from the German right wing. The advance flowed around Maubeuge, which did not fall until 8 September, but the detachment of the two German corps was to be felt on the Marne, as Moltke himself admitted. Joffre maintained a cool grip on a critical situation during the retreat, always looking for some false move on the part of the Germans, to seize the initiative.

Paris mit seinen Festungswerken
Maßstab 1:500000   0 2 4 6 8 10 km

ABOVE: A detail from *Karte des Weltkrieges – Europaischer Kriegsschauplatz* [Map of the World War – European Theatre], showing Paris and its defensive fortresses.
LEFT: The Schlieffen Plan in action: German infantry of the 47th Infantry Regiment advancing through northeastern France, August 1914.

Joffre realized that the key to the situation was on his left wing, which faced the sledgehammer of the German right. At its critical point this was held by the BEF, which was not under his direct control; so he ordered the creation of a new Sixth Army, to the left of the BEF. Commanded by Maunoury, this helped to protect the left flank of the BEF after Le Cateau on 27 August, before being again redeployed to a position near Paris on 1 September. On the twenty-seventh Joffre ordered Lanrezac to take the offensive between Guise and La Fère, towards St Quentin (Battle of Guise–St Quentin). Lanrezac asked Haig on the evening of 28 August to cooperate in the attack, but French denied him permission. French wanted to pull the BEF out of line to rest and reorganize, and agreed with Joffre that it should retire to a position south of the Aisne.

Joffre was already rehearsing in his mind the manoeuvres that were to become the Battle of the Marne, which the new Sixth Army would enable. Moltke now defied the spirit of the Schlieffen Plan by ordering his Sixth and Seventh Armies to attack in the Vosges and at Nancy, hoping to create a successful pincer movement of the right and left flanks, rather than reinforce the right with formations from his left. In the centre, the Germans were advancing through the Champagne country and the Oise valley towards Paris. The German right, however, was in trouble. It had been weakened by detachments, and Kluck and Bülow did not work well in tandem. On 26 August, during the retreat from Mons, the British 2nd Corps was in danger of being overwhelmed. Its commander, Smith-Dorrien, made the bold and justified decision to stand and fight in an improvised defensive position, and give the advancing Germans a bloody nose. With the Germans working around each flank, this was successfully accomplished, not least by the skilful handling of the artillery and French support on his flanks.

While Smith-Dorrien's Corps had done well at Le Cateau, Sir John French believed it had been broken, and was sinking into depression, alarming Joffre who met him during the day. Joffre was worried that the BEF might crumble before he had had time to constitute his Sixth Army on the BEF's left. He realized he had to buy time by yielding space, and his armies continued to retreat between Paris and Verdun. For thirteen days the BEF and the French armies retreated.

As the BEF slipped away from Le Cateau, Kluck lost contact and, believing it was retreating westward, swung his army in that direction towards Amiens but encountered Maunoury's deploying Sixth Army. This contact was fleeting and indecisive and Kluck's manoeuvre created a gap between his army and Bülow's, in the process presenting an exposed flank to the Allies. Haig realized the possibility of his 1st Corps, together with Lanrezac's Fifth Army, making a joint attack, but French refused Haig permission to participate. Joffre, on the other hand, forced Lanrezac to attack by himself going to Fifth Army headquarters. On 29 August, Lanrezac's Army was starting against Kluck's columns when Bülow's army struck its right flank. In this Battle of Guise, Lanrezac wheeled his army to face Bülow and drove his army back. Bülow's appeal for assistance forced Kluck to change his axis south to close on Bülow's army. This allowed Maunoury a breathing space to complete his deployment, and swung Kluck's First Army southeast, presenting its flank to the Entrenched Camp of Paris as it marched on its new axis to pass east of Paris, rather than in a wide enveloping sweep to the west as set out in Schlieffen's Plan. A great opportunity was recognized in the west by Joffre; the Germans had made the false move for which he had been waiting.

On 2 September the French government left for Bordeaux, while Maunoury's Sixth Army had fallen back on the Paris defence, commanded by the redoubtable Galliéni, the Military Governor of Paris, who in this crisis was of the same mind as Joffre. On 3 September the latter instructed Galliéni to set the Sixth Army

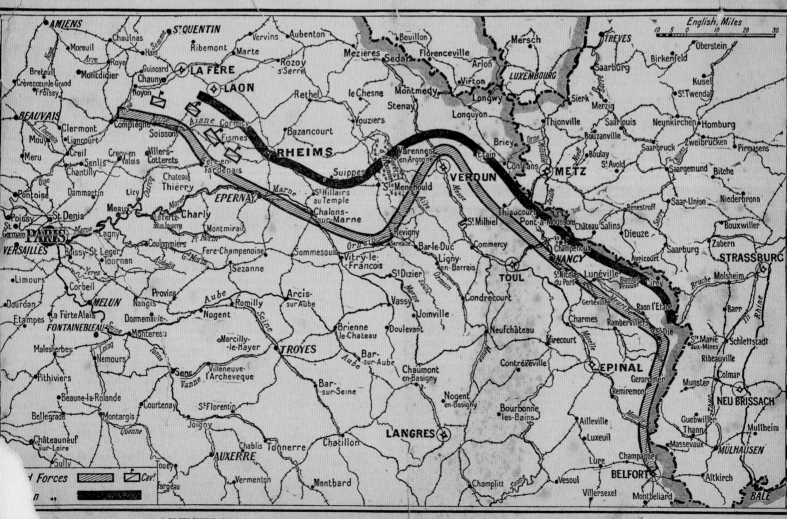

THE MORNING POST, MONDAY, SEPTEMBER 14, 1914.

ON THE FRENCH LEFT WING THE GERMANS CONTINUE TO RETREAT. THEY HAVE EVACUATED AMIENS, AND HAVE FALLEN BACK EASTWARD BETWEEN SOISSONS AND REIMS. THE GERMANS HAVE RETIRED TO THE NORTH OF THE VESLE.
IN THE CENTRE THE ENEMY, WHO HAVE LOST REVIGNY AND BRABANT-LE-ROI, ARE STILL IN THE SOUTH OF THE ARGONNE.

TOP LEFT: The 13-pounder field guns of a Royal Horse Artillery battery at Wytschaete, south of Ypres, 31 October 1914.

BOTTOM LEFT: A newspaper map, showing the development of the Battle of the Aisne, the Germans having retreated from the Marne to the defensive position north of the Aisne. The vital importance to the Allies of the fortress positions along the French eastern frontier, and the pivot point of the Verdun fortress, is clearly shown. Such maps, printed from rapidly produced line-blocks, aimed to show the situation at a glance.

BELOW: British cavalry at Ypres on 13 October 1914, soon after the German cavalry, which had advanced as far west as the Mont des Cats, had withdrawn.

against Kluck's increasingly vulnerable flank. Kluck's army was vulnerable to a flank attack by Maunoury's army and the BEF. Air reconnaissance reports received by Joffre clearly revealed the danger the Germans were marching into on the 150-mile front between Verdun and Paris, the Allied line bending in a great arc to the south, but being reinforced by Foch's new Ninth Army, brought from the French right wing. The weakest link in his line seemed to Joffre to be the BEF whose commander, on 30 August, had told the British government that he intended to pull the BEF out of the line, southwest of Paris. At this, Kitchener came hotfoot to Paris to order Sir John to keep his army in the line and conform to Joffre's plans. Joffre had sacked the pessimistic Lanrezac on 3 September and replaced him with the more positive Franchet d'Esperey ('desperate Frankie' to the British), who was liaising closely with the BEF staff as also, independently, was Galliéni. The BEF responded first to Galliéni's plan, while Joffre had approved proposals put forward by Franchet d'Esperey for an attack by four Allied armies. As a result, the BEF was a day's march behind the other armies when the about-turn came.

On 5 September, Maunoury's Sixth Army attacked Kluck's rear, forcing Kluck to wheel to face west to meet this threat. A gap opened between Kluck's Army and Bülow's into which, on

6 September, Joffre directed his counter-offensive. To reinforce Sixth Army, Galliéni despatched an infantry brigade to the front in a fleet of Paris taxis, while Foch grappled with the Germans in a savage battle in the Marshes of St Gond. The real striking forces were Franchet d'Esperey's Fifth Army and the BEF. Although the latter moved up far too cautiously, it nevertheless drove a decisive wedge between Kluck and Bülow and unnerved the latter, who told Hentsch, Moltke's liaison officer, that a German retreat was inevitable. Kluck's staff were more positive, but Hentsch, knowing that the BEF was behind Kluck's army and that Bülow was in no state to do otherwise, used his delegated power to order Kluck's army to retreat towards Soissons. The whole German right wing now swung back, pivoting on Verdun, so that by 13 September it was across the Aisne, entrenching on the twenty-mile-long Chemin-des-Dames ridge north of the river, on the front facing the British. West of this, the Germans dug in northeast of Compiègne, and to the east on the heights north of Reims and across the undulating plains of the northern Champagne to Verdun.

The BEF, advancing across the Aisne, with Franchet d'Esperey's Fifth Army on its right and Maunoury's on its left, climbed towards the Chemin-des-Dames on 13 September. But not only were the enemy entrenched here, but Zwehl's 7th Reserve Corps, advancing after the fall of Maubeuge, had arrived in strength a couple of hours earlier, having force-marched in twenty-four hours an unbelievable forty miles at the cost of almost a quarter of its infantry, collapsed along the way. The exhaustion of Zwehl's Corps made him ignore Bülow's order to continue eastward to help his right flank, and as a result Haig's 1st Corps could make no further progress, and the gap was further plugged by Heeringen's new Seventh Army, which was directed between Kluck and Bülow. On 14 September, Moltke was replaced at OHL by Falkenhayn who, faced with the results of the Battle of the Marne and the failure of the Schlieffen–Moltke Plan, remarked on taking over that the war was as good as lost. As the German right flank in the West was still open, to transfer troops East to fight the Russians would invite catastrophe in France, so he resolved to continue the Western

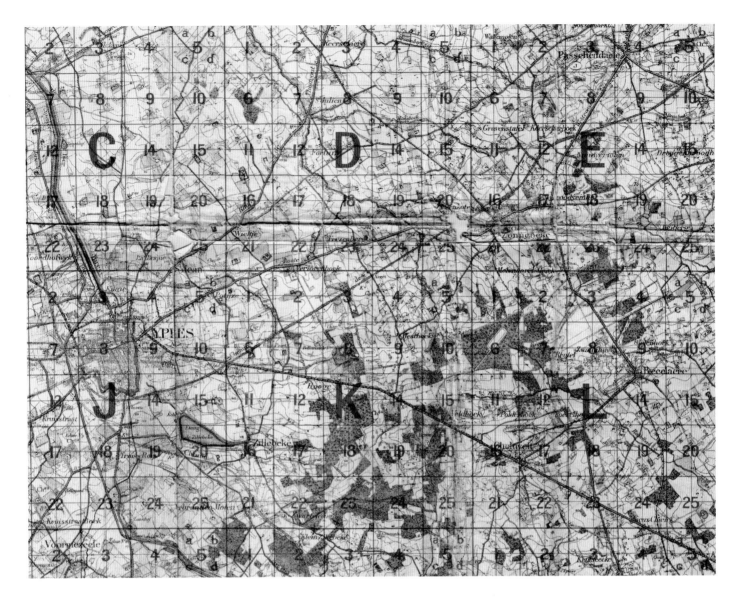

operations and hope that German and Austrian forces could hold out in the East.

Trench, or position, warfare began on the Aisne as did the mutual outflanking attempts known as the 'Race to the Sea'.

While the front east to Verdun and thence south to the Swiss frontier had already solidified, the dense ratio of men to space and the power of modern weapons prohibiting further movement, the zone from Compiègne northward to the fortress of Antwerp on the Belgian coast only contained relatively light forces on both sides. From now on the French were a day and a corps behind the Germans. Joffre furiously transferred troops to his left flank, while Foch took command of Allied forces in the north, including Belgium.

On 1 October, the BEF began to move northward from the Aisne to Flanders where it could operate on shorter communications with Britain and defend the crucial Channel ports, to which Ypres was an outlying bastion. The French already had considerable forces in the area, and these were heavily

engaged, alongside the Belgians and British, in the First Battle of Ypres. On the coast, the Belgian Army remained bottled up in Antwerp, but again the Germans brought up their siege train and crushed the forts one by one. British forces were sent by Churchill to Antwerp and Ostend, and a new British division, the 7th, was landed at Zeebrugge on 6 October, followed the next day by the 3rd Cavalry Division. However, these forces could not save Antwerp, and the Belgian Field Army retreated to the west, finally holding a line along the Yser between the sea at Nieuport and Dixmude, north of Ypres. On 27 October they opened the sluices to create a large flooded expanse as a barrier to further German movement.

Falkenhayn ordered a great attack at Dixmude to break through to the Channel Ports. The failure of this attack led the Germans to shift their axis to one through Ypres itself, in a grand offensive. On 20 October, Haig's 1st Corps arrived from the Aisne just in time to parry a desperate German offensive east of Ypres. In this attack, which opened on 17 October, the four new German volunteer corps made their first appearance, a large proportion being students. Hardly trained, these youths were mown down in much the same way as Kitchener's volunteers were in 1915 and 1916, losing half their strength, and in Germany the battle was remembered as *der Kindermord bei Ypern*, or massacre of the innocents at Ypres.

With the Germans outnumbering the British, though the Indian Corps was moving up by train from Marseilles, casualties were heavy on both sides. On 31 October the Germans captured the Messines–Wytschaete Ridge, but further north German attacks on Haig's 1st Corps were repulsed with heavy losses. The final crisis for the British came on 11 November, when the Germans assaulted astride the Ypres–Menin Road, with some parties breaking through the British position only to be driven back by point-blank artillery fire, and rifle fire. A captured German officer asked a battery commander where the British reserves were; the gunner pointed to the line of guns. The German asked what was behind that, to be told 'divisional headquarters'. His response was '*allmächtiger Gott!*' On the British left, the French 9th Corps stopped the German attacks with well-organized artillery and machine gun barrages.

To the British the battle represented the end of the old regular army. British casualties in the battle amounted to 58,000, and the total since hostilities began in August 90,000. German losses from La Bassée to the sea, including those incurred fighting against the French and Belgians, were around 130,000. At the end of the battle, the Allies were left in possession of an awkward eastward bulge around Ypres, with the Germans holding the high ground. This was the infamous Salient, a murderous and exposed death-trap which was to be the focus of four more great battles in the next four years.

ABOVE: Christmas truce, 1914. British and German officers and men in no-man's-land near Armentières. Christmas truces were a traditional feature of European wars, and there were many such fraternizations during the first Christmas of the war.

RIGHT:: A detail of the Eastern Front from the '*Land and Water*' *Map of the War*. This is a particularly good map for showing the significance of natural features – particularly ground-forms such as mountain ranges.

THE EASTERN FRONT

The major strategic feature of the Eastern Front at the commencement of hostilities was the great westward bulge of Russian Poland, projecting towards German Silesia between East Prussia, a province of Germany, to the north and Galicia, a province of the Austro–Hungarian Empire to the south. To the north of East Prussia lay the Baltic Sea, while in the south of Galicia the ground sloped upwards to the crests of the great chain of the Carpathian mountains.

At the outset, Austria was prevented from concentrating on the defeat of Serbia by the need to respond to the unexpectedly rapid advance of the two Russian armies of Jilinsky's North West Army Group: First Army, under Rennenkampf, in the north and Samsonov's Second Army in the south, which had been precipitately launched against East Prussia in an incomplete state of mobilization. The pressure put on the defending German Eighth Army (Prittwitz) by the Russians forced Conrad von Hötzendorf, Austria–Hungary's Chief of Staff and effective commander-in-chief, to divert his Second Army from Serbia and, partly as a result of this, the Serbs threw back the Austrian force launched against them on 12 August. In the savage fighting in Serbia, the Austrians suffered over a quarter of a million casualties by the end of 1914. While in the west the Germans completed their destruction of the Liège forts on 16 August, opening the way for the advance of their right wing. Russian forces crossed the frontier into East Prussia on the following day. The bulk of the Russian armies were concentrating in the south, facing Galicia. Here Ivanov's Army Group deployed four armies against Austria–Hungary, threatening Galicia and the passes through the Carpathians to Budapest and Vienna, and thereby ultimately posing an existential threat to the Habsburg Empire.

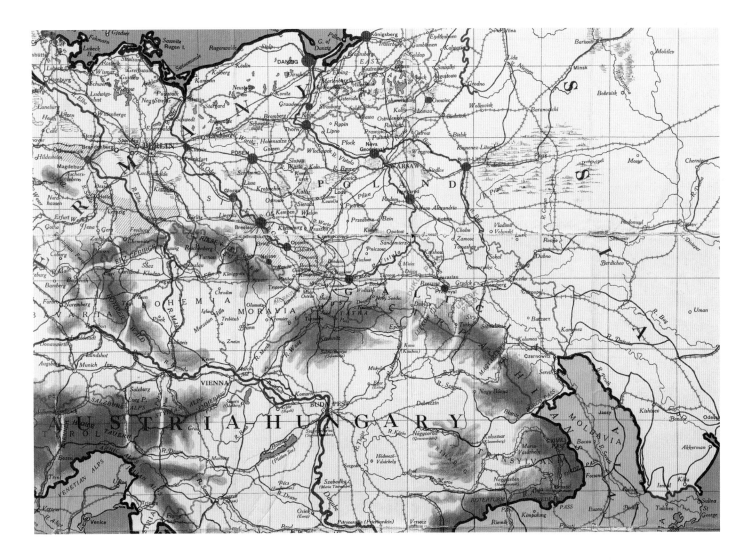

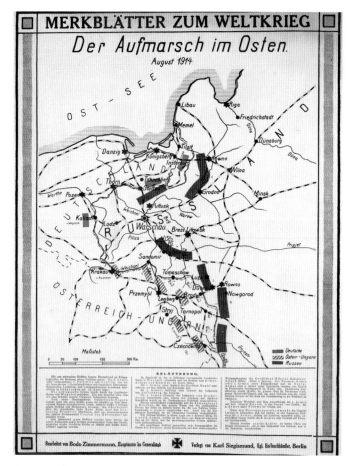

On 19 August, Rennenkampf's First Army defeated the Germans at Gumbinnen in East Prussia. While Rennenkampf continued a slow and methodical advance in the north towards the fortress and entrenched camp of Königsberg, and Samsonov, southwest of the Masurian Lakes, was advancing into East Prussia from the south, the Germans were using signals intelligence to read the Russians' intentions. This guided their measured response: to use the strategic railways of East Prussia to transport troops from the front facing Rennekampf to that facing Samsonov and, by concentrating forces first against one then the other, to defeat Jilinsky's Army Group in detail. While Prittwitz had approved and initiated this plan, this did not prevent Moltke, the Kaiser's Chief-of-Staff at Main Headquarters (OHL) at Coblenz, far away on the Rhine, replacing Prittwitz on the ground of loss-of-nerve.

Here occurred one of the first crises of the war; by 21 August, Prittwitz's gloomy prognostications had so unsettled Moltke that, even at this critical moment in the west when he needed every man in Belgium to strengthen the right wing there, he was thinking of detaching corps from the Western Front to send significant reinforcements to the east. He partially resolved this crisis by sending Hindenburg, pulled out of retirement, and Ludendorff, the latter having recently distinguished himself at Liège, to relieve Prittwitz the following day. Rennenkampf continued his advance towards Königsberg, defeating a German force at Frankenau and entering Insterburg, but the Germans were already responding. On the arrival of the Hindenburg and Ludendorff duumvirate, Hoffmann's plans were approved and the railway and marching movements that led to the German victory at Tannenberg were set in motion.

ABOVE LEFT: A German poster-map showing the August 1914 Advance in the East. The 'Russian Steamroller' into East Prussia was checked at Gumbinnen and stopped at Tannenberg. In the south the Austro-Hungarian armies advanced against the Russians but were pushed back.

ABOVE: A German poster-map showing the Battle of Tannenberg, East Prussia, 24–30 August 1914, which played a decisive part in stopping the Russian advance when Samsonov's Second Army was caught in a German trap and defeated before Rennenkampf's First Army could come to its aid.

At Coblenz, Moltke, who had at one stage been thinking of sending up to six corps (twelve divisions) from the Western Front, was sufficiently reassured to send only two. But their transfer significantly reduced the strength of Kluck's and Bülow's right-wing armies in Belgium and France, perhaps contributing to the failure of the Schlieffen Plan. At this date the Allies were in rapid retreat in the west (the British 2nd Corps had halted to fight the Battle of Le Cateau on 26 August), and the pressure on them needed to be maintained. The two Russian army group commanders, Jilinsky in the north and Ivanov in the south, were worried about the internal strength and cohesion of their forces and so lacked the confidence and the information to take the decisive action that would help their Western Allies.

In Galicia, the encounter operations between 23 August and 12 September are known as the Battle of Lemberg (Lvov). In four big battles, which saw initial Austrian victories in western Galicia, Conrad's three Austrian armies (from their right, Third, Fourth and First) came to grips with the four Russian armies (Fourth, Fifth, Third and Eighth) of Ivanov's South West Army Group. The Austrian Second Army was meanwhile redeploying in Galicia from the Serbian front. The outcome, however, was an Austrian defeat that saw the Russians forcing them back to the Carpathians.

Conrad's forces had advanced, and were engaging Ivanov's Fourth and Fifth Armies at Lublin, southwest of Brest-Litovsk, and Przemysl, west of Lemberg, his First Army fighting the successful Battle of Krasnik on 23–6 August. He had envisaged a manoeuvre to envelop the Russian Fifth Army, under Russki, at Komarów. The climax occurred on the twenty-sixth when, although Conrad's centre and left did well, Ivanov's forces defeated the Austrian right. Conrad concentrated on his left, encouraged by the German manoeuvre against the Russian Second Army in East Prussia, where von François' 1st Corps made an aggressive move against Samsonov's left (west) flank, causing the Second Army to begin a withdrawal to the south.

The promise of a decisive victory over the Russians beckoned, if the Germans could push south from East Prussia and the Austrians drive northward to meet them, thus catching the three Russian central armies – half their total force – between two fires. As the two German reinforcing corps, released from Belgium following the capture of Namur, were only ordered east on 26 August, they arrived too late to take part in these operations. The crisis of Tannenberg for the Russians occurred on 29 August and by the following day the Second Army no longer existed and Samsonov had shot himself. Despite this German victory, no great results followed, for Conrad's Austrians were falling back under Russian pressure. His right flank disintegrated, while his centre

was pushed back to Lemberg. Russki's Fifth Army and Brusilov's Eighth prevailed here against Conrad's troops, forcing an Austrian retreat to avoid Samsonov's fate at Tannenberg.

On 6 September, Hindenburg was pushing north in East Prussia to try to crush the Russian First Army against the Baltic. Rennenkampf, however, aware of this movement, was able to pull back to the east. Further operations in this area in September, the Battle of the Masurian Lakes, forced Rennenkampf's army back on a wide front, and pushed it out of East Prussia. However, an advance by the Russian Tenth Army threatened the German flank and prevented further progress.

In the south, however, the Russians continued their success against Austrian forces, driving their right back to Lemberg, and defeating Conrad's centre at Rawa Russka, northwest of Lemberg. By the end of September, while the Russians had been pushed out of East Prussia, the Austrians had retreated from Lemberg and the Przemysl fortress, leaving a substantial garrison bottled up in the latter, and the Russians had advanced far enough through Galicia and Poland to pose a threat to Silesia and even, perhaps, to Berlin. The Austrians had retreated 200 miles and by the end of this manoeuvre had lost 350,000 men in the fighting against the Russians. With their losses in the Serbian campaign, total Austro-Hungarian casualties were already 600,000, a rate the Habsburg Empire could not sustain. From now on the Austro-Hungarian Empire was moribund – indeed the Germans began speaking of being 'shackled to a corpse'. In future the Austrians would have to be supported by German forces. In the west, the Allied victory on the Marne and the subsequent stalemate on the Aisne, and again following the 'Race to the Sea', had left the Germans to contemplate the failure of their grand scheme for a quick victory in that theatre.

In the east, on 1 October, while the 'Race to the Sea' was in progress, Hindenburg advanced to the support of Austria in the direction of Warsaw, in the heart of Russian Poland, and Ivangorod to its southeast, hoping to envelop the Russian armies. The Russians, however, were well aware of the danger. They retreated in time and regrouped to pose their own threat to Silesia. By 23 October, Hindenburg's troops were being pushed back at Warsaw by the Russian advance, and he was forced to demand reinforcements. On 11 November he advanced again against Warsaw, but with so little success that on his right flank, southwest of Warsaw near Lodz, three of his divisions were temporarily cut off by the Russians. To the north, Russian forces once more entered East Prussia, while in Galicia they forced Conrad's armies southwards as far as the crest-line of the Carpathians, capturing the strategic Dukla pass on 30 November. By now logistical problems intervened to prevent further effective Russian

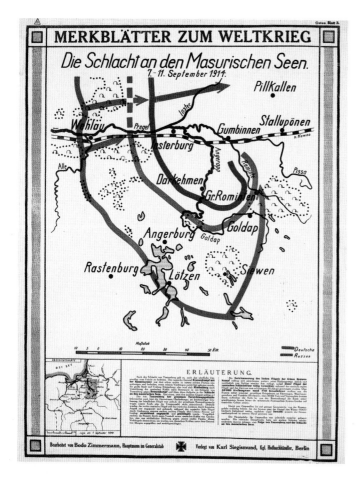

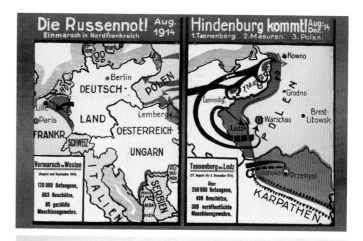

ABOVE: The Russian attack on Germany from east, 1914, and the German victories: Tannenberg, Masurian Lakes, Poland, 1914–15, from a German poster map.

LEFT: A German poster-map showing the Battle of the Masurian Lakes, East Prussia, which followed Tannenberg and led to a temporary stalemate on this front.

RIGHT: The development of trench systems and trench maps in the winter of 1914–15. A British 1:10,000 scale manuscript map of the in-depth defences of Ploegsteert Wood, between Ypres and Armentières, showing trenches, sandbag breastworks, corduroy and brushwood tracks, strong-points, etc. The German front trenches are on the extreme right. The first trench maps were hand-drawn, but were soon reproduced by duplicator or lithography for wider distribution. Maps showing one's own defences were classified 'Secret'.

operations. Shortages of weapons, ammunition and equipment were sapping the hitting power of Russian units and formations, while casualties among junior officers were difficult to replace owing to the shortage of educated men. Russian casualties had been enormous; in the Warsaw offensive alone they had lost 135,000 prisoners.

The failure of the Schlieffen Plan caused a reversal of German strategy. Henceforth she would stand on the defensive in the west, and concentrate on knocking out Russia. Moltke had already made the decision. On 17 November the Germans began the first grand transfer of formations from the Western Front to the Eastern. For three weeks the troop trains rumbled slowly across Germany, carrying the infantry, artillery and supporting services of eight divisions (four corps). Indeed, in France, Joffre saw this as an opportunity to launch new attacks, starting with the First Battle of Artois on 8 December, all of which failed in the usual welter of mud and blood. Joffre's 'nibbling' at the German position in the west had begun.

The German attack against Warsaw, launched in November, was fiercely resisted by the Russians, but the Central Powers

kept up the pressure even in appalling winter conditions. On 6 December the Russians were forced out of Lodz, but stoutly held their trench line to the west of Warsaw. Meanwhile the Serbs had put in a furious counter-attack, and routed the Austrian invaders. At the end of 1914 the Central powers did not appear to be in a strong position on the Eastern Front. The Austrians had performed badly against the Serbs and Russians, and the latter now held much of Austrian Galicia, a greater area in fact than the German territory occupied by Russia. Germany was also now aware that she would have to provide military support to Austria in all future operations. But Russia was weaker than she seemed. Her exposed position in Poland was vulnerable to attack, she had lost a million rifles, and she faced a critical shell shortage. As her shell consumption had, in five months of war, been thirty times greater than the number produced in that period, her stocks were almost exhausted. The stalemate on the Western Front permitted the Germans to shift forces east to concentrate against Russia, while the Russian armies faced a serious crisis of material. Unless they could be re-equipped, Russia could find herself in a desperate situation.

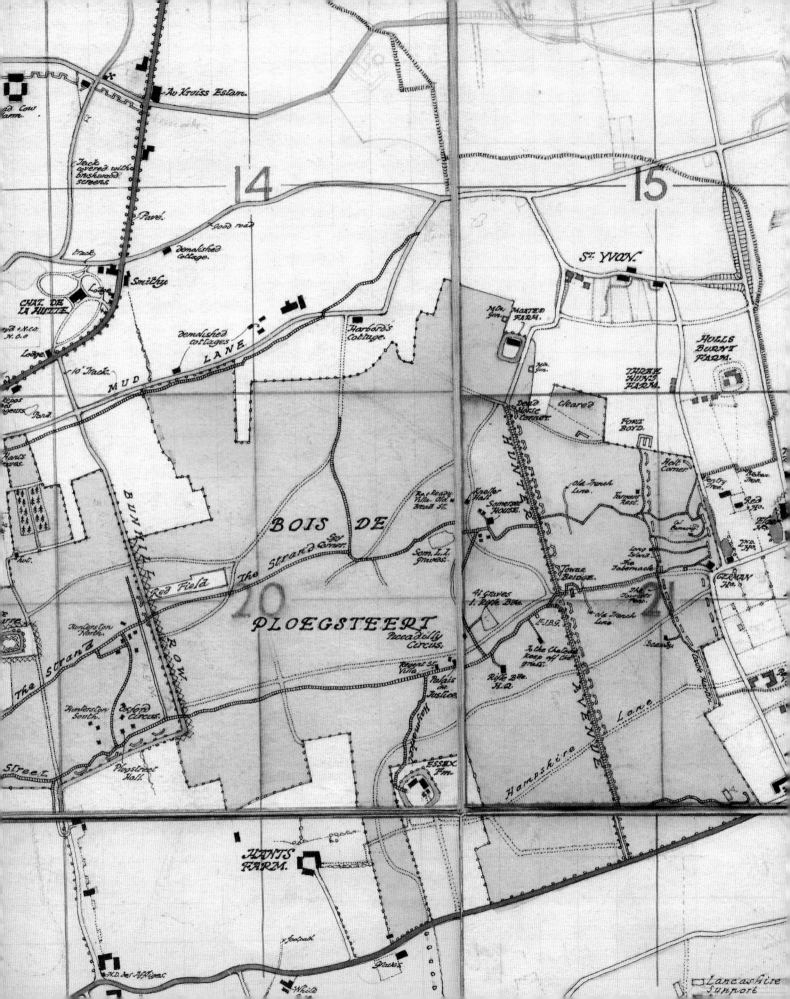

Chapter 3

Italy, Gallipoli, Macedonia, The Caucasus

While the many 'sideshows' or 'other fronts' of the First World War caused much contemporary debate, and have exercised historians ever since, they were all opened for good reasons. Whether for aims of strategy, politics, resources, imperial protection or expansionism, international opinion or internal public opinion, the reasons for the existence and continuation of these fronts must be taken seriously.

The Italian front, while the British and French may have considered it a sideshow, was the main scene of action for Italy and a significant one for the overstretched Austro-Hungarian Empire. It saw four years of heavy fighting, with consequent hecatombs of casualties. Its origin lay in the ancient enmity between Italians and the Austrians, and it is easy to forget how recently large parts of the Italian peninsula lay under Austrian rule. Nineteenth-century nationalism and the Risorgimento were a relatively recent

memory, and Italian nationalists were keen to relieve Austria of more territory that they considered their own.

The Gallipoli campaign was fought to support Russia and knock Turkey out of the war, but it was also fought with Islamic opinion in mind, as were the Palestine and Mesopotamian campaigns. Even the Macedonian campaign had an Islamic undertone: it was fought in a part of the Balkans which had previously been Ottoman, and in which significant Muslim populations still lived. It is often forgotten how global the world conflict was, and how important were global and imperial considerations. To take just one example, Britain, as an imperial power whose empire contained millions of people of the Islamic faith, could not afford to neglect the effect on those populations in India (which then included the territories of modern-day Pakistan and Bangladesh) and elsewhere. Readers of John Buchan's epic espionage adventure *Greenmantle* will recognize the contemporary

concerns. The prospect of a German-controlled Caliphate aroused at the time genuine fears of a *jihad* against the Allies. Likewise the need to protect resources, for instance the oilfield and installations near and at Abadan on the Persian Gulf could not be neglected.

The Caucasus was, and is, a veritable crossroads of humanity. It divided Turkey from Persia and, more significantly, from the Russian Empire. The theatre of operations lay at the south of the ethnic complexities of the Caucasus proper, that is to say the mountainous bridge of land dividing the Black Sea from the Caspian, and at the north of the equally complex ethnic

juxtapositions of Turks, Armenians, Kurds, Persians and other peoples. The Ottoman Empire had gained a grim reputation for its treatment of minorities whom it suspected of disloyalty, notably the Armenians. At the time, and since, the word genocide has been applied to this episode. The fighting in the Caucasus was primarily between Turks and Russians, but towards the end of the war, with the collapse of Russia, the movement of the Germans into the area, and the rise of the Bolsheviks, the British operations in Mesopotamia were extending into this area.

The Italian Front

Before the war Italy was a member of the Triple Alliance with Germany and Austria–Hungary. But Italy and the Habsburg Empire were essentially at loggerheads, and much of Italy had, before the *Risorgimento* in the nineteenth century, been part of that Empire. At the outbreak of war in 1914 Italy had remained neutral on the grounds that neither Germany nor Austria–Hungary had been attacked. To entice Italy away from the Central Powers into the circle of the Allies, she was offered parts of Austrian territory that she coveted. This Allied stratagem was successful, and on 23 May 1915, after Allied attacks in France and

ABOVE LEFT: A detail from a German map, *Vier Jahre Weltkrieg. 3. Italien, Balkan, Vorderasien,* showing phases of the four years of war on the Balkan front.

ABOVE RIGHT: A detail from a German map, *Vier Jahre Weltkrieg 3. Italien, Balkan, Vorderasien,* showing phases of the four years of war on the Italian front.

LEFT: An oblique view of the Italian Front from the south, showing the mountainous terrain north of the plain, and an Italian airship. *Il Teatro della Guerra di Redenzione, Visione Panoramica,* by Mario Stroppa, Milano.

Der Suezkanal.

Übersichtskarte
des
Türk. Kriegsschauplatze
Maßstab

Frontlinie November 19

|||| Von den Russen
besetztes Gebiet

at Gallipoli, Italy declared war on Austria–Hungary but not, at this stage, on Germany.

The strength of the Italian army and her navy, which faced the Austrians in the Adriatic, was a valuable addition to the Allied forces. General Cadorna's army numbered 36 infantry divisions, as well as artillery, cavalry, engineers, etc., and an air force experienced in war since the 1911 operations in Tripoli

(Libya). While this infantry force was superior to the Austrian forces deployed along her frontier, the extreme terrain severely limited offensive possibilities. Italy's war aims were directed towards the Trentino salient, north of Lake Garda, and the part of Friuli, north of Trieste, held by Austria. These areas had substantial Italian-speaking populations, providing Italy with a justification to 'liberate' them from the Austrians. Just as the chain of the Carpathian mountains in the north of Austria–Hungary provided the Habsburg Empire with a natural defensive rampart, so the Alps formed an almost impassable barrier in its south.

As so often in war, terrain proved the decisive factor, the Italian army being forced to advance uphill against defenders in higher and well-protected positions. This was particularly the case in the Trentino, the Lake Garda–Trent front, where in superior positions on the higher ground the Austrian army dominated

ABOVE: Italian *Alpini* mountain troops in a zig-zag column in the snow in the Tyrol.

LEFT: A detail from *So Steht der Krieg an der Ost-u. Orient-Front* (War Situation on the Eastern and Near Eastern fronts), *Feldpostbrief* (Field Post Letter, printed on both sides and designed to be folded and posted), with insets of sub-fronts: Egypt, Suez Canal.

the situation. From their fastnesses in the Trentino, the Austrians observed and threatened the Venetian plain. In the northeast, however, on the Isonzo front in the Friuli, the relatively flat coastal area gave Italy the advantage. Against this, the Austrians were strongly entrenched on the east bank of the Isonzo river, with the bastion of the Julian Alps at their backs, and a field of fire over the Friulian plain in front of them. Between these fronts soared the impenetrable, snow-covered knife-edged ranges of the Dolomites and Carnic Alps. This inhospitable zone provided no communication and supply routes, so all Italian movements and supplies had to run through the bottleneck of Venezia and the railway junctions of Verona, Padua and Treviso.

In the six-month period from late June to early December 1915, the Italians attacked four times on the Isonzo front. Their losses in these battles amounted to over 278,000, for little territorial gain, and there were seven more Isonzo battles to come. Joffre might be nibbling at the Western Front, but Cadorna's army was breaking its teeth. At the Chantilly Conference, held by the Allies in December 1915, it was decided to mount simultaneous offensives on all fronts in 1916, to prevent the Central Powers from moving troops from one front to reinforce another. This strategy had only limited success. In March 1916 the Italians failed again on the Isonzo, while Austria, cock-a-hoop at the defeat of Serbia, decided to put in an attack against Italy while the Russians were recovering from their long retreat. In May 1916, Conrad feinted on the Isonzo front and then, on the fifteenth, made a strong attack, the *Strafexpedition*, or punishment offensive, in the Trentino, between Lake Garda and the Brenta river. Amassing 2,000 guns for the bombardment, against the Italian 850, he failed to achieve tactical surprise against a determined Italian defence. His troops advanced ten miles for the loss of 80,000 men, against crumbling Italian defences. Although Cadorna successfully counter-attacked, the shock of the Austrian attack precipitated a political crisis leading to a change of government. Italian casualties were 147,000.

Cadorna, confident that the Austrians had shot their bolt in the Trentino, attacked again on 6 August 1916 in the Sixth Battle of the Isonzo, and two days later captured the fortress of Gorizia, southeast of Udine. German setbacks at Verdun and on the Somme, coupled with the success of Brusilov's offensive on the Eastern Front, had meanwhile encouraged Rumania to enter the war on the Allied side. Falkenhayn, who because of these German reverses had been replaced as the Kaiser's Chief-of-Staff by Hindenburg and Ludendorff, was, together with Mackensen, to prove Rumania's nemesis. Cadorna's success at Gorizia, reinforced by Rumania's accession to the Allies, created a spirit of optimism in Italy which, together with Allied promises of territory, led on 27

ABOVE: A further detail from *So Steht der Krieg an der Ost-u. Orient-Front* (War Situation on the Eastern and Near Eastern fronts), *Feldpostbrief* (Field Post Letter), showing the Isonzo Front.

RIGHT: The Italian Front, showing Allied and Austrian lines, and dates of battles and movements, in red, from *Harmsworth's New Atlas of the World*, c.1920.

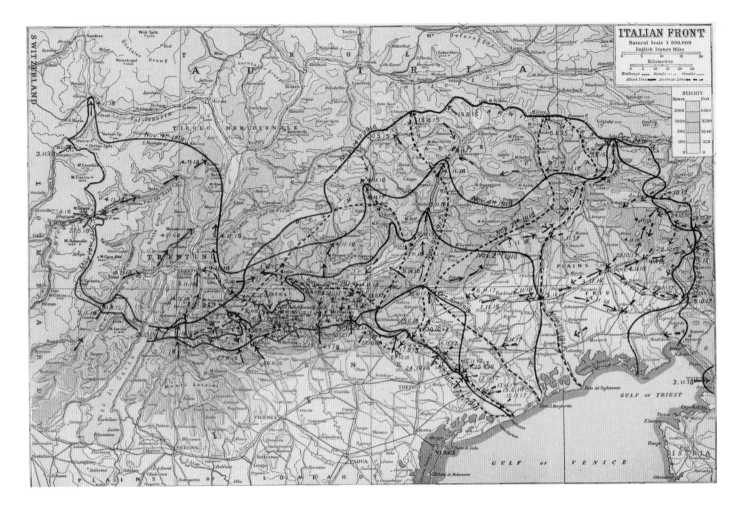

August to a declaration of war against Germany. However, the Seventh (September), Eighth (October) and Ninth (November) Battles of the Isonzo, during the next few months, resulted in little gain apart from expanding the Gorizia bridgehead and edging onto the high ground of the Carso, and stalemate continued on this front.

In December 1916, Lloyd George replaced Asquith as British Prime Minister. At the same time, Nivelle replaced Joffre as French Commander-in-Chief. Appalled by the bloody attrition of the Western Front, Lloyd George was instrumental in suggesting, at the Chantilly Conference of November 1916, that significant numbers of British and French artillery batteries, including personnel, should be sent to Italy to so strengthen the Italian army that it could break through the Austrian lines on the Isonzo. In fact few batteries were sent, Cadorna was in any case not optimistic of success, and the attack, the Tenth Battle of the Isonzo in May 1917, failed. Although they initially took ground, they lost more in an Austrian counter-offensive. The Italian attack had been timed more-or-less to coincide with the British attack at Arras and Vimy

Ridge, and the French Nivelle Offensive. In August 1917, while the British and French were attacking at Ypres, the Italians launched the Eleventh (and last) Battle of the Isonzo. This was a relative success, the Italians capturing the strong Austrian position of the Bainsizzia feature, though at the usual heavy cost in lives.

In terms of attrition, the many Isonzo attacks over two-and-a-half years had bitten deeply into the strength of the Austrian army, to the extent that Straussenburg, Conrad's replacement as Chief-of-Staff, was worried that the Italians might break through. The new Emperor Karl therefore intervened, requesting the Kaiser to provide German assistance – one of many occasions when Germany had been forced to provide help for her weaker ally. This help was duly provided in the form of Below's Fourteenth Army, of two Austro-Hungarian corps and two battle-hardened German corps. Below knew that the Italian army on the Isonzo had extended east-west communications that were vulnerable to an attack from the north. A successful advance here could also drive south to the Gulf of Venice and cut off the bulk of the Italian army on the Isonzo. So on 24 October he launched the Tolmein

Pilot, Lt. Davis.
Observer, Lt. Ellis.

34 Squadron.

May 2. 1918.

34N 638
2·5·18·9

VAL D'ASSA

M. INTERROTTO.

OLD AUSTRIAN FRONT LINE

CAMPOROVERE

This photo gives a good
idea of the VAL D'ASSA, the
main line of approach to
the ASIAGO PLATEAU.
The old No Man's Land is
also clearly visible.

ABOVE: Val D'Assa, the approach to the Asiago Plateau, the old
no-man's-land and Camporovere, 2 May 1918; an oblique air photo.
BELOW: Italian dead after an Austrian gas attack. First used by the
Germans on the Russian front, chemical warfare was widely used

on the Eastern, Western and Italian Fronts.
RIGHT: North of Sculazzon, 11 March 1918, vertical air photo showing
trenches in the snow.

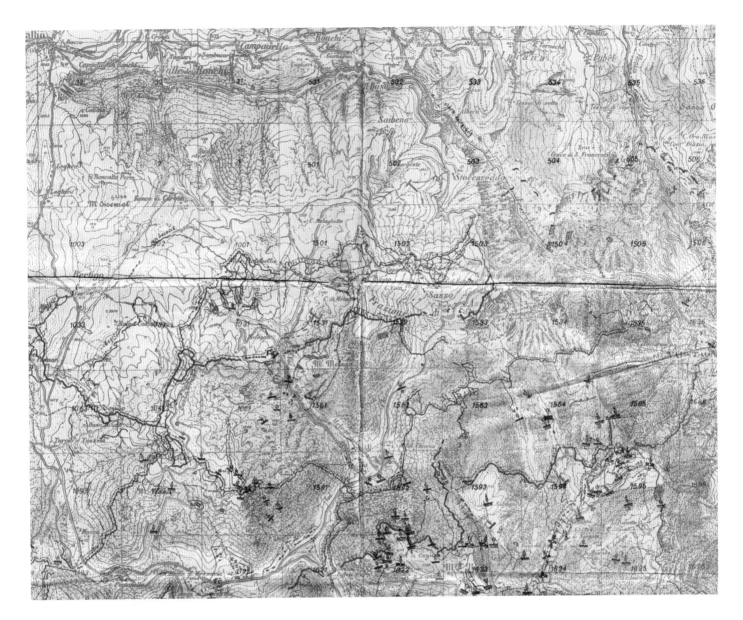

(Caporetto to the Allies) offensive on the Isonzo front. This attack, from Flitsch to south of Canale, on the axis Tolmein–Caporetto–Cividale, broke through the Italian line, the Second Army disintegrating in a rout that spread to the flanking armies.

ABOVE: Austrian *Infanterie-Plan* of 25 July 1918, showing Allied trenches, gun positions, roads, etc., at a time when the British were holding the Asiago front.
LEFT: A British trench map (overprinted in red) of part of the Asiago front. British and French troops were rushed to northern Italy after the Caporetto debacle in October 1917. Survey work on the Italian front was done by 6th Field Survey Company RE.

The stupendous gas and high-explosive bombardment was more intense than anything seen before on the Italian front, and the Italian gas masks were not very effective. By the middle of the afternoon on the first day, Below's army had created a fifteen-mile breach in the Italian defences, and a torrent of Austro-German forces poured through. A complete collapse of Italian morale, and army, followed. Not only had the bombardment torn men and nerves to shreds, but the onset of German troops had been accompanied by the 'force-multiplier' of their reputation for invincibility.

Cadorna attempted to rally his Second and Third Armies many miles to the west across the Venetian plain, on the line of the river Tagliamento, the next big river line before the Piave, just east of Venice, but it was too late for any sort of steady and orderly withdrawal. The Italians had had 1,400,000 men on the Isonzo front, but now most of their formations were little more than a panicky mob. They poured to the rear and lost 650,000 men in an eighteen-day pursuit, of whom some half-a-million were deserters and prisoners. They also lost 3,000 guns.

Although Italian Intelligence had had some forewarning of the attack, the Italian high command neither correctly assessed its strength nor its direction. Cadorna paid the inevitable price, being replaced by Diaz. The Italian army pulled itself together in time to avert a complete disaster, and a new defensive position was formed on the line Adige–Mt Grappa–Lower Piave. This was buttressed by eleven divisions rushed by train through the Alps from France – six French and five British – but these did not need to intervene at this stage. They later entered the line and greatly strengthened Italian morale. Italy had appeared to be heading for both political and military collapse. Fortunately for the Allies, the Flanders offensive was floundering to a close, Passchendaele being captured on 6 November, and divisions could be spared for the time being. However, as the Cambrai fiasco at the end of November showed, the British were desperately short of reserves in France. This shortage had not been made up by March 1918, when the Germans attacked there; the March offensive created a crisis even more acute than Caporetto.

The German and Austrian forces continued to try to force the Allied front on the Piave during November and December 1917, but failed to break through. From the beginning of 1918, the Russian collapse and the peace discussions at Brest-Litovsk focussed German minds on the possibility of a massive offensive in the West. Meanwhile, British forces were holding the Asiago sector, about sixty miles north of Vicenza.

German troops were progressively withdrawn from the Italian front, but the Austrians, enabled by the Russian collapse to concentrate forces in Italy, prepared to put in a decisive attack. This opened on 16 June 1918, but failed to break through. They broke off operations after a week and Diaz started planning a counter-offensive. This – the Battle of Vittorio Veneto – was launched on 24 October, the first anniversary of Caporetto. For four days the Austrians put up a fierce resistance but then, sensing a weakening in front of them, the Italians pushed them back beyond the Tagliamento. Austrian forces were now in headlong retreat, reflecting the more general collapse of the Central powers. The Bulgarians had signed an armistice on 29 September and Turkey on 30 October. Austria–Hungary did the same on 4 November.

Gallipoli

The stalemate on the Western Front from late 1914, and the apparent futility of the Allied attempts at breakthrough, did not deter the British and French generals from continuing their plans for operations in France and Belgium, but others were seeking alternatives. The Grand Duke Nicholas's appeal for relief following the Turkish attack in the southern Caucasus had led Winston Churchill, in particular, to conceive a plan to knock out Turkey by a naval attack through the Dardanelles to link up with Russia via the Bosphorus and the Black Sea. In strategic terms this seemed to some to be very promising in the possibilities it opened up. Turkey at this time could not receive much assistance from Germany, as Bulgaria and Rumania were still neutral and Serbia was holding out against the Austrians. Military weakness and bad communications in northern Turkey and the Caucasus had led to the collapse of the Turkish campaign against the Russians, and an Allied fleet sailing through to Constantinople (Istanbul) could destroy Turkey's sole munitions factory and perhaps force Turkey's surrender. A knockout blow against Turkey would also act as a spur to encourage neutral states in the wider Balkans area – Italy, Greece, Bulgaria and Rumania – to join the Allies. This, in turn, could lead to overwhelming pressure on Austria, and thus a weakening of the Central powers which could, perhaps, be decisive.

In the decade before the war, Britain had been studying closely the possibility of forcing the Dardanelles as a means of putting pressure on Turkey in the event of Turkish threats to Sinai and the Suez Canal. The Akaba crisis of 1906 intensified this effort. Study after study confirmed the view that it would be too risky to undertake, but nevertheless intelligence-gathering on the defences and terrain by the War Office, the Admiralty and the new Secret Service Bureau continued, and several compendious and confidential reports on the Dardanelles and the Gallipoli peninsula were printed. Several clandestine reconnaissances were made,

RIGHT: *Détroit des Dardanelles* (Dardanelles Straits), with inset *Turquie d'Europe*, showing Turkish defences, including the Bulair Lines at the neck of the peninsula, and the forts and batteries at Kum Kale, Seddul-Bahr, the Narrows, etc. Scale of original: 1:120,000, and of inset: 1:2 million.

OVERLEAF: *'The Graphic' Map of the Dardanelles Operations*. Oblique relief map by G. F. Morrell of the Gallipoli Peninsula and Narrows, showing the front lines and Allied ships. The Karachali landing, arrowed at the top, was a feint carried out by Cretan volunteers, to coincide with the Suvla Bay landings.

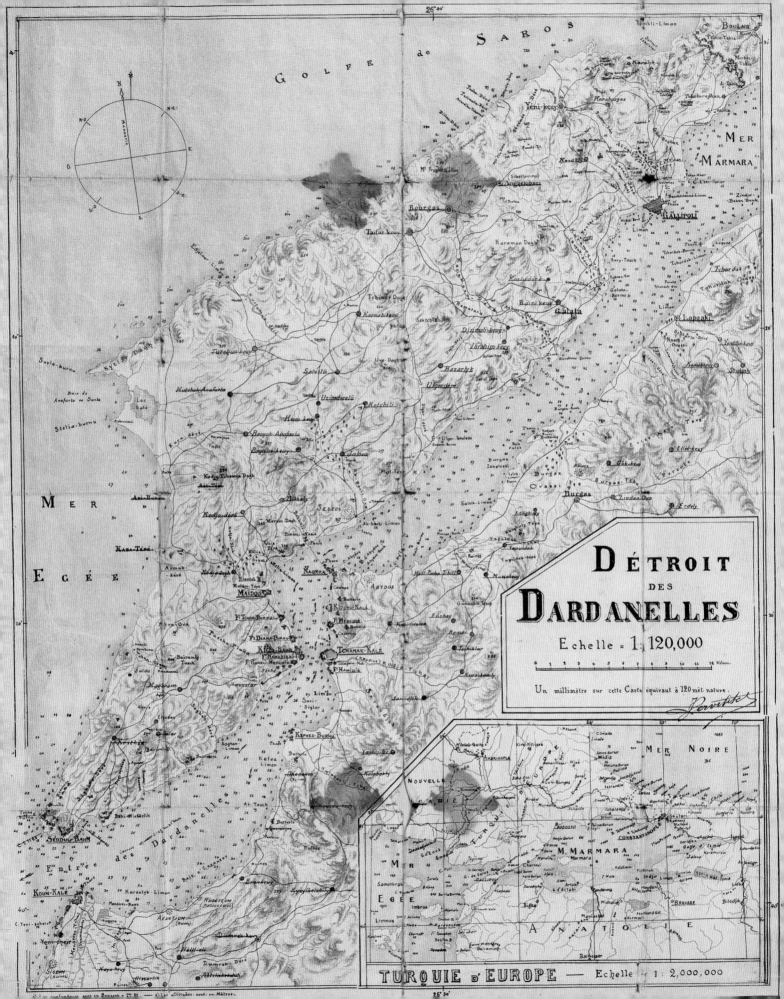

Strictly copyright.;

BATTERING AT THE GATE TO CONSTANTINOPLE: THE PROGRESS OF

This pictorial presentation of the Dardanelles campaign is specially designed to illustrate the joint naval and military operations in the Gallipoli Peninsula, and to enable the Public to follow the movements of the Allies in their progress to Constantinople. Mr. Morrell's drawing illustrates very clearly what Sir Ian Hamilton calls the three dominating features in this section—(1) Saribair Mountain, running up in a succession of almost perpendicular escarpments to 970 feet, and consisting of a network of ravines covered with thick jungle; (2) Kilid Bahr Plateau, which rises, a natural fortification artificially fortified, to a height of 700 feet, to cover the forts of the Narrows

DARDANELLES OPERATIONS

Karachali, the scene of the landing of British troops on August 7.

GULF of XEROS

1322 ft
840 ft
1478 ft
550 ft
BULAIR
BULAIR LINES
Kuku Dagh
1060 ft
932 ft
450 ft
Gallipoli Strait
GALLIPOLI to CONSTANTINOPLE 130 Miles
Chardak Burnu
CHARDAK 500
Burgas
Chaitankeui
Kavakli
Kurtumus Dere
Chinar Dagh 970 ft
Ak Yarlar Dagh 1050 ft
Karanible
Karanible Keui
Uveik Dagh 1160 ft
Bahif
GALATA
GALLIPOLI
991 ft
Ulgar Keui
LAMPSAKI
Karsilar Dagh 820 ft
Usunderleh
Kum Keui
YAILOVA
Ak Bashi Ova
Sarair Tepe 1000 ft
680 ft
Bakajak 820 ft
Mal Tepé 520
BOKALI
Batteries
Bergaz Chai
BERGAZ
Khelia Tepé 450
Bokali Kalessi Fort
Kangarli Tepé 720 ft
FLEE
Maidos Tepé 400 ft
Fort DD
NAGARA Fort Z
CROSS
KELKMAZ DAGH (Mts)
JADA
MAIDOS
Tekeh
Fort KOSSE KALE
Fort MEDJIDIEH
Barracks
CHANAK
Rhodius River
Kilid Bahr Plateau
Cham Kalessi Fort Battery
Fort CC
KILID BAHR
SULTANIEH Fort V
ONE MILE
Corn Fields
HRAM
617 ft Jisoi
Dermaburnu
Fort O
Ft K
Fort T
Fort N
Ft P
Fort S
THE NARROWS
Ft L
Fort R
HAMIDIEH Fort
610 ft
Fort Q
Fort I
Fort F
SARI SIGLAR BAY
Soghan Dere
518 ft
CHANAK to GALLIPOLI 25 Miles
344 ft
Kephez Point
Fort H
Kalabaklr
KEPHEZ BAY
Fort DARDANUS
Ruins of DARDANUS
SEDD el BAHR to CHANAK 15 Miles
Fort G
Kuz Keui
sarlik Point
OSTEMI
1107 ft
AREN KEUI
Where the FRENCH TROOPS first LANDED
on Apr. 25th capturing 500 prisoners, after
ausing a diversion of the TURKISH GUNS
from shelling the European shore. On the
26th they re-embarked & LANDED to the
right of 'V' BEACH where they joined
in the general advance
AREN KEUI BAY
KUM KALE

[Design registered.

THE ALLIED NAVAL AND MILITARY FORCES AT THE DARDANELLES

from an attack from the Ægean; and (3) Achi Baba, a hill 600 feet in height, dominating at long field-gun range the toe of the peninsula. Gallipoli is an ideal place to defend, and the Turks have made the most of their opportunities, the whole peninsula being converted into a network of trenches and small redoubts, well supplied with guns of all calibres and protected by elaborate entanglements. Here is being fought out what Mr. Churchill has well called "the last and finest crusade," and slowly but surely the heroic troops of France and Great Britain are overcoming all the obstacles with which both man and nature have beset the road to Constantinople.

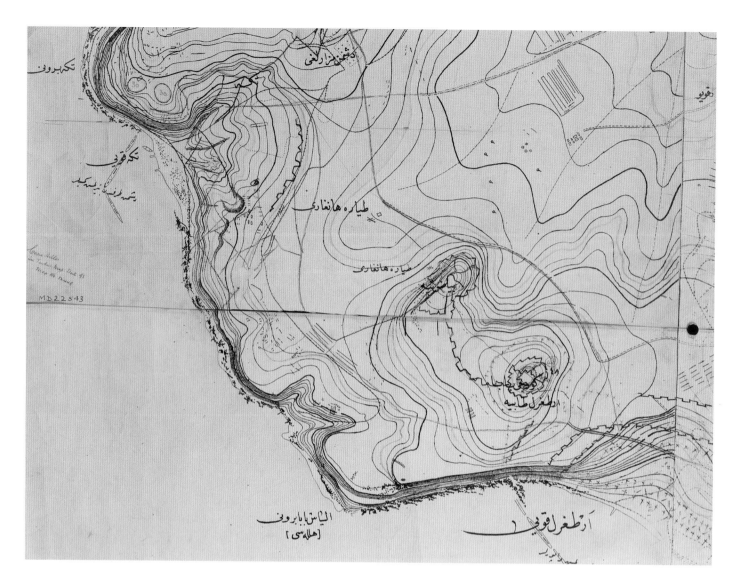

among others by Frederick Cunliffe Owen, the military attaché who was a keen amateur yachtsman, and by Major Rhys Samson, the military consul at Adrianople who, in 1910, provided detailed information and mapping of potential landing beaches and routes across the peninsula to take the forts in the rear. Close cooperation with Greece also took place in this context, as the Greeks themselves had prepared various landing plans.

Churchill's plan at first envisaged only a naval operation, using minesweepers and old battleships to force a passage through the minefields and shore batteries of the entrance to the Dardanelles and the Narrows into the Sea of Marmara, from where the British and French fleet would continue eastward to the Bosphorus and Constantinople.

However, the Turks and their German military advisers had been thoroughly forewarned. Churchill had ordered a British naval

bombardment of the forts at Cape Helles and Kum Kale, at the entrance to the Dardanelles on 3 November 1914. There was a further bombardment from 19 February to mid-March 1915 and there were landings of naval and marine demolition parties.

On 18 March a big attempt was made to push through. Three battleships struck mines, and the fleet, under the British Admiral de Robeck, turned back. Although the Turks were worried enough to make preparations for the government to leave Constantinople for a safer location in Asia Minor, the Allies did not renew the attack. Instead they conceived a new plan, involving the landing of large numbers of troops on the peninsula to capture it before the fleet was sent through.

The Turks had, advised by the German military mission, fortified the peninsula during the Italo-Turkish War and the Balkan Wars, and again following the naval bombardment of 3 November

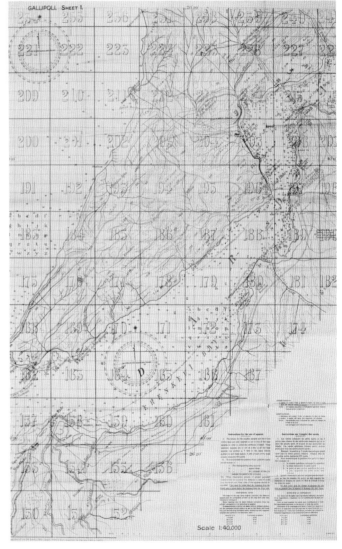

ABOVE: The converted collier, *River Clyde*, aground at V-Beach, Cape Helles, some time after the Allied landings at Gallipoli on 25 April 1915. The 'sally ports' cut in her sides to enable the rapid disembarkation of the assaulting infantry can be clearly seen.

LEFT: Turkish large-scale plan, with Arabic script, of Cape Helles and Sedd-el-Bahr area, made after the evacuation, showing trenches and installations.

RIGHT AND OVERLEAF: *Map of Gallipoli*, Sheet 1, 1915, 1:40,000, reproduced by the Survey Dept. Egypt, from a map supplied by the War Office. An enlargement of a British 1-inch to the mile map, which in turn was taken from a 1:50,000 French Crimean War survey. This sheet shows the Narrows–Cape Helles–Kum Kale. It was the initial assault map for the landings on 25 April 1915, and has a naval squaring system overprinted in red which was different to the one previously adopted by the army. Two details are shown overleaf.

1914. The delays in mounting this operation gave the Turks time to strengthen their defences even further to cover the possible landing places, digging trenches and constructing strong-points, wiring them, and siting machine guns and artillery for maximum effect. A Greek offer to supply three divisions for the landings had to be turned down because of Russian objections – each country rightly feared that the other coveted Constantinople.

After much preparation and some aerial photographic reconnaissance of Turkish defences, the Allies landed on 25 April – henceforth 'Anzac Day'. The main British beaches were at Cape Helles, at the tip of the peninsula, and Anzac Cove on the northwest coast. The French made diversionary landings at Kum Kale on the Asiatic shore, near the ruins of Troy. The troopships of the Royal Naval Division also made a demonstration off Bulair, at the neck of the peninsula where there were strong Turkish

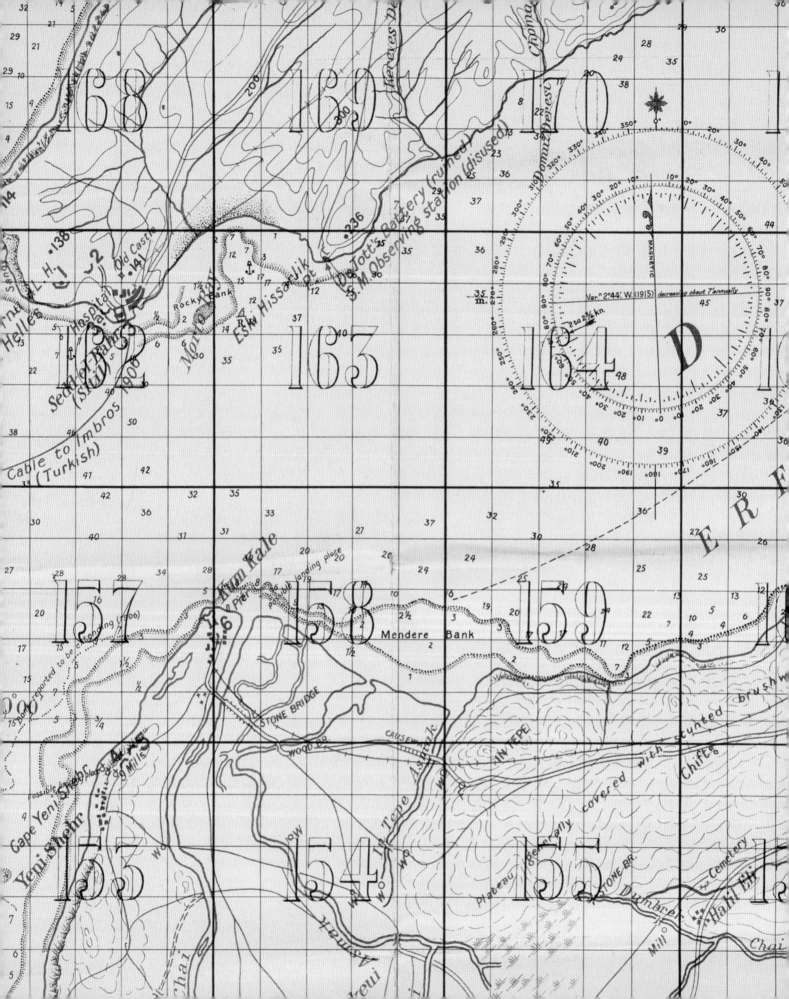

ABOVE: Gallipoli: Anzac sector. New Zealand and Australian Divisional Headquarters, with Plugge's Plateau in the background.
LEFT: Map of the Anzac Position, Gallipoli, showing the main trench lines, British in red and Turkish (as known on 6 August 1915) in blue. As can be seen, before the Suvla landings on 6 August, the northern flank at Anzac was remarkably open. The base map is from the redrawing at the Survey of Egypt of captured Turkish 1:20,000 sheets.

fortifications, before sailing back to land their troops at Helles. The French troops landed at Kum Kale were also transferred to Helles. By attacking Cape Helles, the British were, perhaps foolishly, going for the strongest point. This might have made an effective diversionary operation, but the Australians and New Zealanders of the Anzac Corps were most unfortunately landed a mile north of

their planned points. They became entangled in scrub-covered ravines and ridges, were pinned down by small Turkish forces, and failed to cross the peninsula to attack the Narrows forts and batteries from the rear. The landings had not achieved their aim.

The Helles landings were a massacre. The plan included putting troops ashore from a converted collier, the *River Clyde*, which was run directly towards the beach. Although large sally-ports had been cut in the ship's sides, she grounded some distance from the beach and lighters had to be lashed together, under fire, to get the troops ashore. Rifle and machine gun fire killed most of those who made the attempt. Subsidiary landings at other beaches in the Helles area were relatively unopposed, but because of poor communications were not reinforced and made little progress, and the commanding height of Achi Baba remained in Turkish hands.

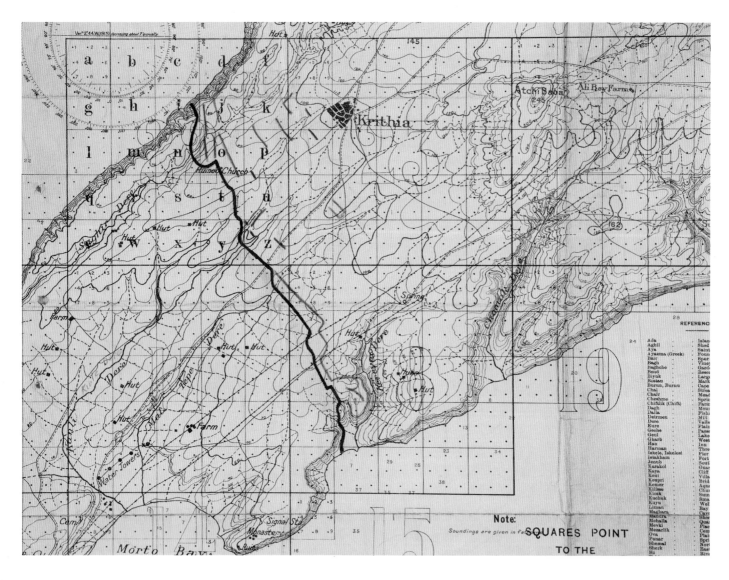

At Anzac the operation was disturbed by the dislocation of the landings and the advance inland was blocked by Mustafa Kemal who, seeing that this was the key to the success or failure of the landings, brought up a regiment by forced march.

However, the very fact of the landings encouraged Italy to join the Allies. With her eyes on significant areas of Austrian territory, she declared war on Austria in May. The landings and the struggle to consolidate the bridgeheads were followed by stalemate. At Anzac the commander was so discouraged by events that he wanted to re-embark his troops. He was prevented. It now became a war of position, as in France and on other fronts, and trenches proliferated, the Turks bringing in more reserves and ammunition, and digging furiously. The Allied trench line at Helles was held by the French and British, while the Anzacs, reinforced with British troops, remained in the bridgehead they had captured. Allied attacks at Helles towards Krithia, and at Anzac, resulted in little except high casualties. The losses were compounded by dysentery caused by heat, flies and lack of sanitation. Landing sufficient supplies and drinking water was a perennial problem.

ABOVE: Taken from captured Turkish map sheets, this Krithia sheet covers most of the Helles front. Trenches in manuscript: British in red, French in blue, Turkish in grey-green. Good, large-scale maps were not available until sheets such as this, the results of a very recent Turkish survey, were captured.

TOP RIGHT: French soldiers in a trench at Cape Helles. The Royal Naval Division shared this trench with the French for some months, their protection being sandbags and dead bodies.

BOTTOM RIGHT: Men of the Royal Naval Division and Australians in the same trench, one using a sniperscope and another a periscope, 28 April–12 May, near Quinn's and Courtney's Posts, Gallipoli.

Large-scale 'trench diagrams' were produced by novel methods, using aerial photographs, at first by Major W. V. Nugent of the Royal Artillery who used such photographs to make a map for his battery, and then with the help of Ernest Dowson of the Survey of Egypt. In Gallipoli, even more than in France, the pre-war maps were very inaccurate for plotting new topographical and tactical detail from photographs, but new triangulation survey by the British and French, and the capture of new large-scale Turkish maps, helped to provide a control framework, and Dowson introduced a light-projection apparatus to assist in the photo-plotting process.

One more attempt to break the deadlock was made on 6 August north of Anzac, at Suvla Bay. This was intended to drive inland behind the Turkish position at Anzac, capture the high ground at Anafarta, and cut the Turkish communications, while the Anzacs drove towards the Sari Bair height. Unfortunately the British landings at Suvla turned into a fiasco. The two inexperienced New Army divisions of Stopford's 9th Corps, despite landing unopposed, failed to move rapidly inland, while Stopford took little interest in events for a crucial two days. A complete lack of urgency characterized the operations, to the thankful disbelief of the Turks who, commanded by the German Liman von Sanders, sat on the high ground watching the British troops sunbathing. This hiatus gave the Turks time to bring divisions up by forced march from Bulair, fifty miles to the northeast, and dig defensive positions on the heights to contain the landing force.

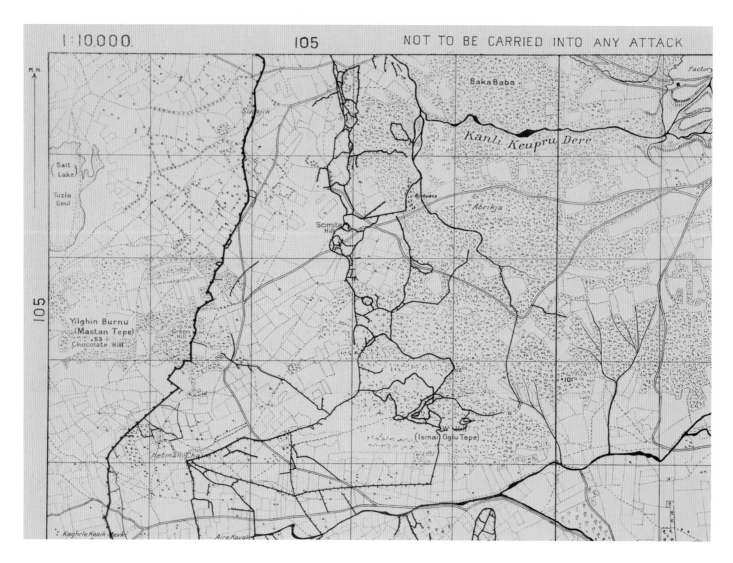

The failure of this landing to achieve Allied aims now encouraged Bulgaria to join the Central Powers and this led to crushing operations by Austria, Germany and Bulgaria against Serbia in September. The failure at Gallipoli also discouraged neutral Greece, which disdained to honour treaty obligations to help Serbia. In turn, and too late to prevent the defeat of Serbia, the Allies landed an occupation force at Salonika.

Meanwhile, the Allies had given up hope of success at Gallipoli, and it was soon decided to evacuate the peninsula and transfer the 134,000 troops to other theatres. Ironically, while so many aspects of the Gallipoli campaign had been characterized by incompetence and sloth, the evacuations were meticulously planned and efficiently carried out. Thinning-out began early, and by 19 December the last man had been taken off from the Suvla-Anzac sector. This alerted the surprised Turks to the reality of the situation, and the evacuation of the Helles position was therefore a more precarious undertaking. Nevertheless, the same thinning-out process went on, a Turkish attack repulsed, and again the last men were re-embarked with the loss of only one man killed, and he by flying debris from a deliberate demolition. To evacuate these huge numbers effectively without loss was a remarkable achievement, as losses of up to 40,000 had been anticipated.

ABOVE: Trench map of the Anafarta Sagir–Suvla Bay area. The British front line (thick, on the left) and all Turkish trenches are shown in red. The Salt Lake at Suvla and Chocolate Hill can be seen on the left.

RIGHT: A map of the Krithia area (Helles front) trench system, 28 December 1915, emphasizing the communication trenches along which men would be withdrawn to the beaches for evacuation, and showing aid posts and dressing stations. The Aegean coast can be seen on the left.

8TH ARMY CORPS
MAP
SHOWING
COMMUNICATIONS TO BRITISH FRONT
FROM
CENTRAL AREA

BASED ON G.H.Q. SURVEY
AND
COMPILED FROM AEROPLANE PHOTOGRAPHS
Nº MS 30

yards 250   0   250   500   750   1000   1250   1500 yards

SCALE 1:10,000

⊕ REGT AID POSTS
▣ R.A.M.C. DRESSING STATIONS

Note: Squares correspond with those
on the 1,20,000 map.

MAP SECTION
8TH ARMY CORPS
28/12/15

AEGEAN SEA

Printing Section G.H.Q. M.E.F.   Nº 19

Macedonia

In 1915 the Allies created a new front at Salonika in then-neutral Greece. This was a direct result of Bulgaria's decision to join the Central Powers, which she did on 6 September, and of her joint attack on Serbia with Austro-German armies in that month. Greece, unsure of Allied victory after the failure of the Suvla landings to achieve anything at Gallipoli, and fearful of the military power of her northern neighbours, refused to help Serbia despite treaty obligations. The internal situation in Greece was volatile, as the King supported Germany while the Prime Minister, Venizelos, was sympathetic to the Allies.

ABOVE: French infantry preparing to march after bivouac in the Franco-Serb area of the Balkan front, December 1916.

LEFT: *Salonika*, 1:100,000, compiled in June 1916 from the surveys of the Allied Armies, showing Salonika and British hospitals, medical installations, etc.

To maintain a foothold in the Balkans, which could act as a possible jumping-off point for an attack into the 'soft underbelly of Europe' (as finally happened in late 1918), the Allies sent a Franco-British force to occupy Salonika in early October. This was despite protests from Greece. An attempt by General Sarrail's advance guard to force a way up the railway, running along the Vardar valley, to Uskub (Skopje) and cross into Serbia was blocked by the Bulgarian thrust to the west, and Sarrail's force retreated towards Salonika. The remains of the Serbian army, evacuated to Salonika via Albania and Corfu, was re-equipped as a fighting force. While the British General Staff in London urged evacuation, the Allies remained for wider political and strategic reasons, not least to maintain prestige in the area. The Salonika front was therefore consolidated, vast camps were laid out, and Italian and Russian contingents joined the Serbs, French and British forces.

Knowing that Rumania was to join the Allies, Sarrail's *Armée d'Orient* prepared to attack the Bulgarians facing the Allies on 20 August 1916. The Germans, equally well-informed, planned a pre-emptive surprise strike in Macedonia which was launched on 17

ABOVE: Serbia – the great retreat. A column passing a lake on the field of Kosovo.

BELOW: Salonika, and Balkans, with inset of the Doiran district, showing Allied lines and movements in red. *Harmsworth's New Atlas of the World*, c.1920.

RIGHT: Macedonia; French trench map, *Front de la 156e Division*, reproduced by the *Armée d'Orient, Service Topographique* from a sketch map produced by the Division. Doiran area, 1917. Detail and trenches in black. Scale of original 1:50,000.

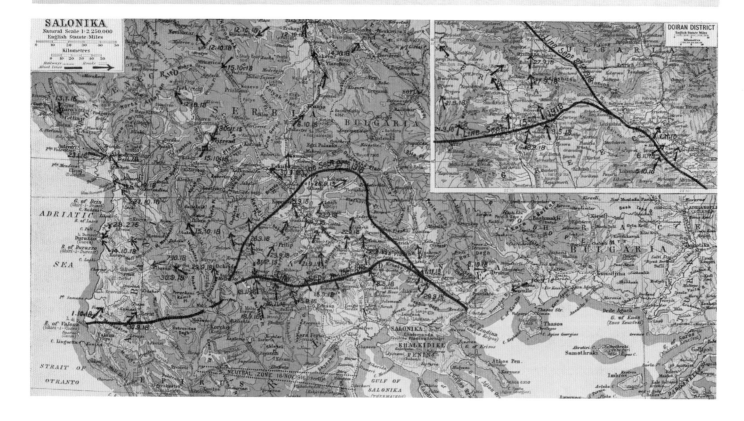

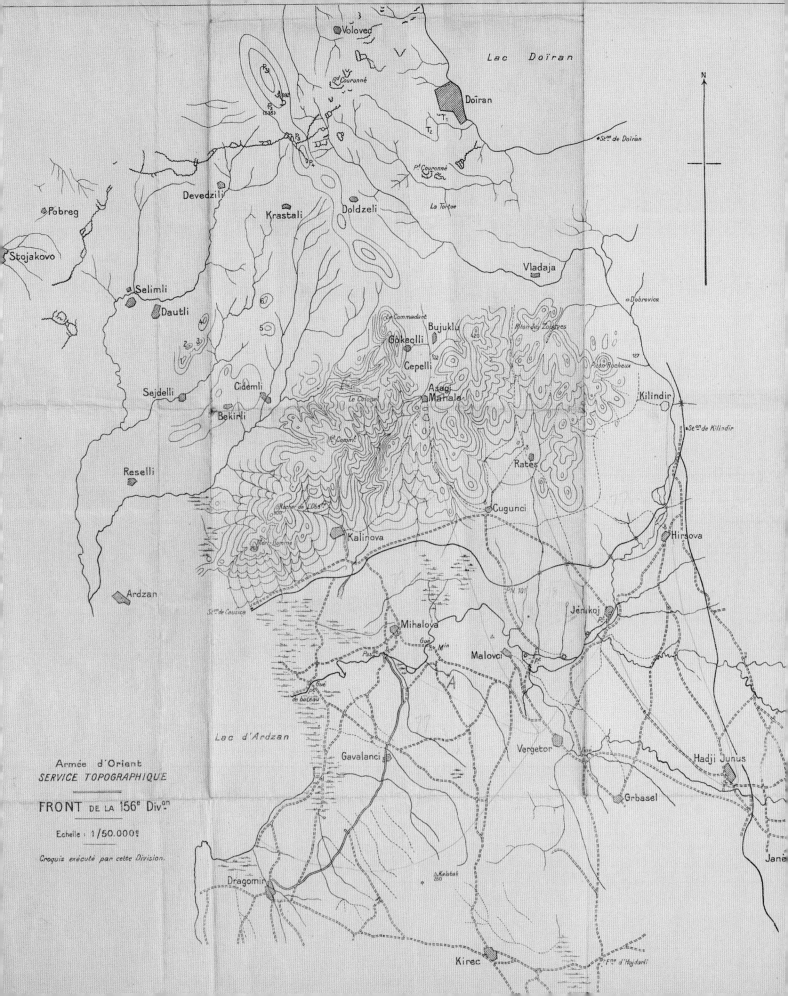

Lac Doïran

N

Voloved
P. Couronné
Doïran
T₁
T₂
♦ Stⁿ de Doïran
P. Couronné
La Tortue

Pobreg
Devedzili
Krastali
Doldzeli

Stojakovo
Selimli
Dautli
Vladaja
Dobrovica

Le Commandant
Bujuklu
Piton des Zouaves
Gökçelli
420
Cepelli
Piton Rocheux
127
Sejdelli
Cidemli
Le Colonel
Asagi
Mahala
Kilindir
Bekirli
♦ Stⁿ de Kilindir
P. Comm.

Reselli
Rates

Rocher de l'Obus
Cugunci
Hirsova
Kalinova
Mort-Homme
P.N. 101
Ardzan
Jénikoj
Stⁿ de Caussica
Mihalova
Malovci
Gué Min
P.
Gué
P.
de Poteau
Lac d'Ardzan
Gavalanci
Vergetor
Hadji Junus

Armée d'Orient
SERVICE TOPOGRAPHIQUE

FRONT DE LA 156ᵉ Divⁿ

Echelle : 1/50.000ᵉ

Croquis exécuté par cette Division.

Grbasel

Kalabak
280
Jane

Dragomir

Kirec
Fⁿ d'Hajdarli

Trenches inserted from aeroplane
photographs up to 17-7-17.

Scale 1 : 20,000

Survey Co., R.E., B.S.F. No. 313

August by the Bulgarians supported by a German division, and also by a Turkish attack on the eastern flank. Early success was achieved, the Serbs were defeated at Florina, and the operation delayed the Allied attack. After two weeks the line stabilized and on 12 September the Allies launched their counter-offensive. Progress was made in difficult terrain, the fighting grinding on into November until winter weather set in. Despite the arrival of two more German divisions, the Allied advance forced the evacuation of Monastir (Bitola), which was entered by the Allies on 19 November 1916. Meanwhile, Italian troops were deployed in Albania against the Austrians.

By the spring of 1917 Sarrail's fighting force comprised twenty-four divisions (seven British, seven Serbian, six French, three Greek, one Italian) plus a Russian contingent of two brigades. An offensive, planned to coincide with Allied attacks in France, was launched towards the end of April. It failed because of the strength of the Bulgarian mountain positions, the Allies' lack of enthusiasm for Balkan operations, and the fact that Sarrail's abrasive personality contributed to poor cooperation between the Allies. Operations were accordingly ended on 21 May. The Allied contingent in the theatre amounted to some 500,000 men, and the international force did little except sit tight and become victim to the malaria endemic to the region. The Germans, watching with some amusement, called Salonika their largest internment camp, while the Allies spoke of 'the gardeners of Salonika'.

In 1918, Franchet d'Esperey replaced Sarrail, and commanded an Allied force of twenty-six divisions (nine Greek, six French, six Serb, four British one Italian). He concentrated a Franco-Serbian force under Serbian command for an offensive starting on 15 September west of the Vardar, where the mountains were strong but the Bulgarian defences weak. The Serbs broke through in two days and advanced twenty miles through the mountains, creating a gap twenty-five miles wide in the Bulgarian line. Further east, a British attack on the Doiran front on the eighteenth failed to break through but pinned down the Bulgarian forces facing them while the Serbs and French continued their advance towards Uskub, collapsing the Bulgarian front. This pressure on the front east of the Vardar now forced a Bulgarian retreat that turned into a rout when British aircraft bombed the Kosturino Pass. With their demoralized army now split into two, and realizing that Germany was heading for defeat on the Western Front, the Bulgarians asked for an armistice. On 29 September this was signed. The Allies, led fittingly enough by Serbia, had knocked away the first prop of the Central Powers, opening the way through Bulgaria for an Allied offensive against Austria. Desperate Frankie had knocked out Foxy Ferdie, and his army continued to move through, and occupy, the Balkans. By the end of the war his forces were advancing deep into Hungarian territory.

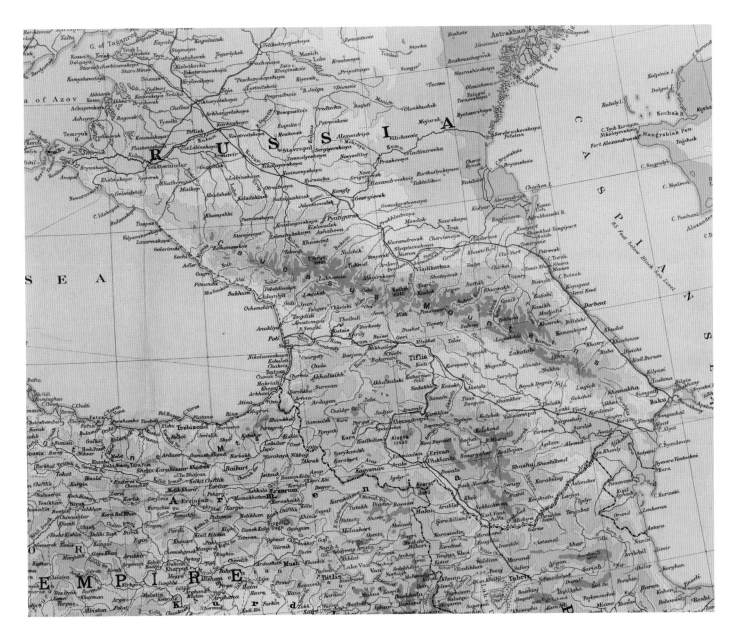

The Caucasus

Turkey and Russia, having been brought into conflict by Russia's inexorable expansion to the south, had fought three wars since 1828. The Caucasus, that great and mountainous land bridge between the Black Sea on the west and the Caspian on the east, was home to different ethnic and religious populations that included Armenians, Georgians and Tartars. Russia had supported, as a defensive measure, nationalist movements in the Balkans and also in the Caucasus. This antagonized the Turks who, in 1914, had just recovered from the Second Balkan War.

Within the Ottoman Empire, the new doctrine of pan-Turkism, which strengthened after Turkey's loss of outlying territories during the Balkan Wars – notably Libya and the Dodecanese Islands to Italy and parts of Macedonia and Thrace to Greece – increased the attraction to Turkey of the Caucasus. Russia had cause enough to know the difficulties of expanding in this fiercely tribal area. A Turkish attack on Russia here would

ABOVE: The Caucasus region from *Philips' Strategical Map of Mesopotamia and Asia Minor, Including the Balkans, Caucasus, Palestine and Egypt*. Scale of original 1:3 million.

LEFT: North of Salonika on the Kireckoj Road; No. 2 Convalescent Depot, 26 November 1917, oblique air photo.

pin down a Russian army and could be accompanied by its claim to be freeing Turkic people from Russian oppression, and also by its cry of *jihad* – holy war. Enver Pasha, Commander of the Ottoman forces, even envisaged a sweep by Turkish forces through Persia and Afghanistan towards British India.

The rugged mountains of the southern Caucasus, freezing and covered with deep snow in winter, were not a wise operational area for the Turks, especially as communications were not favourable to them. Their nearest railhead at Angora (Ankara) was 500 miles further west. Their advanced base of Erzerum, on the upper reaches of the Euphrates, was 650 miles from Constantinople, sixty miles from the Russian frontier and a hundred miles from Trebizond, the nearest Turkish Black Sea port. The main road in the area was the ancient silk route from Teheran, via Tabriz and Erzerum, terminating at Trebizond where goods were loaded onto ships for Constantinople and other western destinations. Trebizond lacked a natural or man-made harbour, had no entrance to a navigable river, and relied on an open roadstead that was subject to frequent and violent westerly winds that made landings impossible. There were no railway links with the interior. Moreover, Turkish shipping was liable to attack by Russian ships, although the Black Sea was dominated by the German-led Turkish navy.

Nevertheless, Enver committed his Third Army to a wide, enveloping movement through the mountains at Sarikamish, rather than the more methodical operations favoured by his German staff officer. Enver's sweep to the left (north), on the axis of Ardahan, took his troops sixty miles further on through hideously difficult terrain and winter conditions, at temperatures sometimes below -30°C. This disastrous manoeuvre saw Turkish supplies exhausted on 25 December 1914, and their army virtually destroyed. The Russians successfully counter-attacked, having held Sarikamish in the battle of 1–4 January. Turkish casualties were between 75,000 and 90,000; most of their force. By 23 January 1915 this only numbered some 12,000 bayonets, with another 8,000 in supporting services. Even now Enver attempted to advance eastwards towards Persian Azerbaijan and Tabriz to encourage the Kurds to stage an uprising against the Russians. This failed.

The Russian 1915 spring offensive aimed south from Kars to the west of Lake Van, in an area of eastern Anatolia partly-populated by Christian Armenians. Antagonism between Muslim Turks and the Armenians had grown in the late nineteenth century, culminating in violent clashes in 1894-6. As the Armenians were supported by the Russians, who in 1914 had encouraged revolt, the Turks suspected treason. Murders of Armenians, with looting and destruction of their villages, by Turkish soldiers, began during the winter. In April 1915, during the Russian advance, an Armenian revolt began in Van. Atrocities by Turks and Kurds followed, and at the end of May the deportation of Armenians south to Syria and Mosul was began. About a million died, either from direct acts of violence or from exhaustion, exposure and disease.

By August 1916, the Russians had pushed as far west as Trebizond, and south to Lake Van, thus creating a large bridgehead in eastern Anatolia. The Caucasus came to prominence again following the 1917 Russian Revolutions, when the Treaty of Brest-Litovsk committed Russia to supplying Germany with oil from Baku, on the Caspian side of the Caucasus, and cotton from Turkestan. The weakening of Russia in the region, consequent upon the revolutions and military incapacity, encouraged the Turks to advance towards Baku. In early 1918 operation Thunderbolt saw the German forces that had moved into eastern Ukraine and the Donetz Basin advancing southeast to Baku. The British were also increasing their presence in the region, following their advance to Mosul and the creation of 'Dunsterforce' in Persia.

Named after its commander General Dunsterville, this was a British military mission of, initially, less than a thousand men, with armoured cars. It was formed after the Russian Revolution had led to the collapse of the Caucasus front to gather intelligence, train and lead tribal militias, and counter German propaganda in Persia. Wilhelm Wassmuss, a German consular official, had long been active in Mesopotamia and Persia, trying to counter Russian and British influence in the area and organize local tribes in an uprising against the British. He has been described as the German Lawrence, a reference to T. E. Lawrence's exploits in Arabia.

Deployed from Hamadan in the middle of western Persia, Dunsterforce was later tasked to secure the Baku oil fields. After being delayed by Russian Bolshevik troops at Enzeli (Anzali), the Caspian port north of Tehran, it sailed to Baku, where it was briefly besieged in September 1918 before being withdrawn.

Chapter 4

Egypt and Palestine, Mesopotamia, Africa

Moving from the northern part of the Ottoman Empire to the southern, several of the themes examined in the previous chapter reappear, for example, the significance of Islam (the context, given in John Buchan's *Greenmantle*, has already been mentioned, and the jihadist activities of the Senussi are included in this chapter), and the need to protect resources such as oil. The oilfields, pipeline, storage tanks and other installations near and at Abadan on the Persian Gulf, on which the Royal Navy increasingly relied for oil fuel, could not be neglected and were the major factor in the British-Indian force being sent to Basra in 1914. However, the Indian government, which had its own agenda not always in tune with that of London, also looked beyond its borders, and had ambitions in Iraq and Persia.

While the Gallipoli campaign was primarily fought to support Russia and knock Turkey out of the war, it was also undertaken with Islamic opinion in mind, as were the Palestine and Mesopotamian campaigns examined in this chapter. The campaigns in Africa were much more imperial in character, though here, as Buchan again pointed out, there was an Islamic element, in the form of possible unrest and worse in the areas bordering on the Sudan and Egypt. The campaign in Egypt and Palestine may have begun to protect the Suez Canal, of vital importance to the Allies, and the British in particular, but its implications were much wider, including its effects on the Arabs within the Ottoman Empire and on Jewish colonies in Ottoman Palestine and, by implication, on the wider Jewish diaspora, such as Jews in Britain and the USA. The question of the Jewish colonies in Ottoman Palestine, which had been established by Zionists from the late-nineteenth century, was sensitive in several respects.

In all of this, the Allies got themselves into a real muddle, making contradictory commitments to a Jewish homeland and to Arab nationalism in the 1916 Sykes–Picot agreement and the 1917 Balfour Declaration. The British, French and Russian governments agreed, in the secret Sykes–Picot agreement in May 1916, to carve up the territories of the Ottoman Empire, outside Asia Minor, between Britain and France, should the Allies succeed in defeating the Ottomans. Britain and France defined and divided the Arab provinces, outside the Arabian peninsula (where the Arab Revolt was already fomenting under the Sharif of Mecca, Hussein ibn Ali), into their proposed spheres of influence and control in Western Asia. They also proposed an international administration of the area that later became the Palestine Mandate. They would decide the type of administration after first consulting Russia, and then the other allies and the Sharif of Mecca. Zionists, when they discovered all this, felt betrayed; their hopes had been ignored. 'Blinker' Hall, Director of British Naval Intelligence, felt the agreement ignored the Jews' strong material and political interests in the future of Palestine. He also held the view that the interests of Egypt had to be taken into account, and the questions of Zionism, and British control of the Palestine railways had to be considered in this light.

The Balfour Declaration, a commitment to the creation of a Jewish homeland, was designed to gain the support of the Jewish population in the Ottoman territories. In a letter dated 2 November 1917, Arthur Balfour, the British Foreign Secretary, wrote to Lord Rothschild, a leading representative of British Jews, for the information of the British Zionist Federation:

His Majesty's Government view with favour the establishment in Palestine of a national home for the Jewish people, and will use their best endeavours to facilitate the achievement of this object, it being clearly understood that nothing shall be done which may prejudice the civil and religious rights of existing non-Jewish communities in Palestine, or the rights and political status enjoyed by Jews in any other country.

This was published in the press on 9 November. The declaration was later incorporated into the Treaty of Sèvres with the Ottomans, and the League of Nations' Palestine Mandate.

Balfour revealed British motives at a War Cabinet meeting on 31 October, two days before his letter, when he suggested that such a declaration would enable Britain to wage an extremely useful propaganda campaign in Russia and the USA. The Cabinet thought it would appeal to Jews in Germany (the home of the modern Zionist movement, founded by Theodor Herzl, a German-speaking Jew born in Hungary, was in central and eastern Europe) and the USA, and help the war effort in various ways. Two of President Wilson's advisors were Zionists, and there was a

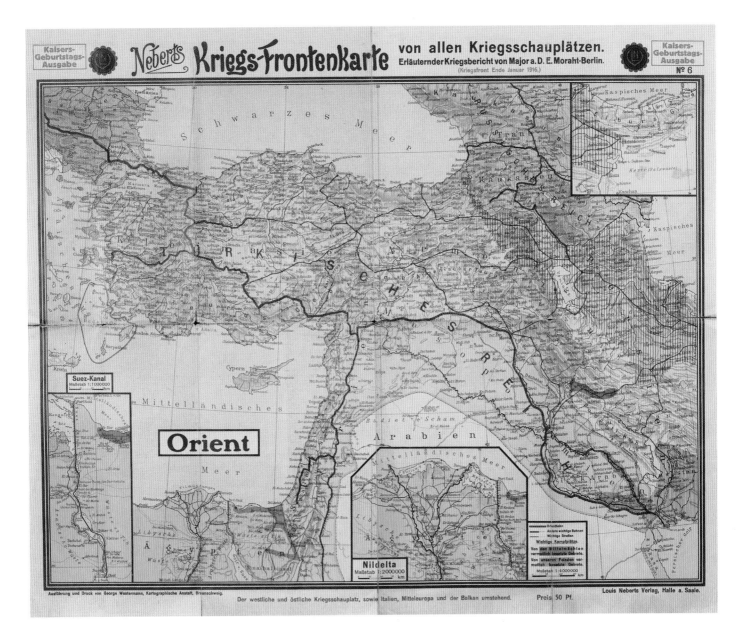

Within the map image:

Kaisers-Geburtstags-Ausgabe

Neberts **Kriegs-FrontenKarte** von allen Kriegsschauplätzen.
Erläuternder Kriegsbericht von Major a. D. E. Moraht-Berlin.
(Kriegsfront Ende Januar 1916.)

Kaisers-Geburtstags-Ausgabe
N? 6

Schwarzes Meer

Kaspisches Meer

Orient

Suez-Kanal
Maßstab 1:1000000

Mittelländisches Meer

Arabien

Nildelta
Maßstab 1:2000000

Ägypten

Ausführung und Druck von George Westermann, Kartographische Anstalt, Braunschweig.

Der westliche und östliche Kriegsschauplatz, sowie Italien, Mitteleuropa und der Balkan umstehend.

Preis 50 Pf.

Louis Neberts Verlag, Halle a. Saale.

---

significant and wealthy American Jewish population. For a British government anxious to raise more war finance, this was a powerful motive, as was Britain's desire, ignoring French and Russian interests, for post-war control of Palestine. Lloyd George echoed the Foreign Office in favouring a Jewish homeland in Palestine as it would help to obtain British control of Palestine after the war, which was strategically necessary to create, in addition to Sinai

ABOVE: *Nebert's Kriegs-Frontenkarte*, showing Egypt, Palestine and Mesopotamia at the end of January 1916.

which was already a British protectorate, a buffer zone to protect Egypt and the Suez Canal.

The Russians also had to be factored in, although they were at a critical point in their Revolution, as several of the key Bolsheviks, including Trotsky, were of Jewish descent. They might keep Russia in the war, especially if their large Jewish population supported this policy. However, the Russian people had other things on their mind. They were desperate for peace, and the Bolsheviks were struggling for power using the slogan of 'peace, land and bread'; they signed an armistice with the Central Powers on 7 November.

In early 1917, the Germans, concerned about the vulnerability of Baghdad to the British advance up the Tigris, warned the Turks

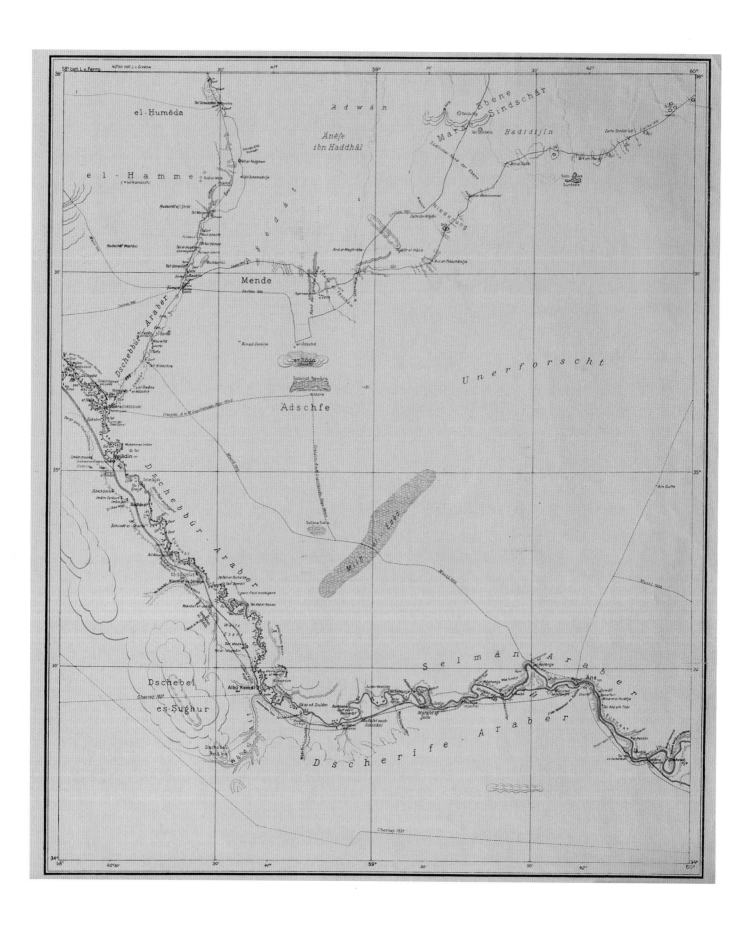

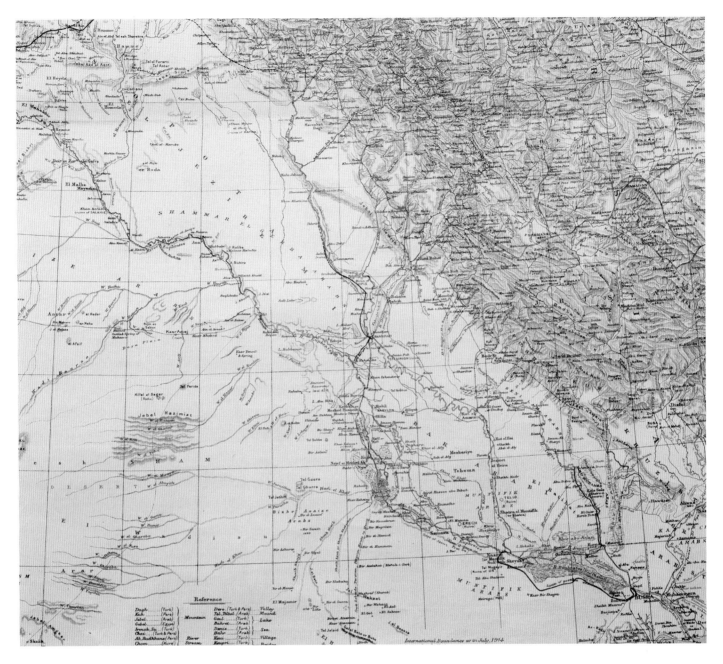

ABOVE: A detail from a general topographical map of the Middle East, and the Ottoman Empire in particular, compiled from travellers' reports, including Captains Aylmer and Butler in the Syrian Desert in 1908, and the surveys of Captain F. R. Maunsell RE, who wrote several reports on the area for the Intelligence Division of the War Office. Originally compiled and published by the Royal Geographical Society (which, like the Palestine Exploration Fund, had a close relationship with the War Office) in 1910, the map was revised to show the railways to 1917.

LEFT: *Karte von Mesopotamien, Sheet 3c. 'Âna* (south-west of Mosul), February 1918, showing the river Euphrates.

of the danger, but to no avail. Following the loss of Baghdad on 11 March 1917, the Germans sent Falkenhayn, the architect of the successful Rumanian campaign, to command the 18,000 German and Austrian troops operating with the Turks in the Middle East. Falkenhayn's initial strategy was to launch a counter-offensive, codenamed 'Lightning' (*Yilderim*), against Baghdad. However, on arrival in the theatre in May 1917, he changed his position. Given that the British had advanced across Sinai and were threatening Palestine – General Murray, Commander-in-Chief, Egypt, attacked on 26 March (First Battle of Gaza) and again on 19 April (Second

Battle of Gaza) – and the fact that the Turks were pinning their hopes on strengthening the Gaza–Beersheba Line, Falkenhayn insisted that the Mesopotamian and Palestine fronts should be unified under his command. He was particularly worried that if he committed his force to the Mesopotamian front, a breakthrough against the Turks in Palestine and Syria would be a threat to his rear and to his communications. His new *Yilderim* headquarters were established at Aleppo in Syria and, in a plan reminiscent of Schlieffen and also of Tannenberg, he intended to defeat the British at Gaza and then switch his weight against Baghdad.

General 'Wullie' Robertson, the CIGS in London, realizing that Falkenhayn intended to strike against Baghdad, supported Allenby's plan for an attack on the Gaza–Beersheba position. To him this was worth devoting resources to, as it would relieve Turco-German pressure against the Baghdad front and secure the British presence and prestige in Persia. Another action of Falkenhayn was his assistance in protecting the Jewish colonies in Palestine from the Turks who, in an attempt to repeat the measures they had taken against the Armenians, planned to 'resettle' the Jews, whom they suspected of espionage. The Turks did hang many Arabs, accused of treason because they expressed support for the Arab rebellion.

During 1918 the Turks maintained the unequal struggle, but were eventually forced back on all fronts (except the Caucasus, where the Russians had crumbled) by sheer weight of resources and numbers. The various British–Ottoman fronts had, during the war, absorbed some two and a half million men. Such profligacy in defending and promoting British imperial interests had nearly led to disaster in France in 1918.

EGYPT, PALESTINE AND ARABIA

In the decade before the First World War, the weaknesses of British and the strengths of German diplomacy had increased the threat from the east to Egypt and the Suez Canal. In 1905, the Turkish High Commissioner in Egypt, Ghazi Mukhtar Pasha, remarked that 'with twelve Army Corps in Syria, and the Germans at our back it should not be difficult to turn the English out of Egypt', and in early 1906 this threat was followed by the 'Tabah' or 'Akaba Incident', a clumsy bluff by the Ottoman Sultan Abdul Hamid II to push the Turco-Egyptian frontier westward from the Akaba–Rafa line into the Sinai desert, towards the Suez Canal. Disturbing elements were detected in British Egypt: boundary pillars had been overthrown and pan-Islamist propaganda was calling on people to support the Caliphate. The Sultan, in fact, claimed the northern Sinai area up to the Tabah–Suez line.

The bluff called, not without Britain threatening the Dardanelles, Britain and Egypt settled down to consolidate their hold on the Sinai peninsula, beginning a military survey which culminated in Newcombe's 'Secret Survey' (his phrase) of the Negeb (Negev) in 1913–14. From the Turkish viewpoint this was correctly perceived as a thinly disguised, cynical and provocative attempt to make a military survey of a crucial strategic area. Nevertheless, they permitted it to go ahead.

It was, from the point of view of British military and imperial policy, a necessary and logical connection between the isolated one-inch to the mile (1:63,360) nineteenth-century survey of Eastern and Western Palestine carried out for the Palestine Exploration Fund (PEF) by the Royal Engineers, and the recent eastern portion of the 1:125,000 (approximately half-inch to the mile) Survey of Egypt and War Office map of the northern Sinai desert, which extended eastward to the Ottoman frontier which ran from Rafa, near Gaza, to Tabah on the Gulf of Akaba. The old PEF one-inch map of Palestine was used by both sides during the war.

This topographical reconnaissance survey of southern Palestine and northeastern Sinai was undertaken by Captain S. F. Newcombe's expedition between December 1913 and May 1914. The work was done by the Royal Engineers officers, Captain Newcombe and Lieutenant J. P. S. Greig, a civilian surveyor from the Survey of Egypt, C. F. Montagu (later, during the war, a captain in 7th Field Survey Company RE), and two Royal Engineers' NCOs, Corporal J. Rimmer and Lance Corporal W. W. McDiarmid. The survey included trigonometrical and topographical work, routes, terrain and 'going' (including water supply, fuel, etc.) and toponymy. In addition, 'cover' was provided by two archaeologists, C. L. (Leonard) Woolley and T. E. Lawrence, who had been excavating at Carchemish in Syria, on the route of the Berlin–Baghdad Railway. The archaeological survey by Woolley and Lawrence, lasting a mere six weeks, was an afterthought, suggested by the War Office to the Palestine Exploration Fund (PEF) in an attempt to generate some convincing 'smoke'. The later exploits of Lawrence, and aspects of his bizarre life, have ensured that, for the 1914 survey of the Negeb desert, the smoke has become substance, and the substance, smoke.

The theodolite and plane-table survey of this inhospitable and desolate area resulted in fine sets of War Office topographical

LEFT: A 1:500,000 sheet of Ma'an, from 1917. Relief shown by hill-shading, but a note stresses the unreliability of sources for terrain east of 35°E and the coastline. Although this map was printed and used during the war, the manuscript annotations are for a post-war (1922) reconnaissance.

maps, and in the Palestine Exploration Fund eventually (in 1921) acquiring a sheet, Newcombe's celebrated 'Map of the Negeb'. The participation of Lawrence and Woolley, and the mysterious title of their subsequent archaeological report (*The Wilderness of Zin*), have distorted the historical perspective and tarred the whole expedition with the brush of clandestine operations. In fact the archaeological cloak was fairly transparent, and was only a six-week episode within the six-month topographical survey. On their way back through Turkey to England, true to form, Woolley and Lawrence reconnoitred and photographed the Taurus Mountains section of the Berlin-Baghdad Railway, still under construction.

British foresight thus provided the army with a military map which proved of crucial importance during the Turkish attacks on the Suez Canal and the subsequent Palestine campaign, and which enormously facilitated the battles of Gaza and operations in the Beersheba area. It is to the credit of the Turks that they permitted such a survey in a strategically sensitive area at a critical geopolitical moment. However, they soon realized that they had been hoodwinked.

Defence of the Suez Canal

Having been resoundingly defeated at Sarikamish, in the Caucasus, at the beginning of 1915, Enver Pasha now turned his attention to the Ottoman's southern frontier with the British Empire – the Sinai desert, so fortuitously surveyed by Newcombe. It formed the only barrier between Ottoman possessions in Syria and Palestine, and the Suez Canal, that vital Allied lifeline to India, the east coast

ABOVE: Kemal Pasha, commander of the Turkish Fourth Army in Palestine, planning to invade Egypt. Attacks on the Suez Canal, across the Sinai Desert, were defeated by the British in February 1915 and August 1916.

OVERLEAF LEFT: Outline Map of Turkish Empire showing the Ottoman possessions, Russian and Ottoman railways including the metre-gauge Hejaz Railway to Medina which was raided by T. E. Lawrence and Arab forces. Scale of original: 1: ten million.

OVERLEAF RIGHT: A British tank in action near Gaza on the Palestine front, 1917. While the new technologies of war were useful, cavalry and mounted infantry played a vital role in the Palestine campaign.

of Africa, the Persian Gulf and the Far East. Australian and New Zealand troops, en route to France, had been diverted to defend the Canal in December 1914, as well as Indian divisions. A weak Turkish attack across Sinai in February 1915 was easily repulsed. The Anzac corps totalled nearly 89,000 men, and was then in prime position for employment in the landings on the Gallipoli peninsula on 25 April.

Siwa and the Senussi

In Egypt's Western desert, a 'sideshow within a sideshow' was waged by British (from Egypt) and Italian (from Libya) troops between November 1915 and February 1917 against the Senussi, mostly Berber-speakers, who claimed a direct lineage to the Prophet Muhammad. Living in Libya and the Sudan, they belong to an Islamic political-religious Sufi order founded in Mecca in 1837 by the Grand Senussi, Sayyid Muhammad ibn Ali as-Senussi, who was concerned with both the decline of Islamic thought and spirituality and the weakening of Muslim political integrity. Between 1902 and 1913, the Senussi had fought against French colonial expansion in the Sahara region, and from 1911 against Italian colonization in Libya.

Influenced by the Turks, who hoped to make another attempt on the Suez Canal, in the summer of 1915, the Grand Senussi, Ahmed Sharif as-Senussi, raised the standard of *jihad* among his tribesmen, and encouraged an Egyptian insurrection, against the infidel occupation of British Egypt. In November 1915 they crossed the Egyptian border in a three-pronged attack. The northernmost was along the coast in November, and this was countered at first by a British withdrawal, but then by a counter-attack in several stages, after being reinforced by South African troops. The coastal strip was regained by March 1916. A Senussi attack in the south, against the Sudan, was defeated, as was another, against the 'band of oases' running southeast from Siwa towards the Nile. The Siwa oases, 30 miles east of the Libyan border and 350 miles from Cairo, were some 50 miles in length and 12 miles wide, and lay between the Qattara Depression and the Egyptian Sand Sea in the Libyan desert. Readers of Michael Ondaatje's book *The English Patient* will recognize the location.

The Arab Revolt

In September 1914, before war with Turkey, Kitchener, then British Agent and Consul-General of Egypt, opened negotiations with Sharif Hussein of Mecca, in Arabia, part of the Ottoman Empire. By offering the Caliphate to Hussein, Kitchener was trying to wean him away from his allegiance to the Turkish Sultan, who was still the nominal Caliph – the politico-religious leader of Islam. In the late nineteenth century, Sultan Abdul Hamid II had reasserted the claim to the title as a tactic to counter the expansion of the Russian Empire into Islamic territories in Central Asia and the Caucasus. The Ottoman Empire at the outbreak of war in 1914 was the largest independent Islamic state. While militarily weak relative to the Great Powers, it was also the most powerful. The Sultan was also influential beyond his frontiers, as Caliph of Islamic populations in the British Protectorate of Egypt and British India, and in Central Asia. The Indian Muslims were particularly supportive, and this was naturally of concern to Britain.

Sir Henry McMahon, the British High Commissioner in Egypt, also promised Arab independence in October 1915 as a spur to bring the Arabs into the war on the Allied side. This offer, and others, illustrates the lack of joined-up policy-making by Britain and its Empire in the Middle East. McMahon's promise came as a shock to the India Office in London and to the government of India, which had its own agenda, namely to annex Mesopotamia. It had already sent troops to safeguard British oil interests in the region. Indeed, in embarking on this expedition, the Indian government had hoped for Arab support. General Townshend had already advanced up the Tigris as far as Kut by the end of September, and Ctesiphon by 21 November. While McMahon had built in some protection for French interests in the Levant – in particular Syria – his promise seems to have been made in ignorance of the Sykes–Picot negotiations of November 1915 to March 1916, which neglected Arab interests and agreed a future partition of Arabia, outside the Arabian peninsula, into British and French spheres of influence.

Hussein had to consider many factors, including the likelihood of the Turks remaining a significant presence in the region, and it was only in June 1916 that he raised the standard of revolt at Mecca with his son Faisal commanding the Arab forces in the field. This was a brave move, as the Allies had abandoned Gallipoli, Kut had fallen to the Turks on 29 April, and the Turks were still strong in Palestine and still posed a threat to the Suez Canal. Turkey was, however, under increasing Russian pressure on the Caucasus front. Following the Allied evacuation of Gallipoli, the Turks concentrated their forces in the Caucasus. The Russians had captured Erzerum, and, on 18 April 1916, reached Trebizond on Turkey's Black Sea coast. In the summer Turkey had twenty-six divisions on the Caucasus front, half of their army, but these divisions were weakened by disease and desertion as well as battle casualties, and in September an army reorganization led to a dramatic reduction in their numbers.

British strategy and operations in the Egyptian and Palestine theatre were aided by the Arab Revolt. An Arab Bureau, part of the

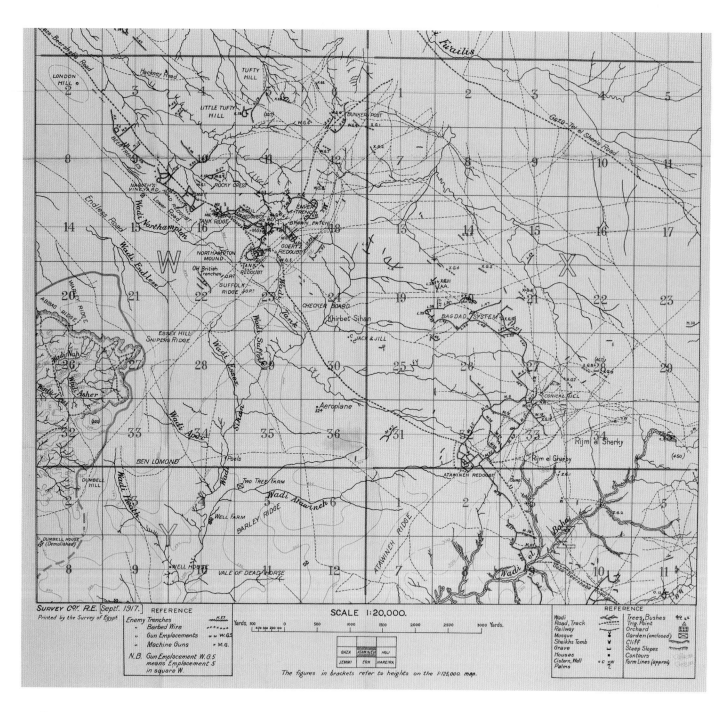

Atawineh, Scale 1:20,000. (September 1917.)
Printed by the Survey of Egypt

SURVEY COY. R.E. [Septr. 1917.]

SCALE 1:20,000.

REFERENCE
Enemy Trenches
" Barbed Wire
" Gun Emplacements
" Machine Guns
N.B. Gun Emplacement W.G.5
means Emplacement 5
in square W.

Yards. 500 400 300 200 100 0   500   1000   1500   2000   2500   3000 Yards.

The figures in brackets refer to heights on the 1:125,000. map.

REFERENCE
Wadi
Road, Track
Railway
Mosque
Sheikhs Tomb
Grave
Houses
Cistern, Well
Palms
Trees, Bushes
Trig. Point
Orchard
Garden (enclosed)
Cliff
Steep Slopes
Contours
Form Lines (approx.)

Intelligence Department in Cairo, was set up, under Gilbert Clayton and David Hogarth, to 'harmonize British political activity in the Middle East', to supply intelligence appreciations of German-Turkish policy to all interested British, Indian and Egyptian government departments, the military and the navy, to liaise with the Arabs and to propagandize on behalf of the Revolt. The Arab Bureau rapidly developed its own agenda: by mobilizing all sources of opposition to Turkey and creating an autonomous Arab

ABOVE: Atawineh, Scale 1:20,000 (September 1917) showing in green Turkish trenches, battery positions, etc., in the Gaza–Beersheba Position, which follows the line of the Gaza–Beersheba Road. The British front line before the attack is shown bottom left in buff. Survey work on the Palestine front was done by 7th Field Survey Company RE.

RIGHT: British horse artillery advancing near Shellal, in south Palestine, in August 1917.

empire, it aimed at the political 'spoiling' of other Allied policies and agencies, notably the Sykes–Picot agreement and the schemes of the India Office. Liaison officers, including T. E. Lawrence, were attached to Arab tribal forces in the Hejaz, in western Arabia, to act as a thorn in the Turkish flesh and worry their eastern flank in the Palestine operations. The Hejaz Railway, from Ma'an, south of Amman, to Medina, north of Mecca, was the main target for guerrilla attacks by Faisal's tribesmen.

Battles for the Gaza–Beersheba Position

The Turkish attempt on the Suez Canal in February 1915, and the Senussi insurrection, had occurred when British policy in this theatre was essentially defensive. During 1916, the British forces in Egypt gradually extended the railway, and built a water pipeline, across the northern Sinai desert towards Gaza. But, while the British government was exerting pressure on General Murray to attack the Turkish defences at Gaza which blocked the route to Palestine, it did not provide the forces. Murray attacked on 26 March 1917 (First Battle of Gaza), but without much success, and again on 19 April (Second Battle of Gaza) with less, and was thereupon replaced by Allenby, 'the Bull', who had aggressively commanded the Third Army in France during the recent Arras offensive. Just as Montgomery, in 1942, replaced a failed commander in Egypt and then made the same requests to Churchill for more time, more guns and more troops as his

predecessor, so Allenby demanded time and resources from Lloyd George, who was determined to present the British electorate with some good news – in this case 'Jerusalem by Christmas'.

Arriving in the theatre in June, Allenby was permitted to build up a force 340,000 strong, of whom some 100,000 represented fighting troops and the rest supporting arms and services. The Turkish fighting strength on the solidly entrenched Gaza–Beersheba line was only 36,000, strengthened by a German *Yilderim* contingent under the command of Falkenhayn. Allenby's artillery concentration for 27 October (Third Battle of Gaza) was as dense, in terms of guns per mile of front, as on the Somme in 1916, and delivered the heaviest artillery bombardment of the war outside Europe. Aerial spotting helped to achieve accuracy of fire, and in the main attack on the Turkish position the sound-ranging sections and observation groups (flash-spotters) of 7th Field Survey Company were particularly successful in locating the enemy artillery positions.

A clever deception plan, evolved by one of Allenby's intelligence officers, indicated that the main attack would be a frontal assault in the coastal sector, starting on 27 October, with a feint inland. In fact this feint developed into the main thrust, a wide, enveloping sweep to the east around Beersheba, involving cavalry and mounted infantry, and it outflanked the Turkish position. The Australian Light Horse played a big part in this manoeuvre. Beersheba was captured on 31 October, and Allenby's force,

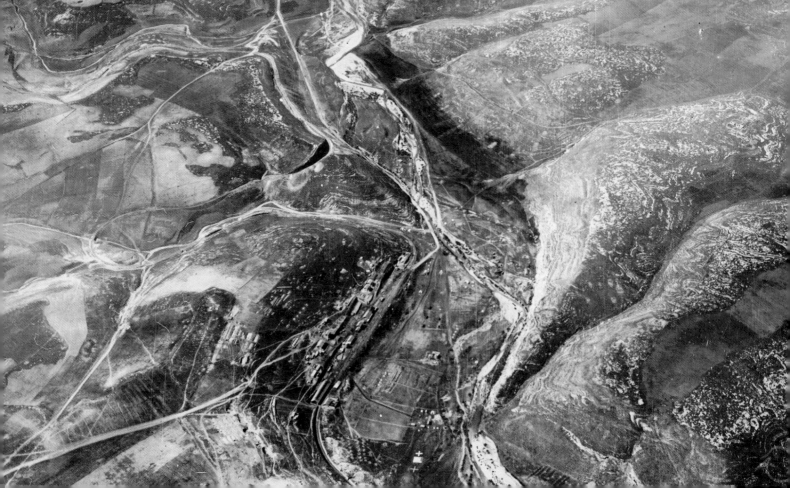

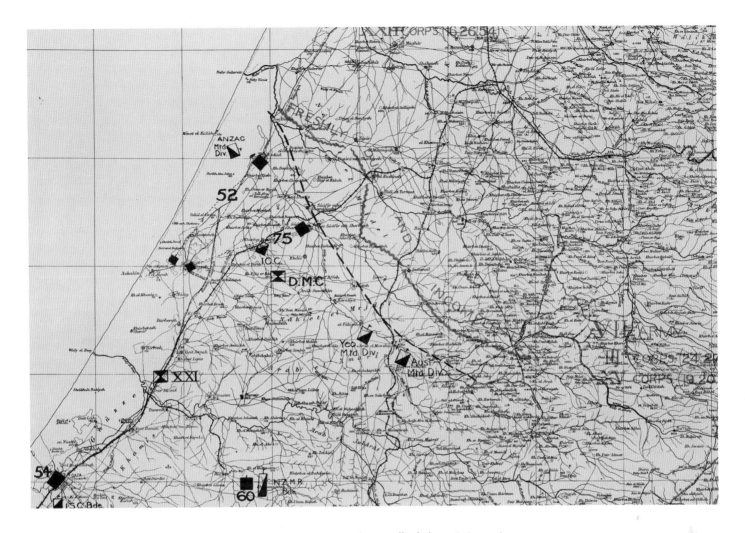

supported by Faisal's Arab irregulars east of the Jordan, captured Jerusalem on 9 December. Following his defeat on the Gaza–Beersheba position, Falkenhayn retreated to a strong position across Palestine, running from the sea at Jaffa eastwards through the high ground north of Jerusalem. He was then recalled to Germany in February 1918.

ABOVE: *Operations Map, Situation at 6 p.m. on 11.11.17*. Black and red, overprinted green with *Notes on enemy formations*. Turco-German Dispositions (7th and 8th Army, its corps and divisions) in green, British in red. Enemy headquarters shown at Ramlegh and Jerusalem, and a freshly dug and incomplete defence line running southeast from the coast, between Jaffa and Gaza. Scale of original 3/8-inch to mile.

TOP LEFT: Jerusalem; a German oblique air photo of the city, captured by the British at *Yilderim* headquarters in Nazareth.

BOTTOM LEFT: Ammon Station, 30 miles NE of Jericho, 20 March 1918, British low oblique air photo showing railway, road, etc.

Allenby's 1918 Campaign

In 1918 Allenby's army had a strength that aroused jealousy at British headquarters in France. At its most intense, in 1917–18, the Egypt and Palestine theatre absorbed over a million British troops. Some of this swollen force, greatly outnumbering the Turks, had to be sent to the Western Front in 1918 to counter the great series of German offensives. Once the crisis had passed on the Western Front, Allenby was instructed to continue his advance. His Palestine campaign was imaginative and successful. He used the technical resources of aircraft, tanks, flash-spotting and sound-ranging, as well as the more traditional striking power of infantry, cavalry (and mounted infantry) and artillery, and had the vision to use Lawrence and Faisal's Arabs to sweep around the Turkish flank.

Allenby broke through the Turkish position at Megiddo (Armageddon), in a battle which began on 1 September, and this forced the Turks to pull back to Damascus, which was then entered by Arab and British forces on 1 October. Faisal claimed it for the Arabs, and the British, as usual when it came to ignoring French

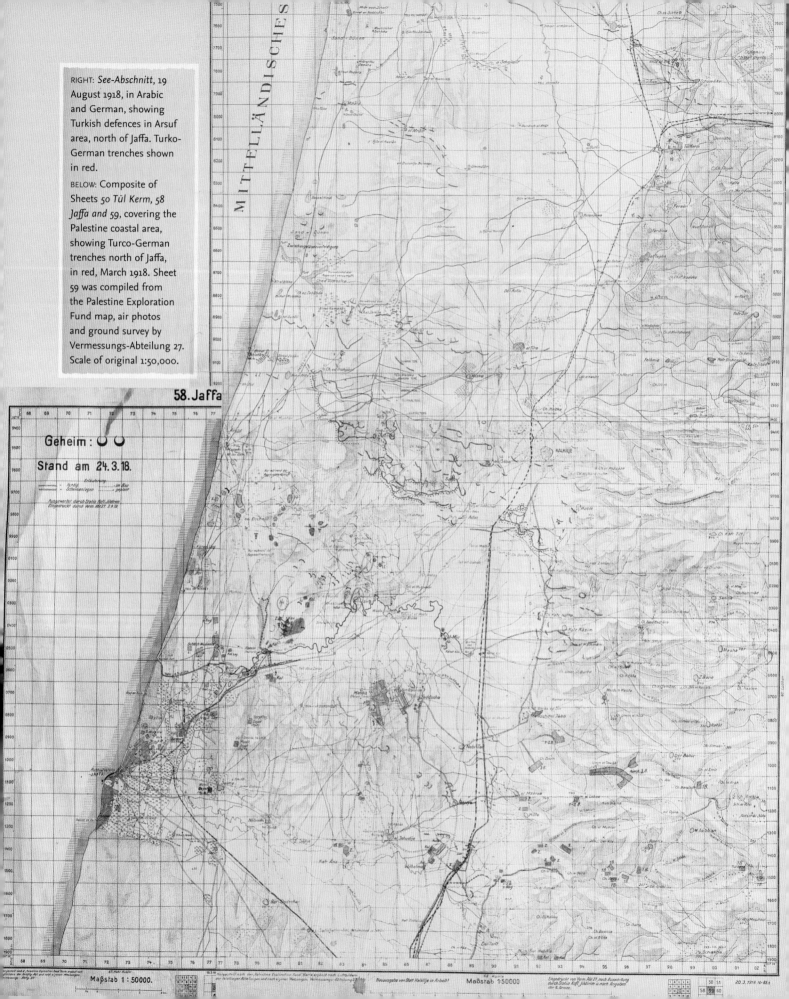

RIGHT: *See-Abschnitt*, 19 August 1918, in Arabic and German, showing Turkish defences in Arsuf area, north of Jaffa. Turko-German trenches shown in red.

BELOW: Composite of Sheets 50 *Tül Kerm*, 58 *Jaffa* and 59, covering the Palestine coastal area, showing Turco-German trenches north of Jaffa, in red, March 1918. Sheet 59 was compiled from the Palestine Exploration Fund map, air photos and ground survey by Vermessungs-Abteilung 27. Scale of original 1:50,000.

MITTELLÄNDISCHES

58. Jaffa

Geheim:

Stand am 24.3.18.

Maßstab 1 : 50000.

Maßstab 1:50000

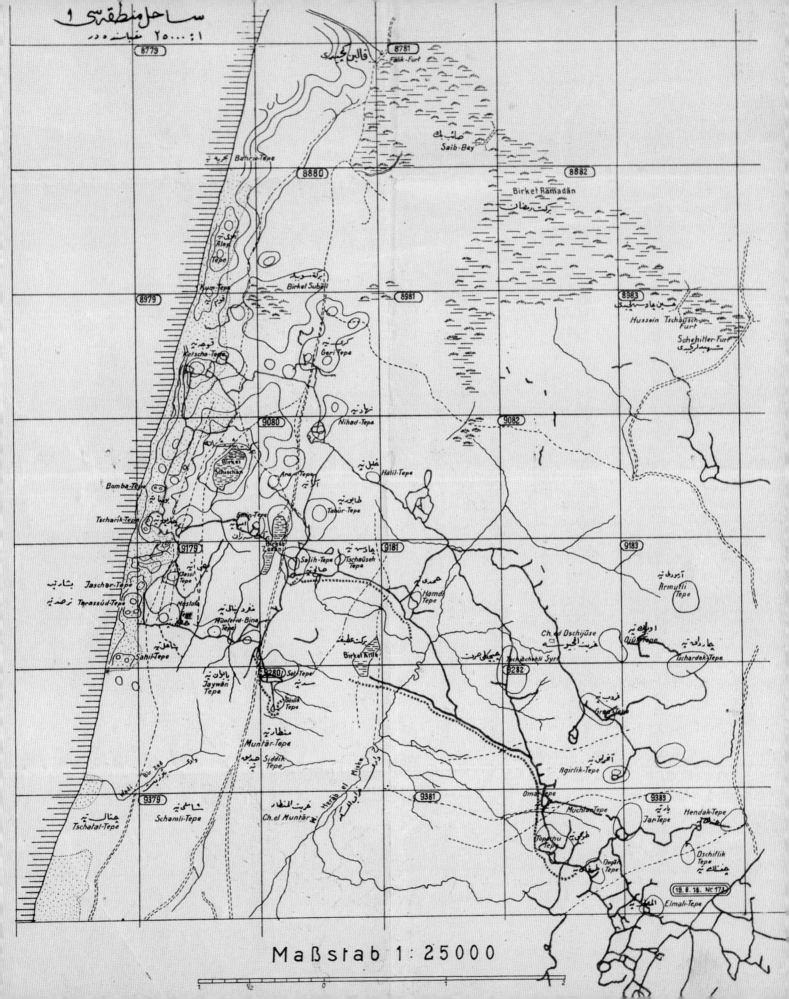

ساحل منطقه سی ۱
١: ٢٥٠٠٠ مقياسنده در

Maßstab 1 : 25000

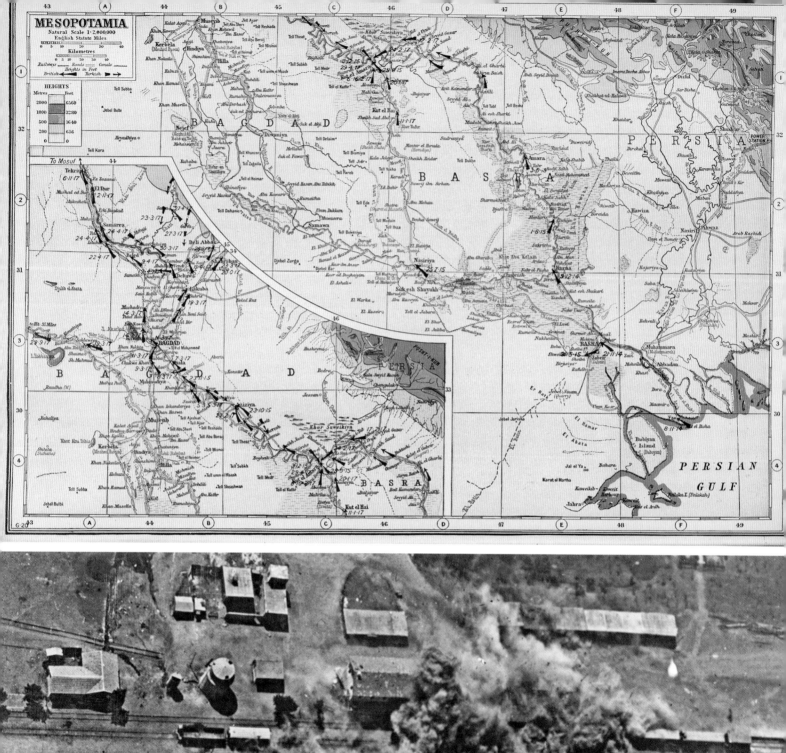

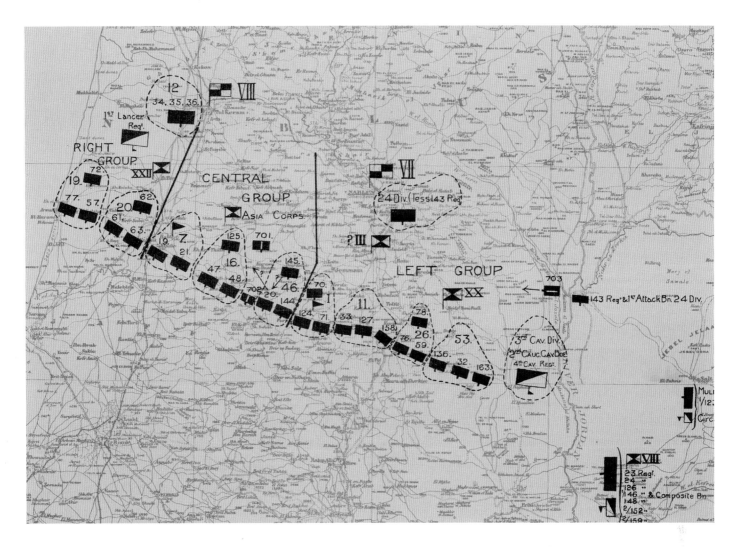

interests in the Levant, concurred. Aleppo was captured on 26 October and, with the Turks defeated in Syria, the stage was set for the British who were advancing up the Euphrates (see below) to join forces with Allenby's army and prepare an attack northward into the Turkish homeland. Turkey, defeated on this front, and with her western flank in Thrace threatened by the armistice signed by Bulgaria on 29 September, herself signed an armistice with the British, in Mudros harbour near Gallipoli, on 30 October.

ABOVE: *Outline Map of Central Palestine. Secret. Estimated Distribution of Enemy Forces 19-4-18. To accompany I.S.* [Intelligence Summary] *267 of 20-4-18. Turco-German dispositions in red. Scale of original 1:250,000.*

TOP LEFT: Mesopotamia, showing British and Turkish movements. *Harmsworth's New Atlas of the World,* c.1920.

BOTTOM LEFT: Bombing a railway station at El Afuleh, north of Jerusalem, 1917–18.

MESOPOTAMIA

The southeastern projection of the Ottoman Empire, in Mesopotamia (Iraq), down the corridor between valleys of the Tigris and Euphrates rivers (hence the ancient name, meaning the land between the rivers), was of great significance to the British Empire as it posed both a threat and an opportunity. The potential threat was to the oilfields in the hinterland of Abadan, and the Anglo-Persian company's installations there. These were of particular interest to Winston Churchill, First Lord of the Admiralty, as the Royal Navy was increasingly dependent on oil fuel. The opportunity which presented itself was that of stimulating a revolt of the Arab tribes against their Ottoman masters. The government of India, which had already sent an Indian Corps to France and troops to other theatres including Egypt, was keen to extend Indian influence in this area, which for many years had been the southern flank of the machinations and intrigue of 'the Great Game' played beyond the borders of India between Britain and

Russia, in the period when Russia was regarded as a threat to the Indian Empire.

It was decided in India, even before Turkey entered the war, to land troops to protect the installations, and this was done on 6 November 1914 from the Shatt al-Arab, the seaway where the Tigris, Euphrates and Karun rivers join the Gulf. When the Turks attacked this force on 17 November they were defeated, and retreated upriver, followed on 22 November by the British-Indian force, which advanced twenty miles to Basra, where it created a base camp. Another advance, of fifty-five miles, to create an outlying bastion, was made as far as Qurna. While the British and Indian governments claimed to have no designs on Baghdad, it was clear that there was a great strategic advantage in occupying that city, and moving beyond it towards the Turkish heartland and to link with the Russians in the south Caucasus. In a good example of what today is called 'mission-creep', the

ABOVE: Vertical aerial photograph of Kut-al-Amara, on the Tigris. A British force under Townshend was besieged by the Turks at Kut from 7 December 1915 to 29 April 1916, when it surrendered.

LEFT: *Turkey in Asia, No. 2c, Baghdad, Rough Provisional Issue, 2nd Edition*, showing river Tigris north and south of Baghdad, and Ctesiphon (at the bottom of the map). Scale of original 1:253,440. Heliozincographed at Survey of India Offices, Calcutta.

first defensive landings evolved into a prolonged campaign which eventually absorbed almost 900,000 men.

In 1915 the failure of the Gallipoli landings to achieve any success was trumpeted by the Turks as an Ottoman victory. To counter the effect of this on opinion in the Islamic world, the British government in October sanctioned an advance on Baghdad. General Townshend advanced up the Tigris, beyond Kut, and attacked the Turks at Ctesiphon on 21 November. His force of 14,000 men suffered 5,000 casualties and was clearly insufficient for the task in hand against the hard-fighting Turks. Realizing that his position and communications were too exposed, and that his troops were worn out, he pulled back to Kut where, from 7 December 1915, he was besieged. Attempts to relieve Townshend's force all failed, and on 29 April 1916 he was forced to surrender, his 10,000 men being herded into captivity on a 'death march' from which few survived.

The new British commander in the theatre, General Maude, advanced up the Tigris, recapturing Kut in December 1916, but it was not until 11 March 1917 that he entered Baghdad. His force, however, was in a precarious position. There were over 400,000 men in the Anglo-Indian forces in Mesopotamia by the end of 1917 and, while the Turks still had to be dealt with, the allies with whom it was hoped to join up with – the Russians – had dissolved in revolution. A new threat from the Turks and their German allies then appeared, aimed at the Baku oilfields on

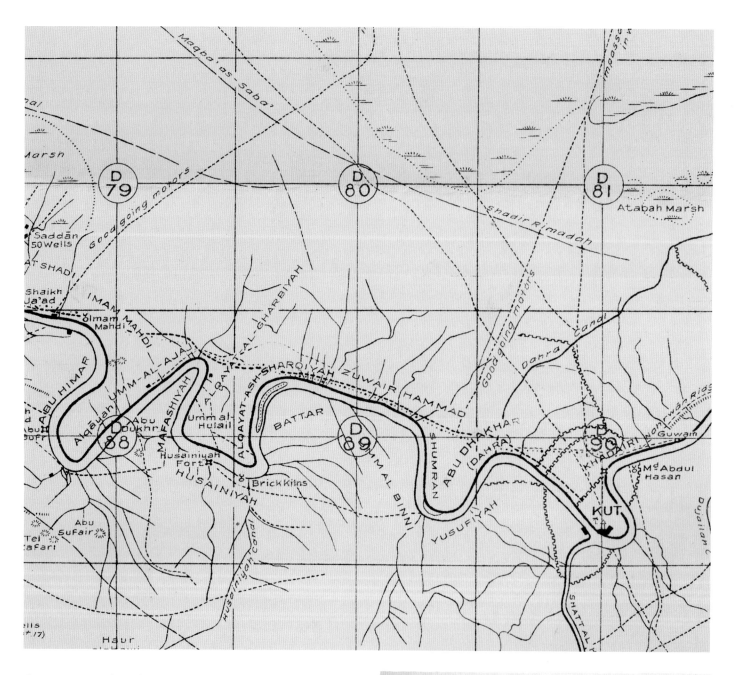

the Caspian and perhaps Persia. An advance northwest up the Euphrates would take the British towards the Amanus mountains and Aleppo in Syria, while one up the Tigris in a more northerly direction would lead them to Mosul, Lake Van and Erzerum.

In the last months of the campaign, the Turkish Sixth Army in Mesopotamia was extremely weak; at 3,500 men in July 1918 it was only at brigade strength. The British faced little real opposition, and speeded their advance, hoping to gain territory and oil before an armistice closed down any further operations. The

ABOVE: A detail from the Tigris Corps map *T.C. 143 Aziziyah–Kut*, *15 December 1917.* Scale 1 inch to 4 miles. Aziziyah is halfway between Kut-al-Amara and Baghdad. The British force under Townshend was besieged at Kut from 7 December 1915 to 29 April 1916, and the new commander, Maude, spent the rest of 1916 reorganizing and training before starting his Tigris campaign which resulted in the capture of Baghdad on 11 March 1917.

RIGHT: Tigris Corps map, *T.C. 144 Baghdad–Karbalā*, 12 October 1917. Scale 1 inch to 4 miles. Karbalā is 60 miles southwest of Baghdad, and west of the Euphrates.

TC 144
Dated 12-10-17
BAGHDAD-KARBALA
Scale - 1 inch to 4 miles

4 MILE SQUARES

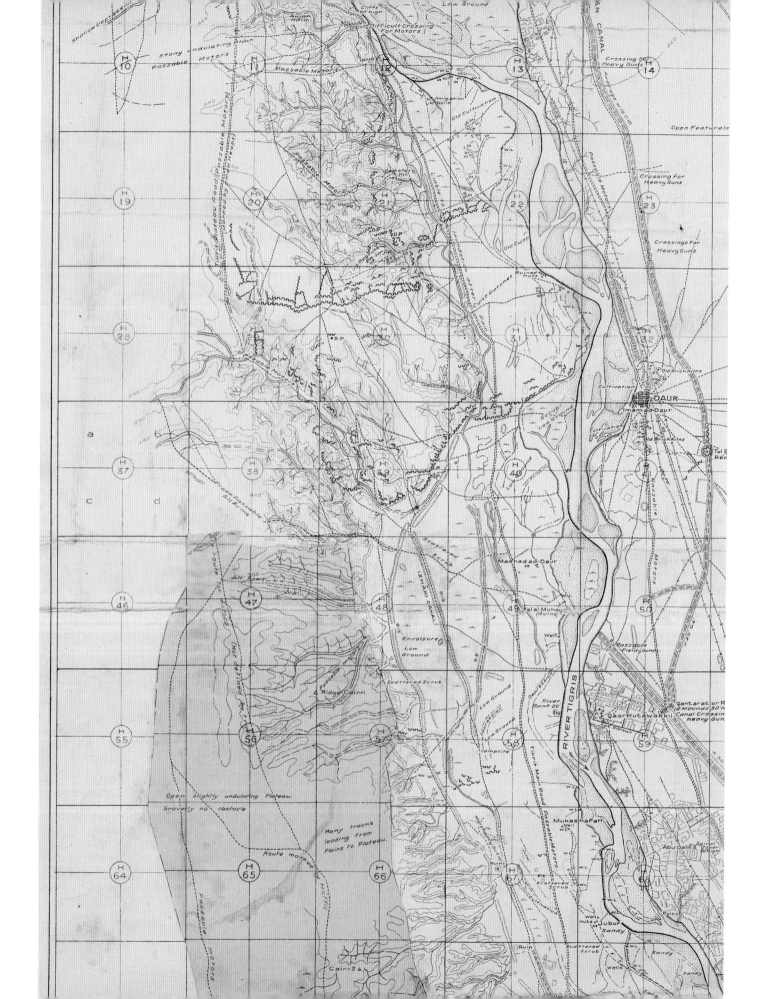

LEFT: Tigris Corps map *T.C. 104(B) Daur*, 20 February 1918, scale 1 inch to the mile.

ABOVE: Photo-map of Baghdad, scale 4 inches to 1 mile, June 1917. A very accurate line plan was similarly compiled from aerial photographs fitted to a series of surveyed control points.

BELOW: A detail from Tigris Corps map, *T.C. 109 Samarrah*, 15 July 1917, scale 6 inches to 1 mile, showing Samarrah, north of Baghdad, and an area of ancient ruins, excavated by the German archaeologist Ernst Herzfeld in 1911–14. The British offensive against Samarrah began on 13 March 1917, capturing Fallujah on 19 March and Samarrah and its strategic railway on 23 April, thus denying its use to the Turks.

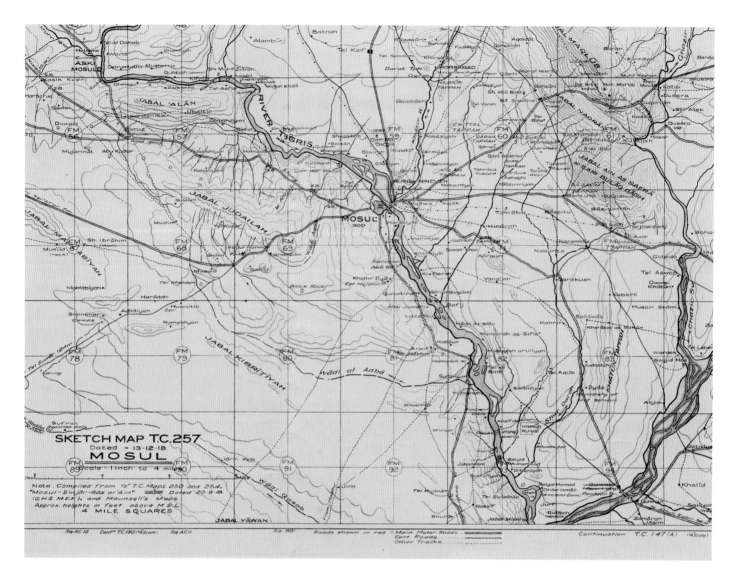

British advance through Palestine had by now moved into what was later called Syria and the Turks signed an armistice on 30 October. On 4 November, days after the Turkish surrender, British troops entered Mosul, supposedly in the French sphere of influence under the obsolete Sykes–Picot agreement.

AFRICA

While European powers had been involved in Africa for centuries, the German colonial connection was relatively recent. It was only after 1884 that German traders had developed quasi-colonial activities in west Africa in the Cameroons (*Deutsch-Kamerun*), Togoland (now Togo and most of the Volta region of Ghana) and South West Africa (*Deutsch-Südwestafrika*, now Namibia), and on the east coast in German East Africa (*Deutsch-Ostafrika*, later Tanganyika, now Tanzania, and Rwanda and Burundi).

Following the outbreak of war in 1914, Togoland was rapidly occupied by Anglo-French forces on 2 August. *Kamerun* was a much more difficult proposition, because of its remote and difficult terrain, and its unhealthy climate. Columns of British African, French and Belgian troops advanced into the interior, but it was not until February 1916 that it was subdued.

ABOVE: Tigris Corps *Sketch Map T.C. 257 Mosul* 13 December 1918, showing the city of Mosul and the Tigris and Greater Zāb rivers in northern Mesopotamia. Scale 1 inch to 4 miles. British troops entered Mosul (which was meant to be in the French sphere of influence under the Sykes–Picot agreement) on 4 November 1918.

RIGHT: A German poster with manuscript German propaganda additions, including a 'Reserved Football Ground for Tame Englishmen' in the Sahara Desert. It was 'Found at Usakos by E Sqn., I L H. 7-5-15.'

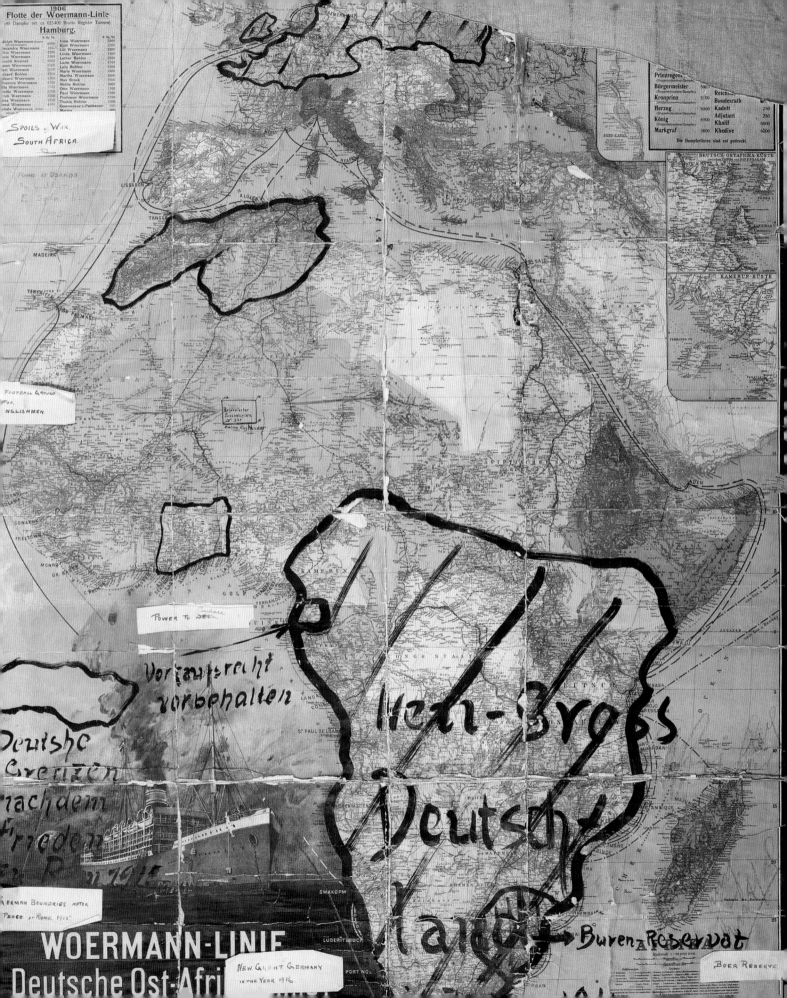

In South West Africa, 'Südwest', where the Germans had bloodily put down the Herero rising of 1904, the picture was again different, both in terms of terrain and geopolitical context. The open terrain of the Namibian desert, and relatively good communications, made for easy operations. Although British South Africa stood on Südwest's eastern frontier, the situation was complicated there by a Boer rebellion against British rule. This, however, turned out to be a damp squib and, once it had been extinguished, South African forces crossed the border into Südwest, faced little opposition from the German settlers and captured the capital, Windhoek, on 12 May 1915. The campaign finally ended with German surrender on 9 July.

In Deutsch-Ostafrika the Allies had great difficulty pinning down the German commander, Colonel Lettow-Vorbeck, whose intrepid and forceful personality and qualities of leadership enabled his force to continue to manoeuvre and fight right up to

the Armistice of November 1918. At the start of the war, Lettow-Vorbeck commanded the local defence force. He had few German troops under him, and a large proportion of his men were local native troops – Askaris. His force launched raids across the frontier into the British possessions of Kenya and Uganda, and when Anglo-British troops tried to land an invasion force at Tanga against a vastly outnumbered German garrison they were so badly led, and behaved so incompetently, that they were forced to re-embark.

ABOVE: Operations of T. E. Lawrence and Arab forces against the Hejaz Railway. Billi Bedouins in Wadi Garm, about 100 miles from the Red Sea coast, in July 1917. Photograph by Col. S. F. Newcombe.

RIGHT: (Provisional) Map of German South West Africa, 1:3,000,000. British official map, prepared for the Geographical Section, General Staff, War Office, London in January 1914.

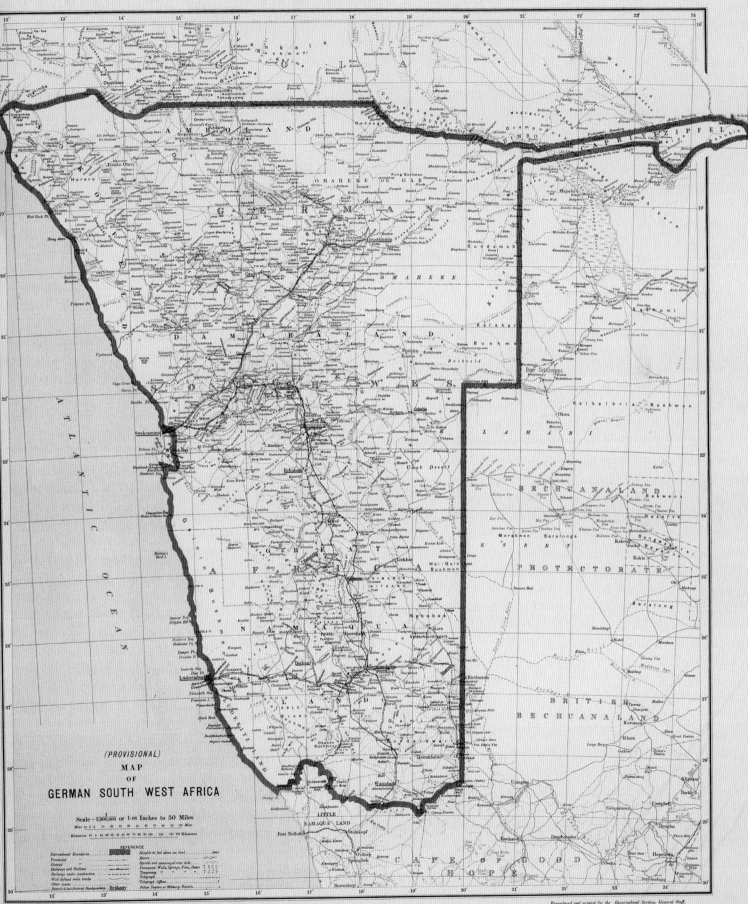

(PROVISIONAL)

MAP
OF
GERMAN SOUTH WEST AFRICA

Scale = 3,000,000 or 1·06 Inches to 50 Miles

Some points have been accurately fixed by the Anglo-German Boundary Commission. No part of the country shown has been surveyed. The information from which the map is compiled is not considered reliable. The positions of towns, rivers, &c., are only approximate.

Reproduced and printed for the Geographical Section, General Staff, at the Ordnance Survey Office, Southampton. Jan. 1914.

After this British failure, Lettow-Vorbeck continued guerrilla operations, and even Jan Smuts's South African troops, brought in after the end of the operations in *Südwest*, could not corner him. Smuts's plan was to send converging columns from three sides – the British, Belgian and Portuguese, all moving in from their respective territories. However, they failed to catch Lettow-Vorbeck's force. After the Armistice the German commander was given a hero's welcome in Berlin, a symbol of the German spirit which, according to the new myth, had not been 'defeated in the field'.

LEFT: Column of African porters in East Africa. Hundreds of thousands of native porters and labourers, notably African and Chinese, served with British forces in many theatres. Apart from casualties from shell and small-arms fire, large numbers died or were disabled by disease.

BELOW: The first trenches dug by the East African Mounted Rifles in September 1914.

TOP RIGHT: *German East Africa, Sheet C.6. Tanga, January 1916*, scale 1:300,000. British map, printed at the War Office in London, of the northeast part of German East Africa, showing the frontier with the British colony of Kenya.

BOTTOM RIGHT: German East Africa. *German Missionary Map, Sheet 3*, redrawn by British No. 6 Topographical Section RE, scale 1 inch to 2 miles.

Chapter 5

The 1915 Campaign in the East and the West

The year 1914 ended with General Winter in command. Operations on the Western and the Eastern Fronts, in the Caucasus and elsewhere had become bogged down, or frozen, and only foolhardy commanders dared to fight against the elements. Things were different in Africa, Egypt and Mesopotamia; in some parts of the world it was the summer that was the enemy, while winter provided the campaigning season. But in Europe, Russia and northern climes generally it was customary, as Caesar knew, for armies to go into 'winter quarters', even if these meant muddy trenches and frozen billets. In any case an operational stalemate had frozen operations: forces matched in weight and firepower had met in battles, had attacked and found no enemy wing to outflank, and had gone to ground. Perhaps in 1915, the generals thought, they would find the key to breaking the deadlock – perhaps more heavy artillery or aerial bombardment, perhaps a new weapon such as gas, perhaps a new front. But for now, no one could go anywhere.

The early months of 1915 were characterized, on the Western Front, by 'tactics without strategy'. As Sun Tzu, the Chinese military philosopher warned, this 'is the noise before defeat'. The Allies' rudimentary strategy consisted of 'nibbling' at the enemy, and later of battering, in an attempt to break through. These attempts were retarded by a 'shell shortage', the result of a failure of pre-war organization to create the necessary stocks, failure to adapt

ABOVE: Well-muffled men of the 2nd Battalion, Royal Scots Fusiliers in a trench at La Boutillerie, Flanders, during the first winter of the war, 1914–15. 'Trench foot', which often turned gangrenous, from waterlogged trenches was a serious problem, largely solved by better drainage, trench boards (duckboards), rubbing with whale oil, and a change of socks.

RIGHT: A detail from *Nebert's Kriegs-Frontenkarte*, showing fronts at end of January 1916.

peacetime production methods to wartime levels, lack of will to make the required expenditure, and an underestimate of the quantity of munitions demanded in modern warfare by quick-firing guns.

Nevertheless, the Allies felt impelled to attack, rather than wait, partly to take pressure off Russia. Joffre maintained his strategy of attacking the flanks of the great German salient in France, in Artois (Arras–Vimy Ridge–Lens) and Champagne (between the Argonne Forest and Reims). In Artois he struck eastwards, and in the Champagne northwards. In successive battles from December 1914 onwards, the scale of these operations increased as the year went on. The big battles of May and June were followed by even bigger ones in September and October. Joffre also required of the British that, as their forces increased, they should take over more front and also launch diversionary supporting attacks.

German strategy in 1915 aimed at increasing pressure on Russia, which was effectively cut off from Allied support: the Dardanelles were closed because of Turkey's accession to the Central Powers, the north Russian ports were icebound for much of the year, and the Far Eastern ports such as Vladivostok were too far away and dependent on the transport bottleneck of the Trans-Siberian railway. Russian powers were weakened by munitions shortages caused by transport and logistical problems and by inefficiencies in civil and military organizations and procurement. The Germans foresaw that Russia would collapse internally if she was unable to import war supplies and export her wheat. At the same time Germany sought to open up new direct routes to supply Turkey and thus increase the pressure on Russia in the Caucasus, and on the British Empire where it faced Ottoman forces – at the Dardanelles and the Gallipoli peninsula, and in Egypt and Mesopotamia.

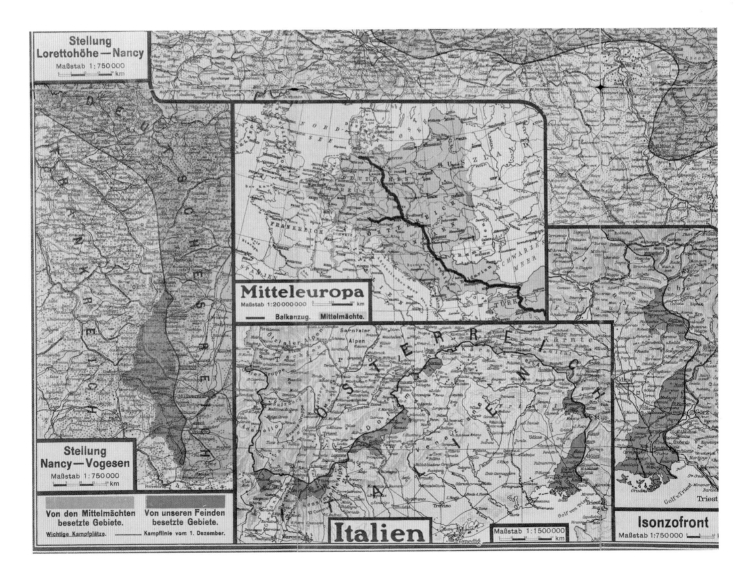

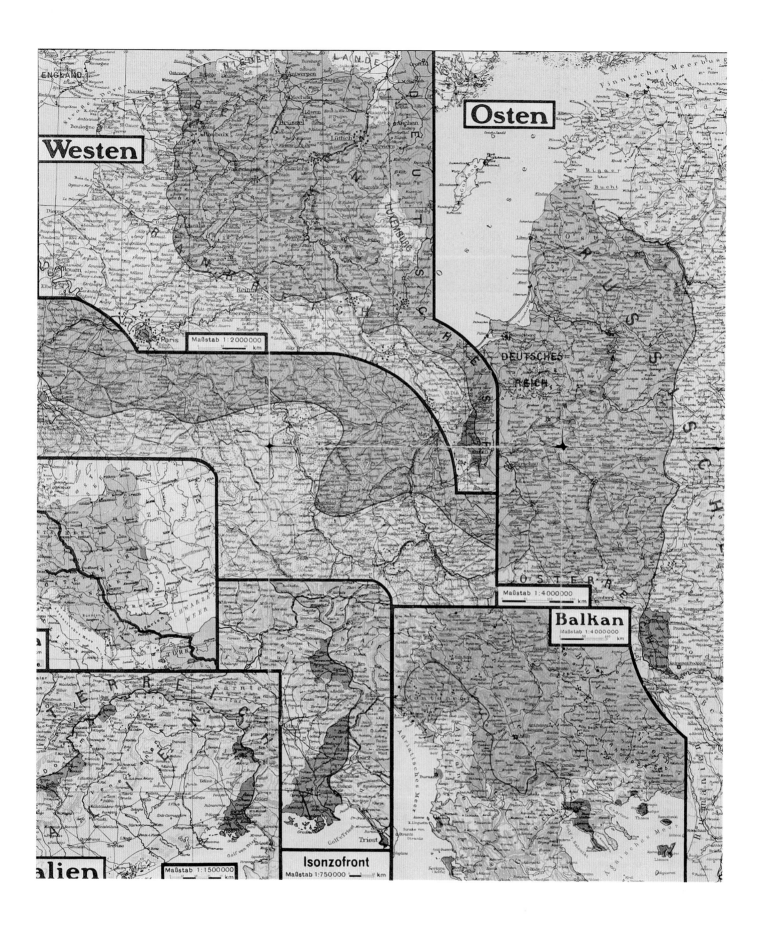

Westen

Osten

Balkan

Maßstab 1:4000000

Isonzofront
Maßstab 1:750000

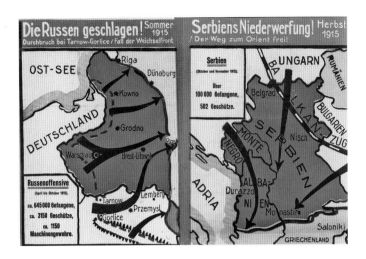

The realities of war on the Eastern Front had been demonstrated by the experiences of 1914. Superior German leadership, efficiency, training and discipline meant that relatively small German forces could defeat larger Russian ones. But Germany was 'shackled to a corpse' inasmuch as Austria–Hungary was the weaker partner and was further weakened by divisive ethnic pressures. To make matters worse, on 23 May Italy declared war on Austria, largely impelled by nationalistic ambitions for territory currently held by the Austrians.

Germany knew that a Russian army could defeat an Austrian army of equal size, and that she would continually have to provide military support for Austria. Falkenhayn had to create his strategy within this framework, and it remained essentially one of opportunism, based on a belief in attrition – the need to wear down the enemy's forces and powers of resistance. In contrast, Ludendorff, Hindenburg's Chief-of-Staff at *Oberost* (*Oberbefehlshaber der gesamten Deutschen Streitkräfte im Osten*, or Supreme Commander of all German Forces in the East), had at this stage a single, clear strategic aim, focused on smashing Russia's ability and will to wage war. In all this the German Kaiser was little more than a puppet, whose strings were being pulled in different directions by these conflicting strategic views.

Meanwhile the Russians were making their plans for 1915, but these were doomed to failure partly by the geographical realities of their exposed position in the Polish salient and partly by their internal contradictions and inefficiencies. The Commander-in-Chief, the Grand Duke Nicholas, ultimately intended to strike westward out of Russian Poland into Silesia, towards Berlin and the German heartland, but before he could do this he had to deal with the Germans in East Prussia on his northern flank and the Austrians in Galicia on his southern flank.

During 1915 on the Western Front the Allies continued to grind their own armies into a bloody pulp against strongly entrenched positions, while on the Eastern Front Austro-German forces were making significant territorial gains from May onwards, having broken through at Gorlice–Tarnów. These, by themselves, were of little account as long as the Russian army could make its traditional strategic withdrawal into its vast expanses, leaving the enemy to extend his vulnerable communications through difficult swamp and forest terrain.

THE EASTERN FRONT

In the harsh Galician winter between January and April 1915, Russian armies fought to capture the Carpathian mountain barrier and its passes through to the Hungarian plain. Success in such an attack would ultimately threaten Vienna itself, the heart of the Habsburg Empire. The Austrian defence, supported by the Germans, was largely successful in holding these attacks, inflicting heavy losses, but at the price of the loss of Przemyśl. Meanwhile, the Central Powers had their own plans.

The Second Battle of the Masurian Lakes (the First had immediately followed Tannenberg), also known as the Winter Battle in Masuria, was the northern part of the early-1915 Austro-German offensive. Its aim was to advance beyond the Vistula and inflict a decisive defeat on Russian forces. Falkenhayn had reluctantly agreed to Hindenburg's plan for the offensive, the latter commanding in the northern offensive while Linsingen attacked in the Carpathians towards Lemberg. A third force would try to relieve Przemyśl. In the north, Ludendorff, commanding Below's Eighth Army and Eichhorn's new Tenth Army attacked to the east on 7 February, against the Russian Tenth Army under Sievers and Twelfth Army under Plehve. This offensive acted as a spoiler to the intended Russian attack north from Poland into East Prussia.

Sievers was surprised by an attack in a snowstorm, and in a week was pushed back in disorder for seventy miles, suffering severe losses. In a sweeping movement east of the Masurian Lakes, the four divisions of Bulgakov's 20th Corps were surrounded by Eichhorn's Army in the Augustów Forest, surrendering on 21 February. However, the rest of Sievers' army managed to create a new defensive position, and on 22 February Plehve's army made a counter-attack that stopped the German advance and ended the German northern offensive. In the south,

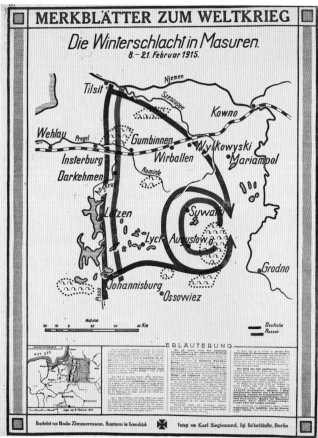

Linsingen's attack failed with heavy losses, and on 22 March the 120,000 men of the Przemyśl garrison, hungry after months of siege, surrendered to the Russians. This was a heavy loss for the Austrians who, compared with the Russians, could ill-afford such manpower depletions.

The Battle of Gorlice–Tarnów

The failure of Allied attacks on the Western Front in the spring of 1915 strengthened German confidence in their ability to defend successfully in the West while attacking in the East. The fly in the ointment was the weakness of Austria–Hungary and her army. After the Second Battle of the Masurian Lakes, the German and Austro-Hungarian commands agreed that their troops on the Eastern Front should operate under a unified command.

Falkenhayn agreed with Conrad that an attack should be launched against the centre of the Russian line, between the Carpathian mountains to the south and the upper reaches of the Vistula river to the north. This was the Gorlice–Tarnów sector, which was placed under the command of the bold and successful Mackensen, with the cool, efficient Seeckt as his Chief-of-Staff.

A joint Austro-German force (Army Group Mackensen) was designated for the attack – the Austro-Hungarian Fourth Army and Mackensen's German Eleventh Army, which had been formed from eleven divisions transferred from the Western Front, a sign of German confidence in its western defences. The attacking force of fourteen divisions, supported by 1,000 guns, was deployed along the river Dunajec, a tributary of the Vistula running north from the Carpathians. On this eighteen-mile front, the Russian defenders had a mere six divisions thinly spread out in several lines of trenches. No man's land in this area was much wider – in places two miles – than on the Western Front, and was still inhabited by the Galician farmers. Their removal by the Germans

for security reasons should have alerted the Russians, as should have the entry into the line of the German Eleventh Army at the end of April. Mackensen's artillery preparation programme allotted each field gun forty-five yards of front, and each heavy gun 132 yards. This may be compared with the British preparation at Neuve Chapelle in March, which directly involved 342 guns and howitzers on a 2,000 yard front (about one gun every six yards), firing a thirty-five-minute 'hurricane bombardment'.

Seeckt had appreciated that the key to a successful breakthrough, apart from surprise, was not just to assault and capture the enemy's first position, but to keep the advance moving through successive positions to the rear before the enemy reserves arrived. This applied to the Western Front as well as the Eastern. Rather than adopt slow and methodical 'bite and hold' tactics as the Allies later tended to do, he envisaged deployment in depth of his attacking forces so that they would all keep moving forward together, and also be positioned to give mutual support wherever the advance was held up. This 'checker-boarding' of assault units,

supports and reserves, all moving forward simultaneously, with an emphasis on flowing around enemy points of resistance and reinforcing success was, in a modified form, to become the basis of German storm-troop tactics in the 1918 offensives in the West.

Surprise could have been lost by the preliminary advance of German and Austrian assault troops across the wide no man's land the night before the attack, and by their digging-in close to the Russian position. But Ivanov, the commander of the Russian army group on this front, disregarded intelligence reports and did not bring up his reserves. An intense four-hour German bombardment began on the morning of 2 May, after which the infantry advanced against the smashed defences and stunned defenders. The crucial elements of firepower, surprise, strength and speed achieved a complete breakthrough, the remnants of the Russian divisions streaming panic-stricken to the rear. A Russian rearguard action on the Wisloka river line, between Tarnów and Przemyśl, was not enough to halt the attacking forces, who continued to drive eastwards towards Lemberg across the farmland and northern slopes of the Carpathians, rolling up the Russian line as they went. The situation, as far as the Central Powers were concerned, cried out for a pincer movement, a 'super-Cannae', to cut off the Russian forces in the Polish salient. But what seemed to be happening was merely a battle that pressed the Russians back along their communications.

The drive eastward in Poland and Galicia led to a weakening of the Russian grip, and a succession of Austro-German attacks followed. By 10 May they had broken all resistance, and by 14 May Mackensen's forces had advanced eighty miles to the river San, which looped north and west of the Przemyśl fortress, and Lodz in central Poland. The attackers crossed the San at Jaroslav, north of Przemyśl, but by now the advance had worn itself out, and there were no more reserves. The problem of maintaining momentum had not quite been solved. Falkenhayn had no option but to transport more divisions from the West, and to impress upon the Austrians that, despite Italy's declaration of war on Austria on 23 May, they should not withdraw troops from Galicia. He knew that he had to maintain the offensive against Russia and so weaken, if not defeat, her so that he could safely shift troops back to the West to meet the expected summer offensives. The German divisions from the West enabled the continuation of the joint offensive. Mackensen put in a new attack that recaptured Przemyśl on 3 June. But logistical problems now intervened. By the close of the first phase of these operations the front hinged on a point south of Warsaw and ran in a southeasterly direction, just west of Lublin and Brody, to the southern pivot north of Czernowitz and the Rumanian border.

On 3 June the Kaiser chaired a conference at OHL, Pless, at which Ludendorff placed a reformulated version of his spring scheme for a grand envelopment of Russian forces before Falkenhayn, Mackensen and Conrad. He asked for sufficient troops to launch a sweeping movement eastward and then southward from the Baltic coast, so cutting the communications and preventing the retreat of the Russian armies, and thus ending the war on the Eastern Front. Falkenhayn rejected the demands of Hindenburg and Ludendorff because he believed that the war should be fought and brought to a conclusion in the West, and

ABOVE: A German poster-map, *Der Durchbruch von Gorlice-Tarnow* (The Breakthrough at Gorlice-Tarnów), *2 Mai 1915*. This successful battle in Galicia led to the crumbling of the Russian position and their withdrawal from Poland to a north–south line just west of the Pripet marshes.

RIGHT: Austrian troops in eastern Galicia. Before the war the Habsburg Empire conscripted relatively small numbers. During the war, ethnic divisions led to questions about loyalty, while poor leadership, language difficulties and heavy casualties reduced its fighting power.

during 1915 he tried to negotiate a peace settlement with the Russians. They contemptuously rebuffed him. Even if Russia was forced to make a separate peace, he believed, Britain and France would carry on the fight; the events of 1918 were to prove him right. His development of this thesis in 1915 was the foundation for his attack on Verdun in February 1916. He therefore refused to release any forces from the crucial Western Front; indeed he asked for divisions to be moved from Poland to France where the Allies were still attacking. Conrad pressed for troops to hit Italy on the Isonzo, while Mackensen (now promoted to Field Marshal), was keen to reinforce his successes in the central sector. Falkenhayn, under pressure from the Kaiser, supported Mackensen on this.

On 22 June the Russians abandoned Lemberg, the Austro-German forces driving a wedge between the northern and southern sections of the Russian front. An attempt was made to cut off the main Russian force, Mackensen changing his axis from east to north, advancing up the corridor between the Bug and Vistula rivers towards the centre of the Russian defence. Meanwhile, Hindenburg was instructed to attack on a southeasterly axis from East Prussia, crossing the Narew and aiming at the

line of the Bug. Ludendorff thought this plan was tactically inept, rather too much like a frontal attack, considering that although it might squeeze their flanks it would not be a Cannae-like pincer movement, cutting off their retreat. Between 23 and 27 June, German forces in Galicia crossed the Dniester, and by 13 July the Russian southern flank had retreated a further 100 miles to the Bug, leaving the Germans in occupation of most of Russian Poland. The Russians now counter-attacked, and Mackensen was forced to halt his offensive.

On 30 June, Ludendorff presented a more ambitious scheme. This involved an even wider enveloping manoeuvre sweeping east from the Niemen estuary in the vicinity of Tilsit, on the Baltic, and then south to the Pripet marshes. Its aim was essentially the same as before – to cut off the bulk of the Russian armies and force their surrender. While Conrad supported it, the plan was refused as before, and all Ludendorff was allowed to mount was a subsidiary frontal attack in Courland on the Baltic to support Mackensen. Ludendorff's northern manoeuvre, had it been launched, would probably have resulted in no great envelopment, as during July the Russians read the writing on the wall. They decided that the poor

condition of their army and their shortage of arms and munitions left them only one option – their time-honoured strategy of withdrawal, in this case from the great Polish salient to the marshes and forests of the Pripet region. Falkenhayn, fearing a repetition of 1812, was resisting the heavy drain on resources and the deeper penetration into the unfathomable reaches of Russia it implied. However, he bowed to the Kaiser's support for Hindenburg and Ludendorff, who demanded that the offensive against Russia continue, while Stavka hoped that a strategic retreat would buy the time needed to build up the Russian war economy. On 2 July, the Kaiser approved the continuation of the offensive. It had three components: the Courland diversionary attack, and the two-pronged main attack aimed at cutting off the Russian forces in Poland, the southern element being Mackenson's attack to the north from the Austro-Hungarian frontier in Galicia, up the Bug–Vistula corridor towards Brest-Litovsk, and the northern element being a powerful attack by Gallwitz across the Narew.

On 13 July the Austro-German armies rolled forward again along the whole Eastern Front. The Austrian Fourth and German Eleventh Armies, attacking from the south, forced the southern part of the Russian front to retreat to the line Ivangorod–Lublin–Cholm. At the north end of the front, three German armies, Scholtz's Eighth, Eichhorn's Tenth and *Armee-Gruppe* Gallwitz (Twelfth Army from 7 August), attacked southeast from East Prussia over the Narew, a tributary of the Vistula. The artillery programme, involving over 1,000 guns firing 400,000 shells,

ABOVE: Russian prisoners being taken by the German pontoon bridge from the Novogeorgievsk fortress, the citadel of which is in the background. The fortress, with 80,000 men, 6 generals and over 7,000 guns, was captured by General von Beseler's troops during the great Austro-German advance in the summer of 1915.

RIGHT: An Austro-Hungarian vertical air photo of trenches near Manajow in the Lemberg–Tarnopol area of Galicia.

Stellungen bei Manajow (Öst.ung. Fliegeraufnahme. 377

was successfully organized by Oberst Georg Bruchmüller. The Germans attacked on a twenty-five mile front with ten divisions and advanced four miles on the first day, taking the main positions and breaking through between two Russian armies around Przasnysz. Bruchmüller's new career was taking off. This attack made the northern front collapse, causing a precipitate retreat of the Russian forces in this area. By 17 July, the Germans had forced the Russians back twenty miles but had suffered heavy losses, and were halted, short of the Narew, by a stubborn Russian defence which thwarted the plan to envelop the Russian armies and allowed the Russians to withdraw from the Polish salient.

On 22 July the Austro-German forces crossed the Vistula, and the Russians were again forced back. In August, Ivangorod was abandoned by the Russian Fourth Army and Warsaw, now isolated, was captured by *Armee-Gruppe* Gallwitz on 5 August. As Ludendorff had feared, the Russian field armies had escaped from the Warsaw salient, and Falkenhayn blamed Ludendorff for not pressing hard

enough. Hindenburg's complaints about the neglect of his status as Ober Ost led to Falkenhayn reducing his command by an army, and using this as the core of a new force. Nevertheless, in a critical period from 17 August to 4 September, the Russians had lost their four most important frontier fortresses guarding the routes into Russia from the west: Kovno, Novogeorgievsk, Brest-Litovsk and Grodno. Novogeorgievsk had been held from 10 to 20 August, with 80,000 men, as a delaying tactic. Brest-Litovsk was captured by the Germans, after significant reserves had reinforced their armies, on 25 August. The Tsar now dismissed the Grand Duke Nicholas as Commander-in-Chief and took command himself.

With the garrisons of these fortresses captured, Russia's losses now included 325,000 prisoners and 3,000 guns (although many of these were obsolete). By mid-August, the Germans had taken Poland and 400,000 prisoners. The Russians, however, had not been defeated. As Falkenhayn had feared, the war in the east was not over.

The Germans followed up with great difficulty, their lines of communication lengthening as those of the Russians were correspondingly reduced. The Germans suffered from lack of good railways, the main routes being broken at the Vistula bridges, which the Russians had blown; beyond the Vistula (which ran roughly southeast to northwest through Warsaw) only temporary field railways continued as far as the Narew. The Germans also had to cope with appalling roads, which disintegrated under heavy military traffic and soon dissolved into mud with the autumn rains. Napoleon's fifth element, mud, would confound the most ambitious plans. Britain and France were to rediscover this on the Somme in 1916 and at Passchendaele in 1917.

During the Russian retreat from Galicia and Poland, four new German armies were formed, giving the Central Powers a superiority of thirteen armies to eleven. The Germans were still applying pressure in the centre, and in Courland by the Baltic, while in the south the Austrians were ripe for a counter-attack that was duly made in September at Lutsk (Luck) on the Styr, south of the Pripet. By September the main offensive had ended and the Russians had withdrawn to a north–south line some 200 miles to

the east of the original front. As they no longer held the Polish bulge, the line was now, at about 600 miles, almost half its original 1,000-mile length, releasing formations to create a reserve to oppose further Austro-German advances. Before Ludendorff launched his forces in the north towards Vilna on 9 September, the front ran from just west of Riga in the north, swinging eastwards towards the river Dvina and then south, passing to the west of Dvinsk, Vilna, Pinsk and the Pripet marshes and Lutsk, to Tarnopol and the pivot point northeast of Czernowitz. At the point of furthest retreat, the Russians were now some 240 miles east of

ABOVE: German 1910 pattern 21-cm (8-in.) *Mörser* (mortar, or howitzer) firing on the Russian front, August 1915. The German army went to war in 1914 with 216 of these heavy howitzers which were, with the 15-cm (6-in.), the backbone of the German heavy artillery on the Eastern and Western Fronts. Large numbers were subsequently constructed. A longer-barrelled version, with greater range, was introduced in 1916.
RIGHT: *Eastern Front (North)*. A general map of the operational area, showing lines and dates. *Harmsworth's New Atlas of the World*, c.1920.

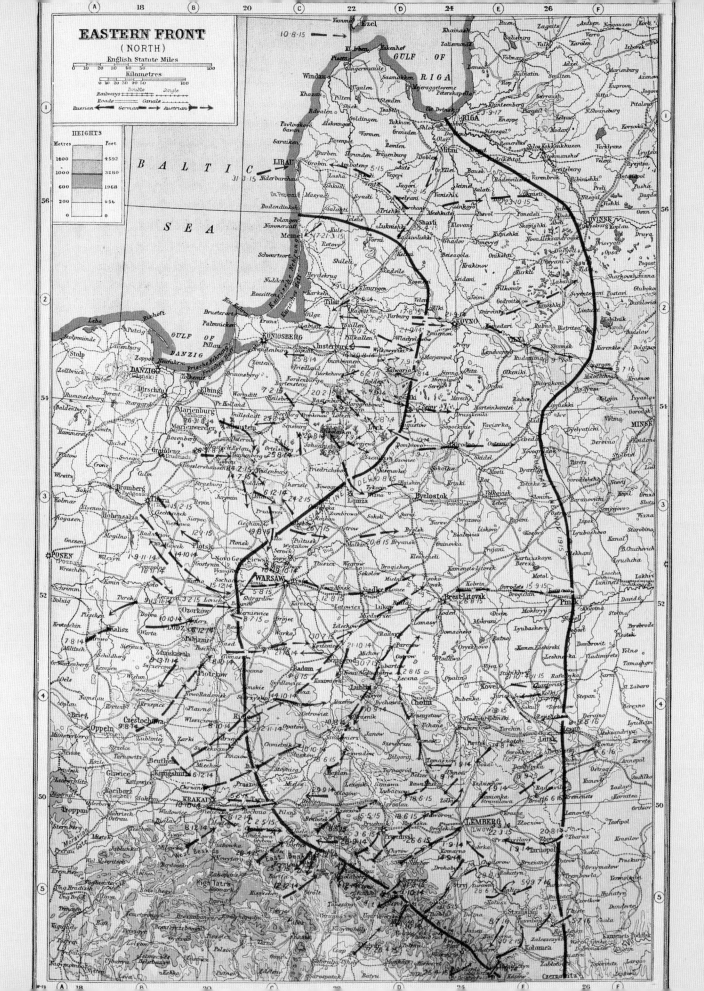

EASTERN FRONT
(NORTH)

English Statute Miles

Kilometres

Railways Double Single
Roads German Canals
Russian German Austrian

HEIGHTS

Metres Feet
1400 4592
1000 3280
600 1968
200 656
0 0

their original line west of Warsaw. Since May they had lost the remainder of Russian Poland and Galicia, and large tracts of western Russia, including the cities and fortresses of Novo Georgievsk, Warsaw, Przemyśl, Lublin, Lemberg, Brody, Brest-Litovsk and Bialystock. On the northern part of the front, where the Germans had earlier pushed their line out from East Prussia to Libau in the north and towards Kovno in the east, the German advance was more in the order of 60 miles.

Falkenhayn, under pressure to redeem his reputation and make up for the lost opportunity to defeat the Russians, at last agreed that Ludendorff's Vilna scheme for a two-pronged manoeuvre against Vilna should go ahead, but without any reinforcements. Starting on 9 September, he therefore launched his under-resourced scheme, using Below's Niemen Army to drive towards Dvinsk to the east, and Eichhorn's Tenth Army against Vilna to the southeast. The Russians were, however, not to be trapped by a Cannae-type envelopment, and withdrew in different directions. Between the two spearheads, the German cavalry pushed ahead beyond Vilna and approached Minsk, an important railway junction. Hindenburg and Ludendorff, continually in conflict with Falkenhayn, now asked him for enough divisions to push northwards to capture Minsk, cutting Russian communications. While German forces captured Vilna on 19 September, shortages of supplies and hardening Russian resistance forced Ludendorff to halt operations. Conrad also attacked from Lutsk on an easterly axis, aiming to envelop Russian forces south of the Pripet marshes, but his offensive did not start until 26 September, losing the value of simultaneity and mutual support, and was a miserable failure. By the middle of October, Austrian casualties had reached 230,000. At the end of these operations, the front extended from the Baltic to Czernovitz on the Rumanian border, via Riga, Jacobstadt, Dünaburg, Baranovichi, Pinsk, Dubno and Tarnopol.

The Conquest of Serbia

The complex historical pressures and tensions of the region explain the behaviour of Italy and the Balkan states in 1915–16. The complicated, volatile, cross-cutting tribal, ethnic and religious fault-lines of the Balkans widened before the war as the Ottoman grip weakened, and these divisions were exacerbated by the application of external levers by neighbouring great powers – notably Austria–Hungary and Russia, who strove to assert their own interests in the region. Similarly, the historical antagonism between Italy and Austria was a key contributory factor in the relations between these two powers.

The crude and naked exercise of national ambitions, even greed, particularly on the part of the newly independent nations,

was demonstrated in the Balkan Wars of 1912–13, and immediately re-emerged following the outbreak of war in 1914; indeed they had never gone away. The states which initially remained neutral in 1914, notably Bulgaria, Rumania and Greece, became the subject of intense competitive lobbying and bribery by the Allies and Central Powers, and watched closely the ebb and flow of the war so that they could jump the right way at the appropriate time. The initial failure of Austria–Hungary against Serbia in 1914, the stalemate on the Western Front, the Allied landings at Gallipoli and the possibility of Allied success in forcing the Dardanelles and sailing through the Straits to cow Constantinople, force Turkey to make peace and open the route to Russia, and the varying fortunes of both sides on the Eastern Front, were all important factors in the calculations of the, as yet neutral, nations in this game of 'rational strategies'.

Serbian resistance to Austria had, since August 1914, provided for the Allies a useful diversion of Austro-Hungarian forces away from the Russian front, effectively creating an 'Austrian ulcer'. While Serbia was undoubtedly a crucial strategic, military and political focus, her communications with the rest of the Allies were very poor; the main railways southward through the mountains to the nearest large port, Salonika, ran through neutral Greece and Bulgaria. During 1915, the Allies had neglected to bolster Serbia's ability to resist Austrian attack by supplying her with technical and material support, and the continued weakness of Serbia thus contributed to her vulnerability when the Austro-German attack came on 6 October. Serbia was particularly vulnerable to Bulgarian ambitions, and had declined Allied suggestions that she relinquish her territory in Macedonia, coveted by Bulgaria, to keep the latter neutral.

The Central Powers could launch an assault at this time because their great 1915 offensives against the Russians, starting with the opening of the Gorlice–Tarnów battle on 2 May, had succeeded to the extent that Russian forces had been driven back 250 miles and were effectively neutralized for the rest of the year. The Austrians felt that they could contain the Italian attacks on the Isonzo front (Italy declared war on Austria–Hungary on 23 May 1915) and, with the Russians no longer a threat, were convinced by Falkenhayn that this was the right time to deal Serbia a

RIGHT: The Austrians failed to crush Serbia in 1914 and the campaign dragged on until 1915 when Bulgaria joined the Central Powers, enabling a 'blitzkrieg' attack on Serbia from three directions, the remnants of the Serbian army evacuating via Albania and Corfu to Salonika. *Harmsworth's New Atlas of the World*, c.1920.

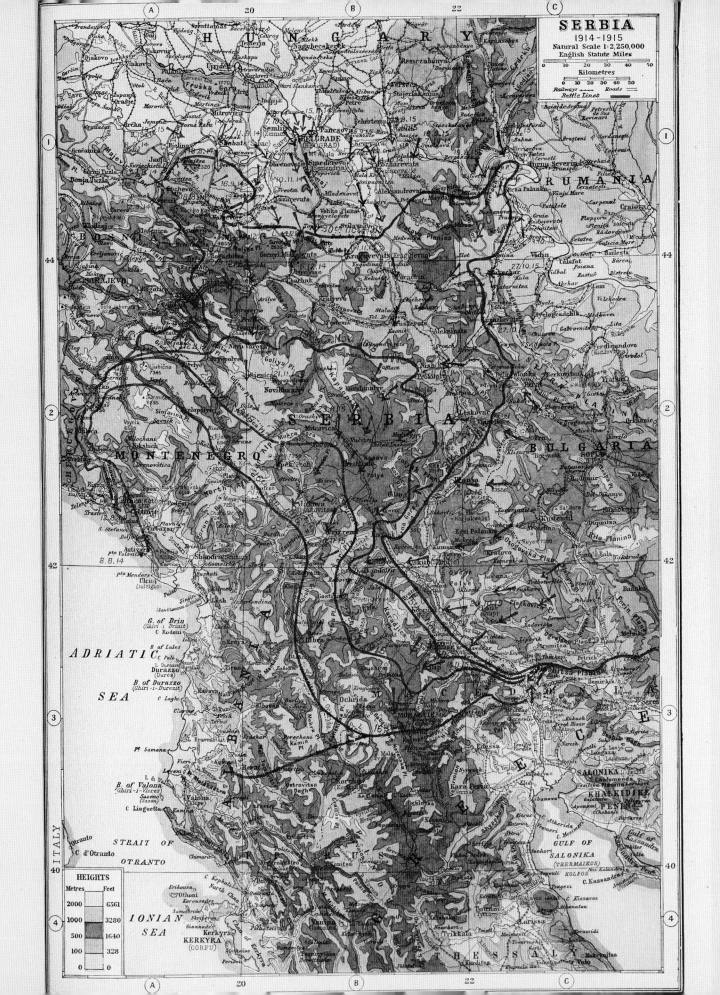

SERBIA
1914–1915
Natural Scale 1:2,250,000
English Statute Miles
Kilometres
Railways   Roads
Battle Lines

HUNGARY

RUMANIA

BOSNIA

SARAJEVO

SERBIA

MONTENEGRO

BELGRADE
(BEOGRAD)

BULGARIA

SOFIA

ADRIATIC

SEA

Durazzo
(Dures)
B. of Durazzo
(Ghiri-i-Duresit)

ALBANIA

MACEDONIA

GREECE

SALONIKA

KHALKIDIKE
PENIN

GULF OF
SALONIKA
(THERMAIKOS)

ITALY

STRAIT OF
OTRANTO

IONIAN
SEA

HEIGHTS
Metres   Feet
2000   6561
1000   3280
500   1640
100   328
0   0

KERKYRA
(CORFU)

THESSALY

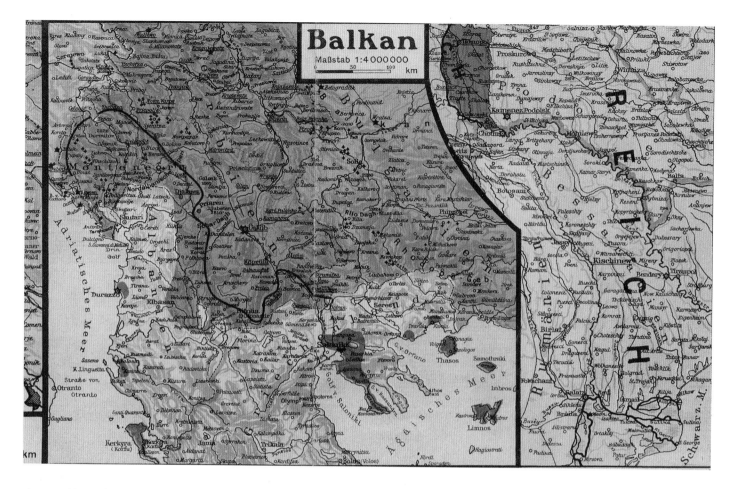

decisive blow. The accession of Bulgaria to the Central Powers enabled Falkenhayn to overcome the resistance of Austria and Turkey to operations against Serbia. They would have preferred to concentrate against Russia and deal her a knockout blow, arguing that from her defeat a favourable Balkan settlement, free from Russian pressure, would naturally follow. Against this, Falkenhayn argued that the defeat of Serbia would eliminate Russian influence in the Balkans. This, together with the opening up of the railway route from Berlin to Constantinople, via Belgrade and Sofia, would be an inducement to the Russians to pull out of the war. It would also enable Germany to supply the Turks directly, bringing the Gallipoli campaign to a close, ending any possibility of the Allies supplying Russia through the Dardanelles, helping the Turks' war against Russia in the Caucasus, and enabling more direct military operations against the British Empire in Egypt and the Suez Canal, Mesopotamia and India.

Seduced by the offer of territory in Macedonia (which Bulgaria had lost to Serbia in the Second Balkan War), Bulgaria joined the Central Powers on 6 September, thus sealing the fate of Serbia, which could now be attacked from a new direction.

Initially the Bulgarians were worried about the stance of Greece and Rumania; if these countries joined the Allies, Bulgaria would be vulnerable to attack from north and south if she attacked Serbia. Bulgaria also held back while it looked as though the British and French might win at Gallipoli, thus opening the Straits, threatening Constantinople and opening up communications with Russia. However, these considerations had changed by the autumn of 1915. The British failure to exploit the Suvla Bay landings of 6 August 1915 sounded the death knell of the whole Gallipoli enterprise. While the defeat of the Russians and the failure of Franco-British offensives in Artois and Champagne in France in September completely changed the strategic balance, weakening the prestige of the Allies in the Balkans and reducing the probability that Rumania and Greece would join them.

ABOVE: A detail from *Nebert's Kriegs-Frontenkarte*, showing the Balkan front at end of January 1916.

Bulgaria, worried about Austria's poor fighting record against Serbia, insisted that the Austro-German assault should be launched before their own armies attacked, and that the whole offensive should be under German command and control. To this end, Mackenson took charge of the operations, with the efficient Seeckt as his Chief-of-Staff. With Russia quiescent, and the Allies not yet ready to launch their autumn offensive in France, Falkenhayn began to organize an assault force by bringing Gallwitz's army from the Russian Front to join the Austrian Third Army. The Bulgarians were to provide two armies to attack Serbia from the east. Against these four strong, confident armies, Serbia could only deploy her own depleted army. Distant promises of help from Greece, to fulfil treaty obligations, and from Britain, France and Russia, echoed feebly through the mountain passes. They were of little help against the immediate prospect of an overwhelming attack. Moreover, the pro-Allied Greek premier, Venizelos, fell from power at just the wrong time for Serbia. Having been overwhelmingly re-elected in June 1915, his appointment grudgingly confirmed by the pro-German King Constantine in August, he ordered the Greek army to mobilize and asked the Allies to supply troops to defend Serbia. However, the arrival of Allied troops at Salonika in October was followed, in December, by the King's decision to dismiss Venizelos for compromising Greece's neutrality. By this time, however, it was too late to save Serbia.

At the end of September 1915 came the overture to the fourth invasion of Serbia, when Austrian forces began to exert increasing pressure against the frontier along the river lines, and against Belgrade. The powerful assault on Serbia, starting on 7 October, came from the north across the Danube, from the west over the Drina, and from the east (the Bulgarians) into southern Serbia. The Bulgarian attack threatened to cut off the Serbian forces facing the Austro-German attacks from any relief force advancing northwards up the Vardar valley, through the mountains from Salonika where the Allies had established a base at the beginning of October. The Bulgarian drive across their rear forced the Serbs to retreat to the west into Albania, through appalling winter conditions in the mountains. From there they were evacuated to Corfu and thence to Salonika. The Austrians, following up, occupied Montenegro and Albania. By the end of this brief Serbian campaign, therefore, the Central Powers had vastly strengthened their position in the Balkans; apart from quasi-neutral Greece they only had neutral Rumania to deal with, one way or another. Rumania's wheat and oil wealth, and the prospect of opening up river communication along the Danube as a further supply line to Turkey, were to prove irresistible to the Central Powers the following year.

THE WESTERN FRONT

In the autumn and winter of 1914, French operations focused on the stretch of front between Reims and the Argonne (First Battle of Champagne), and also on the Lens–Arras front (First Battle of Artois). The BEF was very much the junior partner, and took its lead from Joffre.

Neuve Chapelle

Haig's British First Army mounted a set-piece attack on 10 March that captured the village of Neuve Chapelle and impressed the French. A significant feature of the battle was the prior use of the Royal Flying Corps, which had deployed eighty-five aircraft to help with photography and artillery registration and ranging. Aerial photography had been used for operational mapping since the Battle of the Aisne, and by now the whole British front was well-covered with large-scale trench maps except for the Ypres Salient, which was in process of being taken over from the French. For the Neuve Chapelle operation, trench maps were lithographed at the 1:5,000 scale (12 inches to the mile), showing the German trenches in red. The RFC was also tasked for interdiction during the battle, bombing German headquarters and railways to prevent reserves from intervening.

While the First Army had 530 guns and howitzers in total, including sixty-six heavies surveyed-in by the Royal Engineers' 1st Ranging Section, not all were concentrated on the narrow attack frontage. A brief thirty-five-minute 'hurricane bombardment' by 342 guns and howitzers heralded an attack by the infantry of four divisions – about 40,000 men – on a two-mile front. An indication of the mechanization and intensity of the war, even at this stage, is that more shells were fired in this brief bombardment than in the whole Boer War. The short artillery preparation was the result of the shell shortage as much as a desire to achieve surprise. It had a neutralizing, shock effect on the German infantry and enabled the British and Indian assault troops to overrun the lines of breastworks and get into the village. They were prevented from getting further forward, however, by isolated machine gun detachments and by communications failures.

The French lost 50,000 men for little gain in attacks in Champagne in February and March, and in April lost 64,000 in an attack on the St Mihiel salient, southeast of Verdun, which was a total failure. There was no real coordination to many Allied attacks under Joffre's leadership, and Britain, although her army was growing, was very much the junior partner. However, efforts were made to coordinate Franco-British offensives in Artois in May and Artois and Champagne in September.

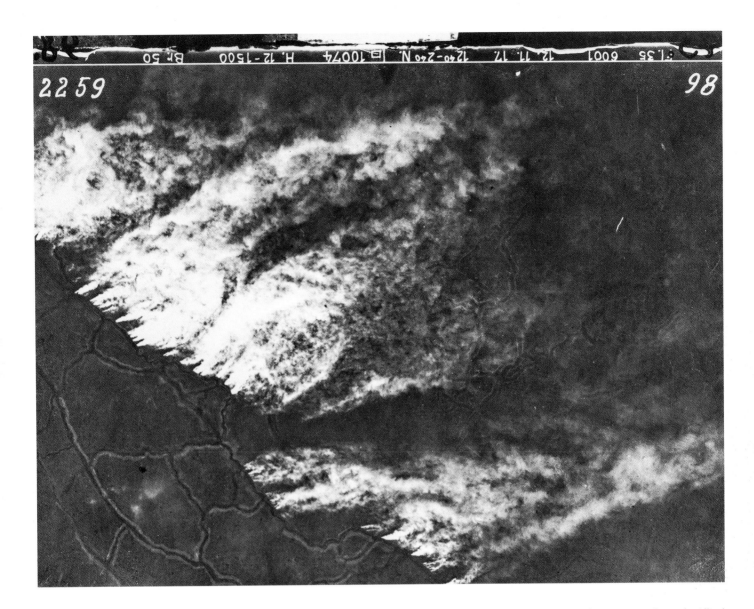

2259

98

Second Battle of Ypres

Meanwhile on 22 April the Germans made a surprise attack with gas at Ypres. Although warned by the French and Belgians that there were intelligence warnings of the possible use of gas at

ABOVE: German air photo of a gas attack. The first large-scale use of cloud gas, released from steel cylinders, was by the Germans at the Second Battle of Ypres on 22 April 1915. Chlorine and phosgene were widely used. From 1916, gas-filled shells were used as a more efficient means of delivery.

LEFT: German high oblique balloon photo looking southwest over Ypres towards Mount Kemmel, 1915. The Germans excelled at artillery observation, battery-location and direction-of-fire from balloons.

Ypres, Smith-Dorrien's British Second Army was the only Allied force to take counter-measures. The French did not bombard the German trenches, where gas cylinders had been emplaced in batteries of twenty every forty yards, though General Ferry, commanding the French 11th Division, in the target Langemarck sector, suggested such action. The British ordered an air reconnaissance, but this did not observe anything significant. It was probably as a result of this failure that, after the Second Battle of Ypres, an Intelligence Corps officer was appointed to each army with the special task of interpreting aerial photographs. As the latter were vital for plotting trench maps, and accurate British trench maps of the Ypres Salient did not yet exist (the British 1:10,000 scale sheets in use had trenches added in manuscript, although the French had previously produced

excellent 1:20,000 scale sheets showing the German trenches lithographed in blue), doubts must be cast on the efficiency of Second Army's staff and its coordination of aerial reconnaissance, maps and survey, and intelligence functions. On 17 April the German wireless accused the British of using gas shells and bombs east of Ypres, perhaps to pre-empt criticism.

But although they thus reinforced the warnings given by deserters to the Allies, the Germans still gained tactical surprise on 22 April. The gas cloud caused the French colonial troops in the Langemarck sector to break and run and, although the Canadians on their right held their position, they had to throw back a defensive flank to cover the gap. Further gas attacks followed, and the Germans actually crossed the canal north of Ypres at one moment, but were soon evicted from the west bank by counter-attack. However, as this was only an experiment with no troops to

follow up the attack, they threw away the opportunity to exploit probably the most complete surprise of the war by failing to provide the reserve divisions which could have broken through to Ypres and perhaps even to the Channel ports.

As it was the Allies, after costly counter-attacks, some made unnecessarily in broad daylight without artillery support, held the Germans. The British artillery was thin on the ground, and had so few shells to fire that batteries had to be withdrawn from the front. Smith-Dorrien was sacked by Sir John French for daring to suggest a retirement to a more defensible line; his replacement did precisely what Smith-Dorrien had proposed. The Second Army lost 60,000 men in these operations, and the Germans at least 35,000. The new Ypres Salient was shallower than the one that had existed from November 1914 to April 1915, and even so was costly to hold, being overlooked by the Germans on the surrounding high

ground. The new line remained relatively static for the next two years, although minor (but always bloody) operations, such as mine warfare at Railway Wood, the Bellewaarde Ridge, Hill 60, St Eloi and the Bluff, and the German attack on the Canadians at Sanctuary Wood in June 1916, caused some local adjustments.

Battle of Artois

The spirited French Artois attack of 9 May, between Arras and Lens, was made by d'Urbal's Tenth Army of Foch's Northern Army Group, and aimed, using nearly 300 heavy guns as well as hundreds of field guns, to capture the important feature of the Vimy Ridge, which dominated the Douai plain to the east. The British, at the same time, made diversionary attacks north of Béthune. D'Urbal's eighteen divisions attacked on a four-mile front opposite the ridge, but only Pétain's 33rd Corps made significant progress,

ABOVE: Vertical aerial photograph of German and British front-line trench systems, mine craters and no-man's-land west of Auchy-lez-la-Bassée (east of Béthune and Cambrin) on 15 July 1915. Mine warfare was particularly prevalent where a rise of the terrain offered an advantage of observation, both sides trying to blow the enemy off the high ground.

LEFT: Sniper and observer from the 1/4th Battalion, Royal Berkshire Regiment in the roof of a barn at Anton's Farm, north of St Yvon (St Yves) and Ploegsteert Wood, spring 1915. As the British were initially poorly equipped with loopholes and frequently changed sector, Battalion snipers had a very high casualty rate compared with the German snipers who stayed for long periods in a sector which they knew intimately.

FOLLOWING PAGES: *The Daily Mail Bird's Eye Map of the Front*: Section 1: Ypres-Béthune-Lille; Section 2: Béthune–Vimy–Arras–Albert–Somme. Scale of original: 1 inch to 1 mile.

The · Daily · Mail

Bird's · Eye · Map · of · the · British · Front — Section 1

COMPANION MAP.

For Southern Section of British and Allied Line (La Bassée Arras Albert), buy the 'DAILY MAIL' BIRD'S-EYE MAP OF THE FRONT

SECTION 2

Price 6d. net

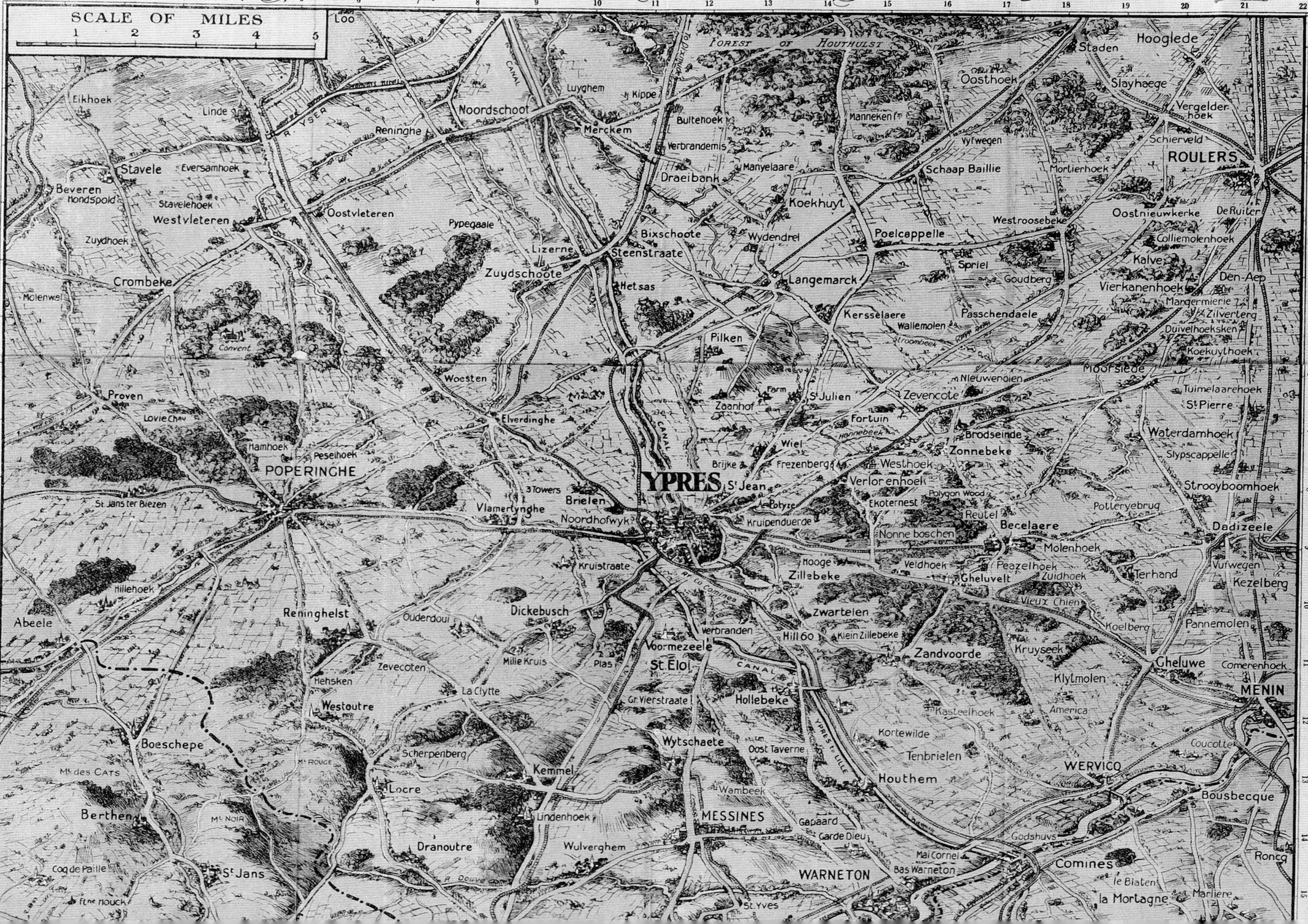

MILES 0 1 2 3 4 5 6 7 8 9 10 11 12 13 14 15

SCALE OF MILES
1 2 3 4 5

ROULERS
YPRES
POPERINGHE
MENIN
WERVICQ
MESSINES
WARNETON
COMINES

Hooglede
Staden
Oostnieuwkerke
Westroosebeke
Poelcappelle
Passchendaele
Langemarck
Becelaere
Zonnebeke
Gheluwe
Pilken
S.Julien
Hooge
Zillebeke
Hollebeke
Wytschaete
St.Eloi
Kemmel
Dranoutre
Locre
Reninghelst
Vlamertynghe
Dickebusch
Brielen
Noordschoot
Oostvleteren
Pypegaele
Elverdinghe
Zuydschoote
Bixschoote
Steenstraate
Boesinghe
Woesten
Proven
Abeele
Berthen
Westvleteren
Stavele
Beveren
Elzenwalle
CANAL
FOREST OF HOUTHULST

No. 2

The · Daily · Mail
Bird's · Eye · Map · of · The · Front – Section 2

COMPANION MAP

For Northern Section of British Line buy the
'DAILY MAIL' BIRD'S-EYE MAP OF THE BRITISH
FRONT — SECTION 1   Price 6d. net

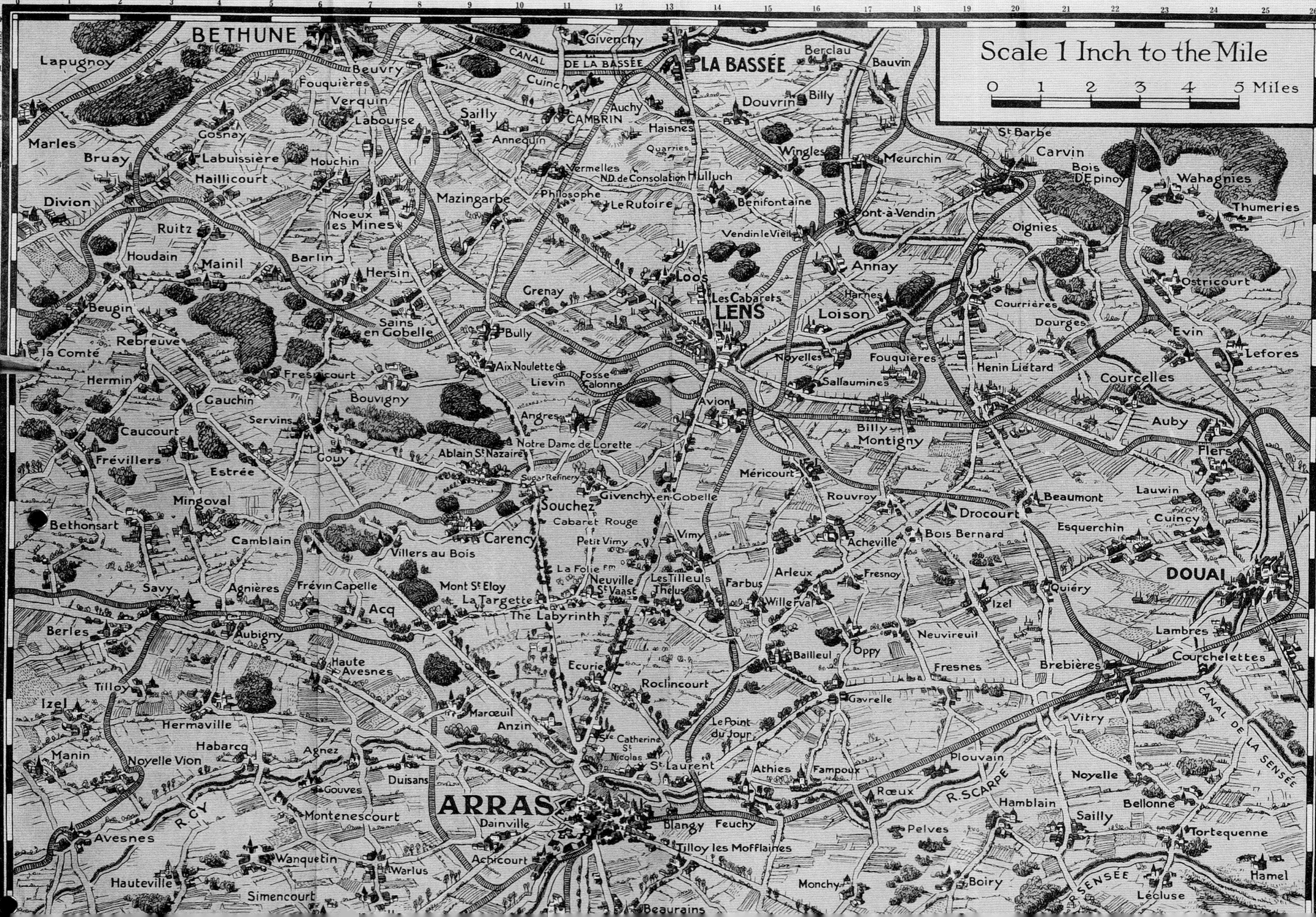

Scale 1 Inch to the Mile

Scale 1 Inch to the Mile

0   1   2   3   4   5 Miles

MILES

BETHUNE

LA BASSÉE

CANAL DE LA BASSÉE

CAMBRIN

DOUAI

LENS

ARRAS

CANAL DE LA SENSÉE

R. SCARPE

R. SENSÉE

Lapugnoy, Marles, Bruay, Gosnay, Labuissière, Houchin, Hallicourt, Divion, Ruitz, Rebreuve, Houdain, Beugin, Hermin, Mainil, Berlin, Noeux les Mines, Fouquières, Beuvry, Verquin, Labourse, Sailly la Bourse, Annequin, Cuinchy, Givenchy

Fressecourt, Caucourt, Frévillers, Camblain, Servins, Gauchin, Estrée, Mingoval, Savy, Agnières, Aubigny, Haute Avesnes, Acq, Villers au Bois, Mont St Eloy, Frévin Capelle

Bethonsart, Tilloy, Izel, Berles, Manin, Noyelle Vion, Hermaville, Habarcq, Agnez, Gouves, Wanquetin, Duisans, Montenescourt, Simencourt, Warlus, Beaurains, Achicourt, Dainville, Anzin, Marœuil, Ecurie, St Catherine, St Nicolas, St Laurent, Athies, Fampoux, Feuchy, Blangy, Tilloy les Mofflaines

Auchy, Haisnes, Quarries, Vermelles, ND. de Consolation, Hulluch, Philosophe, Le Rutoire, Loos, Les Cabarets, Avion, Liévin, Angres, Bully, Aix Noulette, Bouvigny, Notre Dame de Lorette, Ablain St Nazaire, Carency, Souchez, Cabaret Rouge, Petit Vimy, La Folie Fm, Neuville, St Vaast, Thélus, Vimy, La Targette, Les Tilleuls, Farbus, Willerval, Bailleul, Roclincourt, Le Point du Jour, St Nicolas

Berclau, Bauvin, Douvrin, Billy, Wingles, Vendin le Vieil, Bénifontaine, Loison, Noyelles, Sallaumines, Méricourt, Rouvroy, Acheville, Arleux, Fresnoy, Oppy, Gavrelle, Rœux, Pelves, Monchy

St Barbe, Carvin, Bois de Épinoy, Oignies, Courrières, Hénin Liétard, Billy Montigny, Fouquières, Courcelles, Dourges, Auby, Beaumont, Esquerchin, Drocourt, Bois Bernard, Neuvireuil, Fresnes, Quiéry, Izel, Plouvain, Vitry, Brebières, Courchelettes, Lambres, Flers, Cuincy, Lauwin, Noyelle, Hamblain, Sailly, Bellonne, Boiry, Boiry

Wahagnies, Thumeries, Thumeries, Ostricourt, Evin, Leforest, Meurchin, Mons-à-Vendin, Annay, Bois

Mortequenne, Hamel, Lecluse, Écourt, Goeulzin

Published by the "Daily Mail," Carmelite House, London, E.C. PRINTED BY GEORGE PHILIP & SON, LTD.

PRICE 6d. NET.   COPYRIGHT.

PERONNE

R. SOMME

R. TORTILLE

R. ANCRE

ALBERT

BAPAUME

R. HIRONDELLE

REXUETTE

Rumaucourt · Lestrée · Sauchy · Villers · Baralle · Sains · Inchy · Pronville · Moeuvres · Boursies · Demicourt · Dognies · Havrincourt · Bois Havrincourt · Ruyaulcourt · Neuville · Metz · Fins · Sorel · Heudicourt · Lieramont · Villers · Longavesnes · Roisel · Bussu · Driencourt · Mt St Quentin · Allaines · Moislains · Rancourt · Bouch. avesnes

Saudemont · Vis · Chérisy · Fontaine · Hendecourt · Croisilles · Riencourt · Bullecourt · Quéant · Cagnicourt · Ecoust · St Léger · Noreuil · Lagnicourt · Vaulx · Morchies · Beaumetz · Hermies · Vélu · Bertincourt · Haplincourt · Baraste · Bus · Ytres · Etricourt · Manancourt · Equancourt · le Mesnil · Rocquigny · Sailly · Aizecourt le Haut · Aizecourt le Bas · Nurlu

Wancourt · Héninel · St Martin · Hénin · Mercatel · Boiry · Boyelles · Hamelincourt · Ervillers · Mory · Behagnies · Sapignies · Favreuil · Biefvillers · Frémicourt · Reincourt · Beugny · Villers · le Transloy · Morval · le Mesnil · Lesboeufs · Ginchy · Combles · Le Forest · Maurepas · Cléry · Curlu · Vaux · Suzanne · Hem · Frise

Neuville · Ficheux · Boisleux · Boiry · Moyenneville · Courcelles · Ayette · Gomiécourt · Achiet le Grand · Bilmcourt · Grévillers · Ligny · La Barque · Le Sars · Flers · Longueval · Guillemont · Hardecourt · Maricourt

Rivière · Blairville · Ransart · Hendecourt · Adinfer · Douchy · Ablainzevelle · Bucquoy · Achiet · Puisieux · Irles · Warlencourt · Pys · Courcelette · Martinpuich · Bazentin · Montauban · Carnoy · Mametz

Monchiet · Bavincourt · Basseux · Bailleulval · Bienvillers · Monchy · Hannescamps · les Essarts · Fonquevillers · Gommécourt · Hébuterne · Serre · Miraumont · Beaumont · Grandecourt · Thiepval · Pozières · Contalmaison · La Boisselle · Fricourt · Bécordel · Meaulte

Bailleulmont · Berles · La Cauchie · Humbercamp · Souastre · Bavencourt · Courcelles au Bois · Colincamps · Auchonvillers · Hamel · Beaucourt · Ovillers · Aveluy · Mailly · Mesnil · Englebelmer · Médauville · Martinsart · Dernancourt · Ville · Buire · Treux

Gaudiempré · Hénu · Couin · St Amand · Coigneux · Sailly · Bus · Courcelles au Bois · Acheux · Bertrancourt · Beaussart · Forceville · Senlis · Bouzincourt · Millencourt · Laviéville · Ribemont · Mericourt

Sauty · La Herlie · Berles · Varennes · Hénencourt · Baizieux · Warloy · Bresle · Morlancourt · Bray · Buire · Helly

Bord · Baizeux

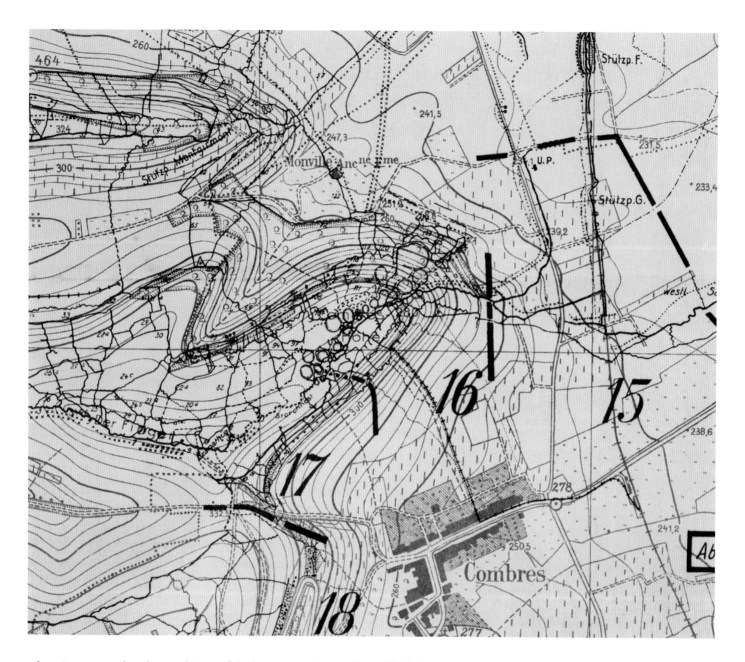

advancing two miles due to his careful planning and use of artillery, and briefly reaching the crest of the ridge. Such a breakthrough, on too narrow a front, became the focus of heavy flanking fire from the Germans and the gap was soon plugged. The Germans were alarmed as they had not yet constructed strong rear positions to contain such attacks, and the danger of breakthrough was real. They immediately began to construct a second trench position, wired and with strong-points at intervals, all along the Western Front. French casualties were appallingly heavy, but this did not deter Foch from continuing the attacks into June, again with heavy losses. The French offensive was finally

ABOVE: *Stellungskarte* (Trench Map), *Geheim* (Secret), *Combres-Höhe* (Les Eparges, south-east of Verdun), 19 August 1916, showing trenches and mine craters. French trenches in red, German trenches in blue. Like Vauquois and many other fiercely contested sectors, mine warfare was the result of a struggle to occupy the high ground to gain observation, particularly for the artillery, and deny it to the enemy.

RIGHT: French troops in a trench in front of Mont Herniel in the Bois de Beaumarais, Aisne, on 21 August 1915. The French introduced steel helmets that summer. The big Champagne offensivebegan on 25 September.

called off on 18 June, after losing 100,000 men. German casualties were around 75,000. Only mass populations could absorb these levels of casualties, but over the next few years, as the casualty figures increased much more, people began not only to question, but to resist, the whole hideous strategy of attrition. In the end, though, it was not casualties but hunger that accelerated revolution and the collapse of empires.

Aubers Ridge and Festubert

To the north of the French, a subsidiary British attack was made on 9 May, by Haig's First Army, on either side of Neuve Chapelle against the slight rise of the Aubers Ridge, in the direction of Lille. Following the Neuve Chapelle attack in March, the Germans had significantly strengthened their defences, in particular by building concealed machine gun positions into the base of their breastwork parapets. High sandbag breastworks, protected by the usual barbed wire entanglements, were constructed in this area of Flanders because the surface water level was very high, and trenches flooded. Lacking heavy artillery and sufficient high explosive shell, the British assaults on 9 May failed totally in a massacre of the infantry, but Joffre insisted on a further British effort that Haig launched on 15 May at Festubert, just north of the Béthune–La Bassée Canal, in the same area as the southern British attack of 9 May. Despite the shell-shortage, this utilized a more prolonged artillery bombardment, and developed into a series of local attacks which took some ground, lasting until 27 May,

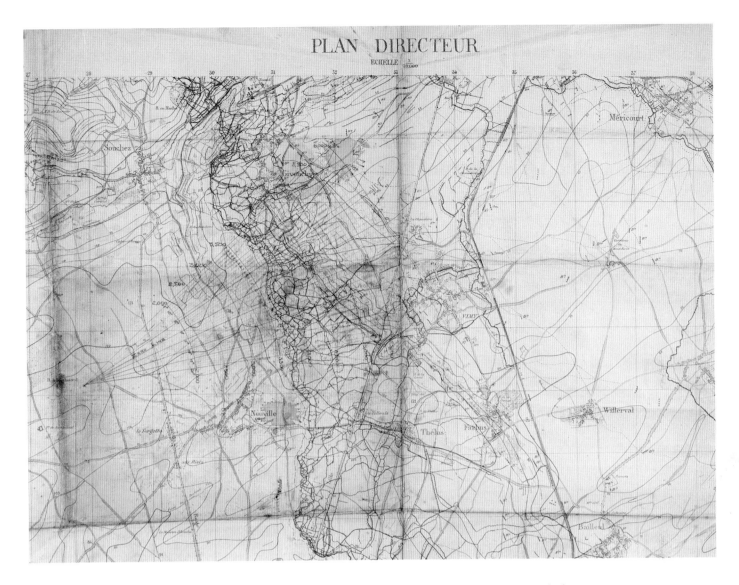

PLAN DIRECTEUR
ECHELLE $\frac{1}{20,000}$

followed by yet another small attack near Givenchy-lès-la-Bassée on 15–16 June. The British attacks by First Army in May had cost 27,000 men.

In July the British inserted a new army, the Third, to the south of the French Tenth Army which held the Vimy–Arras sector, taking over the front north of the river Somme from the French.

ABOVE: French trench map (*plan directeur*), Vimy Ridge–Arras area. German trenches printed in blue, and manuscript British artillery arc, showing battery position at the Bois de Berthonval, arc of fire over Vimy Ridge, etc. The British relieved the French in this sector in February–March 1916.

LEFT: French soldiers in 'Entente Cordiale Trench', southeast of Loos, after the battles of Loos and Artois in September–October 1915.

September Battles in Artois and Champagne

The French and British attacked yet again in Artois and Champagne in the late summer. Joffre launched thirty-five divisions northward in Champagne, and in Artois twelve British divisions attacked on a front between the Béthune–La Bassée Canal and Lens, while to their right eighteen French divisions again assaulted on the Lens–Vimy Ridge–Arras front. The axis of these Artois attacks was eastwards, Foch's strategy being, as before, to cut off the German forces in the great Noyon bulge by these converging attacks from the south and west. Joffre had created the artillery reserve for his attacks by dismantling the French fortresses, even those in the front line such as Verdun, which had been declared obsolete after the success of the super-heavy German and Austrian howitzers at Liège and elsewhere. By so doing, he transferred 2,000 heavy and 3,000 field guns to the field armies. In addition, ten cavalry

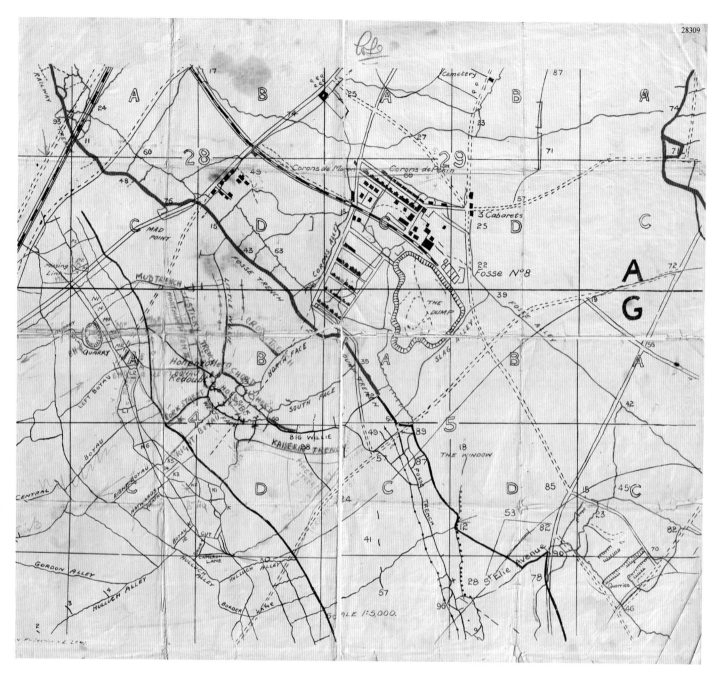

Map labels (as visible): 28309, Railway, Cemetery, Corons de Maroc, Corons de Pekin, 3 Cabarets, Fosse Nº8, THE DUMP, Fosse No 8, FOSSE ALLEY, SLAG ALLEY, MAD POINT, MUD TRENCH, FOSSE TRENCH, LITTLE WILLIE, CORON TRENCH, Missing Link, Hohenzollern Redoubt, NORTH FACE, SOUTH FACE, BH QUARRY, LEFT BOYAU, WEST FACE, YORK STREET, BIG WILLIE, KAISERIN TRENCH, THE WINDOW, RIGHT BOYAU, HAYWARDS TRENCH, CENTRAL, GORDON ALLEY, HULLUCH ALLEY, CAMERON LANE, BORDER LANE, SCALE 1:5,000, St Elie Avenue, Quarries, A B C D, 28 29 4 5, AG

divisions were brought up to pour through the expected gap that would be created. Allied commanders were still under the illusion that the artillery bombardment would destroy all opposition, that the infantry could merely walk through the pulverized enemy position, and that the cavalry could then exploit far into the enemy's rear, disrupting his command and communication infrastructure and forcing a retreat, or even achieving an encirclement. If a gap were somehow created, cavalry was the only arm capable of rapid exploitation. The fast cross-country motor

ABOVE: Secret British 1:5,000 trench map produced during the Battle of Loos, of the Hohenzollern Redoubt, Fosse 8, Dump, Quarries area, around 7 October 1915. Drawn and lithographed in the field, with German trenches in red, British blue, and manuscript additions showing operational use.

RIGHT: Faces of battle: men of 'B' Company, 1st Scots Guards, with the new Mills bombs (hand grenades) in trenches very close to the German position at the Hohenzollern Redoubt, in the later stages of the Battle of Loos, October 1915.

vehicle had not yet been developed, and the prototypes of the slow, clumsy, first models of the tank were only just beginning to be produced and tested.

Kitchener, concerned about the possibility of a Russian collapse, opposed British offensives in the west, but wanted to take pressure off Russia and Italy where things were going badly. The British contribution to the September offensive, while small, taxed her resources. More shells were now forthcoming, but trained and battle-experienced troops were lacking. The British had also progressively taken over more front from the French, as well as sending divisions, guns and ammunition to Gallipoli and elsewhere. Joffre also required active British attacks, so despite the unfavourable semi-industrial terrain of the Loos

coal-mining area where he wanted them to attack as a flank guard to the French assault on the Vimy Ridge, Sir John French and Haig had no option but to agree. Short of artillery and ammunition, the British also used an 'accessory', chlorine gas, to compensate.

On 25 September, 800,000 French and British soldiers attacked. In Champagne, where the Germans had created an elastic defence system, thinning out the first position (front, support and reserve trenches) and making their second position (also three trench lines) over a mile behind the main one, the attack surged over the first position but came under heavy fire in the open ground beyond it, and were then stopped by the second. This had been cleverly sited beyond the range of the French field artillery. The furthest advance was 3,000 yards. A similar result obtained in Artois. Again troops broke through to the top of Vimy Ridge, but once more were forced back.

The Battle of Loos

To their north, Haig's British First Army, including divisions of the New Armies, broke through the German first position on 25 September, even though the gas cloud did not did not carry smoothly across no man's land, and captured the mining village of Loos and, briefly, Hill 70 beyond it. But withering German fire and lack of reserves caused them to retire to the reverse slope of the hill. The German second position, with its wire and *Stützpunkte* (strong-points), was too strong. The British reserve divisions, the inexperienced 21st and 24th divisions of the New Armies, were held by French too far back, and released to Haig too late to intervene quickly at the right moment on the first day, despite Haig's entreaties. And when they did attack, on the morning of the next day, after an exhausting and hungry march, they had no time to make a proper reconnaissance and broke under heavy German fire, retreating in some disorder. The gap was filled by cavalry and by the Guards Division, which had also been in reserve. This fiasco led, after some behind-the-scenes intrigue by Haig, who had the ear of the King, to Haig taking over from French as Commander-in-Chief of the BEF in France and Belgium on 10 December.

The battle continued into October, but although heavy fighting at the Hohenzollern Redoubt, Hill 70, Hulluch, the Quarries and elsewhere along the line continued into October, little further progress was made. British casualties at the Battle of Loos were 50,000 while the French lost nearly 200,000 in Artois and Champagne. Total German losses were perhaps 200,000. In the balance of attrition, typical of the Western Front battles, it was a close-run thing.

Chapter 6

The 1916 Campaign in the East and the West

The year 1916 was one of drama and of blood, and ended, as 1914 and 1915 had done, in stalemate. In 1915 the Allies had tried and failed to break through in the West, and sought or had been drawn into various 'sideshows', notably the Gallipoli, Egyptian and Mesopotamian theatres. At the beginning of 1916, at Kut on the Tigris the British-Indian force under Townshend was still besieged. While the Turks had reached the Suez Canal, it was secure. The Arab Revolt was soon to begin. The Central Powers, defending in the West, had defeated Russia to the extent that Russian Poland and much of Galicia had been captured, and German troops were on the Gulf of Riga and close to Pinsk.

Falkenhayn, the Kaiser's Chief-of-Staff, had made some serious strategic errors, perhaps the worst of which was not attacking the British in 1915, permitting them to expand their army to the extent that it was becoming a real danger. The introduction of conscription in Britain meant that Germany had to contend not just with the remains of Britain's Regular and Territorial Armies, reinforced with Kitchener's volunteers of the New Armies, but also with a mass 'peoples' army' akin to those of the Continental powers. The Somme battle, however, demonstrated that even without the conscripts, the BEF was already a formidable opponent. Another error was that, by failing to finish off Russia in 1915 and turning to the West in 1916 with his Verdun offensive, Falkenhayn had created a rod for Germany's back, as Brusilov was to demonstrate.

The year 1916 began with the final evacuation of the British and French from Gallipoli, and ended with Germany's peace proposals. It was to see not just the titanic battles of Verdun, the Eastern Front and the Somme, but also the 'Easter Rising' in Dublin, the first appearance of the tank in battle, more bombing of London by the Germans, the indecisive fleet action at Jutland in the North Sea at the end of May, the drowning of Lord Kitchener in HMS *Hampshire* early in June, and the fall of Asquith, Joffre and Falkenhayn, and the death of the Emperor Franz Joseph. The British Commander-in-Chief, Sir John French, had already been replaced by Sir Douglas Haig in December 1915, and Hindenburg and Ludendorff were to replace Falkenhayn. Just as 1915 saw the entry of Serbia on the side of the Allies, and her rapid defeat, 1916 was to repeat this experience for Rumania. The USA was still neutral. The year was to see millions of men killed, millions more maimed and many more fall sick and die in prison camps. Millions of civilians were also beginning to die of hunger and disease as a result of the war.

THE EASTERN FRONT

The Eastern Front at the beginning of 1916 ran approximately north–south for 600 miles from the Gulf of Riga on the Baltic to Czernowitz, near the junction of Galicia, Rumania and Bessarabia, in the Carpathians. The Russians had been driven back to this line in the summer of 1915 by the great series of Austro-German offensives which began with the breakthrough at Gorlice–Tarnów in May 1915 and ended with Ludendorff's Vilna manoeuvre in the autumn. By the end of 1916, after Rumania had entered the war and been defeated, the front extended to the Black Sea and was 1,000 miles long.

It is a common misconception that the Eastern Front, unlike the Western, was characterized by movement and manoeuvre and that trench warfare, as known in the West, was not a feature of war in the East. Nothing could be further from the truth, as many of the contemporary trench and operations maps make clear. While there were phases of movement, when these stopped the trench lines immediately solidified, and trench systems as intricate as those in France and Belgium developed rapidly. Indeed, the conditions of modern warfare could lead to little else. Where firepower dominated the field, men had no option but to dig in, and this was seen on every front during the war.

In January 1916, on the southern part of the front, the Russians made a strong feint attack towards Czernowitz, in northern Bukovina, whilst to the north they pushed across the upper reaches of the Dniester river and there were inconclusive operations in the Riga area. The Russians captured Erzerum, on the Caucasus front, on 15 February. The Grand Duke Nicholas, by smashing the main Turkish army here, helped to offset the Turkish victory over the British and French at Gallipoli. Following this success, the Russians pushed forward to capture Trebizond, on Turkey's Black Sea coast, on 19 April, and then advanced south to Lake Van.

Following the 1915 successes of the Central Powers, led by Germany, Ludendorff began initiating a plan to 'Germanize' the

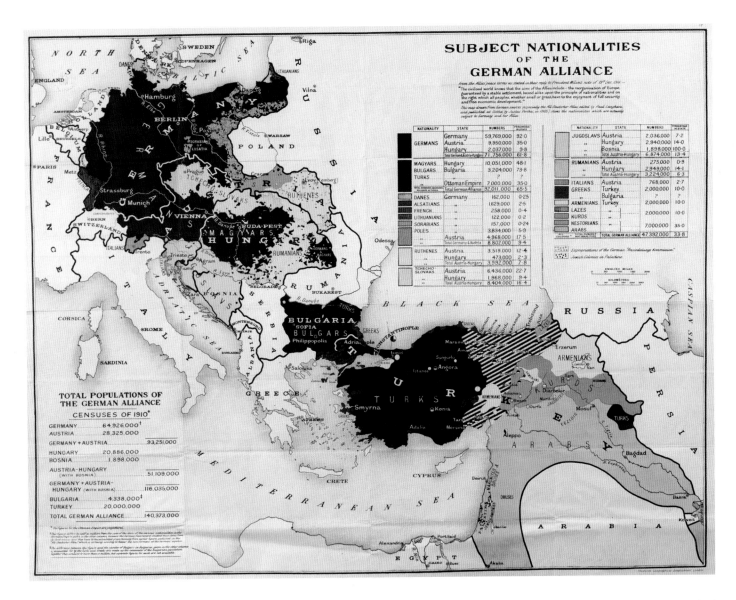

ABOVE: A propaganda map, based on *'the Allies' peace terms as stated in their reply to President Wilson's note of 19 December 1916'*, illustrating the various 'nationalities' to be liberated from the grip of the Central Powers. The Jewish colonies in Palestine are worth noting.

occupied territories in Russian Poland and the Baltic lands, as part of a longer-term programme effectively to make them German economic colonies. A Russian offensive, which started on 18 March, as a resumption of the northern offensive, was partly planned by the Stavka with Ludendorff's scheme in mind, but was also intended to take pressure off the French at Verdun. This attack, north and south of Lake Naroch, had Vilna, the capital of Polish Lithuania, as its immediate objective. The Russian army had recovered well from its 1915 defeats, and was numerically stronger than its opponents in the northern sector (north of the Pripet marshes) by a margin of 300,000 to 180,000 men, and in the central sector by 700,000 to 360,000. In Brusilov's southern sector the opposing forces were more even, about half-a-million each. But while the Russian army as a whole was still short of rifles, artillery and ammunition (not least stocks of shells), in the north it had had 5,000 guns with 1,000 shells per gun, more than the Germans had at Gorlice–Tarnow in May 1915.

Despite this superiority, the northern attack, which lasted nearly two weeks, failed as it was launched on too narrow a front and suffered from bad artillery–infantry cooperation, and was then pounded from three sides by the German artillery, while more

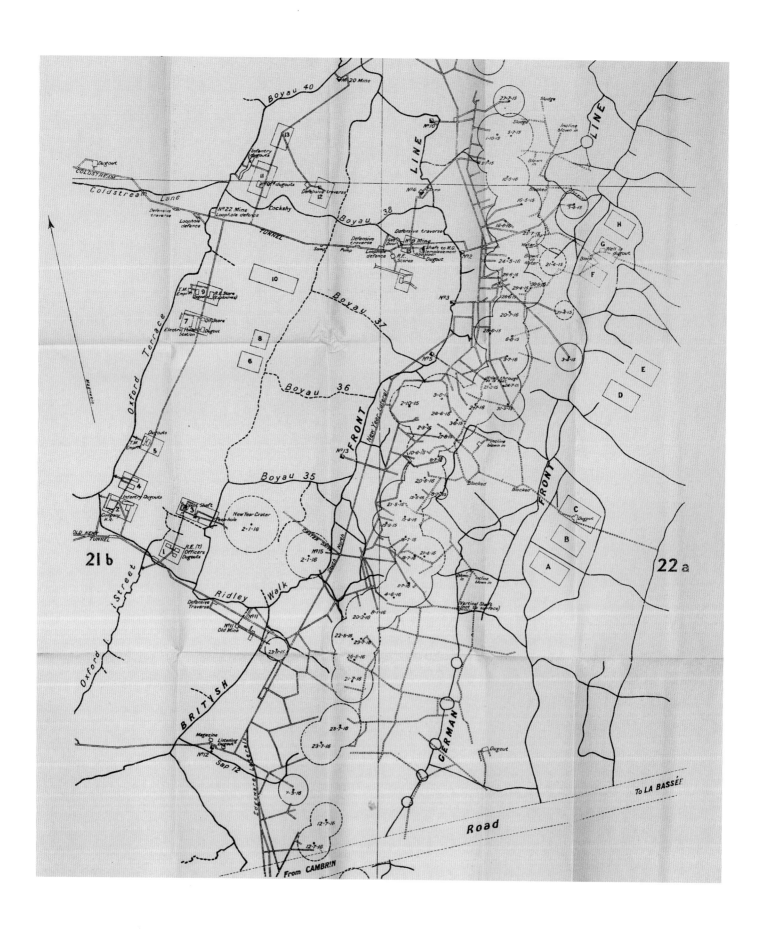

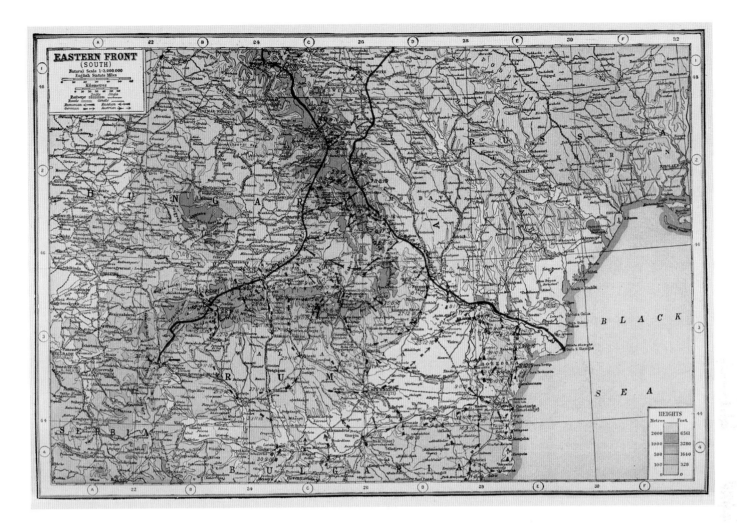

EASTERN FRONT
(SOUTH)
Natural Scale 1:3,000,000
English Statute Miles
Kilometres

men were fed in to become casualties to the German guns. By the end of the battle on 31 March, the Russians had lost 100,000 men. In April, Bruchmüller controlled over thirty batteries during the Tenth Army's brutal counter-attack, which was spearheaded by 40th Corps, and he was able to centralize the army's artillery command and control, and arrange a creeping barrage. The effect of his intelligent artillery preparation was to stun the Russian defenders senseless, and to help make his reputation. He was now the rising star of German offensive artillery technique, and

ABOVE: *Eastern Front (South)*. A general map of the operational area, including the South-Eastern Front (Rumania, etc.) with lines and dates. *Harmsworth's New Atlas of the World*, c.1920.

LEFT: *Craters on Cuinchy Front*, 1916. This sector, north of Lens and Loos and south of the Béthune–La Bassée Canal, was, like others, subject to mine warfare. A key feature was the Brickstacks, described among others by Robert Graves and Edmund Blunden.

later in the year planned the fire support for several of the counter-attacks against the Brusilov offensive.

On 14 April, Tsar Nicholas presided at a conference of his army-group commanders, when it was agreed that Evert's centre group would launch the main offensive, Kuropatkin's northern group swinging south to support it, while Brusilov's southern group, its front not considered suitable for an attack, would hold fast. Brusilov, however, reasoned that, precisely for this reason, the Austrians would not be expecting an attack and that, therefore, he should attack, not least to prevent the Central Powers from concentrating on defeating Evert's attack. Given permission, Brusilov began to prepare twenty widely spaced attacks to conceal the true location, and also divided his reserves.

In mid-1916 both the Russians and the Central Powers had adopted essentially offensive postures in the East, even though, in the West, Germany was heavily committed at Verdun and was anticipating the forthcoming Allied attack on the Somme, while Austria–Hungary, after the defeat of Serbia, was also looking to the

Italian front. The Russian army, while weak after its 1915 defeats, was rebuilding its strength and seeking to help the French beleaguered at Verdun. German and Austro-Hungarian armies, commanded by the Bavarian Bothmer (*Südarmee*) and Pflanzer-Baltin (Seventh Army), under Archduke Frederick's overall command, held the front south of the Pripet marshes and in Galicia, while facing them was Brusilov's southern army group. Bothmer took command of the Südarmee on 7 July and was to hold it until 1918.

Brusilov's preparations were thorough, along a wide front so as to confuse the Austrians as to the location of the main attack and to make them disperse their reserves. He insisted on deep dugouts being provided, like the German *Stollen* before the Verdun battle, to save casualties among the waiting assault troops, and also instructed the infantry to sap forward to reduce the width of no man's land, a standard siege-warfare procedure. The British had done the same before the Battle of Loos. Along the twenty miles of his main attack frontage, the Russian superiority over the Austrians was not great – 200,000 men to 150,000, and 904 guns to 600.

Brusilov attacked, or rather launched a series of probing attacks, on 4 June, having advanced the date because Cadorna, the Italian Commander-in-Chief, had appealed for a relief attack to draw away Austrian forces from the offensive Conrad had started on 15 May in the Trentino. The Austrians were taken by surprise. Four Russian armies were launched along the southern front from Pinsk, in the Pripet marshes, south towards Kimpolung and Czernowitz on the Rumanian border, and the attack frontage eventually extended to 300 miles. The axis of the main attack was westward towards the railway centre of Kowel. The attack immediately broke through the Austrian Eighth and Ninth Armies.

By 6 June the northern flank of Brusilov's armies had reached the important railway and road centre of Lutsk (Luck) on the river Styr, and crossed that river and also the Ikva. Kaledin's Eighth Army cut through Archduke Joseph Ferdinand's Fourth Army, whose positions had been so pulverized by the Russian artillery that his troops surrendered in droves. The Archduke was removed from command at the insistence of the German High Command after this fiasco. Kaledin then went on to capture Lutsk and advanced forty miles to the Stochod river, forcing a wedge between the Austrian Fourth and First Armies. In the Lutsk area the greatest gains were made between Kowel and Dubno, and by mid-July the Russians had advanced fifty miles. The Russian armies north and south of Kaledin's also advanced, pushing back the Austrians who lost 30,000 prisoners in two days. These armies were Lesh's Third Army in the Pripet region, Sakharov's Eleventh and Scherbachev's

Seventh in eastern Galicia and Lechitsky's Ninth along the Dniester on the front from Tarnopol south to Czernowitz, the capital of Bukovina.

Pflanzer-Baltin's Austrian Seventh Army was overwhelmed by the force of the Russian Seventh and Ninth Armies, being cut in half and pushed out of East Galicia. Scherbachev's and Lechitsky's armies drove through for seventy miles to Stanislau, in the Dniester valley, and on past Kolomea and Kuty. Scherbachev's army pushed the Austrians back across the Strypa. By mid-June, Pflanzer-Baltin's army was retreating fast, and had lost 100,000 men, a large proportion as prisoners. Lechitsky's army broke through in the Bukovina and rapidly advanced on Czernowitz, which it captured on 17 June, and by 21 June it had advanced another thirty miles to capture Radautz.

The pessimistic Evert was to have attacked on 14 July but, using bad weather as an excuse, postponed until 18 July, and there was then a further delay while the Tsar and his Chief-of-Staff, Alekseyev, prevaricated. Still Evert and Kuropatkin marked time, so Alekseyev tried to shift their reserves south to reinforce Brusilov's successes. Poor railway communications prevented them from arriving before the Germans could counter-attack, but the Germans struck first. Linsingen hit at the northern flank of the

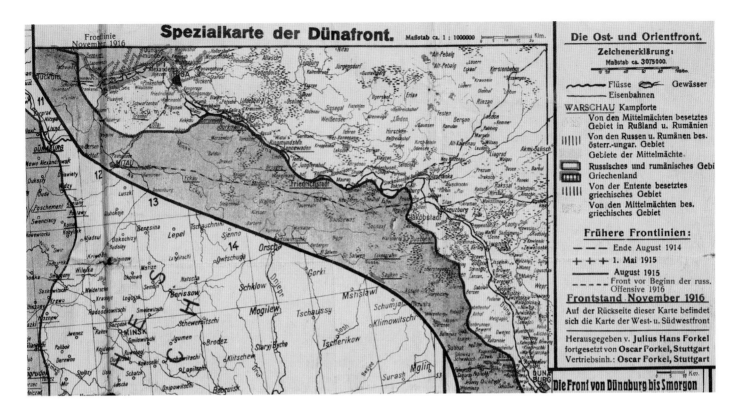

Russian breakthrough at Lutsk, stopping the Russian advance in this vital sector, but further south in the Bukovina the Russians pressed on until they reached the very edge of the Carpathians.

The success of Lechitsky's army was a serious threat to Bothmer's *Südarmee*, which was being pushed back remorselessly towards Rumania, and forced him to retreat hastily. By 23 June the Russians occupied all of the Bukovina, and by the next day Lechitsky had pushed the Austrians even further back, practically to the Rumanian border, to Kimpolung in the eastern Carpathians. Kuty, in northwest Galicia, also fell. Lechitsky, who had changed his axis, now pushed north towards Lemberg (Lvov) and on 28 June attacked the Austrians in the new defensive positions they had taken up after being driven from the Bukovina. Kolomea was captured by the Russian on 29 June, but Lechitsky's army was now forced to slow its pace westward.

The effects of the Russian attack were, as intended, widespread. The British and French launched their great attack on the Somme on 1 July, and further attacks by Russia were welcome as a diversion. Falkenhayn had already been forced to suspend offensive operations at Verdun, and the need to face the Russians had stopped Austria's offensive against Italy, which had already been counter-attacked by the Italians.

In early July, another Russian offensive finally began under Evert, north of the Pripet marshes, driving towards Baronovitchi, southwest of Minsk. The Germans soon halted this attack, but in the south Brusilov's attacks continued their run of successes into September. Floods delayed Lechitsky for a week, before he moved again on 9 July. Towards the end of July the Russians attacked again. Initially Sakharov advanced in the centre in the direction of Brody and Lemberg, and this push was followed by attacks further north by the Russian Guard Army, towards the river Stochod and Kowel. Through August the attacks continued with heavy losses but for no particular strategic gain, except that they had the Central Powers by the throat and were thereby loosening still more Falkenhayn's grip on the situation in the West. To meet these attacks, Falkenhayn had to transfer seven divisions from France, being forced to abandon the Verdun offensive and also his plans to launch a spoiling attack against the British offensive on the Somme.

Lechitsky's offensive continued on 7 August, two days later capturing the railhead of Khryplin, in Galicia near Stanislau, which was itself captured on 10 July. Bothmer now found both his flanks under threat, and retreated from the river Strypa to the Ziota–Lipa line. At the end of August, Russian forces advanced in the Carpathians, to the north and south of the Jablonica Pass, and captured the important height of Ploska. Between June and August, Lechitsky's army in the Bukovina captured over 100,000 prisoners and nearly 600 guns.

Meanwhile, on 27 August, Rumania, encouraged by the Russian successes, declared war, with her twenty-seven divisions, on Austria–Hungary. On 17 August, Rumania had agreed with France and Russia that she would enter the war in return for land. The Central Powers' territories she coveted, and was granted in this venal transaction, were Transylvania, the Bukovina, and part of southern Galicia and southwest Hungary. But the perfidious France and Russia had no intention of delivering on this agreement. While Rumania did not realize this, she was still foolish to stick her neck out between the hostile Bulgaria and Austria–Hungary. She was relying on the Russian offensive, and in particular that towards Kowel in the southern Pripet marshes, to keep German reserves away from the Southeast theatre, and was strangely dismissive of the possibility of having to make war against Bulgaria and Turkey. The latter, in fact, shipped two divisions to the Rumanian front. The Russians gave Rumania little help, being already heavily engaged themselves, and Alekseyev considered Rumania an unwelcome burden. Neither did the British and French at Salonika come to her immediate assistance, as the Bulgarians, Germans and Turks attacked in Macedonia on 17 August, defeating the reconstituted Serbian army at Florina, and delayed the planned attack by the British and French until September, by which time it was too late.

The entry of Rumania led to Falkenhayn's dismissal as the Kaiser's Chief-of-Staff, and his replacement by the Hindenburg–Ludendorff duumvirate. Ironically, Falkenhayn was now sent, as a consolation prize, to join Mackensen to command the Central Powers' forces against Rumania. On 4 September, Mackensen invaded the Dobrudja, and on 4 October the Rumanians were defeated in a battle near Nagyszeben (Hermannstadt). The Rumanian situation was so serious by early October that the Russian General Sakharov was placed in command of the joint Russian–Rumanian armies fighting the German–Bulgarian armies in the Dobrudja, and further Russian progress was halted. On the border of Rumania and the Bukovina, in the Dorna–Watra region, Russian forces fought remorselessly to take the pressure off Falkenhayn's campaign further south. The Central Powers, however, had the upper hand and on 6 December occupied Bucharest.

As the Germans deployed more troops in the Eastern and Southeastern theatre, despite the Allied offensive on the Somme and France's counter-offensive at Verdun, the Russian advance lost impetus. Rumania's accession to the Allies came too late to affect the situation, and merely invited an Austro-German counter-offensive. Indeed, the Germans were now counter-attacking remorselessly. At Tarnopol in July they launched a savage thrust, heralded by one of Bruchmüller's brief but crushing

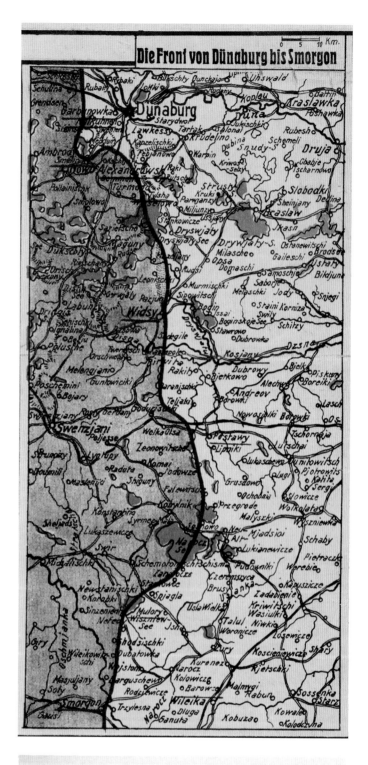

Die Front von Dünaburg bis Smorgon

ABOVE: A detail (continued from previous page) from *So Steht der Krieg an der Ost-u. Orient-Front, Feldpostbrief,* showing part of the Dünafront.

RIGHT: German troops moving up to forward positions in Russian Poland in the driving snow of the Eastern Front.

bombardments, and soon Austro-German counter-attacks were hammering away along the line. South of the Pripet, the Austrian Fourth Army put in an attack to the southeast against the Russian offensive that had been directed at Kowel. Bruchmüller was instrumental in organizing the German artillery in more ferocious counter-attacks, notably at the Zarzeize bridgehead, at Korytnica–Swiniuchy in September, and most significantly at Witonitz on the Stochod river on 1 November.

Although the Russians had initially achieved a great tactical victory, Brusilov's logistical problems prevented strategic exploitation, for the bulk of Russian reserves had been concentrated in the north for Evert's main offensive; the other army groups failed to take advantage of the situation. The Russian command, logistical and administrative systems had not performed well. Apart from the change of gauge at the frontier, the Russian and Galician railway systems were not appropriate to the Russians' needs, which were for north–south connections, as well as east–west lines to support the advance. The primitive roads could not take heavy traffic and there was a shortage of

motor lorries. Support divisions, ammunition and other supplies could not, therefore, keep the advance moving. Russia was greatly weakened by the Brusilov offensive. In four months she suffered nearly a million casualties, and by the end of 1916 her army's power had been further sapped by over a million desertions.

The offensive had also greatly sapped the power of the Central Powers and Austria–Hungary was a spent force. By the end of September, the Central Powers had lost well over a million men, including large numbers of prisoners. Austrian losses were about a million, including 400,000 prisoners, and the Germans had lost 350,000. German resources were, however, still sufficient to counter-attack the Russians and support the Bulgarians and Austria–Hungary against Rumania. The Habsburg Emperor Franz Joseph, who had been born in 1830, died on 21 November. He had ruled for nearly 68 years. The new Emperor, his grand-nephew Karl, was destined for a brief rule over a crumbling empire. Meanwhile, the Allied blockade was biting, and Central and Eastern Europe were in for a cold and hungry winter.

THE WESTERN FRONT

Battle of Verdun

Falkenhayn's plan for an attack on Verdun, as outlined in his 'Christmas memorandum', may have been an attempt, as has been claimed, to 'bleed the French army white' by attacking an objective the French, for historical and emotional reasons, would be forced to defend. By setting limited objectives, he hoped to draw in French reserves to be ground down by overpowering German artillery, thus destroying Britain's 'keenest sword'. His perception was that, after the failure of the 1915 battles, the French army was at the end of its tether, and that the Verdun operations would cause its morale to collapse. The French, he thought, could therefore be induced to make a separate peace, thus isolating Britain – the 'arch-enemy'. An alternative view is that Falkenhayn actually intended to capture Verdun, thus precipitating a crisis within France and causing her collapse.

Like Liège, Namur, Antwerp and other fortresses, the city and ancient citadel of Verdun was surrounded, at a distance of several miles, by a ring of masonry and concrete forts, each further protected by a thick layer of sand and earth. The vulnerability of the Belgian forts to bombardment in 1914 by the German and Austrian super-heavy howitzers had led the French to declare their Verdun and other fortresses obsolete, and to strip them of their guns to strengthen the artillery of the field armies for the September 1915 offensives. Only a few turret guns were left in position. But here a great error had been made. The Verdun forts had only recently been modernized and strengthened, and had a great deal more resisting power to heavy plunging fire than the Belgian forts. What the Verdun forts offered (and this was quickly grasped following the loss of Fort Douaumont on 25 February) were massive, protected blockhouses capable of harbouring large numbers of troops, command and first-aid posts, vital artillery observation posts, ammunition and supplies, so acting as key anchor positions for the defence. The whole Verdun fortress

RIGHT: Produced in November 1924 for post-war tourists to Verdun, this plan shows clearly barracks and cemeteries, the old Vauban fortifications, and also the important standard and metre gauge (*Meusien*) railway installations. Scale of original: 1:7,000.

OVERLEAF: The French defences of the Fortified Region of Verdun, as they stood on 21 February 1916 at the start of the battle. Many of the trench systems shown were poorly constructed and discontinuous, relying on the barbed wire in front, the 75-mm field guns behind, and the (disarmed) forts in rear. German maps dated January 1916 show all these defences in detail.

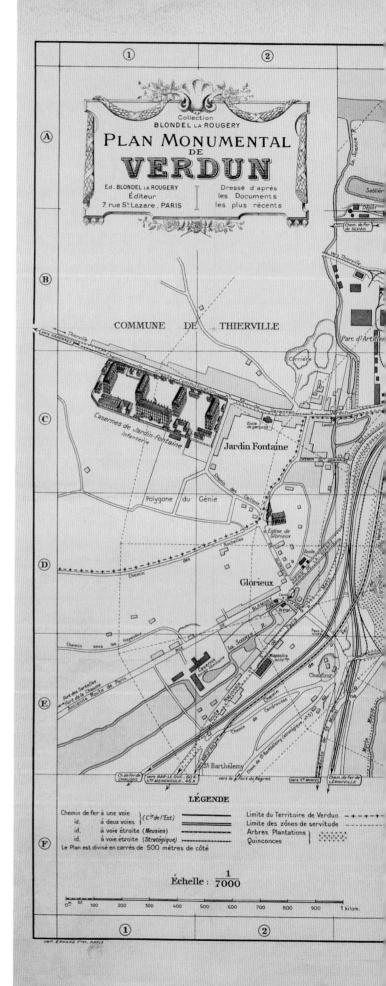

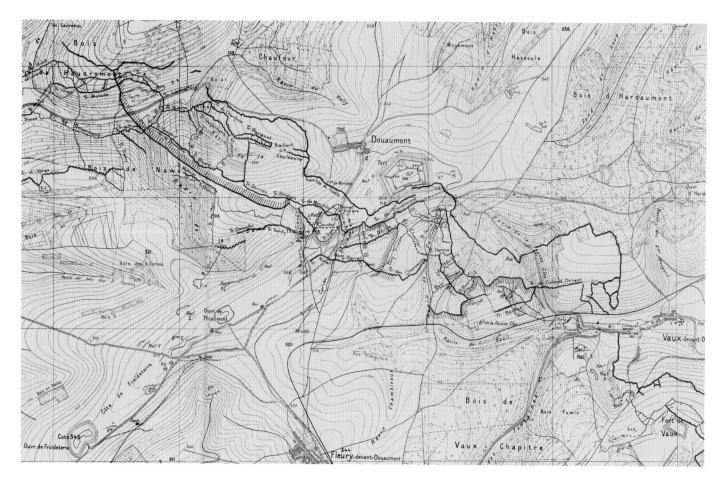

region had acted as such an anchor during the Battle of the Marne in 1914, and during the 1916 Verdun battle the forts took on such a role on a local level.

Not only had the Verdun forts been disarmed, but the defence, under General Herr, of the whole exposed Verdun salient had been neglected. This was hardly Herr's fault, as he had for months been demanding men and resources. Its defending infantry divisions were low-grade and thinly spread, as were the physical defences. Apart from the forts, other concrete works and disarmed flanking battery positions, the outlying trench system was extremely rudimentary, consisting of short, disconnected sections of trench and isolated redoubts, strong-points and command posts. There were few communication trenches, and little supporting artillery. Concern for the vulnerability of the sector grew in late 1915 and early 1916, and its weaknesses were pointed out to the government, even by Driant, a regimental commander (who was also a member of parliament), whose chasseurs held the key forward position of the Bois des Caures. Politicians and staff officers, notably Joffre's deputy, Castelnau, visited the Verdun region to investigate. Some measures were taken to strengthen the defences, including the beginning of an intermediate trench position on the right (east) bank of the Meuse. This was, of course, noted by the German reconnaissance aircraft which photographed all the defences to bring the *Stellungskarte* up to date.

On the right bank the terrain was dominated by the Meuse heights, which to the east and south of Verdun presented a steep, scarp slope to the Germans in the Woeuvre plain. The French defences in the north were on more rolling down-like terrain, in an area which included several forests and woods, and it was in this densely forested area that the Germans were able to hide their concentration artillery, and from here that they made the main

ABOVE: French trench map (*plan directeur*), Verdun, Fort Douaumont area, 1:10,000 scale, showing French (red) and German (blue) trenches on 1 April 1916, with red-hatched trenches on 2 April and blue-hatched on 17 April.

RIGHT: Although new standard and narrow gauge railway links were built during the battle of Verdun, motor transport columns on the *Voie Sacrée* between Bar-le-Duc and Verdun were the mainstay of supply for the French Second Army.

assault. Facing them were the important forts of Vaux and Douaumont crowning the heights a few miles behind the front line, in a more open zone. Douaumont, the most important fort of the whole Verdun fortress, stood on a dominating ridge which extended westward past Froideterre to the Meuse. Closer to the front line and parallel to it was the significant Côte de Poivre ridge, while closer to the city of Verdun was a ridge marked by the forts of Tavannes, Souville and Belleville; the steep reverse slope behind this ridge was to provide protection for the mass of French batteries during the battle. The ground on the left (western) bank was more open and rolling, but was marked by two features of great importance: close to the front line was a range of high ground which included the Côte de l'Oie, Le Mort Homme and Côte 304, and a few miles behind this was the Bois Bourrus ridge studded with forts; like the Belleville ridge, this provided protected battery positions for the French during the battle. The river Meuse, and its parallel canal, ran from south to north through Verdun, and through the centre of the battlefield. It was impassable except where bridged.

The German attack was made by Crown Prince Wilhelm's Fifth Army, under the control of its Chief-of-Staff Schmidt von Knobelsdorf. Benefiting from their experience on the Eastern Front, the German artillery preparation, at nine hours, was much shorter than the long bombardments that were becoming usual for the Allies. The influence of Bruchmüller may perhaps be perceived at Verdun. The brief, but extremely intense bombardment was calculated to optimize destruction and neutralization effects. The massive artillery concentration of 1,200 guns, howitzers and

mortars included 512 heavies and 30 super-heavy howitzers. Two-and-a-half-million shells were fired on an eight-mile front, a density of 150 guns per mile. While the bombardment extended to the left bank, the infantry assault was initially confined to the right.

The assault had originally been planned for 10 February but was delayed by winter weather until 21 February. Meanwhile, the assault infantry had been sheltering in deep dugouts, or *Stollen*, specially prepared during the winter. The bombardment opened at 7 a.m., French infantry positions, command posts and batteries being systematically pounded in turn; the German guns and their targets had been well-surveyed. French airmen, trying to locate the German artillery, reported that the Spincourt forest was spouting a mass of flame from the concentration of German batteries firing. At 4 p.m., far too late in the day at this time of the year for rapid exploitation, the infantry assault began, as ordered by Falkenhayn, with probing fighting patrols on two of the three attacking corps fronts to test the French resistance. These felt their way forward, infiltrating between the wrecked French posts in the smashed woods, avoiding centres of resistance which were earmarked for further bombardment; only when all resistance was dealt with would their infantry advance in mass. The 18th Corps was held up by Driant's chasseurs in the Bois des Caures. The assault of Von Zwehl's 7th Reserve Corps, however, directly followed up the patrols, and made rapid progress through the Bois d'Haumont. This success, and patrol reports from the other corps urging an immediate advance, rather startled Knobelsdorf, who quickly ordered the attack to be pressed. Slow communications and the end of daylight, however, postponed progress to the following day. The bombardment, for all its intensity, had not silenced all the defenders, and Falkenhayn's cautious tactics, reminiscent of those used by the Germans in the Second Battle of Ypres, had given the French vital time to regroup.

A more vigorous assault might have rapidly broken through the defences, and reached Verdun the following day. Immediate French reserves were few and over the next four days could not prevent a German advance of five miles and the capture of the key position of Fort Douaumont. However, by advancing on the right bank only, the Germans exposed their right flank to increasingly heavy fire from the French artillery on the left bank, notably from batteries in protected positions behind the Bois Bourrus ridge which were consequently difficult to engage with counter-battery fire. These batteries were part of the concentration ordered by Pétain, who now, in the crisis period during which Douaumont was lost, took over command from Herr. Now it was Pétain's Second Army, brought up from reserve, which was to bear the brunt of the defence of Verdun.

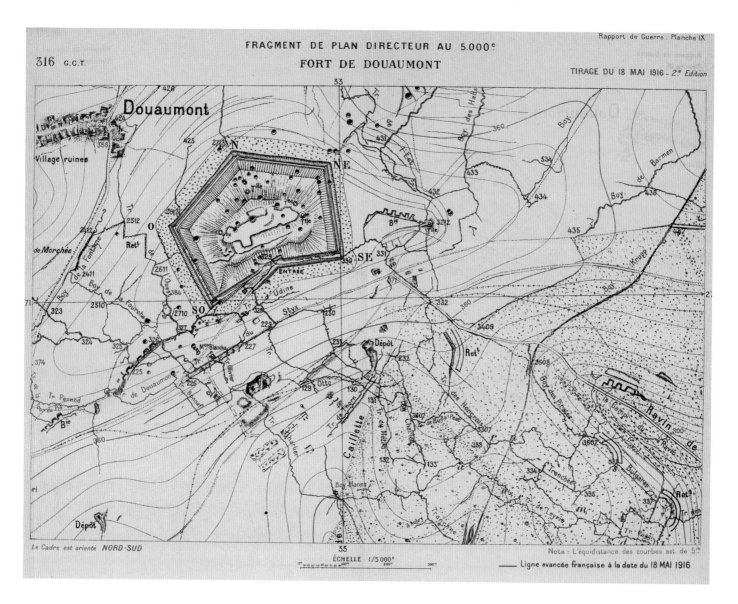

Le Cadre est orienté NORD-SUD

ÉCHELLE 1/5.000ᵉ

Nota : L'équidistance des courbes est de 5ᵐ

——— Ligne avancée française à la date du 18 MAI 1916

On 25 February, Castelnau arrived on the spot, made a rapid assessment of the situation and decided that the important ground and forts on the right bank could be held, though the exposed French position in the Woeuvre plain would have to be evacuated. Pétain, though suffering from pneumonia, got an immediate grip on the situation, allocated sectors to his corps commanders, took control of the artillery and enforced measures instigated by Herr to ensure reliance on Verdun's fifty-mile road link from Bar-le-Duc in the rear, later called the *Voie Sacrée*.

At the same time, new standard- and narrow-gauge railway construction was begun, in particular a new standard-gauge line, branching from the Révigny–St Ménehould railway, which would link up with the routes severed by the Germans on either side of the Verdun salient. Intensive use was also made of the Meusienne

metre-gauge line from Bar-le-Duc to Verdun, and this was also extended. On the *Voie Sacrée*, a continuous lorry convoy system, using 12,000 vehicles, was inaugurated, and a territorial division ceaselessly shovelled stone under the wheels of the trucks to maintain the surface. At one stage it was touch-and-go whether the road would hold. Had it disintegrated, the right bank would have been abandoned.

ABOVE: French trench map (*plan directeur*) of Fort Douaumont. German trenches in blue. *Ligne avancée française à la date du 18 mai 1916* in red. Note the huge shell holes plotted on and around the fort. French counter-attacks all failed at this time, the fort not being recaptured until the autumn.

RIGHT: Fort Douaumont in German hands, 9 April 1916; vertical air photo.

Having captured Fort Douaumont, the Germans now extended the attacks to capture more of the ridge which the fort dominated, southwest to the Ouvrage de Thiaumont, and east to Fort Vaux. Southwest again of Thiaumont was the Ouvrage de Froideterre, and between these two small forts another connecting ridge ran south from the main ridge towards the village of Fleury and a lateral ridge on which stood Fort Souville. The latter was flanked, on the same high ground, by Forts Belleville, St Michel and Tavannes, and beyond these was the city of Verdun, only four miles from Douaumont. However, German advances on the right bank, where these ridges and forts blocked the way, were being cut up by French artillery fire, not just from behind the protected Belleville ridge, but from the left bank, dominated by the heights of Le Mort Homme and Côte 304, and not least the Bois Bourrus ridge to their south, on which stood yet more forts.

Between 11 March and 9 April, therefore, the Germans switched the weight of their attack to the left bank. Attack and counter-attack led to the German assault waves creeping ever closer to these summits, though at horrifying cost. A massive German assault, presaged by a two-day bombardment, began on 5 May, and Côte 304 was taken a few days later. The German infantry on the captured position, recoiling from the smell of rotting corpses, demanded more tobacco to counter the stink. After further weeks of successive pulverizing bombardments and infantry attacks and counter-attacks, in which corpses were continually dismembered and ploughed once more into the ground, Le Mort Homme was continually attacked, a particularly strong effort being made on 22 May. It was captured by the end of May, as were the powdered remains of its neighbouring village of Cumières. It must be emphasized that these conditions applied equally well to many localities on the right bank, where the shelling was so intense, and the density of men on the ground so high, that the landscape consisted of a gruesome mixture of chalky soil, shattered trees, bodies and mud.

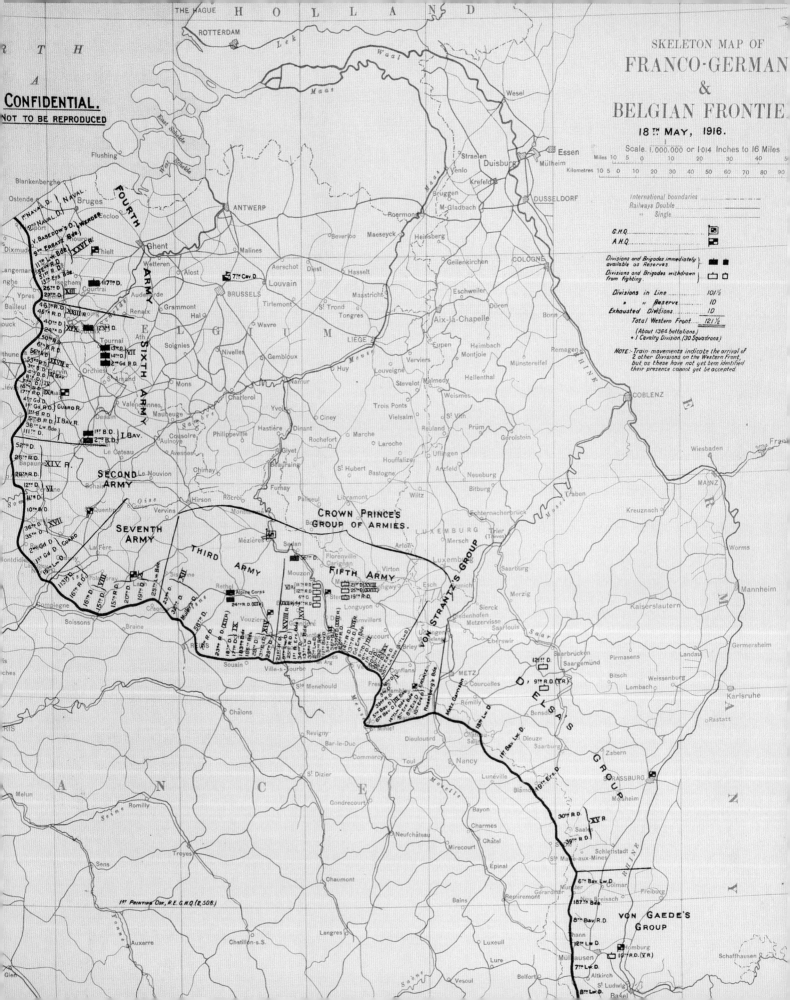

ABOVE: The Battle of Verdun, 1916. A German soldier aims his rifle, with a dead French soldier on his left. Most casualties during the war on the Western Front were from shellfire, rather than small-arms.

LEFT: *German Order of Battle, Western Front, 18 May 1916*. British map showing the situation at the height of the Verdun battle, when critical fighting was taking place on both banks of the Meuse. Scale of original: 1:1 million.

On 1 May, Pétain had been promoted from the Second Army to command the Group of Armies of the Centre, and replaced with General Nivelle. With his right-hand-man, Mangin, Nivelle represented a more aggressive spirit, that of relentless counter-attack. On 22 May, Mangin launched an attack on Douaumont, but failed. By the end of May the Germans had 2,200 guns at Verdun against the French 1,777. The imminence of the Somme offensive meant that Joffre was husbanding his artillery, but at great cost to his infantry. That said, the poor '*poilus*',

'*biffins*' or '*bonhommes*' were not always thankful for artillery support, as only too often French shells fell among their own front-line troops.

Having gained Le Mort Homme and Côte 304 at a gruesome cost, the Germans once more switched the main thrust of their offensive to the right bank. They attacked on 1 June with five divisions on a three-mile front, against Fort Vaux and eventually captured it on 7 May, the garrison having run out of water. The following day the Germans captured Thiaumont, but were ejected. It changed hands fifteen times during the summer. A great German attack on 23 June, in which they fired large numbers of shells filled with phosgene gas, surged south towards Souville and captured Fleury, which changed hands sixteen times during the summer, but was finally recaptured by the French on 8 August. This attack brought the Germans alarmingly close to Verdun, and, as a precaution, Nivelle began moving some of the French artillery (a third of which was on the right bank) to the left bank.

On 3 July the Germans captured the Damloup High Battery, which was blocking their advance from the east on Fort Souville. In a last German effort on 11 July, they also used phosgene, but by now the French were equipped with more effective gas-masks. Although a few German infantrymen reached the glacis of the fort, from where they could see the battered spires of Verdun, they failed to capture the fort or advance beyond. With the Somme battle increasing in intensity, the tide at Verdun had already turned, and a series of French counter-attacks soon pushed them back. Douaumont was recaptured on 24 October, and Vaux on 2 November.

Most of the French army was dragged through the mill on the Meuse by Pétain's 'noria' system of rapid divisional reliefs, and as a result the supreme experience of Verdun epitomized the bloody butchery, and also the heroism, of the war. It generated a crisis of army morale which was to erupt the following year. In the inter-war period it became a place of pilgrimage, as did Ypres, and to a lesser degree the Somme, for the British. French casualties at Verdun during 1916 were 61,289 killed, 216,337 wounded and 101,151 missing, giving a total of 378,377. German casualties were about 330,000.

RIGHT: A huge British mine exploding under the German front line at the Hawthorn Ridge Redoubt, west of Beaumont Hamel, Somme, at 7.20 a.m., 1 July 1916. This explosion, 10 minutes before zero, alerted the German garrison to the impending attack by the British 29th Division. This error was compounded by the early lifting of the heavy artillery bombardment in this sector.

BELOW: A detail from *So Steht der Krieg an der Ost-u. Orient-Front. Feldpostbrief*, showing the Verdun front.

The Battle of the Somme

It was originally intended that France would provide the largest contribution to the Somme offensive, but the Verdun operation had forced her to divert huge resources of manpower, guns and ammunition to the Meuse. Joffre had first suggested that a British offensive should be made before the main attack on the Somme, or with the French but in a subsidiary role. While it meant postponing his preferred Flanders offensive, Haig ensured that the British fought on the Somme alongside the French. The Verdun battle forced the French to accept that the British would bear the main brunt of the offensive.

While the plan was simple, it lacked any specific strategic objectives. It envisaged a long and overwhelming artillery bombardment on a wide front, followed by an infantry assault and exploitation to break through the German first and second positions, which had a combined depth of about two-and-a-half miles, and then an onrush of cavalry through the gap to recreate a war of movement. Previous Allied offensives on narrow frontages had suffered seriously from flanking fire, so the Somme plan specified a broad attack frontage to obviate this. This unfortunately spread the artillery fire too thinly, and the weapons and, particularly, the ammunition available, were insufficient in quantity and of poor quality. The eight-inch howitzers were improvised, the eighteen-pounder field guns frequently suffered from weak or broken buffer springs, and shells burst prematurely or not at all, either because their fuses were faulty or because they unscrewed in flight. There was insufficient high-explosive shell to destroy the

OVERLEAF, TOP LEFT: German 1:10,000 trench map of the British and German defences, giving a very detailed picture of the German defence scheme in the key Thiepval sector, where the positions were very strong. British trenches in red, German trenches and names in black, with coloured shading. The Reference (*Erläuterung*) in the bottom right corner gives much information about the defences, including machine gun positions. Correction dates are not given, but early–mid 1916.

BOTTOM LEFT: A German 1:10,000 trench map of La Boisselle, 2 July 1916. British trenches and batteries in red; German trenches and names in blue. Despite the date, no sign of any British break-in is indicated at, for example, the *Leipzig Salient* (*Granat-Loch*), on the spur south of Thiepval.

RIGHT: *Western Front* 2, scale 1:100,000, overprinted in red with German dispositions on 1 July 1916, the first day of the Somme battle. An important note states: *The regiments underlined have been identified by contact since 20 June.* This refers to the trench raids carried out by the British to identify the German units and formations opposite, to enable GHQ Intelligence to compile an accurate enemy-order-of-battle. It is noticeable how, compared with later stages of the battle, the German formations are thin on the ground.

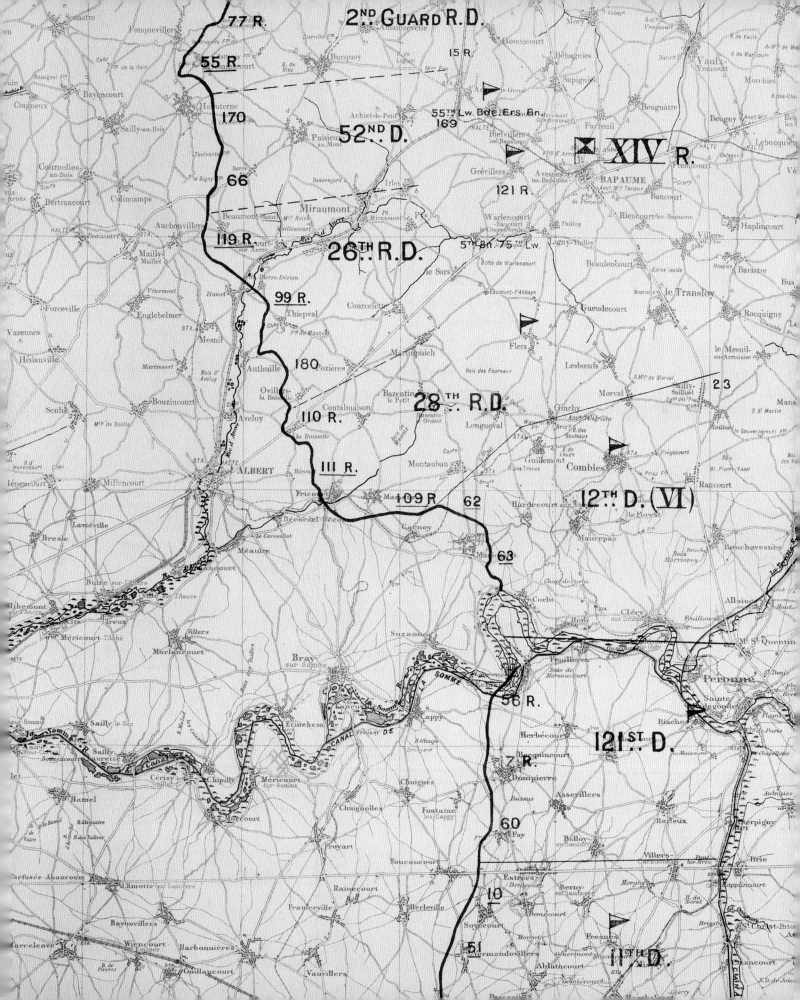

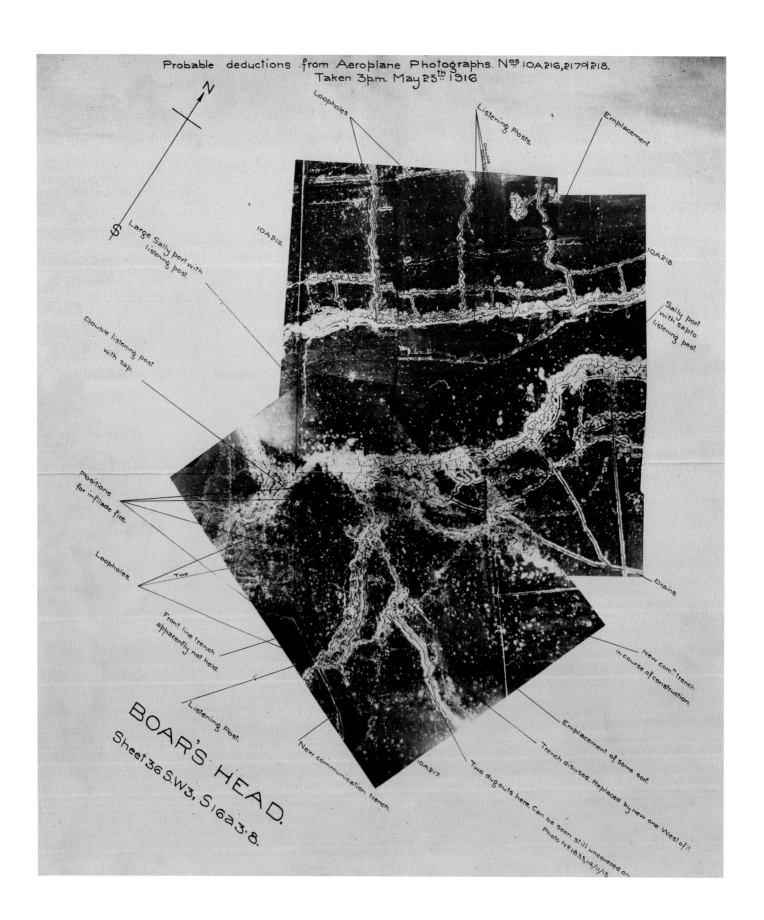

Probable deductions from Aeroplane Photographs. Nos 10AP16, P17 & P18.
Taken 3pm. May 25th 1916

N

S

Loopholes

Listening Posts.

Emplacement.

Double Bank

10AP16.

10AP18.

Large Sally port with listening post.

Double listening post with sap.

Sally port with sap to listening post.

Positions for inflade fire.

Loopholes.

Two

Drains.

Front line trench apparently not held.

New com.n trench in course of construction.

Listening Post.

New communication trench.

Emplacement of some sort.

Trench disused. Replaced by new one West of it.

Two dugouts here. Can be seen still uncovered on

Photo No 1833, 14/11/15

10AP17.

BOAR'S HEAD.
Sheet 36 S.W3, S16a 3.8.

ABOVE: A British sentry and sleeping soldiers in a captured German trench at Ovillers, Somme, July 1916.

LEFT: *Boar's Head, 25 May 1916, Probable Deductions from Aeroplane Photographs*. Vertical air photo mosaic with interpretation. The Boar's Head was a sharp salient in the German front line opposite Richebourg. A feint attack was made here by 11th Royal Sussex on 30 June 1916, the eve of the Somme battle. Edmund Blunden described the shambles in his classic memoir *Undertones of War*.

RIGHT: Elevation of Hawthorn Ridge Redoubt and La Boisselle Craters, 1916. This diagram shows cross-sections of the two largest mine craters blown by the British under German strong-points at the outset of the Battle of the Somme on 1 July 1916.

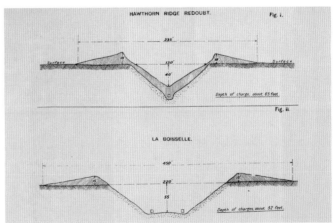

German trenches, deep dug-out entrances and battery positions, and in any case the ground was littered with duds. Most of the field-gun shell was shrapnel, whose balls were useless against earthworks and fortifications and not very effective, despite encouraging trials, against barbed wire. The New Army gunners had not had the long practice needed to set the shrapnel time-fuses accurately, and in any case the fuses were unreliable due to hasty and unregulated manufacture. Neither were the gunners sufficiently experienced to fire a creeping barrage with the precision necessary to give the infantry confidence.

From 26 June to 1 July, during the last week of the preliminary bombardment, the Allied artillery fired two-and-a-half million shells onto the German positions. The British artillery concentration comprised 1,000 field guns, 180 heavy guns and 245 heavy howitzers. These last were the most important for destruction of enemy positions, but it was their ammunition which was most likely to be unreliable. The density of guns on the attack frontage was a field gun for every twenty yards, and a heavy gun or howitzer every sixty yards. Three million shells were fired during the

preparation, but considering the multiplicity of German trenches, wire entanglements and other works (each German position had at least three trench lines, and there were two main positions, plus communication trenches, switch lines, redoubts, and mortar and battery positions) the bombardment was in fact rather thin. British commanders and staff were overoptimistic, and British Intelligence ignored reports from front-line units that much of the German wire and deep dugouts were largely intact.

With insufficient and imperfect guns and inadequate ammunition, and with inexperienced infantry frequently using unimaginative tactics, on too wide a front and with a complete lack of surprise against a well-entrenched and thoroughly prepared enemy, the attack in broad daylight by Rawlinson's Fourth Army was bound to be a massacre. And so it proved. The disaster, particularly on the British centre and left, was made more certain by the deliberate premature explosion of the mines at La Boisselle (Y Sap and Lochnagar) and Beaumont Hamel (Hawthorn Ridge Redoubt), the latter ten minutes before zero, and the similarly deliberate premature lifting of the heavy artillery bombardment on

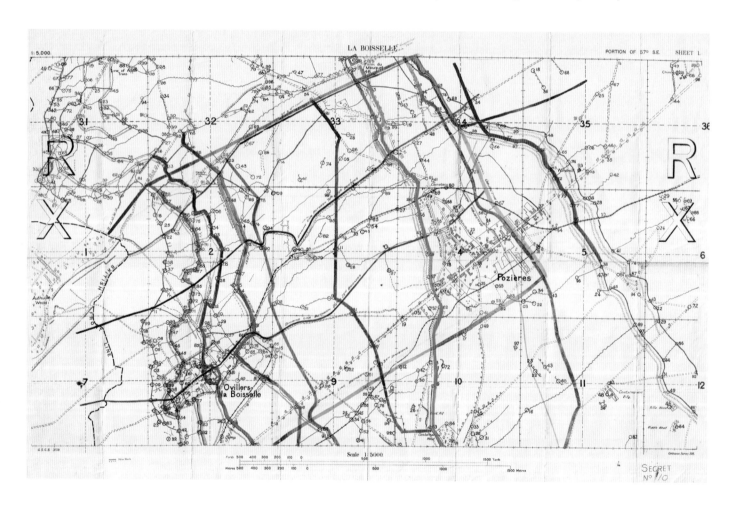

the 8th Corps front (also ten minutes early), which alerted the Germans to the impending attack. The field artillery bombardment here also lifted two minutes early.

The principle of fire-and-movement was poorly applied, if at all; in some sectors a rudimentary creeping barrage and overhead machine gun fire had been arranged, but in others the barrage just lifted to the next trench line and the infantry advanced across no

ABOVE: French troops advancing under the protection of smoke at Vermandovillers, Somme, 10 October 1916.

LEFT: British special 3rd Corps 1:5,000 trench map, *La Boisselle*, Sheet 1, showing (in manuscript) objectives, and corps, division and brigade boundaries for 8th Division's attack on 1 July 1916, the first day of the battle of the Somme, and also recent German work in green. Towards the top of the map, the hand-written note should read 'Dividing Line Between 3rd Corps and 10th Corps' (not 13th Corps).

man's land with little or no covering fire. Infantry tactics varied between formations, but in many sectors the battalions crossed a wide no man's land in linear waves, and were mown down by machine guns, rifles and the German field artillery firing on their SOS lines. Many soldiers were caught on the barbed wire where it had been badly cut.

German defence doctrine was simple; keeping only sentries in the trenches during the bombardment, the garrison sheltered in deep dugouts until the alarm was raised, when they would rush up the steps and out into the battered trenches and nearby shell-holes, mount their machine guns, snap in the ammunition belts and traverse their guns along the advancing lines of infantry. Only too often this defence was successful. The Allies advanced furthest, and with fewer casualties, south of and astride the river Somme (the French sector) and on the southern part of the British front around Montauban, Mametz and Fricourt.

This was because the Germans were not expecting a serious assault south of or near the river, and because the French in particular, benefiting from their experiences at Verdun, had adopted more flexible, infiltration-like tactics. Total British casualties on the first day were 57,000, of whom 20,000 were killed. The British attack on their centre and left, including a diversionary attack by the Third Army at Gommecourt, was a total failure.

Just as Bruchmüller revolutionized German artillery tactics, so Colonel von Lossberg did the same for the defence. Brought in by Falkenhayn to replace the Chief-of-Staff of the Second Army astride the Somme, which had experienced a limited Allied breakthrough and lost ground on 1 July, Lossberg quickly appreciated that the stubborn German linear defence tactics were too rigid, and replaced them with a defence-in-depth based on organized shell-holes which presented a much more difficult target to the Allied artillery. The attack would be met by machine guns in the thinly held forward zone, but the weight of the defence lay in the counter-attack formations held back out of field-gun range, ready to intervene at the critical moment.

Haig now gave Gough's Reserve Army (soon to be renamed Fifth Army) the northern sector of the attack frontage, allowing Rawlinson's Fourth Army to concentrate against the high ground of the German second line on the Bazentine ridge which could be attacked from the ground already taken in the south. Here imagination led to results. A surprise night attack, supported by well-surveyed artillery firing a creeping barrage, succeeded in placing the Fourth Army on the high ground and gaining the admiration of the French. Brigadier-General Tudor used a creeping barrage fired by surveyed-in batteries for 9th Division's attack. Wire cutting and strong-point destruction occupied several days before the assault, but Tudor was determined to achieve tactical surprise so that the Germans would not put down their protective

ABOVE: Battle of Albert (Somme), 1 July 1916: British troops making a bombing (grenade) attack on German trenches near Fricourt. A soldier is silhouetted against the chalk, and smoke from the grenades can be seen. The ground is seamed with a maze of trenches.

RIGHT: A Vickers medium-machine gun crew of the Machine Gun Corps (MGC), wearing PH gas helmets as a protection against phosgene gas, in action at Ovillers, Somme, in July 1916. Machine guns increasingly adopted artillery-type indirect-fire barrage tactics during the war.

barrage on the infantry forming up for the dawn attack in no man's land. He wanted a brief intense bombardment by the Corps' medium and heavy artillery which would cover the infantry advance, with the field artillery creeping barrage opening on the German front line at the moment this ceased.

A further innovation was that the creeping barrage was fired by eighteen-pounders and 4.5-inch and medium howitzers with high explosive shell and delay fuses to avoid short bursts. Thus the infantry would be covered by fire during their approach up to and through the German front line, and would have confidence in the barrage. Powell, the artillery commander of 3rd Division, supported Tudor in his contention that the 13th and 15th Corps artillery should only fire an intense bombardment for five minutes, instead of the usual thirty, in order to achieve surprise. The Third Division,

which was only in a supporting role, did not fire a creeping barrage advancing at a constant rate, but contented itself with a series of lifts. A barrage map was provided, 8th Brigade of 3rd Division noting in its operation order that barrage maps had been issued to infantry battalions, that exact times should be passed to all concerned and that the infantry should keep strictly to the timetable. While the set-piece stage of the operation was successful, its exploitation failed. An attempt to put the cavalry through the gap to capture the commanding point of High Wood failed due to poor communications and lack of initiative.

Operations in the second half of July turned into a bloody slogging match as attempts were made to gain more of the high ground and the German second position, the Australians suffering massive casualties in their slow progress through Pozières village

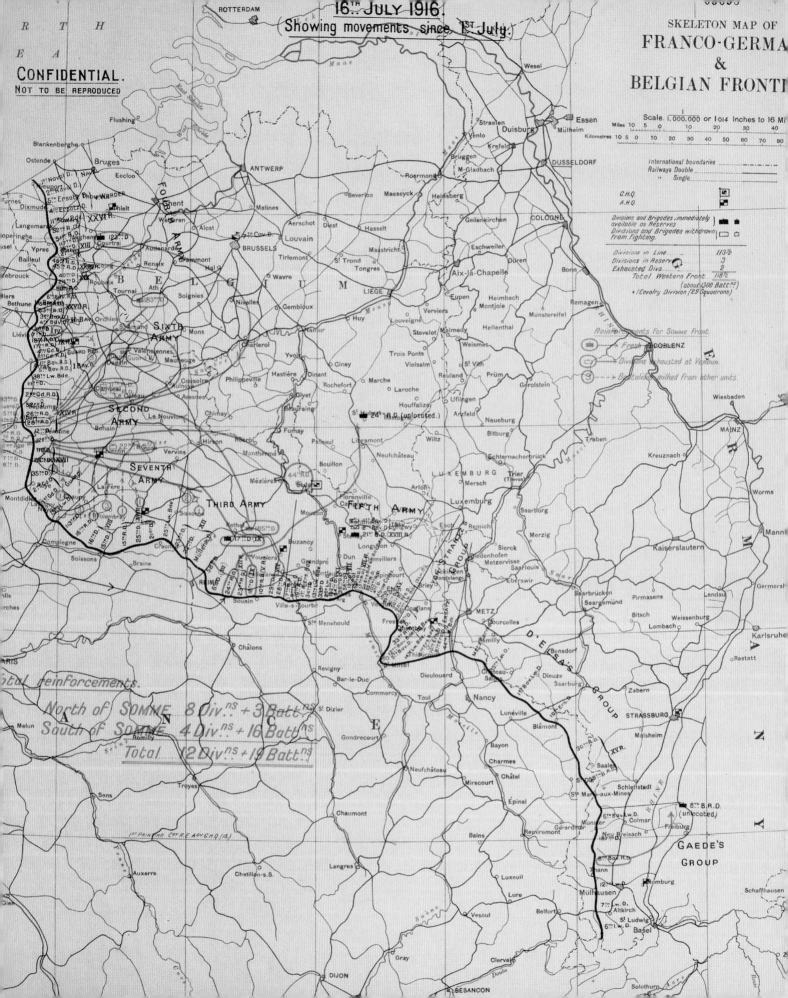

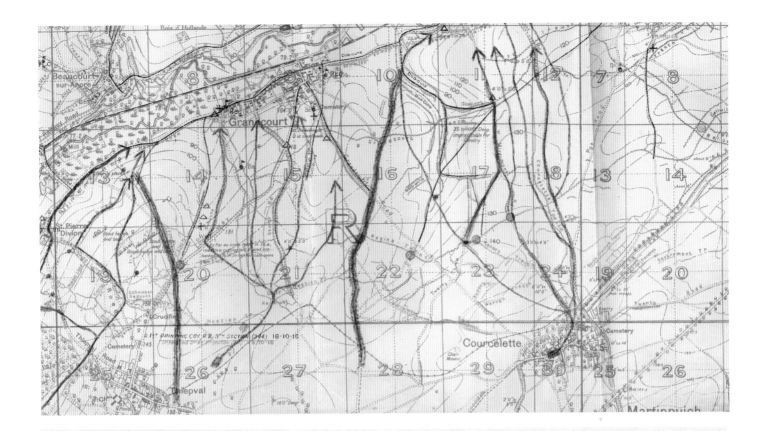

ABOVE: Manuscript annotations showing planned routes of tanks prepared for the Battle of the Ancre Heights on 21 October 1916, in which Regina and Stuff Trenches, east of Thiepval, were captured.

BELOW: Four British Mark I tanks before the Battle of Flers-Courcelette. Armed with 6-pounder guns and machine guns (male) or just machine guns (female), these machines were very slow and cumbersome to manoeuvre. Hydraulic wheeled steering gear at the tail was soon abandoned.

LEFT: *German Order of Battle, Western Front, 16 July 1916* during an early stage of the Somme battle, after the successful Allied attack of 14 July, which placed the British Fourth Army on the Bazentin ridge.

and onto the ridge beyond. August was similarly characterized by uncoordinated attacks by various corps, which allowed the Germans to concentrate all their artillery against narrow fronts, to crush these attacks. Little was achieved, though villages and woods were turned into household names as they were erased from the map – Longueval, Guillemont and Ginchy, Flers and Courcelette, Morval and Lesboeufs, Thiepval and Beaumont Hamel, Leuze (Lousy) Wood, Delville (Devil's) Wood (where the South Africans made a name for themselves), High Wood. Meanwhile the French role was that of left flank guard, and they progressed slowly and painfully towards Péronne, on the river Somme, and Combles north of the river, over an equally devastated landscape.

During the battle the British artillery was getting stronger, ammunition supplies were increasing, and fuses were slowly becoming more reliable. But all this was a long process. From 2 July to 15 September, the date of the first tank attack, British guns and howitzers fired more than seven million shells, and the German army suffered terribly, not least because of the doctrine of immediate counter-attack, and began to speak of the *Materialschlacht*, or battle of guns and ammunition, while Ludendorff was to call the Somme battle 'the muddy grave of the German field army'. British enemy-order-of-battle maps showed the magnetic effect of the Allied offensive, as the Germans sent in reinforcements. In July and August, Falkenhayn directed forty-two fresh German divisions to the Somme. Attrition was working, grinding down German men and morale, but at a ghastly cost to the Allies. By the end of July, Allied casualties were over 200,000, while those of the Germans were perhaps 160,000.

The next phase was more coordinated and occasionally more imaginative. While British artillery and aerial photography were becoming even more effective, there was still a lack of effectiveness in counter-battery work, despite the spotting efforts of the Field Survey Companies' flash-spotters and of the Royal Flying Corps. The sound-ranging sections of the Field Survey Companies, with their excellent Bull apparatus, were only gradually being equipped with the new Tucker hot-wire microphone over the summer, and microphone cable was continually being cut by shellfire. The continuous noise during operations also confused the film record of the arrival of gun-waves at the microphones. It was also a matter of organization. Corps artillery commands concentrated on their own, relatively narrow, fronts and neglected opportunities to cooperate with flanking corps and use enfilade fire, while artillery intelligence was not yet fully efficient.

The plan for the attack by Fourth and Fifth Armies between Flers and Courcelette on 15 September left wide gaps in the creeping barrage, to create 'lanes' along which the tanks were to move, and as a result much German opposition remained unsubdued.

Thirty-six tanks actually crossed the British front line. The attack broke through two German positions, the average advance on the six-mile front being a mile. In this first vital test in battle, the tanks, while proving occasionally useful, and having an initial damaging effect on German morale, also demonstrated their mechanical weaknesses, their lack of speed and manoeuvrability and their proneness to ditching.

Ten days later, in the Battle of Morval on 25 September, another big attack was made, capturing Morval, Lesboeufs and Martinpuich, and Gueudecourt and Combles on the following day. The French meanwhile were attacking on the British right, and shared in the capture of Combles. The same day also saw successful Fifth Army attacks against Thiepval and the ridge on which it stood, both of which had resisted attacks on 1 July and subsequently. Zollern and Stuff Redoubts were captured, and the Schwaben Redoubt on 28 September.

The last complete German defence position, although the Germans were feverishly digging others further back, was west of Le Transloy, and Haig hoped that, if this could be ruptured, an exploitation might be possible. But in October and early November the weather turned wet, and operations bogged down in conditions that many participants thought were worse than at Passchendaele the following year. Not only this, but bad visibility made artillery work very difficult. A dry spell in mid-October made it possible for the Fifth Army to attack again on 21 October, when four British and Canadian divisions went over the top, after an excellent artillery preparation and covered by an equally good creeping barrage, to 'capture and consolidate' Regina and Stuff trenches. The German artillery, as usual, made occupation of the captured trenches as difficult as possible.

Finally, on 13 November in the Battle of the Ancre Heights, after four days of dry and frosty weather, the Fifth Army attacked after two days of artillery preparation and again under a creeping barrage. Assisted by tanks and protected by fog, the infantry went forward astride the river Ancre north of Thiepval. St Pierre Divion, Beaucourt-sur-Ancre and Beaumont Hamel were captured, the

RIGHT: *Western Front 2*, overprinted with German dispositions on 15 September 1916, the day of the first tank attack on the Somme. This sheet was printed at Haig's Advanced GHQ at the Château de Val Vion at Beauquesne, between Rawlinson's Fourth Army HQ and Gough's Reserve Army HQ. Scale of original: 1:100,000.

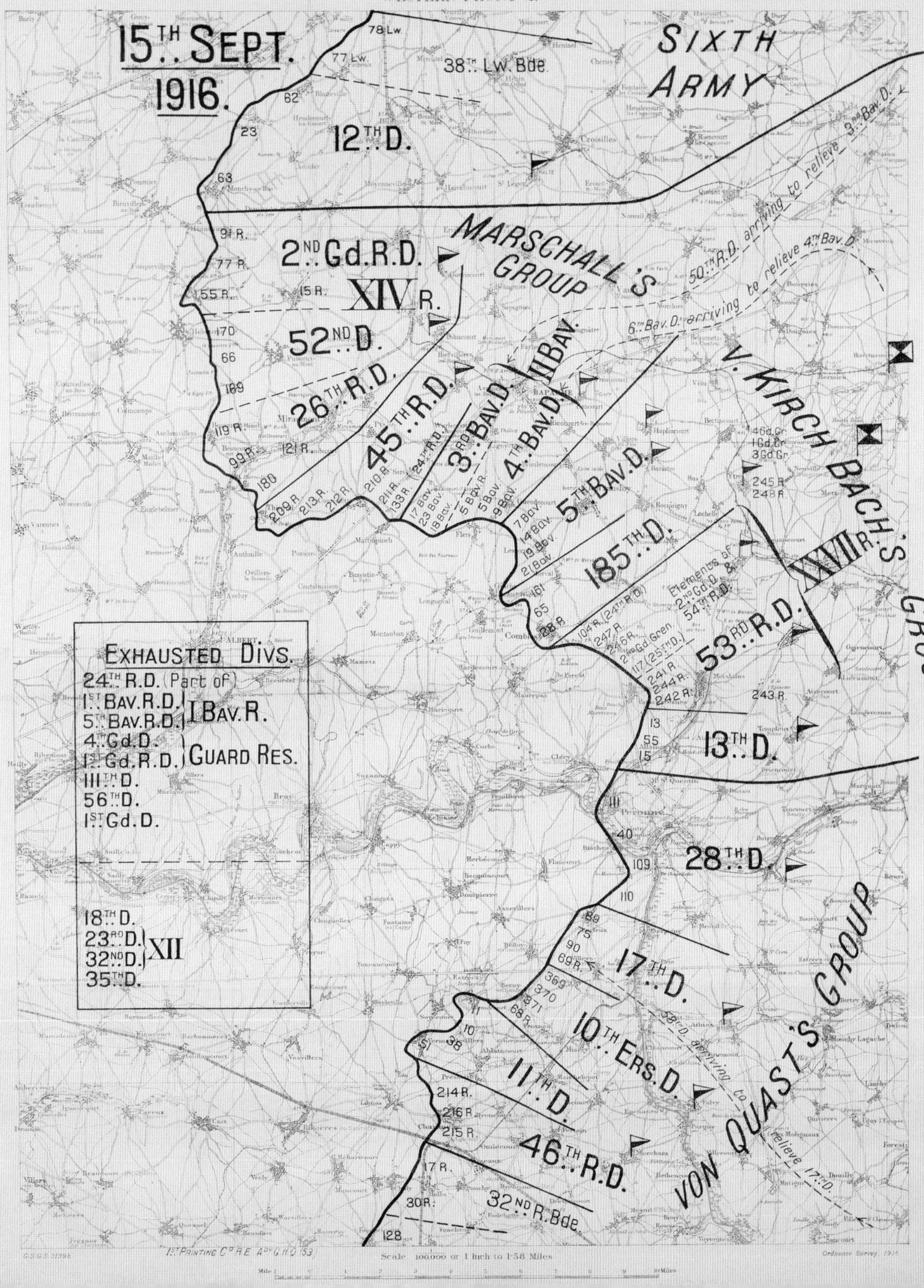

15TH SEPT. 1916.

SIXTH ARMY

FIRST ARMY

SECOND ARMY

78 Lw.

77 Lw.

38TH LW. Bde.

62

12TH D.

23

63

3RD BAV. D. arriving to relieve 3RD BAV. D.

50TH R.D. arriving to relieve 4TH BAV. D.

6TH BAV. D. arriving

91 R.

2ND Gd.R.D.

MARSCHALL'S GROUP

77 R.

XIV R.

55 R.

15 R.

52ND D.

170

66

189

26TH R.D.

119 R.

99 R.

121 R.

45TH R.D.

180

209 R.

213 R.

212 R.

210 R.

211 R.

133 R.

24TH R.

17 Bav.

23 Bav.

13 Bav.

3RD BAV. D.

5 Bav. R.

5 Bav.

99 Bav.

4TH BAV. D.

7 Bav.

14 Bav.

19 Bav.

21 Bav.

5TH BAV. D.

185TH D.

V. KIRCHBACH'S GROUP

46 Gr.

1 Gd. Gr.

3 Gd. Gr.

245 R.

248 R.

XXVII R.

161

65

68 R.

104 R. (24TH R.)

247

246 R.

2 Gd Gren.

117 (25TH D.)

241 R.

244 R.

242 R.

Elements of

1 Gd D.

54 TH R.D.

53 RD R.D.

243 R.

13

55

15

13TH D.

EXHAUSTED DIVS.
24TH R.D. (Part of)
1ST Bav.R.D.
5TH Bav.R.D. } I Bav.R.
4TH Gd.D.
1ST Gd.R.D. } GUARD RES.
III TH D.
56TH D.
1ST Gd.D.

18TH D.
23RD D.
32ND D. } XII
35TH D.

III

40

28TH D.

109

110

Be

75

90

69 R.

17TH D.

58 R.D. arriving to

VON QUAST'S GROUP

369

370

371

68 R.

11

10

51

38

10TH Ers. D.

214 R.

216 R.

215 R.

11TH D.

46TH R.D.

relieve 17TH D.

17 R.

30 R.

32ND R. Bde.

128

Scale 100000 or 1 inch to 1.58 Miles

Ordnance Survey 1916.

G.S.G.S. 31398.

1ST Printing Co. R.E. 4TH G.H.Q. 53

new line pivoting on Stuff Redoubt, and extending to a point southwest of Serre, the scene of a terrible massacre of British infantry on 1 July. Here the wet ground proved so bad that the attack was soon abandoned. On 18 November operations were continued in the Ancre valley, in the Beaucourt valley and towards Pys and Grandcourt. Atrocious weather and abominably muddy terrain prevented much progress over the next few weeks, and the hard winter of 1916–17 actually provided some relief by freezing the ground. But as Wilfred Owen documented in his poem 'Exposure', written from experience in this very sector, the icy conditions were as much the enemy as the Germans. On 6 February 1917 the Germans were found to be withdrawing on the Grandcourt–Stuff Redoubt front. This was a preliminary to a much greater withdrawal.

The Royal Flying Corps began ground-strafing to assist the attacking infantry, and contact patrols to locate their progress,

and made great advances in aerial photography, though this was primarily for artillery and intelligence purposes rather than mapping. The Field Survey Companies were crying out for wide-angle, high-altitude, vertical photographs to be taken to provide a control framework onto which the myriad of lower-altitude photographs could be fitted, but it was not until early 1917 that the RFC began to oblige. The creation of new, accurate maps

ABOVE: The remains of a German soldier at Beaumont Hamel, Somme, November 1916. Beaumont Hamel was captured in the Battle of the Ancre on 13 November 1916.

RIGHT: An inset map of the Somme from the *So Steht der Krieg an der Ost-u. Orient-Front* (War Situation on the Eastern and Near Eastern fronts), *Feldpostbrief* (Field Post Letter, printed on both sides and designed to be folded and posted).

and of more extensive survey, which had been developing since 1915, opened up the possibility of predicted fire ('map shooting'), and at Loos in 1915 battery survey and the provision of artillery boards (rigid, gridded boards, often mounted with sections of the trench map, fitted with a graduated arc and rule pivoted on the directing gun, showing the battery position and targets) facilitated and improved fire by quickly determining the precise bearing and range of targets. Preliminary bombardments, and lifting and creeping barrages to cover the advancing infantry, became more accurate and effective. Counter-battery work was greatly improved by developing artillery intelligence organizations, working in close cooperation with

the flash-spotters and sound-rangers of the Field Survey Companies, and also with the aeroplanes and observation balloons ('sausage balloons') of the Royal Flying Corps. Hostile battery maps became a regular feature of counter-battery work, and began to distinguish between occupied and unoccupied, and active and inactive, positions. Wireless-fitted machines, cooperating with corps' counter-batteries, would indicate active enemy batteries by sending 'NF' ('now firing') calls using the battery's code number. This process was aided by the introduction of 'zone call' maps, with specially designated areas.

During the battle of the Somme, the artillery staff, and the personnel of the many new batteries learned to use these techniques effectively. The Cambrai battle in 1917 involved the extensive first use of trigonometrically fixed bearing pickets (they had been used on occasions since mid-1916 if not before) which enabled bearing to be passed to the guns using a director (a simple theodolite) for parallel laying. Accuracy was enhanced by adapting sound-ranging apparatus for calibration, measuring and enabling variations from the normal to be noted, so that corrections for range could be applied to short-shooting worn guns. To achieve this, calibration ranges were established by the autumn. Calibrated guns of similar muzzle velocity were allotted to the same battery, ensuring that when the appropriate corrections, including those derived from meteorological data, were applied they would all shoot together 'to the map'. While the Somme battle saw accelerating progress by the British army in infantry tactics, cooperation with tanks and technical gunnery, these developments were made in the white heat of battle and the cost was correspondingly terrible. Allied casualties on the Somme were between 600,000 and 650,000, including 420,000 British and 195,000 French, while German casualties were perhaps 550,000.

As a result of his failure at Verdun, and of the Allied successes, such as they were, on the Somme, and also of the Rumanian entry into the war on the side of the Allies, Falkenhayn was dismissed by the Kaiser and replaced by the Hindenburg–Ludendorff duumvirate. Two years after he and Hindenburg had been called from the Western Front to retrieve the situation at Tannenberg following Prittwitz's failure of nerve, Ludendorff returned to the West, on 6 September 1916, with his chief. The battlefield conditions of Verdun and the Somme came to him as a profound shock. The ratio of men, artillery and shells to space was much higher in the West than on the Eastern Front, resulting in the 'confluent smallpox' shell-pitted landscape, riddled with rotting corpses, which was becoming the paradigm for battles on this front.

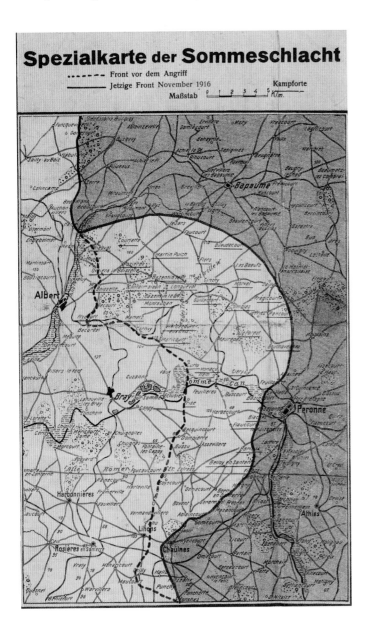

Chapter 7

The War at Sea and in the Air

As a projection of national power, a means to create empires and a form of defence, sea power is as ancient as civilization itself. But the First World War saw a new dimension being exploited: beneath the waves. Above them there was also the novel arena of air warfare.

Submarines and torpedoes had been prefigured in the American Civil War of the 1860s, and the air dimension had already been entered by reconnaissance balloons in various conflicts. However, the First World War witnessed the first development of all these, plus airships and aeroplanes, as regular weapons of war. In this sense it was the first mechanized, three-dimensional war. Aircraft were also becoming amphibious, being designed with floats or special hulls to take off from, and land on, water.

New operational applications of sea and air technology required new counter-measures. Searchlights and anti-aircraft guns were improved, balloon barrages introduced and air defence command and communication systems set up. Acoustic anti-submarine and anti-aircraft detection apparatus and wireless-direction-finding were developed, enemy codes and ciphers were broken, and the convoy system to protect merchant shipping (used with success in the Napoleonic Wars) was introduced by the Royal Navy, along with airships to spot submarines. Mines and depth charges became more efficient. Strategic bombing was introduced, first by the Germans with their Zeppelin airships and Gotha bombers, and later by the Allies. In short, much of the sea and air activity of the Second World War was prefigured in the First.

THE WAR AT SEA

The completion of the Kiel Canal, connecting the Baltic with the North Sea, has been seen by some as a signal that Germany was now ready, after many years of fleet-building, and the years of the 'naval race', to challenge British naval supremacy. The critical factor was control of the North Sea, on the far side of which lay Germany, and the waters surrounding the British Isles, including the English Channel and, especially, the Western Approaches to British ports. Blockade and counter-blockade, whether by surface vessels or submarines, mostly occurred in these zones. While a decisive fleet action between Britain and Germany might affect the

course of the war (Churchill said of Admiral Jellicoe that he was the only man on either side who could lose the war in an afternoon), the success or failure of either side's blockade would have a more certain effect. A successful British blockade would reduce Germany's war potential by cutting off raw materials, fuel and food, while a successful German blockade of Britain would halt British manufacturing and munitions production and starve her into submission. The British were more dependent on imported food and materials, and loss of these would cause the Alliance to collapse and the war to end. Loss of surface naval supremacy would render Britain's long coastline liable to invasion, while Germany's North Sea coast was short and heavily defended.

HMS *Dreadnought* was the first all-big-gun, turbine-powered warship when she was launched, in 1906. In the years following, the Royal Navy maintained its lead in battleships and armed them with heavier guns. In 1914, the British Grand Fleet had twenty-one Dreadnought-type battleships against Germany's thirteen, supported by nine of the faster and lighter battle-cruisers against four. While the British battle-cruisers were faster and more heavily armed than the German, they lacked the armour of their German equivalents and were, in other aspects of their construction and operation (notably unsafe cordite-handling in the turrets, barbettes and magazines, which made them vulnerable to flash-explosions), weaker. The Germans aimed to reduce the Grand Fleet's numbers through mines and torpedoes. When it had been sufficiently weakened, a challenge could be mounted by the *Hochseeflotte* – the High Seas Fleet.

TOP RIGHT: The crew abandoning ship as the German heavy cruiser *Blücher* turns over prior to sinking at the Battle of the Dogger Bank on 23 January 1915.

BOTTOM RIGHT: The German light cruiser *Emden*. Germany's initial campaign against Allied commerce was the 'cruiser war', and the *Emden* sank or captured thirty merchant ships in the Indian Ocean, shelled Madras in southern India and sank two warships at Penang (Malaya) before she was run aground after engaging the Australian light cruiser *Sydney* at the Battle of the Cocos on 9 November 1914.

OVERLEAF: *The Naval War in the North Sea*, Stanford map showing minefields, submarines, etc.

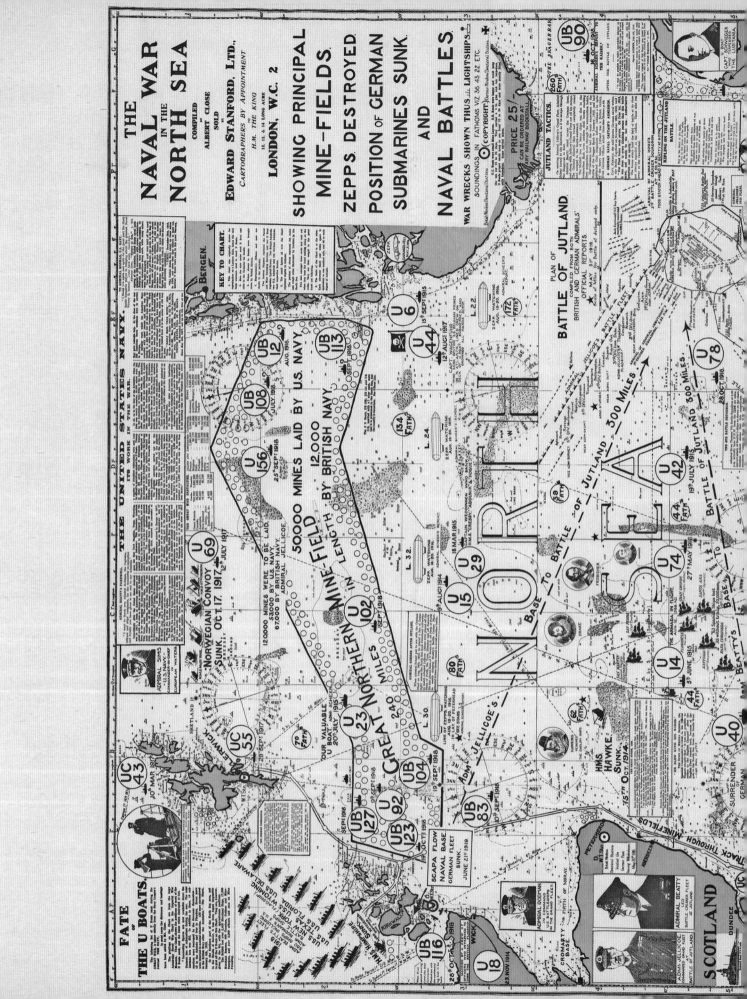

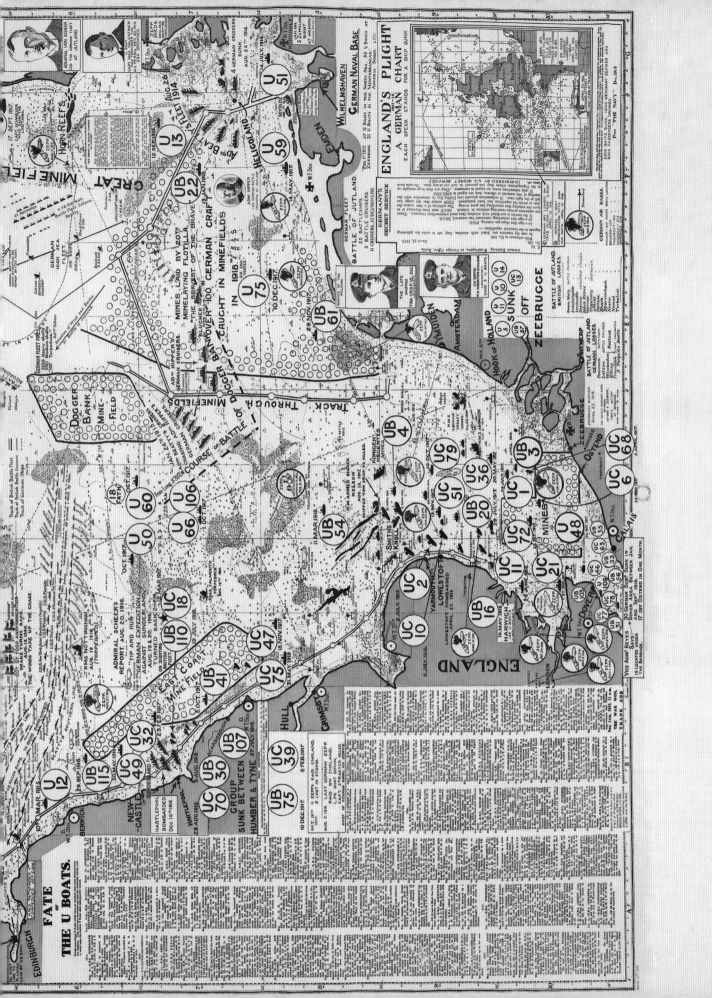

Battles of the Dogger Bank and Heligoland Bight

The German shore and naval bases were heavily defended by minefields and coastal batteries, and the island of Heligoland acted as a heavily-armed block-ship defending Cuxhaven and Wilhelmshaven. But the British had until recently neglected its North Sea defences, and lacked defended east coast deep-water ports and dockyards for heavy ships. New harbours and facilities were improvised, for Admiral Beatty's battle-cruisers at Rosyth near Edinburgh and for Admiral Jellicoe's battleships at Scapa Flow in the Orkney Islands and Invergordon on the Cromarty Firth, north of Inverness. As none of these was ready or safe from submarine attack in 1914, the Grand Fleet was pulled back out of the danger area to the west coast of Scotland where it was worse-positioned to protect the east coast. German battle-cruisers made three provocative raids during the winter of 1914–15, hoping to draw the Grand Fleet out over submarines and mines. First came a small raid on Yarmouth on 3 November, followed by one on a much larger scale on 16 December when Hartlepool, Whitby and Scarborough were bombarded and the whole *Hochseeflotte* was at sea. Bad weather prevented a British intercepting force (six battleships and four battle-cruisers) from engaging a German fleet double that number and risking the loss of the British naval margin.

The third raid, on 24 January 1915, was intended to destroy the British fishing fleet, and developed into the Battle of the Dogger Bank. This time the British Admiralty's 'Room 40' – its signals decrypting service – was ready. Room 40 had been passed a German code-book, captured in the Baltic by the Russians and they were able to inform Naval operations staff that the Germans were preparing to sail. A trap was set. Beatty's battle-cruisers surprised the Germans, sank the heavy cruiser *Blücher* and badly damaged two others. The ambiguous flag-hoists of Beatty's Flag Lieutenant, Commander Ralph Seymour (he had already caused similar confusion at the Battle of the Heligoland Bight, and was to repeat the error at Jutland) enabled German fire to be so concentrated on Beatty's flagship *Lion* that she had to be towed home. The Germans, alerted to the vulnerability of their signals, kept in port for the next year.

Meanwhile the strength of the German defences kept the British out of the Heligoland Bight. It was impossible to mount a close blockade, as was found when three old British cruisers, *Aboukir*, *Hogue* and *Cressy* (nicknamed 'the live bait squadron' for performing such exposed patrol duties) were torpedoed on 27 September 1914, by one German U-boat, within two hours of each other, with the loss of 1,459 men. However, early in the war the British had made offensive sweeps here, one of which, on 28 August 1914, developed into the successful Battle of the Heligoland Bight.

Battles of Coronel and the Falkland Islands

At the start of the war, various German warships were far from home. Admiral Spee's China Squadron, of five cruisers, was in the Pacific, two light cruisers were in the West Indies, another was off east Africa, and one more off east India. These, while not a serious threat, could still wreak havoc amongst merchant shipping and in bombarding ports. Japan's early declaration of war on Germany, on 23 August, deprived the China Squadron of its base in the Germany colony of Kiaochow on China's Shandong peninsula. Spee therefore determined to sail for Germany. The Royal Navy was prepared, sending Admiral Craddock from his base at the Falkland Islands. The squadron comprised *Canopus*, a slow, old battleship mounting four twelve-inch guns, three cruisers including two old ones, and an armed merchantman. Craddock, leaving *Canopus* in harbour, encountered Spee's squadron on 1 November, off Coronel in Chile, losing two of his ships. Stung by this, the British Admiralty sent a task-force of two battle-cruisers which arrived at the Falklands on 7 December, where *Canopus* was preparing for a German attack. Spee's squadron appeared the next day, and in a running fight the British battle-cruisers sank two German heavy cruisers and two German light cruisers. One German cruiser escaped into Chilean waters, where she was dealt with three months later. The German warships remaining at sea succumbed one by one, the last, *Emden*, being sunk by *Sydney* on 9 November in the Cocos Islands.

Goeben and *Breslau*

In the Mediterranean, in the very first days of the war, occurred the most dramatic sea chase of the war, with the most fateful results. The German battle-cruiser *Goeben* and light cruiser *Breslau* had been stationed in the Mediterranean, under Admiral Souchon, to intercept French transports carrying colonial divisions from North Africa to southern France. However, early on 4 August, Souchon was informed by Tirpitz, the German naval minister, that an alliance with Turkey had been made, and ordered him to sail immediately for Constantinople. This dash eastward was not expected by the Allies, who believed that, after bombarding French North African ports, Souchon would sail west. Souchon headed east to Messina to coal.

Two battle-cruisers of Admiral Milne's Mediterranean Fleet had passed the German ships, travelling in the opposite direction, at 9.30 on the morning of 4 August, but as Britain did not declare war on Germany until later in the day they could not engage.

Nevertheless, the British ships started to shadow the German vessels. While Milne informed the Admiralty of their position, he failed to report their direction. They were heading east. British ships shadowed them and attempted to intercept, but lost them in bad visibility off the Sicilian coast.

At Messina, which he was forced to leave by the Italians after 24 hours, still short of coal, Souchon now heard from Tirpitz that Austria refused to help Germany in the Mediterranean, and that

ABOVE: Admiral von Spee's squadron – *Scharnhorst, Gneisenau, Leipzig, Nürnberg* and *Dresden* – in line ahead off the Chilean coast, 26–29 November 1914. All but *Dresden* were sunk off the Falklands on 8 December 1914.

the Ottoman Empire had not yet declared war. Indeed she would not enter the war until 29 October, when her fleet, under Souchon, bombarded Russian Black Sea ports. Tirpitz therefore ordered him not to head for Constantinople. Rather than sail for Pola, the Austrian naval base in the Adriatic, and run the risk of being bottled up there for the duration, Souchon decided to strike out for Constantinople. He intended to take action to force the Ottomans, even if they had no such intention, to carry the war into the Black Sea against the Russians. In this he succeeded.

Sailing into the eastern Mediterranean on 6 August, the German ships encountered the light cruiser *Gloucester*, which began to shadow them. *Gloucester* was soon joined by Admiral Troubridge's East Mediterranean Squadron of four armoured cruisers and eight destroyers, which was slower, outranged and vulnerable to *Goeben*'s guns. Troubridge appreciated that his only chance was to engage *Goeben* at dawn when she would be east of his ships and therefore silhouetted against the sun while his own ships would be less visible, and launch a torpedo attack with his destroyers. But his destroyers had insufficient coal to keep up with the cruisers in a long chase. Before dawn on the seventh, Troubridge realized he could not intercept before daylight and, bearing in mind an order from Churchill to avoid engaging an undefined 'superior force', signalled Milne that he intended to break off the chase.

While Milne ordered *Gloucester* to disengage, still expecting Souchon to turn west, it was obvious to *Gloucester*'s captain that *Goeben* was racing east. By aggressive moves, *Breslau* attempted to force *Gloucester* to break off, but *Gloucester* retaliated, hoping to force *Goeben* to drop back to protect her. The action was then broken off after a shell from *Gloucester* hit *Breslau*, although without causing damage, and Milne ordered *Gloucester* to cease pursuit at Cape Matapan off southern Greece, which *Goeben* passed steering northeast towards the Dardanelles. Soon after midnight on the eighth, Milne, who had remained in the western Mediterranean, took his three battle-cruisers and a light cruiser east. At 2 p.m., he received an incorrect signal from the Admiralty stating that Britain was at war with Austria (in fact war was not declared until 12 August). Though this was soon cancelled, Milne chose to guard the Adriatic rather than continue the search for *Goeben*. On the ninth, Milne was at last ordered unequivocally by the Admiralty to chase *Goeben*. But it was too late. The careers of both Troubridge and Milne were damaged by their failure to close with the enemy.

Arriving at the entrance to the Dardanelles on 10 August, *Goeben* and *Breslau* were granted permission by the Minister of War, Enver Pasha, to pass through the Straits to Constantinople. As Britain had just impounded in UK shipyards two battleships being completed for the Turkish Navy, she was not popular with the Ottomans. The German offer of *Goeben* and *Breslau* to replace those confiscated by 'Perfidious Albion' was eagerly accepted by the Young Turks in power. The Straits were closed behind the German ships, Enver ordering that the British ships, which were now in view, should be fired on if they tried to follow. *Goeben* and *Breslau*'s welcome in Constantinople signalled the accession of Turkey to the Central Powers. British pre-war diplomatic failures in her relations with the Ottoman Empire, her influence being gradually replaced by Germany's, cannot be ignored. But the strategic consequences of the failure of the British naval pursuit were immense, Ludendorff stating that Turkey's entry prolonged the war by two years.

Following Turkey's declaration of war (bombardment of Russian Black Sea ports), British warships bombarded the forts at the entrance to the Dardanelles on 2 November, on Churchill's orders. Further bombardments were ordered on 19 and 25 February 1915, before the major attempt to force the Narrows on 18 March. In support of the landings on the Gallipoli peninsula on 25 April, British and French battleships bombarded the forts and tried, with the aid of minesweepers, to force their way through the Straits. They lost ships and gave up the attempt, following which an amphibious attempt was made to capture the peninsula.

The First German Submarine Campaign

The British Admiralty had not expected submarines to be used against merchant shipping. To do so contravened the international rules of blockade, which restricted naval action to seizure of 'war contraband' (arms, munitions and equipment, and war materials). Under these rules, a suspect ship could be boarded, and a prize crew could take it into port for investigation. Submarines, because of their limited size and small crew, could not do this. British blockade doctrine had not considered the possibility of merchant ships being sunk and their crews drowned. Britain's warships operated according to international law, and her submarines did not attack German merchant ships. The German navy, having only a limited number of ships, could not operate a counter-blockade of this kind.

On 18 February 1915 they began their first U-boat campaign, declaring British waters a war-zone within which merchant shipping could be sunk without warning. But of their twenty-four long-range U-boats, only eight could be at sea at one time. Allied and neutral ships were equally vulnerable, especially as Allied ships often flew neutral colours. Some U-boat skippers were too gentlemanly to sink at sight, preferring to surface and let the crew take to their boats before sinking the ship. However, the introduction of armed 'Q-ships' by the British put an end to this chivalrous practice. Others were more ruthless, and torpedoed at sight, a victim being the Cunard passenger liner *Lusitania*, which was also carrying cargo for Britain. She was deliberately sunk on 7 May 1915 as a terror tactic, to scare shipping from the Atlantic sea-lanes. This action, which was partly counter-productive, shocked Allied and neutral opinion, and created powerful anti-German sentiment in the USA. The fact that almost 1,200 passengers and crew were drowned, including 100 American citizens, was a turning point in US-German relations and, when a similar sinking occurred three months later, President Wilson threatened to break off diplomatic relations. This frightened the

German government into diluting her policy, and it stated that in future it would give a liner warning before sinking, enabling crew and passengers to be taken off in boats.

German sinking policy remained unchanged for cargo vessels. British counter-measures were soon devised, including the fitting of merchant ships with guns to fight off surface attacks, and a barrage of nets and mines was laid from England to France across the twenty-one-mile Strait of Dover. As this had to be sufficiently deep for surface vessels to pass, it was not very effective as U-boats could cross on the surface at night. This was later prevented by lighting the barrage at night, and providing 24-hour surface patrols. 'Q-ships' were another anti-submarine device, small merchant ships with hidden guns in collapsible deck-houses, which would appear to conform to the wishes of U-boat commanders, the crew taking to the boats, but leaving concealed gun-crews to engage the surfaced U-boat. Sinking eleven submarines in two years, these were initially successful but in the long-run counter-productive as they encouraged U-boats to torpedo immediately rather than surface to sink by gunfire. This in turn rendered useless the arming of any merchant ships, and increased losses among crews.

For years the Royal Navy, despite the successful experience of the convoy system during the Napoleonic Wars, resisted its introduction after 1914. Losses were considered small and destroyers could not be spared as escorts, being needed in the North Sea to protect the Grand Fleet. Germany's first attempt at a submarine blockade against Britain's food supplies was therefore met with a blockade of Germany's food imports. Germany was not building U-boats quickly enough – fifty-four were constructed during 1915 against nineteen lost – to starve Britain into submission, and Germany was also hamstrung by her unwillingness at this stage to face a complete breakdown in her relations with the USA. Thus during 1915 and 1916 a stalemate obtained in the blockade war at sea.

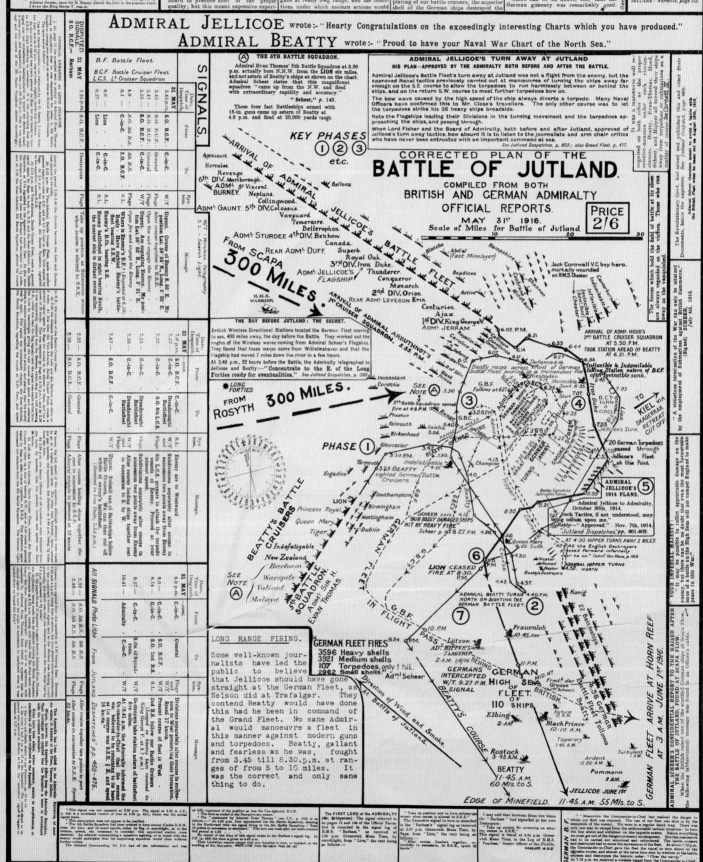

The Battle of Jutland

The inaction of the *Hochseeflotte* ended in 1916 when a new and impatient commander, Admiral Scheer, was appointed. As the U-boat campaign had been in abeyance from April, following American protests, submarines were now available to cooperate with the fleet. Scheer intended to use them to form lines outside the British fleet anchorages at Rosyth (Beatty's battle-cruisers) and Cromarty and Scapa Flow (Jellicoe's Grand Fleet), and also to sow mines in the approaches. Having set the trap, he would then sail into the North Sea hoping that part of the Grand Fleet, or Beatty's battle-cruisers, could be tempted to come out. British capital ships might then be damaged or sunk by mines or torpedoes, and

ABOVE: Battleships of the British Grand Fleet cruising in line abreast columns in the North Sea. At the battle of Jutland on 31 May 1916, Jellicoe deployed the main body of the Grand Fleet from a formation of six columns in line abreast into a single battle line just before the battleships of the German High Seas Fleet came into sight.

LEFT: *Battle of Jutland*, a Stanford map, published in 1927.

perhaps Beatty's battle-cruiser squadron, which had been strengthened with the four dreadnought battleships of the Fifth Battle Squadron, could be engaged before Jellicoe could reinforce from Scapa and Cromarty.

Scheer's first attempt was a bombardment of Lowestoft in April, but this failed to entice Beatty's ships over a sixteen-strong U-boat line. His next try, at the end of May, led to the fleet action both sides so desired, without the result that either side hoped for. Room 40, decrypting the German wireless traffic, reported to the Operations staff that the *Hochseeflotte* was sailing. On 16 May, Scheer had deployed eighteen U-boats, including three mine-laying submarines, from the Orkneys (Scapa) to Holland, to act as scouts but also to attack. The light cruiser *Hampshire*, carrying Kitchener to Russia, was sunk by one of their mines off the Orkneys on 2 June. Their sailing was known from signal intercepts, and as they were not reported on shipping routes, Room 40 deduced that they were part of a new plan by Scheer. Then, on the morning of 28 May, Room 40 decrypted Scheer's signal putting the *Hochseeflotte* in a state of special readiness. On the afternoon of 29 May a signal to a U-boat was read, asking for information

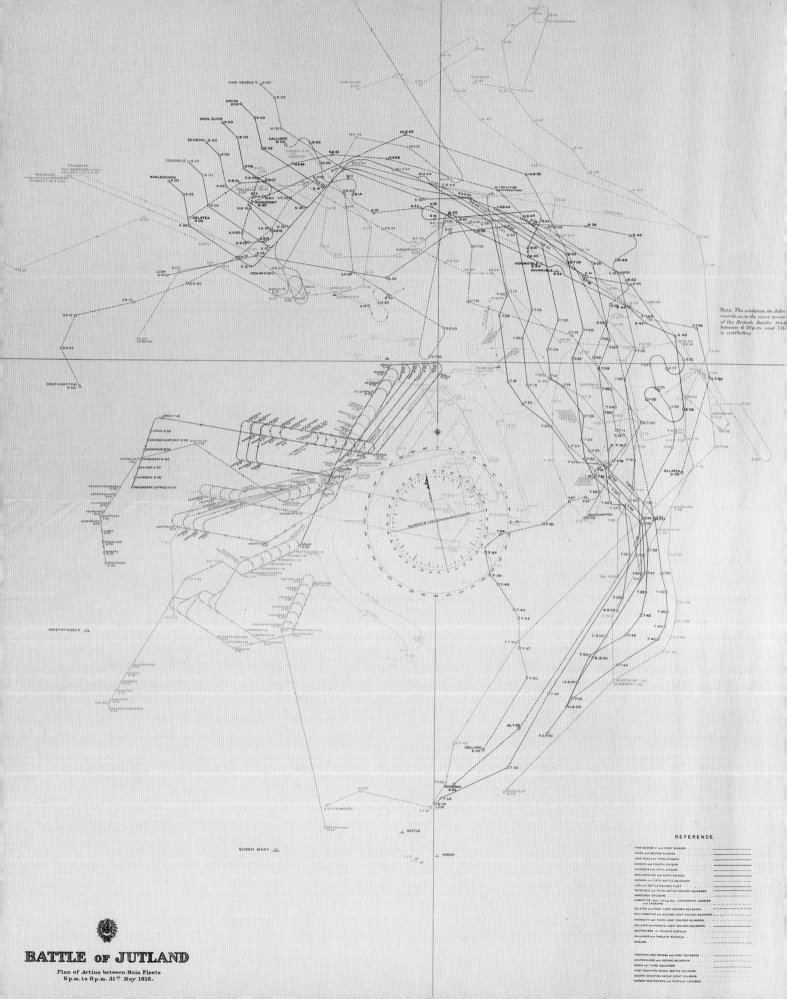

BATTLE of JUTLAND

Plan of Action between Main Fleets
6 p.m. to 8 p.m. 31ˢᵗ May 1916.

Note. The evidence in Adm
records as to the exact move
of the British Battle Crui
between 6.30 p.m. and 7.1
is conflicting.

REFERENCE.

about British defences in the Firth of Forth (i.e. Beatty's base, Rosyth). Finally, on the morning of 30 May, a signal instructed the German fleet to assemble in the outer Schillig Roads, off Wilhelmshaven, and the Bruges wireless station warned all U-boats that their, or the British, fleet would be at sea for the next two days (the ambiguity was caused by uncertainty in Room 40 over the meaning of a code group). In any case, the British were sufficiently alerted, and at noon the Admiralty warned Jellicoe and Beatty that the Germans would probably sail early on 31 May. The Grand Fleet was accompanied by a seaplane carrier, the *Engardine*,

but as she could not keep up she was sent back to Scapa, thus depriving the fleet of vital reconnaissance capability.

Beatty sailed immediately from Rosyth to intercept the German fleet and draw it within range of the big guns of the Grand Fleet, following sixty miles astern. The U-boats were ineffective against Beatty, who engaged Hipper's five battle-cruisers with his six, before the Fifth Battle Fleet's four dreadnoughts had caught up. Hipper turned away, starting his 'run to the south' to draw Beatty onto the guns of the *Hochseeflotte*. Three of Beatty's battle-cruisers were soon hit on their thinly armoured turrets, leading to cordite explosions, and flash penetrating to the magazines. Two, *Indefatigable* and *Queen Mary*, blew up, while the third was only saved by flooding the magazine. Yet another, *Invincible*, was hit and blew up at a later stage. Although the German battle-cruisers received nine hits on their turrets, none was lost. Apart from better fire-control, gunnery and ammunition, the Germans avoided flash-explosions by using heavier armour, having their cordite propellant not in silk-bagged cartridges but in brass cases, and

better-protecting their magazines from flash with special scuttles and doors. The British, to accelerate their rate of fire, had deliberately adopted risky cordite-handling, leaving scuttles and magazine doors open and having plenty of bagged charges stacked ready in the handling rooms and turrets where they were all too liable to be ignited by a bursting shell.

Beatty's four battleships came within range too late to save his battle-cruisers, and in turn the arrival of the *Hochseeflotte* saved Hipper's battle-cruisers. The light cruiser *Southampton* sighted Scheer's fleet at 4.30 p.m. and signalled this to Beatty and Jellicoe, but with faulty reporting of position. Beatty now turned towards Jellicoe, who was racing down from the north, to draw Scheer's sixteen dreadnought battleships and six older ones within range of the heavier broadsides of Jellicoe's twenty-four dreadnoughts. Together with Beatty's four, these should have been more than capable of crushing the German fleet as the British ships carried heavier guns – the weight of their broadside was double that of the Germans – and significantly outnumbered the Germans. Confused by *Hampshire*'s report, Jellicoe nevertheless divined the situation and ordered the Grand Fleet to deploy across the bows of the German line in the classic manoeuvre of 'crossing the T', enabling his ships to concentrate their fire against Scheer's leading ships, which could not concentrate against his. This manoeuvre also put Jellicoe's ships to the east, from where they could cut off Scheer's escape.

The fire-fight lasted a mere ten minutes before Scheer turned away to the west, covered by torpedo-firing destroyers and smoke. Only one torpedo hit a British ship, but did no damage. Jellicoe, however, turned away from the torpedo attack, according to British doctrine, rather than towards it, 'combing the tracks' of the torpedoes. Fearing for the security of his fleet, he avoided risks that might destroy British naval superiority and, bearing in mind the possibility of encountering further torpedo attacks or mines sown by the fleeing enemy, did not pursue. As Scheer had withdrawn to the west, Jellicoe believed he was in a position to prevent Scheer from returning to base. Scheer now attempted a breakthrough to the east, leading with his battle-cruisers and destroyers, but failed when he found the Grand Fleet again 'crossing his T'. At this point Scheer ordered Hipper's battle-cruisers on a 'death-ride' towards Jellicoe, with his destroyers laying a smoke screen, and managed to turn away and disengage. Jellicoe again turned away from the torpedo attack. At nightfall Scheer appeared to be in a hopeless position.

During the night, there were sudden and confused encounters. Jellicoe avoided a night action, for which the British navy was not trained, and was uncertain of Scheer's position and movements.

ABOVE: A German poster-map showing the Battle of Jutland, *Die Seeschlacht vor den Skagerrak*, 31 Mai–1 Juni 1916.

The German navy had star shell, which illuminated an area without giving away the position of the firing ship. The British only had searchlights. Waiting for dawn, he set a course that he calculated would cut off Scheer's escape. Scheer, however, eluded the British battle fleet by crossing the rear of their line, encountering only light forces, and British ships that made contact did not always report, or failed to send Scheer's position and course. Before dawn, the *Hochseeflotte* had forced its way through the rear of Jellicoe's fleet and set a course for the swept channel at Horns Reef, 120 miles northwest of Wilhelmshaven.

Scheer's escape need not have happened. Had Room 40's intercepts been correctly interpreted and rapidly passed to the fleet, Jellicoe and Beatty could have cut off his escape, and that of Hipper, on 1 June. A key intercept sent to the Grand Fleet in the evening gave the course and speed of the *Hochseeflotte*, leaving no doubt that it was heading for the Horns Reef channel, and this was immediately followed by another reporting that Scheer had asked for a Zeppelin reconnaissance of the Horns Reef area. This last message, although decrypted by Room 40 and passed to Operations, was never transmitted to the British fleet. It is obvious now, and clear at the time, that there was incompetence in the high echelons of the Admiralty when it came to the relationship between the excellent staff of Room 40 and the hide-bound Operations staff, who often treated Room 40 and its decrypts with contempt.

Both sides naturally claimed a victory, but the Germans got their claim in first. The Germans, with inferior forces, had done well to sink twice as many ships (including three battle-cruisers), twice as much tonnage, and kill twice as many men as they lost, although they had suffered an adverse balance of serious damage. On the other hand, the British were left 'masters of the field' and the Germans had run for home. While the British fleet was ready to sail again with in a few hours of reaching port, the Germans took much longer to recover. Scheer had not achieved his objective, to destroy part of the Grand Fleet to equalize the balance between the fleets. One American summed it up by saying that the German fleet had assaulted its jailer, and was now back in jail. Scheer told the Kaiser, a month after the battle, that even the most successful fleet action would not force Britain to capitulate, and he added that only a U-boat blockade could defeat Britain by breaking her economy. Jutland was therefore a strategic victory for Britain, and a strategic defeat for Germany. The *Hochseeflotte* came out again twice during 1916, and once more in 1918, but achieved nothing. The British failure to defeat it in 1916 meant, however, that they had to keep the Grand Fleet and its escorts in readiness throughout the war, and they had to give up any hope of opening the route to Russia through the Baltic, though this always seemed an unrealistic proposition.

In other theatres, the French looked after the Mediterranean, the Allies had the Austrian navy bottled up in the Adriatic, and the Japanese and Americans (from April 1917) assisted the British, particularly by escorting convoys. American battleships even joined the Grand Fleet.

The Second German Submarine Campaign
By the end of 1916 Germany had reached an impasse. The failure of land operations to force a decision, coupled with the worsening effects of the Allied blockade at home, suggested that more drastic action was needed. Furthermore, Russia did not yet appear to be near collapse and the German peace proposals, based on terms unacceptable to the Allies, had been contemptuously rebuffed. Germany therefore decided to rescind her relaxation of the U-boat

blockade, and reintroduce the 'sink-at-sight' policy. By now she had more U-boats, about 120 long-range craft, and the German Admiralty calculated that sinkings would starve Britain into submission within six months and that, even though this would probably entail the USA declaring war, the risk was worth taking. The Germans had taken into account the time it would take for the USA to raise, train and equip a large enough army, and set against that their belief that the European Allies would collapse before this US army could take the field. The Russian Revolution in March 1917 assisted the Germans, pressed by Ludendorff, in their decision to take the plunge – a disastrous one as it turned out. The six-month period the Germans reckoned it would take to starve Britain was four months shorter than that arrived at by the British authorities.

The newer German U-boats had greater range and were more heavily armed. Later in 1917 the Germans launched a new, ocean-going type that carried ten torpedoes, two 5.9-inch guns and also lighter guns, and could cruise several thousand miles from port. On 1 February 1917 they declared British Home Waters, the French Atlantic coast and the Mediterranean an unrestricted zone, within which all ships could be sunk at sight. Losses began to accelerate to critical levels, and many neutral ships simply refused to enter the zone. Despite a reduction in tonnage crossing the zone, catastrophic losses ensued. In February, 260 ships were sunk, in March 338 and in April, the month Germany enjoyed a devastating air superiority in France, a peak of 430. By April, British corn reserves were down to six weeks' supply, and the government was informed in secret that Britain could not hold out beyond November. This led to a crisis in the war cabinet, and the First Sea Lord, Jellicoe (who had been transferred to the Admiralty from the Grand Fleet at the end of November 1916), used the German submarine threat to urge the importance of Haig's Flanders offensive to seize Zeebrugge and Ostend which were being used as U-boat bases. Jellicoe created for the first time a much-needed Anti-Submarine Division of the Naval Staff. Equally vital was the inclusion of Room 40 into the Intelligence Division in May 1917. It took a long time, however, before Room 40 became a proper intelligence centre as opposed to a mere decrypting function.

The shipping crisis forced the Royal Navy to introduce merchant convoys and, as their advocates had predicted, sinkings fell rapidly. By May the monthly figure had fallen to 280, and by December to 150. They continued to fall up to the Armistice in November 1918, in which month they were down to 20. The efficiency of escort vessels improved as better depth charges and hydrophones were developed. The entry of the USA made more escorts available, and where possible airships, seaplanes and flying

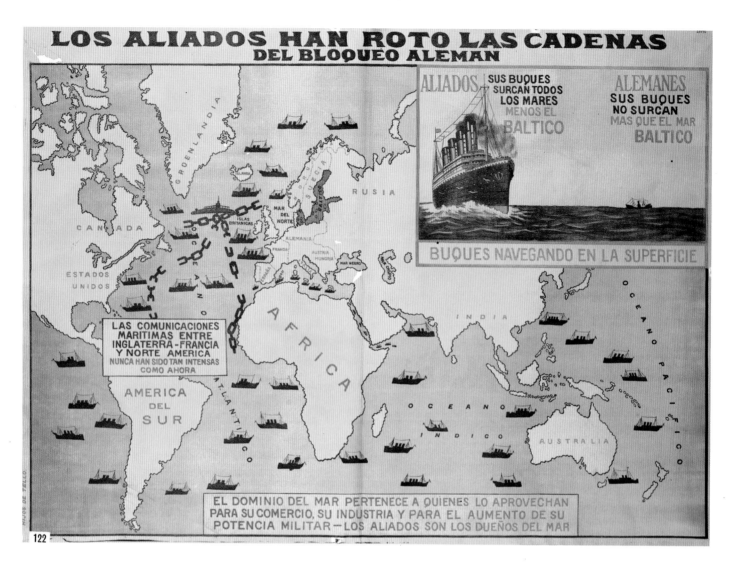

LOS ALIADOS HAN ROTO LAS CADENAS
DEL BLOQUEO ALEMAN

ALIADOS SUS BUQUES SURCAN TODOS LOS MARES MENOS EL BALTICO

ALEMANES SUS BUQUES NO SURCAN MAS QUE EL MAR BALTICO

BUQUES NAVEGANDO EN LA SUPERFICIE

LAS COMUNICACIONES MARITIMAS ENTRE INGLATERRA-FRANCIA Y NORTE AMERICA NUNCA HAN SIDO TAM INTENSAS COMO AHORA

EL DOMINIO DEL MAR PERTENECE A QUIENES LO APROVECHAN PARA SU COMERCIO, SU INDUSTRIA Y PARA EL AUMENTO DE SU POTENCIA MILITAR—LOS ALIADOS SON LOS DUEÑOS DEL MAR

122

boats provided additional cover. U-boats were kept at a distance, reducing the proportion of torpedo hits. By October 1917, tonnage sunk was only half that of April and, while in the period January to April 1917 only twelve U-boats were sunk, in the period September to December the figure was thirty-six.

The convoy system proved so successful that up to the war's end sinkings of ships that sailed in convoy were only 0.5 per cent, or 1 in 200. Toll was taken of U-boats by various weapons. New, horned mines sank thirty-six during 1918. British submarines stalked U-boats and torpedoed them when they surfaced. The effectiveness of the Dover barrage, which U-boats had been crossing at the rate of twenty-four per month, was increased by night-lighting. But attempts failed to lay minefields to block the exits from the Heligoland Bight into the North Sea, and therefore stop-up the naval bases of Wilhelmshaven at the mouth of the Jade and Cuxhaven at the mouth of the Elbe. Here the Germans

were able to use heavy ships to protect their minesweepers. New minefields were laid where the Germans could not sweep them, to keep U-boats out of the Western Approaches. To avoid the Dover barrage, where U-boats submerging to avoid lights and patrols were striking the submerged mines, they were ordered to reach the Western Approaches by rounding Scotland and, in the final months of the war, British and American minelayers laid a mine barrage across 300 miles of the North Sea between the Orkney Islands and Norway.

ABOVE: *Los Aliados Han Roto las Cadenas del Bloqueo Aleman* [The Allies have broken chains of German blockade], poster-map showing chains attached to U-boat.

RIGHT: The spectacular result of a British bomb hitting a German ammunition train, east of Mericourt-sur-Somme, July 1918, during the preparations for the Allied counter-offensives.

THE WAR IN THE AIR

The great contribution of aircraft at the beginning of the war, while the initial manoeuvres were being made, was in strategic reconnaissance. During the war their greatest value was more in operational and tactical functions, particularly aerial photography for intelligence and mapping, and artillery cooperation. At sea they made a vital contribution in reconnaissance, anti-submarine work and spotting for the navy's guns. The use in warfare of various types of aircraft had been developing since the eighteenth century, when hot air and, later, gas-filled balloons began to be used in strategic reconnaissance. In the nineteenth century photography from balloons and kites, and later from powered airships (dirigibles, made possible by the invention of the internal combustion engine) was also applied to military purposes, including mapping and the direction of artillery fire. Photography from balloons was a feature of the American Civil War (1861–5), the Franco-Prussian War

(1870–1) and other conflicts. The control of artillery fire was particular assisted by the invention of the telegraph, and later the telephone, providing direct communication from an air observer to the gunners as in the Boer War (1899–1902).

While airships in particular offered great possibilities for reconnaissance and photography, and for bombing, they were large and relatively slow-moving. They made easy targets for the first anti-aircraft guns, then known as 'balloon guns'. It was the internal combustion engine that enabled power to be applied successfully to gliders, thus producing the first aeroplanes. The Wright brothers' innovations of 1903–5 created the controllable fixed-wing aircraft which, by 1914, had already seen service in the Italo-Turkish War in Tripoli (Libya) in 1911–12 and the Balkan Wars (1912–13).

The decades before the First World War saw the powers creating military and naval organizations for balloons, kites,

airships and aeroplanes. Primarily used for reconnaissance (formerly one of the main roles of cavalry), as the war approached there was an increasing awareness of their offensive and defensive roles. Aeroplanes were also fitted with floats rather than wheels, enabling them to take off and land on water. Then aircraft – flying boats – were designed with special boat-like fuselage (or hull) shapes for the same purpose. From now on, fleets at sea could vastly extend their range of observation by using accompanying aircraft for reconnaissance. It would only take a couple more decades before these same aircraft, usually carrier-based and equipped with bombs and torpedoes, would sound the death-knell of the capital ship.

It was recognized early that the aircraft was a new weapon, and the air a new battlefield. Indeed, H. G. Wells had written of just

such an idea in his 1898 science fiction work *The War of the Worlds*, though his aerial invaders had come from Mars. In Britain, fear of invasion, however misplaced, increased in the period up to 1914 as tension with Germany intensified. Not only were large-scale maps of potential invasion areas prepared (particularly East Anglia), but serious thought was given to creating a ring of fortifications around London and to possible naval and air defences.

The war in the air was not confined to the air only; it represented another dimension to the ground war, just as the war at sea was ultimately related to the terrestrial operations of the great powers. The air combats that have captured popular imagination were actually incidental to the main roles of the air forces: strategic and tactical reconnaissance and denying this to the enemy, supporting ground operations and countering the

ABOVE: A British FE2D pusher aeroplane on the ground, with the observer standing to fire backwards over the top plane; a camera is mounted on the port side. Aerial photography and ranging for the artillery were the main tasks of all air forces.

LEFT: An RE8 of No. 69 (later No. 3) Squadron, Australian Flying Corps, preparing to set out on a night bombing operation from Savy near Arras, 22/23 October 1917.

enemy's air operations, and strategic bombing. Interdiction, or preventing the enemy's air force from carrying out its functions, became of great importance, and 'aerial barrages' through intensive patrolling were created for this purpose.

The air dimension also acted as a 'force multiplier' for existing arms and techniques. Aerial photography provided a massive advance over ground reconnaissance for intelligence purposes. Aircraft also enabled better observation and correction of artillery fire, which previously could only be done by forward ground observers or rear observers on a rise of the ground.

In the first months of the war, pilots and observers flying reconnaissance sorties started carrying pistols and sporting rifles for protection in case they should have chance encounters with enemy aircraft. It was not long before machine guns were

mounted, as weapons both of defence and offence. It soon became standard to fit these with interrupter gear to fire through the propeller, the whole machine being aimed at the enemy. At first, metal anti-personnel darts were carried to drop on close-packed enemy troops, and these were followed by grenades, modified shells and purpose-made bombs with flight vanes which aided their descent, ensuring that they landed on their percussion-fused noses. Rockets were mounted on wing-struts to fire against enemy airships and observation balloons, and seaplanes were fitted to drop torpedoes. Wheeled aircraft began to take off from ships (though not land on them) and special seaplane carriers were built. On land, aeroplanes were fitted with wireless sets from the start of the war, to report the fall of shell for the artillery. The systematic photography of enemy positions for intelligence, mapping and planning purposes also developed early. Indeed, experiments with most of these innovations had been made by all powers in the pre-1914 period.

When war began in August 1914, the European powers each had around 300 aircraft, mostly a motley non-standard assortment of makes and types, both monoplanes and biplanes, with many only suitable for training. The Royal Flying Corps (RFC) initially took four squadrons to France with the BEF, and by 15 August, while the BEF was moving up to its concentration area around Maubeuge, they were located at Amiens. They moved to Maubeuge on the sixteenth, and three days later flew the first reconnaissance sortie in an attempt to locate the advancing German columns. At this stage of the war, and indeed throughout it, reconnaissance was the air force's primary role. The other roles that developed were usually to protect one's own reconnaissance machines or to blind the enemy by preventing him from carrying out his own reconnaissance sorties.

The ability to project one's own eyes (and, soon, cameras) above and beyond the battlefield – indeed into the enemy's rear areas and homeland – was crucial for many reasons. It built up a reliable intelligence picture: developing a map of the enemy's territory; his strength, dispositions and order-of-battle; defences; organization and logistics infrastructure; intentions (offensive or defensive). For exactly the same reasons, it was vital to deny such observation to the enemy. The value of air observation, and the frequent failure of cavalry in the same role, was demonstrated several times in the early encounter battles on the Western and Eastern Fronts. The day before the Battle of Mons, the RFC flew twelve sorties which spotted German forces moving round the flanks of the BEF, which had taken up an advanced position along, and to the east of, the Mons–Condé Canal. To its right, Lanrezac's French Fifth Army, engaged in the Battle of Charleroi, was already retiring – the airmen observed the German advance driving back the French from the river Sambre – and to its left were only scattered French cavalry and territorial infantry formations. Late on 23 August, the day of the battle, Sir John French, realizing that his flanks were both threatened, ordered the retreat.

The advance through Belgium and northern France of the all-important German right wing – the great wheel of the Schlieffen–Moltke plans – was closely observed by French and British airmen. In early September their air reports enabled the French to attack, from the direction of Paris, the vulnerable German western (right) flank when von Kluck swung his First Army to the southeast to close the gap between his and Second Army. French fliers, although they failed to observe the great concentration of German forces moving through the Ardennes in the week before serious encounter battles on 22 August, supplied vital information during the subsequent operations. In February 1915, a French seaplane made a vital contribution to the defence of the Suez Canal by detecting the Turkish force approaching across the Sinai desert.

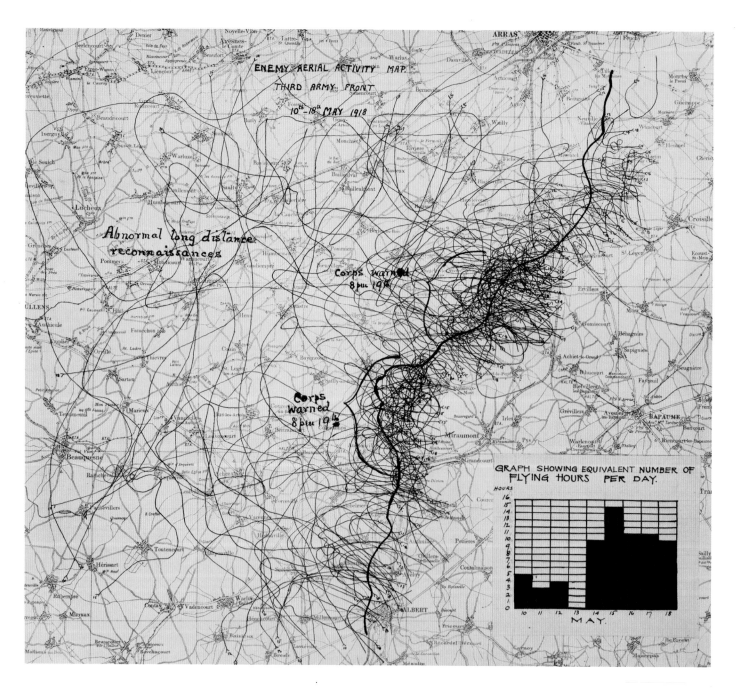

For the Germans, aerial reconnaissance was equally important. Although in the West it failed at first to detect the presence of the BEF, it did observe Lanrezac's forces moving north towards the Meuse, and thus helped Moltke to divine Joffre's intentions. On the Eastern Front it was crucial in supplying the information that

ABOVE: A British aeroplane over a gridded photo-mosaic of the *Moorslede* 1:10,000 map sheet, east of Ypres, 1917–18, showing the process of map compilation from aerial photographs (fitted to multiple control points). In the relatively flat terrain of Flanders, little distortion was caused by undulating ground. Apart from practice trenches and tracks, the landscape shows little sign of war.

LEFT: *Enemy Aerial Activity Map, Third Army Front, 10–18 May 1918.* Intense air reconnaissance over the front and battery area, and abnormal deep reconnaissance sorties, were indications of an impending attack.

won the Battle of Tannenberg. In August 1914 the German army deployed on the Eastern and Western Fronts some 200 operational aircraft in 33 *Feldflieger-Abteilungen* (flying units of six aircraft). Each of these units served either an army or a corps headquarters, there being eight German armies and thirty-three corps in total, the bulk of them in the West as Schlieffen and Moltke had planned. There were also ten *Festungsflieger-Abteilungen* (fortress flying units) attached to German frontier fortresses in West and East – for·example Thorn, Posen, Graudenz and Königsberg in the East, and Cologne, Strassburg and Metz in the West. Two airships, from Posen and Königsberg, and the 2nd Aircraft Battalion, reported correctly, from 9 August onwards, the movements of Russian columns approaching East Prussia while the Russian armies were still on their own territory. The crucial intelligence they supplied was that the movements of the two Russian armies

Longuenesse · Ht · Arques · Staple · Meteren · Neuve Eglise · Warneton
Visques · Arques · Renescure · Ebblinghem · la Kreule · Pradelles · Strazeele · Merris · Bailleul · Ploegsteer
Blendecques · Wizernes · Campagne · Wallon Capel · Borre · Strazeele · la Creche · Nieppe
Helfaut · Pt. Bois · Heuringhem · Quiestede · Quiestede · Blaringhem · la Belle · Morbecque · Vieux Berquin · Bleu · le Verrier · le Pt Mortier · Exinghem · Armentières
Sientques · Inghem · Ecques · Roquetoire · Forêt de Ni · Neuf Berquin · Estaires · Fleurbaix
Herbelle · Clarques · Rebecq · Rincq · St Floris · Calonne · Lestrem · L'Avenne · Aubers
Thérouanne · Manetz · Aire · Isbergue · Molinghem · Robecq · Vieille Chapelle · Richebourg · La Bassée
Nielles · Marthes · Blessy · Lambres · Mazinghem · Busnes · Mont · les Lobes · Lacouture · Locon · Richebourg
Delette · Enguinegatte · Estrée Blanche · Guarbecque · la Flandrie · Bernenchon · Lillers · Gonnehem · Hinges · Béthune · La Bassée
Enquin-les-Mines · Erny St Julien · Norrent-Fontes · St Hilaire · St Rely · Lières · Chocques · Oblinghem · Essars · Givenchy
Bomy · Flechin · Ligny · Westrehem · Amettes · Burbure · Allouagne · Lozinghem · Cauchy · Marles · Bruay · Labuissière · Houchin · Noyelles
Beaumetz · Laires · Felvin · Nédonchel · Ferfay · Auchel · Calonne-Ricourt · Divion · Hersin · Grenay
Prédefin · Fiefs · Bailleul les Pernes · Sachin · Pernes · Bours · Ourton · Houdain · Barlin · Bully
Heuchin · Equirre · Boyaval · Tangry · Marest · Beugin · Maisnil · Sains en Gohelle
Anvin · Erin · Fleury · Fontaine · Diéval · Ranchicourt · Rebreuve

Humerœuil · Pierremont · Troisvaux · la Thieuloye · Fresnicourt · Bouvigny · Servins · Gouy · Souchez · Vimy
St Pol · Roëllecourt · Marquay · Villers Châtel · Camblighul · Carency · Mont St Eloi · Acq · Neuville
Ligny St Flochel · Bailleul · Tinques · Villers Brulin · Agnières · Prévin Capelle · Aubigny · Habarcq · Agnez · Duisans · ARRAS
Ecoivres · Nuncq · Buneville · Maizières · Penin · Tilloy · Hermaville · Avesnes · Marœuil · Ecurie · Ste Catherine
Hautecote · Sibiville · Gouy en Ternois · Villers · Givenchy le noble · Manin · Gouves · Montenescourt · Dainville · Tilloy les Mofflaines
Boubers · Ligny · Ambrines · Magnicourt · Lignereuil · Noyelle · Vion · Lattre · Achicourt · Beaurains · Boiry
Trevent · Pt Bouret · Estrée · Liencourt · Avesnes · Hauteville · Wanquetin · Warlus · Rivière · Wailly · Neuville
Rebreuviette · le Cauroy · Grand-Rullecourt · Barly · Simencourt · Gouy · Beaumetz · Mercatel · Rensart
Bonmeres · Ivergny · Beaudricourt · Sombrin · Monchiet · Basseux · Ransart · Blairville · Hamelincourt
Neuvillette · Sus · Warhizel · Bavincourt · Coullemont · Saulty · Bailleulval · Adinfer · Boiry · Hamelin · Ervillers
Doullens · Brevillers · Humbercourt · Bellevue · la Cauchie · Humbercamps · Berles · Monchy · Boiry · Mory
Occoches · Gronches · Pommera · Gaudiempre · Pas · Bienvillers · Douchy · Ayette · Courcelles · Bilmicourt
Authie · Warlincourt · Grincourt · St Amand · Hannescamps · Bavencourt · Bucquoy · Ablainzevelle · Achiet le Grand
Halloy · Authieule · Coigneux · Sailly · Puisieux · Gommecourt · Behagnies
Fienvilles · Candas · Amplier · Thievres · Anthies

were not synchronized. Rennenkampf's First Army was a few days' march ahead of Samsonov's Second, so they could be defeated one by one.

During position warfare and operations on all fronts, most machines were employed on the vital routine tasks of photography and artillery work. These fulfilled many requirements – general intelligence, artillery intelligence (locating enemy battery positions and determining which were active), artillery cooperation and counter-battery work (ranging one's own guns onto enemy batteries and other targets), and tactical mapping.

The mapping function was particularly important, and involved not merely the plotting of enemy trenches, batteries, pill-boxes and other features of the enemy's defensive organization, but also the creation of a new, accurate, large-scale topographical maps from photographs which could be fitted to a framework of ground control points. In theatres such as the Middle East where such control points were lacking, new techniques were developed for mapping from aerial photographs, which depended upon accurate determination of height, speed and flight-path.

Above the photographic and artillery work-horses flew the protective fighters and their pilots, some of whom became known internationally as 'aces'. Huge aerial 'dogfights' developed over the battlefields, particularly in 1917, while the rival air forces fought for aerial supremacy and to drive the enemy's photographic reconnaissance and artillery machines from the sky. The French ace, Georges Guynemer, was killed during the Third Battle of Ypres in 1917, while German aces in that year were the 'Red Baron' Manfred von Richthofen and Werner Voss. Among British pilots, some aces were Edward Mannock, Albert Ball and James McCudden. Even before the USA entered the war, American pilots flew for France in the *Escadrille Lafayette*, named to commemorate the help France had given in the American War of Independence. The American pilot Eddie Rickenbacker became a famous ace. These aces caught the imagination of the public, and were a godsend to national propaganda efforts.

At sea, seaplanes, balloons and airships were all used for fleet reconnaissance, and the Royal Navy provided a seaplane carrier, the *Engardine*, for the Grand Fleet. Experiments were also made with spotter-aircraft taking off from turret-mounted ramps. In the U-boat war in 1917 and 1918, the British allocated 685 aircraft and 103 airships for anti-submarine patrol work. The first convoys coincided with the entry of the USA into the war in April 1917 and, as a result of the convoy system, which made attacking deep-water shipping a riskier business, the U-boats switched to attacking smaller, unescorted ships in shallower inshore waters where they were more vulnerable to sightings from the air.

ABOVE: A raid on a German aerodrome between Haubourdin and Santes, three miles southwest of Lille, showing a British aeroplane with bombs exploding below.

LEFT: An August 1916 secret War Office map extract showing British airfields in France during the Battle of the Somme. On the complete map, four large stations (see key) are shown by red rectangles (there were five British armies on the Western Front at this time), and many squadron aerodromes by red circles. Scale 1:250,000.

Zeppelins

Zeppelins and other airships, while proving increasingly vulnerable to attack from the ground and the air, performed valuable reconnaissance work on both the Eastern and Western Fronts in the early years of the war. The first Zeppelin raid on Britain took place on the evening of 19 January 1915, when two airships, L3 and L4, bombed Great Yarmouth and King's Lynn in Norfolk, killing nine people. Civilian morale suffered because of shock, a feeling of helplessness and also a heightened fear of invasion. More raids followed on coastal towns, and also on London, during 1915 and 1916. In all there were fifty-two Zeppelin raids on Britain during the war, killing over 500 people. Little significant damage was done, and the main effect was the diversion of scarce military resources to air defence.

Air Defence

The air defence of Britain was at first in the hands of the Navy. The London Air Defence Area (LADA) was formed in September 1915, initially under Admiral Sir Percy Scott, a naval gunnery expert, to defend London from the increasing threat from airships. Existing naval and land-service guns were adapted for high-angle fire. The

LADA was taken over by the RFC in February 1916. Deploying searchlights and anti-aircraft guns, it was at first remarkably ineffective, and RFC squadrons had to be brought back from France to provide London with some protection. Some fourteen airfields around London and the Home Counties were used for squadrons defending London. Existing aeroplanes were adapted as night-fighters.

In early September 1916, William Leefe Robinson, flying a BE2c two-seater converted into a single-seater night-fighter, was the first British pilot to shoot down a German airship over Britain. His machine gun fire caused the airship to burst into flames, and it

ABOVE: German Naval Airship L13. She took part in a raid on London and the Home Counties on the night of 13/14 October 1915. Her commander dropped most of his bombs, mainly incendiaries, in the Woolwich area, presumably intended for the Royal Arsenal.

RIGHT: Air Raid, 6 December 1917, showing the routes of German bombing planes over London and the Thames Estuary. The paths of sixteen aeroplanes, in four detachments, are shown. An official map, overprinted on an Ordnance Survey base map, not for public consumption.

crashed in a field in Hertfordshire, killing Commander Schramm and his fifteen-man crew of Schütte-Lanz SL11, one of sixteen airships on a mass raid on England. Civilian morale, which had been suffering because of the apparent immunity of the raiders, received a great boost, the effect being helped by the large number of witnesses and the triumphant celebrations. It was a propaganda victory as well as a successful demonstration of the capabilities of night-fighters. Robinson was awarded the Victoria Cross.

Among the anti-aircraft defence techniques tried was a balloon apron, which involved a chain of tethered barrage balloons from which were suspended a curtain of cables. The Germans had tested a kite or balloon barrage in the winter of 1914–5, and in 1917,

in response to Allied air raids, used balloon barrages to protect important industrial targets. The Italians used a similar system to protect Venice and, in September 1917, General Ashmore (who had visited Venice) outlined his London balloon barrage plan. German twin-engine Gotha bomber planes had begun to raid London. Two balloon aprons were soon deployed to the east of London. In October 1917, the Commander-in-Chief Home Forces initiated a scheme for five balloon squadrons, and a further cordon of twenty balloon aprons in an arc from northeast to southeast London. By April 1918 seven were in operation and the eighth was almost ready. The morale effect was considerable, as the balloons reassured civilians.

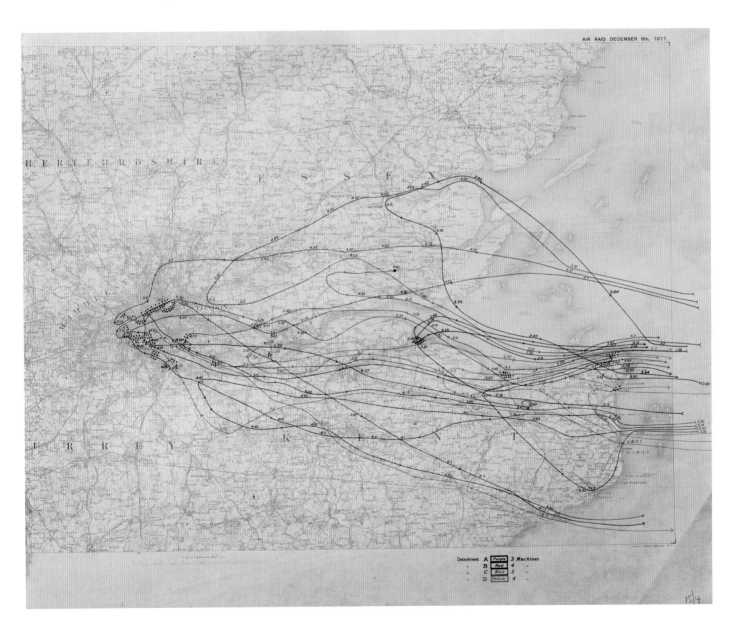

THE *Daily Mail* MAP
OF
ZEPPELIN AND AEROPLANE BOMBS ON LONDON.

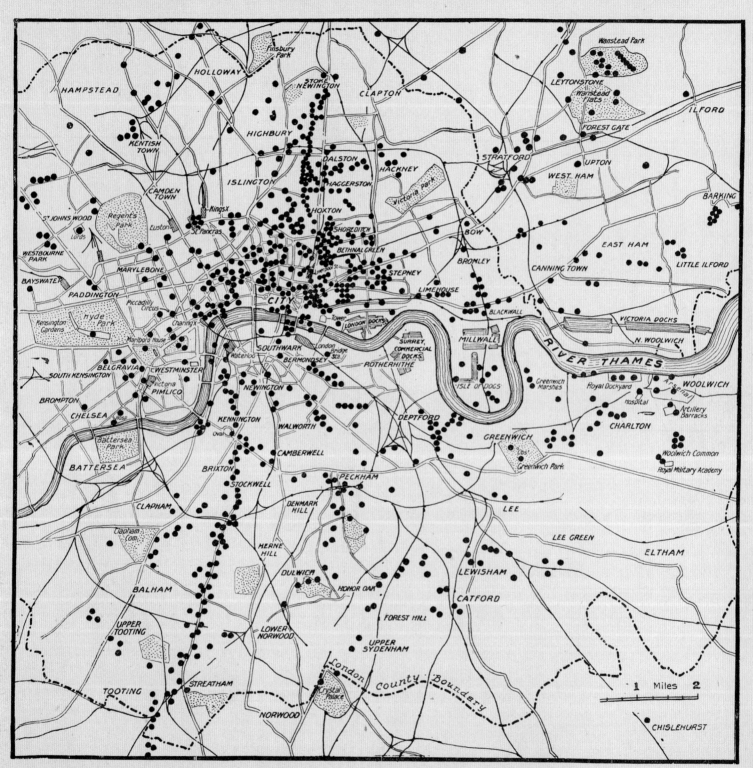

Reprinted from "The Daily Mail," January 31, 1919.

Strategic Bombing

Since the beginning of the war, certain long-range airship and aeroplane bombing operations had been carried out by both sides – notably the German Zeppelin and Gotha attacks on London – and suitable maps or charts had to be prepared for these. The Royal Naval Air Service mounted several unsuccessful

ABOVE: Balloon apron for the defence of London, 1917–18. In 1917, copying German and Italian ideas, the British deployed two balloon aprons east of London. By April 1918 seven more were in operation and the eighth was almost ready.

LEFT: *The Daily Mail Map of Zeppelin and Aeroplane Bombs on London,* 31 January 1919. The scale of original is approximately ½ inch to 1 mile.

raids against targets in Germany in late 1916 and early 1917, and worsening German air raids on Britain led to British retaliation raids into Germany from 17 October 1917, when 100 Squadron RFC, the pioneer night-bombing squadron, started operating from Ochy, near Nancy, against German towns. It was expanded into 41st Wing RFC, and then, on 1 February 1918 it became 8th Brigade RFC, still under Haig's command.

On 1 April 1918 the Royal Flying Corps was merged with the Royal Naval Air Service to become the Royal Air Force, under the new Air Ministry. Between 17 October 1917 and 6 June 1918, 8th Brigade and its antecedents carried out fifty-seven raids against targets in Karlsruhe, Mannheim, Cologne, Mainz, Stuttgart, Coblenz, Diedenhofen (Thionville) and Saarbrucken. On 6 June 1918, 8th Brigade became, by Air Ministry instruction, the core of a new Independent Air Force, also known as the Independent Bombing Force, specifically for deep penetration 'strategic bombing' of targets within Germany. On 26 October 1918 it was renamed the Inter-Allied Independent Air (or Bombing) Force, and now included French, Italian and American squadrons. In August, Frankfurt was attacked, and in November operations by four-engined Super-Handley Pages from Prague (the Austro-Hungarian Empire had capitulated on 4 November) were planned against Berlin

BELOW: Handley Page bombers at Coudekerque near Dunkirk, 20 April 1918. By the end of the war, these machines were preparing to bomb Berlin from an airfield near Prague.

RIGHT: German vertical aerial photograph (*Reihenbildner*), 21 May 1918 (full image and detail), showing ships in the Victoria and Albert Docks, and the George V Dock under construction. Much industry was concentrated in Silvertown, between the docks and the Thames, where an explosives factory blew up on 19 January 1917. The Royal Arsenal was at Woolwich, on the south bank.

Chapter 8

The 1917 Campaign in the East and the West

By the end of 1916 the war had ground to a bloody and exhausted halt, and no end to the deadlock was in sight. On the Russian front, Brusilov's offensive, despite bringing Rumania into the war, had petered out under a series of counter-attacks, and the Germans were everywhere ascendant. The Russian armies were, in fact, beginning to disintegrate through their loss of belief in the Tsar and in the war. The Verdun and Somme battles on the Western Front had been victories of nothing but attrition, resulting in a dreadful total of 1,200,000 casualties.

It might have made more strategic sense, and saved more Allied lives, to use the naval blockade of Germany to starve Germany into suing for an armistice rather than launch more frontal assaults on strongly wired and entrenched German positions. Indeed, the German people had already suffered terribly through the 'turnip winter' of 1916–17. Germany had put

out peace feelers in late 1916, but had refused to give up any of the foreign territory in which it stood. This intransigence merely hardened the resolve of the Allies. Before Christmas 1916, Woodrow Wilson, the US President, had asked all the belligerents to state their peace terms. But Germany's declaration of unrestricted submarine warfare in January 1917 and the

ABOVE: Surrounded by maps, Field Marshal Prince Leopold of Bavaria, Commander-in-Chief, Eastern Front, seated, with his Chief-of-Staff, General Max Hoffmann, in Russia, August 1917. Before the war Hoffmann, as a general staff officer in Berlin, had been an expert in Russian matters.

RIGHT: German trench map (*Stellungskarte*), 30–31 March 1917, German trenches in blue, Russian in red. The Kadlubiska area is in eastern Galicia, west of Brody and south of Pripet marshes.

Zimmerman telegram (a crude German attempt to incite Mexico to attack the USA) angered and exasperated the USA. On 6 April 1917, Wilson led his country into the war, effectively ending any chance of a negotiated peace.

After the appalling Somme battle, Ludendorff had decided that the German doctrine for the defensive battle (*Abwehrschlacht*) in the West should be reconceived to give the infantry far more protection. While defence-in-depth had already been adopted, the new posture envisaged a withdrawal from the stinking, shell-churned morasses of these battlefields to newly constructed, heavily wired rear positions equipped with concrete shelters and underground accommodation for the trench garrison. At the same time, there developed a doctrine of holding the advanced positions lightly, with machine gun positions checker-boarded in depth behind, stronger support forces in rear and beyond these, out of range of Allied artillery fire, even stronger counter-attack divisions. This was the genesis of the *Siegfried*

Stellung (Hindenburg Line to the British) to which the Germans retired in March 1917, and also of the tactics with which they fought the defensive battles during 1917.

In Britain, Asquith's Liberal government had become another victim of attrition, and also of Lord Lansdowne's letter to the War Cabinet of 14 November 1916, questioning the possibility of a knockout blow by the Allies and proposing a negotiated peace. While Balfour and Churchill felt that Lansdowne's paper should be considered, the fire-eating and ambitious Lloyd George, realizing that the press and voters would not support a coalition government on a peace platform, soon took over as prime minister. Haig and Robertson (Chief of the Imperial General Staff) were totally committed to the view that Germany should be defeated in battle. Pledged to a policy of total war, and of ceaselessly hitting at the enemy, Lloyd George was responsible for that nadir of British offensive strategy in 1917, the Third Battle of Ypres, popularly known as Passchendaele.

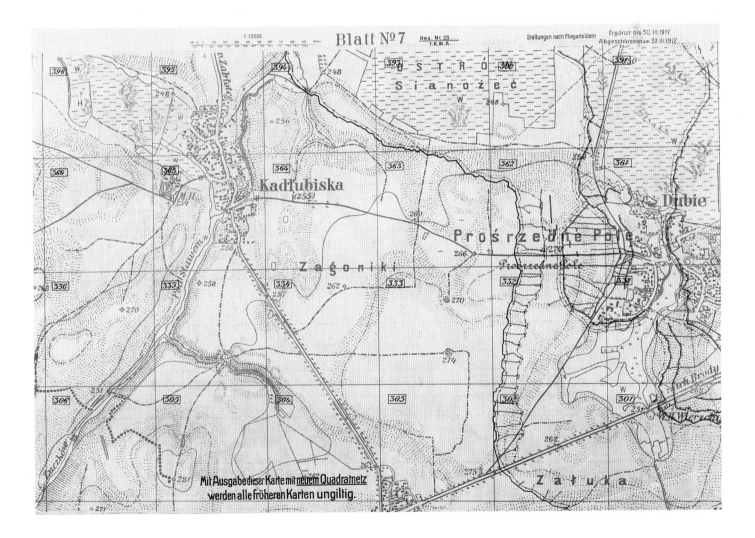

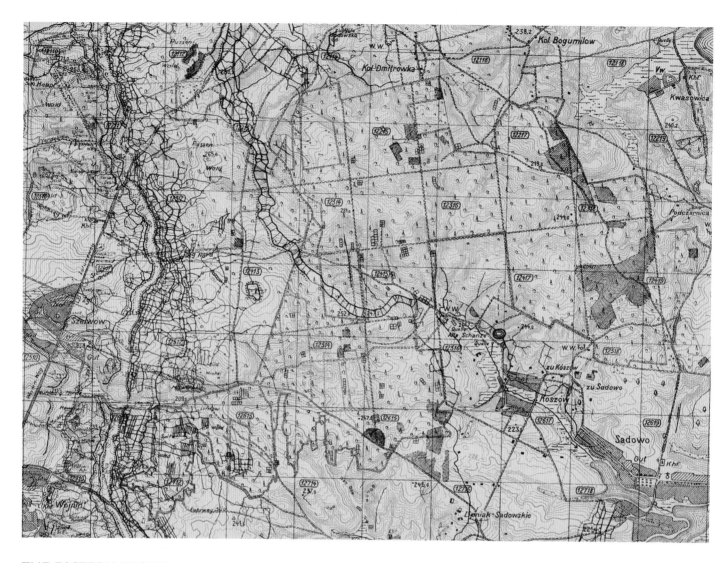

THE EASTERN FRONT

The Rumanian campaign finally ended on 6 December 1916 with the fall of Bucharest. Rumania, with Russian support, only retained a small part of Moldavia. Her fighting capability from now on was minimal, and Russia had little hitting power left. In the West the Germans spoiled Allied plans for their spring offensives by withdrawing to the Hindenburg Line. This shorter line could be held with fewer divisions, the balance either being kept as reserves in the West or deployed against Russia in the East. Germany and her allies were feeling the effects of the blockade, but at least Germany and Austria were soon able to reap the benefit of the agricultural resources of Rumania and the Ukraine.

A great Russian offensive had been scheduled to start on 1 May, as agreed with the Allies. The concentration of reserves and artillery had begun in the late winter and spring, and sixty-two divisions had been assembled by the beginning of March.

However, it was already apparent by then that the army was hardly capable of the planned effort; morale was low and falling, the railway system was in crisis and revolutionary ideas were spreading. In two months the number of deserters soared to two million.

The Russian Revolutions (March and November)

Prefigured by an earlier revolt in 1905, the Russian Revolution had about it a certain inevitability. Tsarist rule was autocratic, and the social system aristocratic, sycophantic and inflexible. Tsar Nicholas II was weak, and his German wife, the Tsarina Alexandra, was a fervent supporter of autocracy and was under the baleful influence of the charismatic monk Rasputin until he was murdered by aristocrats in December 1916. Rigid social barriers prevented the professional and intellectual classes from integrating into the aristocratic elite, and they perceived the power structure as

ABOVE: Revolution in Petrograd: car with soldiers on footboards and mudguards, with red flags on their bayonets during the 1917 October/November Bolshevik coup.

LEFT: German trench map (*Stellungskarte*, 1:25,000), Sadowo, 4 July 1917. The sector, between Vladimir–Volynsk and Luck (Lutsk), of Army Group Linsingen, showing the depth of the trench systems which had solidified towards the end of 1915 after the great Russian retreat. Austro-German trenches blue, Russian trenches red. Traces of these trenches can still be made out on modern satellite imagery.

undemocratic (which it was, despite the parliament or Duma created after the 1905 revolt) and corrupt. The franchise was very limited, ministers could only be appointed by the Tsar and lack of upward mobility created resentment among the middle classes. During the war, men from the lower middle class were admitted to the officer corps, but not socially accepted by the aristocrats. While there was a growing industrial sector, the urban industrial working class were still a small part of the predominantly rural peasant population.

The war had not been going well for Russia; the high command was inefficient and junior officers often brutal to their men, while a vast swathe of territory had been lost, and each year had taken a terrible toll in casualties. In common with much of Europe, the winter of 1916–17 was severe enough to curtail food supplies. These had already been shrinking because of labour shortages caused by conscription and by wartime transport problems. Food shortages, compounded by rising prices, led to strikes. The peasants, hungry and angry, wanted land. The urban population, restive because of falling real wages, demanded bread. By using the slogan 'Peace, Land, Bread', Bolshevik agitators were able to maximize their support from soldiers, urban workers and peasants.

In the cold, short, dark days of early 1917, desperation was growing among Russians. In Petrograd (St Petersburg) bread riots, in which soldiers of the garrison joined, turned into revolution on 8 March. This challenge became a crisis when Cossacks refused to shoot at rioters. Four days later the Soviet (Council of Workers' and Soldiers' Deputies) was set up, which regarded itself as independent of the liberal opposition.

The Soviet quietly planned to undermine the army and seize power. The Tsar, trying to return to Petrograd from his military headquarters, was stopped and turned back. On 15 March the liberals convinced the generals that the Tsar no longer had the support of the army and forced him to abdicate. In Petrograd power was taken by the Soviet. They authorized the appointment of a Provisional Government founded upon principles of liberal constitutionalism and led by Kerensky. This government still supported the prosecution of the war, and had the support of the Allies and the USA. But the Bolsheviks, led by Lenin who was soon to return from in exile in neutral Switzerland, were becoming increasingly powerful within the Soviet. On 6 April, the USA declared war on Germany, and the Germans, perceiving some considerable advantage to their cause, shipped Lenin back to Petrograd across their territory in a sealed train, 'like a bacillus'.

The Central Powers were not just looking on while events unfolded in Petrograd. General Hauer, with artillery support orchestrated by Bruchmüller, the rising star of German offensive operations, captured the Toboly Bridgehead in a surprise counter-attack on 3–7 April. On 1 July 1917, Kerensky, convinced that a military victory was imperative to give his government the authority and credibility it needed within Russia and to impress the Allies, ordered Brusilov, his best general, to attack. At short notice Brusilov unleashed forty-four divisions in an ultimately disastrous offensive against the Austro-German forces in Galicia. While some initial success was achieved, further Russian attempts made no progress as morale collapsed in the supporting formations. The offensive broke down within days, succumbing to violent counter-attacks along the front between Tarnopol and the Carpathians.

A brief quiescent stance by the Allies on the Western Front between the Messines operation on 7–14 June and the opening of the Third Battle of Ypres in July enabled the Germans to transport four divisions from the West to spearhead a counter-attack on 19 July at Tarnopol. Supported by 134 batteries, they delivered a crushing artillery bombardment. This rout was again organized by Bruchmüller who, the following day, was transferred by Hoffmann, Chief-of-Staff of *Oberost*, to the Eighth Army to plan the fire support for the forthcoming northern

attack at Riga (1 September). The Austro-German counter-attacks led to a breakthrough and the retreat, if not the immediate disintegration, of the Russian southern armies. Ironically, what was left of the Rumanian army had by now been reconstructed, and during July and August 1917 it successfully resisted Mackensen's push against the Sereth Line. However, the Bolshevik coup in November and the collapse of Russia forced Rumania to ask for an armistice on 9 December. The subsequent settlement enforced by the Central Powers was punitive.

The Germans were heartened by the success of the July operations in Galicia and even though they were heavily engaged in Flanders from late July, made another attempt to knock out Russia. This was the long-planned offensive by Hutier's Eighth Army, focused on Riga, against Kornilov's Twelfth Army. It followed the Bruchmüller model of a deep and disruptive hurricane bombardment, followed by an overwhelming storm-troop attack and the simultaneous forward move of reserve echelons. Riga was captured on 3 September, and the battle developed into exploitation and pursuit as Kornilov's army retreated rapidly along the Dvina river with the Germans following close on its heels.

This defeat destroyed any remaining Russian morale and cohesion, and shook the Provisional Government and high command. German forces, advancing in Courland, their left flank on the Baltic, now threatened Petrograd itself. Brusilov was dismissed after the failure of his offensive in the south and replaced by Kornilov, while senior Russian officers were now more against the Provisional Government than the Central Powers. The crisis caused by a disobedient army, urban industrial workers in revolt, and peasants' demands for food and bread, all led to the collapse of Kerensky's government and the seizure of power by the Bolsheviks. In October, Lenin, who had prudently left Petrograd for Finland in the summer, returned to Petrograd and took control of events. The Bolshevik coup, or Second Russian Revolution, was mounted on 7 November, after which the Bolsheviks asked the Germans for an armistice, granted on 16 December. This effectively took the Russians out of the war, though the Germans continued to advance to enforce their will, and a punitive peace treaty was finally signed at Brest-Litovsk on 3 March 1918.

LEFT: German trench map (Stellungskarte, 1:25,000), Tarnopol, corrected to 18 November 1917, Austro-German trenches, blue; Russian trenches, red; map corrections, black; woods, green; Tarnopol is off the map, near the top of the blue pecked line on the left. Galicia, part of the Austro-Hungarian Empire, was covered by pre-war Austrian surveys, from which the topographical base of this sheet is derived.

THE WESTERN FRONT

Allied strategy for 1917 had been determined at a conference in November 1916. As in December 1915, the Allies agreed a strategy of simultaneous attacks on all fronts, and also that in 1917 the British contribution would be an attack in Flanders. But events in France soon changed all this. The French had lost confidence in their Commander-in-Chief, Joffre, after the horrifying battles of 1916. Desperate politicians replaced him with the supremely confident, charming and English-speaking Nivelle. After achieving a local success in counter-attacks at Verdun, against an enemy who had already thinned out his forward troops, Nivelle had been hailed in France as a bright new hope. He and his staff claimed to have the formula, based on the 1916 development of the creeping or rolling artillery barrage, to achieve a cheap and quick victory.

Nivelle's plan was based on the grand illusion that he could, by his 'new methods', smash through the German position on the Aisne. He would launch a supremely heavy and violent attack employing twenty-seven divisions and, for the first time in a French battle, tanks. It envisaged the French providing the main war-winning attack, with the other nations merely supplying diversionary attacks – the British, for example, at Arras. The Allied political leaders, shocked by the monstrous casualty lists of the 1916 Verdun and Somme battles and desperate for a speedy solution, were seduced by Nivelle's dubious scheme. Even the hard-bitten and cynical Lloyd George was taken in by Nivelle's assurances of rapid victory. Lloyd George had hitherto vehemently opposed offensives on the Western Front, proposing instead support for attacks in Palestine or Italy. But having met Nivelle after the Rome Conference in January 1917, he invited him to London and was duly convinced. He informed Robertson and Haig that they should follow Nivelle's plan. The generals duly cooperated, but as they were already preparing for their big Flanders offensive, including coastal landings, to drive the Germans from their U-boat bases at Zeebrugge and Ostend, they were not pleased. Lloyd George went further; determined to enforce the status and authority of the British War Cabinet over the generals, he proposed placing Haig under Nivelle's command, effectively subsuming the BEF into the French army. When Nivelle outlined the new command-structure proposals, the shocked British generals rebelled. A compromise was agreed whereby the BEF was only temporarily placed under Nivelle for the duration of the offensive. Henceforth, however, there was great suspicion and mistrust between the British generals and their political masters.

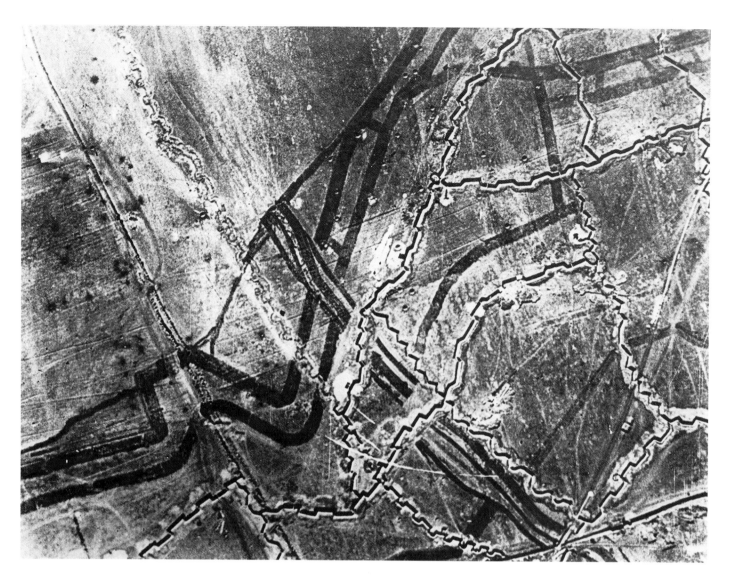

German Retirement

Meanwhile, the Germans knocked away the underpinnings of Nivelle's whole concept by withdrawing to their new, shorter, rear position, the Hindenburg Line. This economized on men, created a formidable and well-sited new defence position, and disrupted Allied preparations. Verdun and the Somme had left the Germans temporarily exhausted, and they had prepared rear defence systems, notably the *Siegfried Stellung* (Hindenburg Line) to which they could retire if Allied pressure continued. The *Siegfried Stellung*, more or less in the centre of all these systems, was eventually only one of a series of highly sophisticated, linked defensive trench positions constructed by the Germans. Ludendorff calculated that the *Siegfried Stellung* saved ten divisions and fifty batteries of heavy artillery from the front line garrison, and shortened the front by nearly thirty miles.

The *Siegfried Stellung* was based on the newly developed German doctrine of elastic defence-in-depth and swift and heavy counter-attacks. The forward zone comprised, on the front, or west, side, a wide and deep trench behind a broad barbed-wire entanglement. This formed an anti-tank ditch, behind which were five or more additional wire entanglements. Then came the deep main, or battle, zone, anchored by forts and blockhouses sheltering machine guns. After this came the rear zone, in which the last major barrier boasted an intricate system of zigzag trenches designed to prevent enfilading fire. Two lines of artillery were sited in the rear zone – on reverse slopes wherever possible – and later in trenches and tunnels. These rear positions, largely constructed by German workers and Russian POWs during the winter of 1916-17 under Operation *Alberich*, were:

Flandern Stellung	Belgian coast to Lille.
Wotan Stellung	Lille to Cambrai.
Siegfried Stellung	Cambrai to St Quentin; this was the strongest of all the positions.
Alberich Stellung	St Quentin to Laon.
Hermann Stellung	East of German Sixth Army.
Hunding Stellung	Craonne (Chemin-des-Dames ridge) to Verdun.
Brunhild Stellung	East of German Third Army, protecting the Champagne front; the northern portion of the *Hunding Stellung* (southern part of which was behind Seventh Army), from near Craonne to near Reims in the Champagne.
Kriemhilde Stellung	East of German Fifth Army; the southern portion of the *Hunding Stellung* (northern part of which was behind Seventh Army), from near Reims to near Verdun.
Michel Stellung	Southward extension of the *Hunding Stellung*, from the Argonne Forest running east of Verdun and then south to Metz.

Operation *Alberich* was the First World War's greatest construction project. It lasted four months, employing over half a million workers, supplied by 1,250 train-loads of material, to dig the trenches and dugouts, and build the reinforced concrete blockhouses. *Alberich's* final phase was the 'scorching' of the intermediate country and the retirement of the troops holding the old front line to the new positions. Photographing these positions, covering a band of terrain from the North Sea to Switzerland, and plotting the new defences from the photographic images onto large-scale maps, was a task which severely challenged the overstretched air forces and survey organisations of the Allies. Superior German aircraft inflicted heavy casualties on the Allied aircraft during their vital photographic sorties.

Allied Command and the Nivelle Plan

Nivelle's original plan for his main attack on a wide frontage between Reims and Roye, targeted at the Chemin-des-Dames ridge in particular, involved some 7,000 guns and over a million men. The British subsidiary attack was to be against Arras and Vimy Ridge. By retiring their line between these points, the Germans had disrupted Allied preparations. (Lapses in French security had helpfully gifted them a complete set of attack plans.) The Allies failed to exploit the German withdrawal through a combination of lack of initiative, bad ground conditions, rearguard actions and booby traps. The withdrawal deprived Nivelle of a third of his attack frontage in the Roye area. While Haig questioned the

ABOVE: Battle of Arras, April 1917. This photograph clearly shows all-arm cooperation: a field battery in action, with tanks, cavalry and infantry moving up. The air element was also present, though for the RFC it was 'bloody April'.

LEFT: Vertical air photo showing German trenches and barbed wire belts, southwest of Wancourt, in the area of the Hindenburg Line. Special tactics, used by the British at Cambrai in November 1917, were developed to get tanks and infantry through such defences.

advisability of going ahead with the attack (he favoured his own offensive in Flanders), Nivelle refused to make any significant changes. His position was weakened by a change of government in France. Painlevé, the new Minister of War, opposed the offensive. So too did the French army commanders who had to execute it – Franchet d'Esperey, Micheler and the saviour of Verdun, Pétain. On 6 April the new French President, Poincaré, with his prime minister and war minister, met Nivelle and his army commanders to find a way forward. Nivelle's offer of resignation was refused, and things proceeded as before.

Battles of Arras and Vimy Ridge

Those who believe that British commanders in the First World War lacked imagination have to contend with some uncomfortable realities. The surprise, hurricane bombardment at Neuve Chapelle in March 1915; the use of gas at Loos in September 1915; the launching of the first tank attack in history on the Somme in September 1916; the thoroughly planned capture of Vimy Ridge in April 1917; the great simultaneous mine explosions at Messines in June 1917; and above all the surprise attack at Cambrai in November 1917, whose success was based on scientific predicted fire as well as a mass tank attack, all give the lie to many of the old

assumptions. The bloody, slogging matches of most of the Somme and Third Ypres (Passchendaele), battles whose only successes were in terms of attrition, have to be set against these.

Before the Battle of Arras, GHQ vehemently opposed a short preliminary bombardment, and removed Allenby's artillery commander, Holland. He had dared to suggest that they could achieve greater surprise through a 48-hour bombardment with shooting based largely on the map. The British bombardment on the Arras–Vimy front began on 4 April, and on 9 April the British Third (Allenby) and First (Horne) Armies jumped off. The latter's Canadian Corps (Byng) seized the heights of Vimy Ridge and the former gained its continuation southwards and a wide area of terrain astride the river Scarpe, east of Arras. Gough's Fifth Army to the south put in a diversionary attack.

The battle opened, despite unseasonable snow and sleet, with a stunningly successful set-piece. This deep and well-planned artillery bombardment used 3,000 guns and howitzers for destruction and neutralization, with a creeping barrage to cover the infantry assault, supported by tanks. Clever use was made of interconnected caves and subways for bringing up the assault troops. The Royal Flying Corps, meanwhile, was suffering heavy losses because of faster German fighters; this was their 'bloody April'. The tanks were little better than those used on the Somme in 1916; they were slow, difficult to manoeuvre, subject to breakdown and ditching, lacked firepower and were particularly vulnerable to direct artillery fire. Of the sixty that were ready in time for 9 April, many broke down or ditched before they reached the front line. While cavalry were brought up to exploit a possible breakthrough, as in all Western Front battles they achieved little, proving all-too-vulnerable to enemy fire when they were used to help capture vital high ground at Monchy-le-Preux, east of Arras.

The gunners and their material had improved substantially since the Somme. There were more and better guns, much more ammunition, of better quality, with more efficient fuses (including the new 106 'burst-on-graze' fuse for wire-cutting and anti-personnel use, which did not crater the ground). The flash-spotting and sound-ranging used to locate the German guns was more effective, as were the survey, calibration and meteorological

techniques that enabled predicted fire. There was also an impressive creeping barrage of great precision. While the artillery intelligence and counter-battery organisation was very effective in the initial phase of the operations – over 90 per cent of German battery positions were located – the flash-spotters and sound-rangers were slow to move forward during the battle, and then had to pinpoint an array of enemy batteries in new positions. The German artillery was not very effective in the early stages of the battle, due to British counter-battery fire and ammunition stocks being kept too far back.

The Canadian Corps, of four divisions, supported by nearly 1,000 guns and mortars that had fired a million shells during the artillery preparation, was particularly successful. Most of Vimy Ridge was captured in a few hours, and this pattern was repeated by Third Army to its south. The four Canadian divisions captured 4,000 prisoners and fifty-four guns in six days, suffering 10,500 casualties in the process, while Third Army, on a wider front, captured 7,000 prisoners and 112 guns.

British infantry tactics had improved since the Somme. They were more flexible and efficient, particularly in their use of supporting waves to 'leap-frog' captured positions. However, while successful set-piece attacks were proving easier to achieve, breaking through was quite another matter, and many subordinate commanders couldn't handle troops in a war of depth and movement. Questions were also raised about the conduct of operations by corps and army commanders. Gough and his Fifth Army staff were not popular, and Allenby, 'the Bull', was faced with a rebellion by some of his divisional commanders. As on the Somme, it was often felt that army and corps staffs were ordering attacks without knowledge of local conditions and without listening to those who had to carry out the attacks. Heavy casualties for little or no gains had become a common experience, and generals had come to feel that if they did not 'drive' their subordinates they would be sacked.

Nivelle Offensive

On 16 April, Nivelle unleashed his great attack on the Aisne involving fifty divisions, 5,000 guns and a complete lack of surprise. The key German position on the Chemin-des-Dames ridge was a tunnelled and galleried fortress, studded with concrete pillboxes and protected gun positions. The threat of attack had been countered by defence-in-depth reinforced with a mass of new, more mobile, machine guns, covered by counter-attack divisions, and finally by a spoiling attack on 4–5 April. Most of the French infantry jumped off with a great spirit, quite surprising after the 1916 battles, but many, particularly African troops, were

TOP LEFT: British trench map, Arras, with German trenches corrected to 4 March 1917, showing in manuscript the barrage and tank routes for 6th Corps' attack on 9 April 1917, the first day of the Battle of Arras, as far east as the Wancourt–Feuchy Line (the German *Monchy–Riegel*); 6th Corps attacked with 3rd, 12th and 15th Divisions.

BOTTOM LEFT: French St Chamond tank, armed with a 75-mm gun, at Condé-sur-Aisne, 3 May 1917, during the Nivelle Offensive.

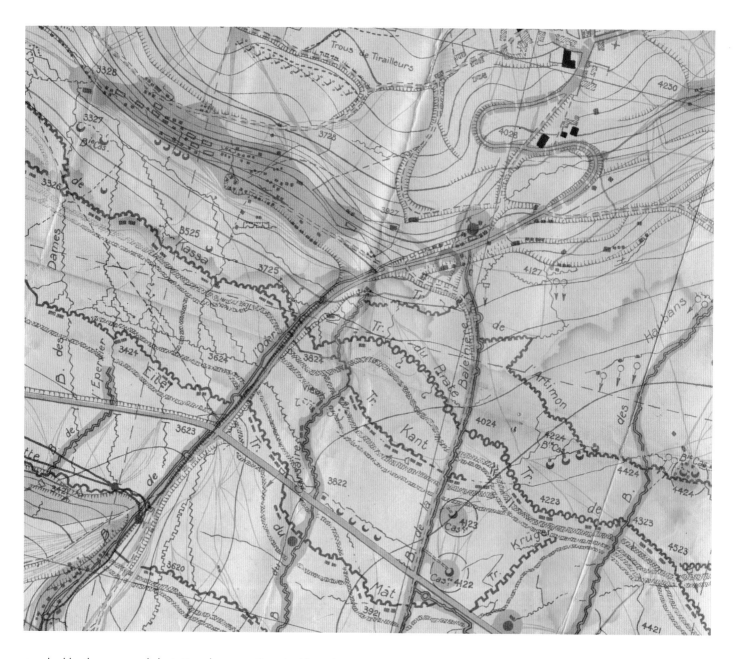

numbed by the snow and sleet. French preparations had been less than thorough, the artillery bombardment had been much less effective than promised and the many surviving German machine gunners mowed down the attackers.

The eighty new French tanks were delayed by bad terrain, arrived too late for the exhausted infantry to rally to them in new attacks and were soon targeted by the German artillery, often being turned into fireballs by direct hits. German air superiority caused a failure of French artillery cooperation and, as at Verdun in 1916, the gunners often bombarded their own infantry. Towards the end of April another French attack was made along the thirty-

ABOVE: French tactical intelligence map of 25 February 1917 of the Chemin-des-Dames ridge ahead of the Nivelle Offensive, with German trenches and batteries in blue, wire entanglements in purple, dugouts, pillboxes, machine guns, etc., in red and tracks in yellow ochre.

TOP RIGHT: French trench map (plan directeur, 1:10,000), 9 June 1917, of the Mort Homme area, French trenches in red, German trenches in blue. The French recaptured the Mort Homme later that year.

BOTTOM RIGHT: The French offensive at Verdun in 1917 retook the Mort Homme and Côte 304. German trenches are in blue, and French in red. This plan of 19 August 1917 shows the zones bombarded, partially and completely destroyed by French artillery fire prior to the attack.

five-mile front, advancing four miles in one sixteen-mile sector and capturing 29,000 prisoners and 150 guns. The new German defence organization had been thoroughly systematized, and a huge investment in machine guns, concrete and artillery achieved greater success here in the defensive battle than at Vimy Ridge and at Messines Ridge in June. French casualties rose to horrifying levels – perhaps 120,000 men were lost in the first few days. Total French casualties for the battle, which continued into May, were some 187,000 against 163,000 German. The Germans counter-attacked from the start, much ground gained by the French was quickly lost and the battle dragged on.

The shock to the nervous system of the French army was staggering. Its morale terribly weakened by the experience, the army soon erupted in manifestations of 'collective indiscipline', if not outright mutiny. The infantry expressed themselves willing to hold the line, but not to be massacred in hopeless attacks. Nivelle was sacked and replaced by Pétain who, on 28 April, had been made Chief of Staff, and was given the task of nursing the army back to health. Sixty-eight of the 112 French divisions were affected but Pétain managed to rebuild morale by visiting them, by instituting more leave and better rations, and by establishing for the present a defensive policy. Only about sixty mutineers were executed. Later in the year the French army was capable of carrying out attacks at Ypres at the end of July, to recapture Côte 304 and the Mort Homme on Verdun's left bank on 20 August, and at Fort Malmaison on the Chemin-des-Dames ridge on 24 October.

Battle of Messines

During the first half of May the British kept up the pressure on the Arras front, and after that north of the Vimy Ridge against Lens. The first phase of Haig's Flanders offensive began at the end of May when Second Army's massive preliminary bombardment began against the German positions on the Armentières–Ypres front, and on 7 June the Battle of Messines opened. The ultimate aim of Haig's offensive was to clear the Belgian coast, eliminate the German submarine bases at Zeebrugge and Ostend, and force a German withdrawal from northern Belgium.

The capture of the Messines–Wytschaete Ridge, taken by the Germans at the end of October 1914, would eliminate the southern half of the Ypres salient, and would not only provide a secure flank for the forthcoming attack at Ypres but also superb observation posts for the British artillery and the flash-spotters locating the German batteries. British Royal Engineers tunnelling companies had for two years been driving deep mine galleries through the blue clay under selected German strong-points in advance of the

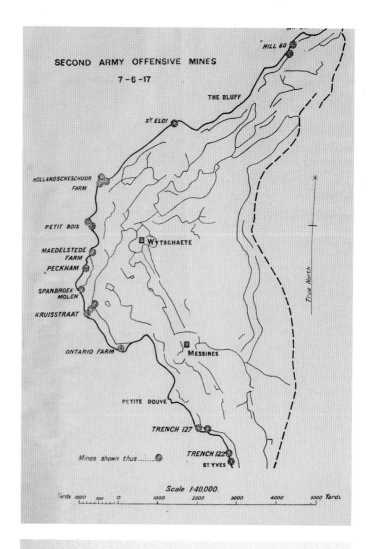

ABOVE: Diagram of Messines Ridge, 7 June 1917. Nineteen great mines were blown at zero under German strong-points. Most of the craters can still be seen.

RIGHT: *Enemy Dispositions, Second Army Front, 4 June 1917*, overprinted in red. The secret map prepared by Second Army Intelligence, shows the situation just before the Messines battle, which opened on 7 June.

main ridge. Many of these mines had been ready and charged a year earlier, but the operation planned for 1916 had been postponed. The deep mines were a well-kept secret, and although the Germans were aware of some mining, and had considered pulling back to a rear position, they had no idea of the real scale of the operation. They knew an attack was coming, for the artillery bombardment started twelve days before the assault, and the barrages were rehearsed during this period.

This attack was to be Vimy Ridge plus mines. The explosion of nineteen huge mines, containing 500 tons of high-explosive,

C.D.C Corps Command.

PART OF SECOND ARMY FRONT.

ENEMY DISPOSITIONS SECOND ARMY FRONT.

JUNE 4th, 1917.

DIVISIONS IN LINE.

195th DIV. (PRUSSIAN). Good troops. Two regiments of Jägers. Division arrived from Galicia end of April, when they came into line; has not much experience of hard fighting.

204th DIV. (WURTTEMBERG). Fair troops. Only the 120th Res. Regiment has had much fighting experience. Division formed June, 1916, and has remained in Ypres salient since October, 1916.

35th DIV. (PRUSSIAN). Moderate division. Contains some Poles. Lost heavily on the Somme. Fought near Arras in April, 1917. Into line end of May.

2nd DIV. (E. PRUSSIAN). Division in Russia until February, 1917, and came into line in April. Was in many successful engagements Tannenberg, etc. Has shown little spirit or enterprise on Western Front; its morale, although improved lately, is not high.

40th DIV. (SAXON). Good Division when fighting on the defensive, but passive in attitude like all Saxon Corps. Losses on Somme estimated 70% of establishment. Has been on Messines front since Nov., 1916.

4th BAV. DIV. (BAVARIAN). A good division. Seen considerable amount of fighting, including Somme. Opposite this Army front since Sept. 1916.

DIVISIONS IN RESERVE.

11th DIV. (SILESIAN). Not a good division. Suffered very heavily on the Somme and on the Scarpe in April. Contains number of Poles who desert frequently. Came middle of May.

23rd RES DIV. (SAXON). Had good reputation early in the war but not distinguished itself since. Was engaged on the Somme and came here from Arras Battle in April.

3rd BAV. DIV. (BAVARIAN). The remarks re 4th Bavarian Division also apply to this division. Was also engaged heavily at Arras and returned end of May.

24th DIV. (SAXON). Sister division to the 40th Division (XIX Saxon Corps). Same remarks also apply.

COMPOSITION OF DIVISIONS THOUGHT TO BE IN RESERVE.

24th Division	179 I.R. 133 I.R. 139 I.R.	Withdrawn from Wytschaete end of May.
23rd Res. Div.	100 Res. Grenadier Regt. 102 R.I.R. 392 I.R.	Withdrawn from Boesinghe end of May
11th Division	10 Grenadier Regiment 38 Fusilier Regiment 51 I.R.	
3rd Bav. Divn.	17 Bavarian I.R. 18 23	

TWO DIVISIONS from Russia have arrived in Belgium but have not yet been identified; possibly one may be the 1ST RESERVE DIVISION (prisoner's statement, June 4th) composition: 1 R.I.R., 3 R.I.R. and 59 R.I.R.

REFERENCE.

Divisional Boundaries	
Regimental Boundaries	
Regimental Headquarters	
Battalion Headquarters	
Companies	

195TH DIV.

204TH DIV.

35TH DIV.

2ND DIV.

40TH DIV.

4TH BAV. DIV.

16TH BAV. DIV.

YPRES

8 JAG. R.

6 JAG. R.

120 R.

414 I.R.

413 I.R.

61

176

141

44 I.R.

33 FUS R.

4 GREN R.

104 I.R.

181 I.R.

134 I.R.

9 BAV I.R.

5 BAV.I.R.

21 BAV. R.I.R.

14 BAV. R.I.R.

233 I.R.

ONE BN. RESTING AT MOORENHOEK. REGT. HDQ. ALSO THERE

8 JAG. R.

ONE BN. RESTING AT TERHAND

6 JAG. R.

120 R.

414

413 AT WERVICQ

61 AT WERVICQ

44 AT WERVICQ

141 176

4 GREN. 33 FUS.

104 181

134

9 BAV. I.R.

I BN. S.E. OF QUESNOY

5 BAV. I.R.

I BN. IN WAMBRECHIES

21 BAV R.I.R.

I BN. IN MARQUETTE

OOSTTAVERNE LINE

WARNETON LINE

2ND I.S.Co. 2118 4-6-17

Scale 1:40000

2ND ARMY INTELLIGENCE

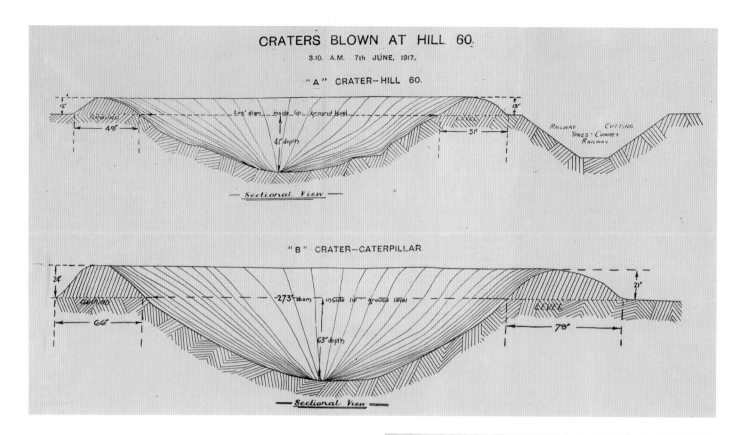

CRATERS BLOWN AT HILL 60.

3.10. A.M. 7th JUNE, 1917.

"A" CRATER—HILL 60.

— Sectional View —

"B" CRATER—CATERPILLAR.

— Sectional View —

on the morning of 7 June, signalled the infantry assault. This was covered by a devastating series of creeping and standing barrages and intense, neutralizing counter-battery fire by the British artillery, which had already taken a heavy toll of the German batteries in the preliminary bombardment. The devastating effect of the mines surprised and shocked the German defenders, while the attacking infantry were supported by tanks, overhead machine gun fire, gas bombardment and burning oil drums projected onto the enemy positions. The attack was a complete success, marred later only by heavy casualties when supporting troops crowded the top of the ridge in full view of German machine gunners on the plain to the east. From Ploegsteert Wood in the south to Hill 60 near Ypres in the north, the Germans were forced back, and soon withdrew further to better-sited defence positions.

Third Battle of Ypres

Despite the need to keep pressure on the Germans to divert their attention from the mutinous French army, to assist the troubled Russian Kerensky Offensive and to strike again in Flanders before the German defences became even stronger, there was a disastrous delay between the Messines attack and the start of the main offensive at Ypres. Worse, Haig gave the responsibility

ABOVE: Elevation of Craters blown at Hill 60 at 3.10 a.m. on 7 June 1917 ('A' Crater–Hill 60 and 'B' Crater–Caterpillar). These were two of the nineteen mines blown at zero hour under the German front line. These huge craters are still key features of this memorialized landscape.

RIGHT: *Second Army Barrage Map, June 1917, Secret,* overprinted in blue. One of the sheets of the barrage map for the Battle of Messines, 7 June 1917, showing the field artillery fireplan for 9th Corps (36th, 16th and 19th Divisions).

of spearheading the attack to the young, impetuous Gough's Fifth Army, rather than to the older and more cautious Plumer and his Second Army. Plumer's Chief-of-Staff, Harington, was respected as most efficient, unlike Malcolm, Gough's equivalent. The Germans, meanwhile, made a spoiling attack at Nieuport, on the coast, on 10 July, which eliminated the Allied bridgehead intended to be the launching place for an attack along the coast to link up with planned landings further east. The coastal operations were later abandoned when the attack at Ypres bogged down.

Allied preparations for the Ypres offensive continued. Roads and railways were pushed up to the front; causeways and bridges for transport, guns and tanks were built across the canal north and south of Ypres; batteries and ammunition dumps established; and hospitals and hutted camps extended. From

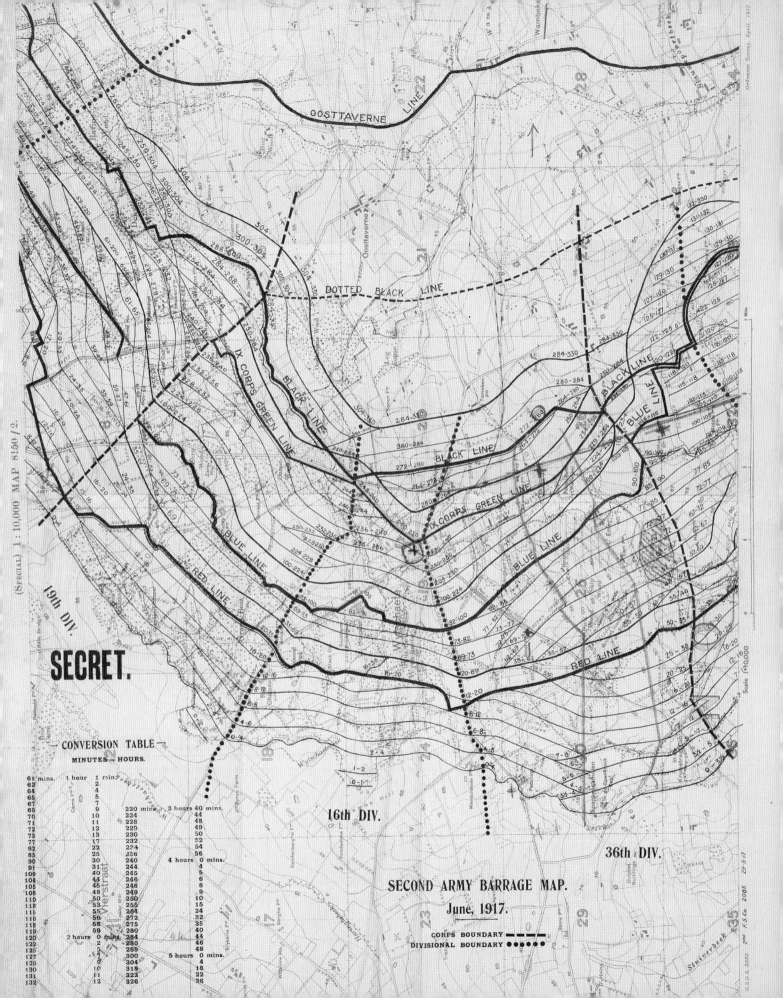

SECRET.

SECOND ARMY BARRAGE MAP.

June, 1917.

CORPS BOUNDARY -----
DIVISIONAL BOUNDARY ••••••••

19th DIV.

16th DIV.

36th DIV.

CONVERSION TABLE

MINUTES = HOURS.

their positions on the ridge east of Ypres the Germans could see much of this, and they also had the evidence of their aerial photographic reconnaissance and of their artillery intelligence organization. The German flash-spotters (*Lichtmesstrupps*) and sound-rangers (*Schallmesstrupps*) located more and more Allied batteries in action, and still more were identified on aerial photographs by their distinctive signatures. In some areas of the Ypres Salient, the British batteries were packed so closely together that the Germans targeted them en masse with 'area shoots', which harrowed the whole battery zone with high explosive and drenched it with mustard gas. British counter-battery fire began early in July, and the main Allied artillery preparation (Anthoine's French First Army were on the northern flank facing the Houthulst Forest) lasted for a stupendous eighteen days, so the Germans were in no doubt as to what was coming. Despite their firepower, and the grinding artillery duel, the Allies failed to locate many of the German batteries, and never mastered the German guns before the battle or during it.

The long delay before the bombardment began at Ypres sacrificed what little surprise had been left after all this preparation

work. The delay was caused by the need to bring up French and British artillery from the south, and it gave the Germans a breathing space to further strengthen their already formidable Flanders positions – strongly wired and studded with concrete pillboxes built into trenches and the ruins of farm buildings. While Haig's original plan was for a step-by-step attack with the infantry never advancing beyond the range of its supporting artillery, Gough was now encouraged to envisage a rapid breakthrough, smashing across the German defences to the Passchendaele

ABOVE: Australian officers and men on a duckboard track through the shell-blasted remains of Chateau Wood, Hooge, east of Ypres, on 29 October 1917. This had once been a picturesque area of sun-dappled greenery, close to the chateau and its decorative gardens, ponds and lake. Plank roads and duckboard tracks formed the main communications over the mud.

RIGHT: *Ypern. Paasche's Specialkarten der Westfront*, September 1916; a detail showing the Ypres Salient, with the line after the Third Battle of Ypres (July to November 1917), and other actions, in manuscript. Scale of original: 1:105,000.

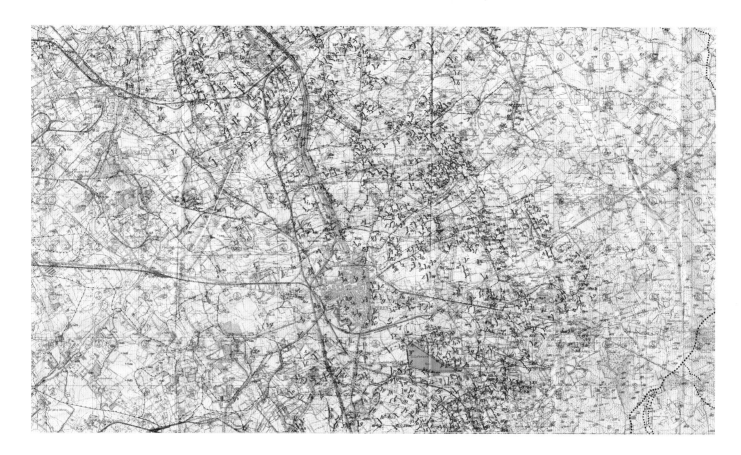

Ridge in four days (it eventually took three months) and launching the cavalry towards the key railway junctions of Roulers, Thourout and Bruges.

One of the supreme ironies of the Flanders offensive was the creation by the British Army of its own worst obstacle; the artillery preparation and covering barrages cut up the country so much that tanks were soon not able to operate effectively, and ultimately had to be withdrawn from the battle (at least those which had not become totally bogged down). Field guns sank beneath the mud, their position only marked by red flags, and the infantry suffered worst of all and even drowned in the mud. Units found it difficult to locate their positions in the wasteland, even after the close study of maps, aerial photographs and models, and the multiplicity of similar concrete blockhouses or pillboxes caused confusion as to which was the objective for a particular attack. Many of these had been so well covered with earth before the attack that they were not shown on the maps. Position-finding was impossible when no fixed points could be recognized from which to take bearings. Divisions detailed parties of sappers to follow up attacks and plant signboards with names and map references on prominent points.

The use of tanks to capture the Gheluvelt Plateau, the central feature of the Ypres Salient, had long been envisaged, and some

of the problems had been foreseen. Special topographical and 'soil', or 'going' maps, showing where water would collect in the event of heavy rain, or the destruction of the drainage system, or both, were prepared by the Tank Corps, and by Fifth Army's field survey company at their instigation. The bombardment created a terrible obstacle for tanks and infantry in the form of a crater field which, soaked by rain and the spreading streams or beeks, turned into swamp. Hotblack of the Tank Corps monitored the damage to the ground done by the preliminary bombardment that began on 16 July (counter-battery work had begun on 7 July), and arranged for aerial photographs to be taken of the operational area. Information was also obtained from local inhabitants, refugees and the Belgian authorities. He daily plotted the spread of the 'swamp area' of the Steenbeek river onto a large-scale 'swamp map,' with wet areas marked in blue, and Plasticine models were also kept up-to-date. He sent copies of the swamp map to GHQ to try to convince the Army staff that tank operations in the area were futile; the response from Fifth Army was ostrich-like: 'Send us no more of these ridiculous maps.' The 'swamp maps' were produced into November. The Tank Corps prepared its own maps after reference to the geologists at GHQ, geological considerations often being crucial when considering moving tanks over the

ground. Many tanks became bogged down in the waterlogged, soft, sandy clay east of Ypres.

The assault went in on 31 July, and was partly successful in that it captured the Pilckem Ridge, northeast of Ypres. But the vital high ground of the Gheluvelt Plateau and Menin Road Ridge, which the Germans recognized as the key to the whole position, resisted attempts by the British 2nd Corps infantry and tanks to capture it. Gough's staff had not given the attack in this crucial sector sufficient weight and, appallingly, the centre division (30th Division) of the three allotted for its capture had been recognized as exhausted before the attack but had not been replaced.

According to their new doctrine, the Germans held their forward zone lightly, relying on defence-in-depth, with scattered

machine gun posts giving interlocking and supporting fields of fire. Counter-attack divisions waited further back to assault once the thinned and exhausted Allied infantry had reached their objective but before they had had time to consolidate. In this, timing was everything. The main German position was on the high ground, with artillery and reserves behind the ridge in dead ground, beyond the observation and reach of most Allied artillery. Where the crucial high ground was close to the front, as at Hooge on the western edge of the Gheluvelt Plateau, the German pillboxes, machine guns and anti-tank guns were denser on the ground and deployed closer to the front, as well as in depth. If the main position was captured, the counter-attack divisions had to wrest it back and, as on the Somme, it was often the high casualties suffered by these divisions, once the British machine guns and artillery had adapted their tactics to meet them, which contributed most to German losses. The Germans had also constructed several well-wired rear positions, extending many miles back, studded with concrete pillboxes for machine guns and troop shelters, and regarded the whole Flanders defensive zone as capable of resisting an attack. British ideas of the cavalry pouring through a gap showed that certain generals had not grasped the reality of the German defences,

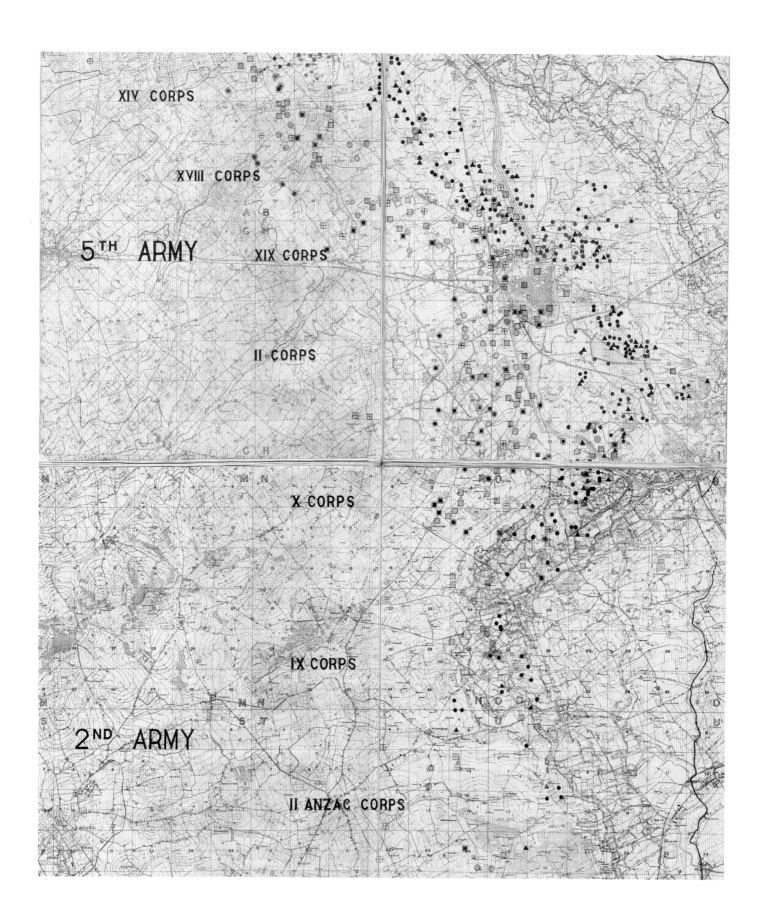

XIV CORPS

XVIII CORPS

5TH ARMY   XIX CORPS

II CORPS

X CORPS

IX CORPS

2ND ARMY

II ANZAC CORPS

LEFT: British Artillery Dispositions for the Third Battle of Ypres, 31 July 1917 (Haig's HQ map). Gough's Fifth Army batteries in red, and Plumer's Second Army's in blue. Different signs are used for batteries of different types and calibres. A large proportion of all these batteries could easily be located by the Germans. The base map shows the German trenches before the Messines attack of 7 June.

ABOVE: Derelict British tanks in the 'Tank Graveyard' at Clapham Junction, on the Menin Road east of Hooge, on 23 September 1917, during the Third Battle of Ypres. Tanks were particularly susceptible to ditching, bogging and shell-fire – sometimes all three.

BELOW: British transport wrecked by German shell fire, on the Westhoek Ridge in the devastated landscape of the Ypres Salient during the Third Battle of Ypres, September to October 1917.

despite excellent reports by Second Army Intelligence during the year before the battle.

Ground was another factor in halting the advance. The prolonged Allied artillery bombardment had destroyed the ground surface and the drainage system and, when the rain started on the afternoon of 31 July, pools of water collected as the Tank Corps staff had predicted. Over the next few days, as the rain continued, tanks, horses, guns and men began to sink into the churned mud. In the shattered and tangled woods around Hooge and on the high ground of the Menin Road Ridge, troops found it difficult to keep direction and make progress. The tanks, negotiating the narrow defiles between the woods, became ditched in old trenches or bogged down in shell holes, and were easy targets for German anti-tank fire. The German gunners on the Somme had begun to use captured Russian field guns

in the direct-fire anti-tank role, but any gun, howitzer or even mortar could easily destroy or disable these slow, thinly armoured machines. In the notorious 'Tank Graveyard' at Clapham Junction, on the Menin Road southeast of Hooge, seventeen tanks were soon knocked out, many by one anti-tank gun in a giant concrete blockhouse.

ABOVE: A vertical air photo of the Tank Graveyard at Clapham Junction, Ypres Salient, 9 August 1917, showing the 'confluent smallpox' terrain, pitted with millions of shell-holes.

RIGHT: Corpses around a pill-box at Stirling.Castle, Ypres Salient, during the Battle of the Menin Road Ridge (part of the Third Ypres battle), 20 September 1917. Casualties from shell-fire formed the majority of battlefield casualties.

The Germans took advantage of the shell-pocked terrain to develop a new defence system, based on 'organized shell holes', which replaced the old linear trenches. These defended shell hole zones were, at first, difficult to locate on aerial photographs, but the interpreters soon learned how to identify them on large-scale, low-altitude photographs by the squared-out modifications to some holes, and by the tracks made by men moving from the rear and between holes. Often the helmets of the occupants, which reflected light very well, could also be identified. When located, these zones were subjected to special bombardments.

Throughout much of August the rain continued, turning the ground into even more of a quagmire and preventing the Allies from developing the operations. Attempts by 2nd Corps to advance further onto the Gheluvelt Plateau all failed, as did the many minor attacks on the flanks. The beeks broke their banks,

trenches and shell holes flooded, and men who sank into the mud could often not be pulled out. Many of the wounded drowned, as did men who fell off the duckboard tracks which replaced communication trenches in this slough of despond. A big attack, the Battle of Langemarck, was launched on 16 August but made little progress. The rain now stopped, and by 20 August the ground was dry enough for a few tanks to operate and help the infantry to get forward, capturing some concrete strong-points. But little progress was made on the Plateau, where the German defences were thickest.

The battle had reached a turning point. From 24 August Haig, very disappointed by the failures so far, and aware that ugly rumours had reached London, took a firmer grip of the operations which had been floundering under Gough. He transferred control of the next phase of the battle to Plumer's Second Army, which

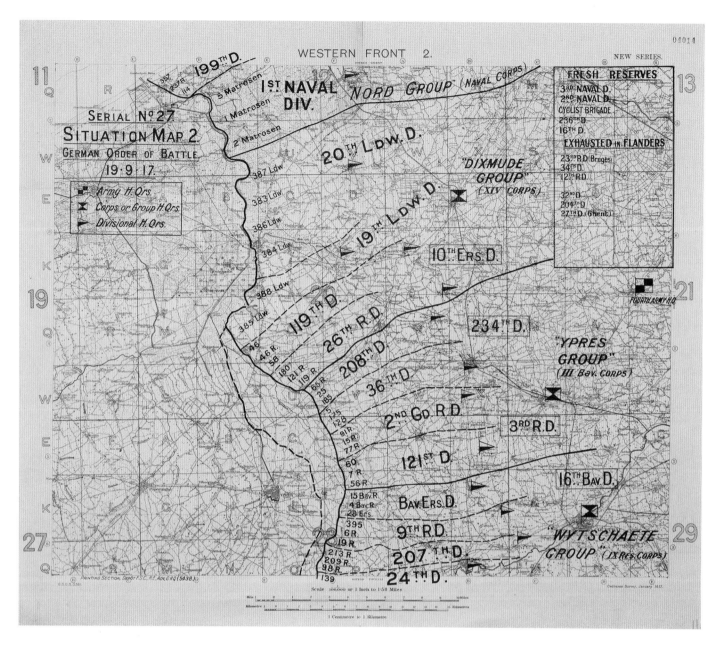

WESTERN FRONT 2.

199TH D.

1ST NAVAL DIV.

"NORD GROUP" (NAVAL CORPS)

5 Matrosen
1 Matrosen
2 Matrosen

SERIAL Nº 27.
SITUATION MAP 2.
GERMAN ORDER OF BATTLE.
19·9·17.

■ Army H.Qrs.
✕ Corps or Group H.Qrs.
➤ Divisional H.Qrs.

20TH Ldw. D.

"DIXMUDE GROUP" (XIV CORPS)

387 Ldw.
383 Ldw.
386 Ldw.
384 Ldw.
388 Ldw.
385 Ldw.

19TH Ldw. D.

10TH Ers. D.

119TH D.

26TH R.D.

234TH D.

"YPRES GROUP" (III Bav. CORPS)

FRESH RESERVES
3RD NAVAL D.
2ND NAVAL D.
CYCLIST BRIGADE
236TH D.
16TH D.

EXHAUSTED IN FLANDERS
23RD R.D. (Bruges)
34TH D.
12TH R.D.
32ND D.
204TH D.
27TH D. (Ghent)

FOURTH ARMY H.Q.

208TH D.

36TH D.

2ND Gd. R.D.

3RD R.D.

121ST D.

16TH Bav. D.

Bav. Ers. D.

9TH R.D.

207TH D.

24TH D.

"WYTSCHAETE GROUP" (IX Res. CORPS)

46
46 R.
58
180
121 R.
119 R.
66 R.
25
185
5
128
91 R.
152
77 R.
60
7 R.
56 R.
15 Bav. R.
4 Bav. R.
28 Ers.
395
6 R.
19 R.
213 R.
209 R.
98 R.
139

PRINTING SECTION, DEPOT F.S.C., R.E. ADV. G.H.Q.(5438.)
G.S.G.S. 3361

Scale 100000 or 1 Inch to 1·58 Miles

Ordnance Survey, January 1917.

1 Centimetre to 1 Kilometre

11 Q R
12
13
W E
K G
19 Q M
27 Q R M
21
29

took over the crucial central area (2nd Corps front) from Fifth Army. This phase was a series of set-piece attacks, each with overwhelming artillery support, with gaps between them for guns and ammunition to be moved up. Plumer asked for, and got, three weeks to make his meticulous preparations. The Battle of the Menin Road Ridge (20 September), Battle of Polygon Wood (26 September), and Battle of Broodseinde, (4 October) succeeded in gaining much of the high ground and defeating German counter-attacks, but an important section of the ridge from Broodseinde northeast to Passchendaele, Westroosebeke and Staden remained in enemy hands. Meanwhile the coastal landings

had been abandoned, the Germans were constructing further rear defence lines and there appeared no prospect of breaking through to clear the coast.

The weather now broke again and by the next attack on 9 October (Battle of Poelcappelle) the shell-churned battlefield had been transformed into a stinking, nightmare morass of wreckage, bodies and water. Field gun and small-arms ammunition, water and rations had to be carried up, on mules or by men, by duckboard tracks which had long supplanted communication trenches. Metalled roads had completely disappeared, and were replaced by beech-plank roads which could support the weight of

LEFT: *Western Front 2, scale 1:100,000*, overprinted in red with German dispositions on 19 September 1917 at a critical stage of Third Battle of Ypres, on the eve of Plumer's great series of attacks starting on 20 September (Battle of the Menin Road Ridge).
BELOW: Exhausted Australian soldiers sheltering in the railway cutting near Tyne Cott, 11 October 1917, during the First Battle of Passchendaele. The ground was drier and firmer here on the higher ground of the Broodseinde–Passchendaele Ridge.

field guns, ammunition wagons and their horse teams, and ambulances and limbers. Light railways and narrow-gauge 'foreways' were constructed to carry ammunition to medium- and heavy-gun positions, and getting guns forward through the mud was almost impossible away from the main roads along which the heavy batteries were arrayed. These concentrations of British guns made easy targets for the German artillery, firing in enfilade so that if they missed one gun or battery they would hit the next.

As the attack on 9 October was a bloody failure, largely because of uncut barbed wire, the rain and ground conditions, the Anzacs were brought up to capture the remaining German-held part of the Passchendaele Ridge. The First Battle of Passchendaele, starting on 12 October, achieved little. Vast areas of the battlefield

west of the ridge had become impassable swamps, and the attackers were restricted to the higher and dryer ground on the narrow spurs, commanded by German machine gunners in pillboxes and shell-holes. The exhausted Anzacs were replaced by the Canadian Corps, with its magnificent record of success at Vimy Ridge in April, and at Hill 70 near Lens in August. Now it was the Canadians' turn to attack the German positions in and around the destroyed village of Passchendaele, which over the last few months had been gradually pulverized by shellfire, in the Second Battle of Passchendaele (26 October–10 November).

Now the remaining stubs of wall were ground into the mud by the artillery, and when the village was captured on 6 November all that remained was a heap of rubble where the church had been. The Canadians worked their way up the spurs onto the drier ground of the ridge, and pushed beyond the village to establish infantry, machine gun and observation posts, and strong-points, to repel the inevitable counter-attacks. Their success was helped by an accurate barrage, a near-miraculous achievement in such appalling ground conditions. Gun platforms had to be constructed, survey carried out (extremely difficult when most landmarks had disappeared) and ammunition laboriously brought up over the exposed and waterlogged wasteland. From their new position the

Canadians had an excellent view of the Flanders plain to the east, but northwards the Germans still held the ridge towards Westroosebeke and Staden.

While the Canadian achievement had been magnificent, the result of the later phases of the Third Battle of Ypres had been to create an even more acute and vulnerable salient jutting into the German Flanders position. With its terrible and exposed ground conditions, it formed a much longer line to hold and exacerbated British manpower shortages. GHQ recognized that it could probably not be held against a strong German attack, and in April 1918, under German pressure in the Battle of the Lys, ordered a withdrawal to a more defensible line close to the ruins of Ypres. In the ghoulish balance of attrition, the casualty figures were, as usual, difficult to establish. British casualties had been perhaps 280,000, and German 240,000.

The Battle of Cambrai

The attack at Cambrai on 20 November was based on the key principle of surprise. This was achieved through predicted artillery fire and tanks, rather than bombardment, destroying the wire. The Tank Corps, during the Ypres operations, had looked for more

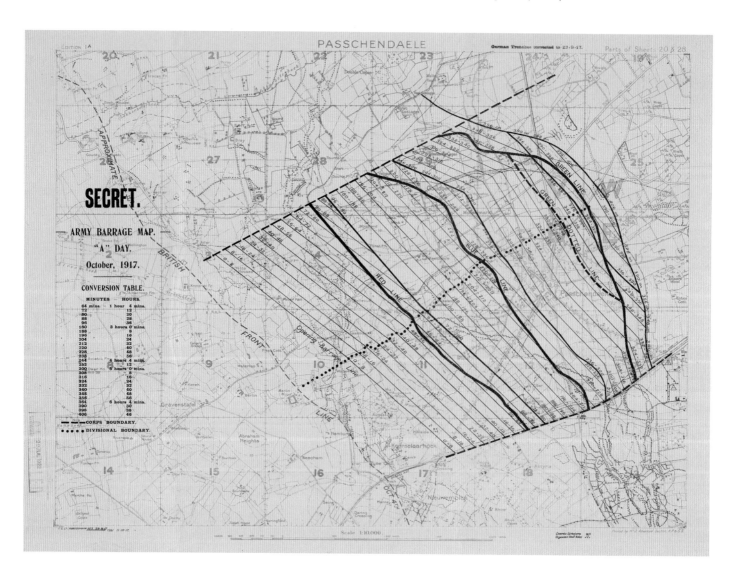

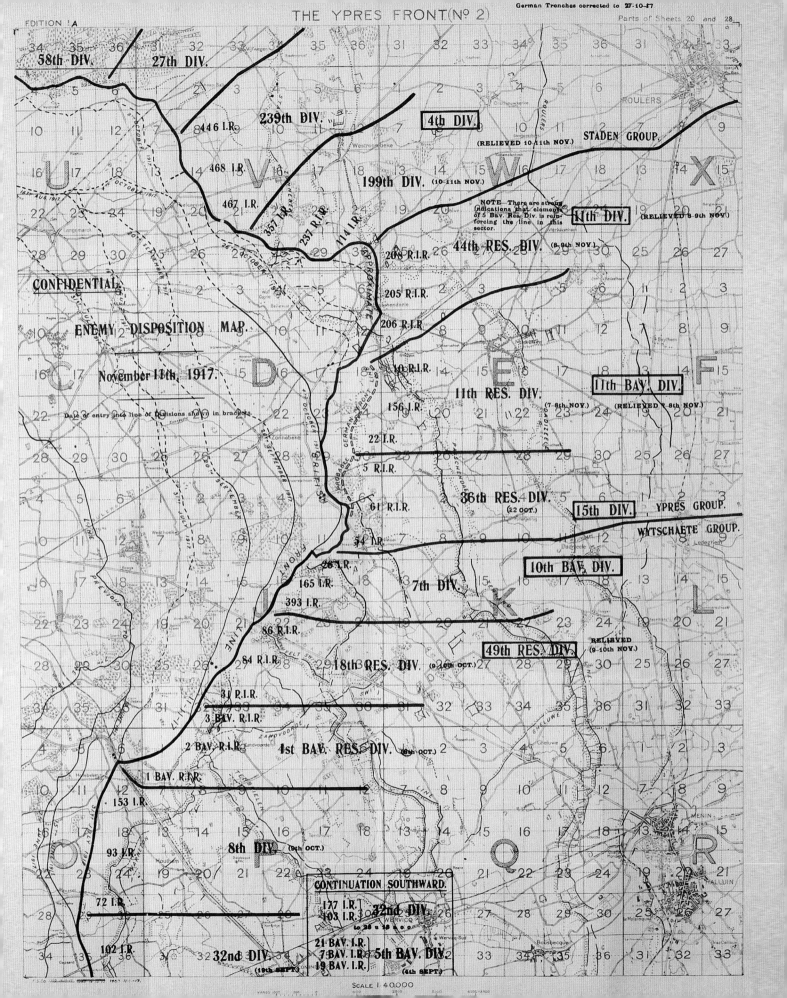

EDITION A

58th DIV.   27th DIV.

239th DIV.

4th DIV.
(RELIEVED 10/11th NOV.)   STADEN GROUP.

ROULERS

U   V   W   X

199th DIV. (10-11th NOV.)

11th DIV.
(RELIEVED 8-9th NOV.)

8446 I.R.

468 I.R.

467 I.R.

357 I.R.

237 R.I.R.

114 I.R.

208 R.I.R.

NOTE.—There are strong indications that elements of 5 Bav. Res. Div. is reinforcing the line in this sector.

44 RES. DIV. (8-9th NOV.)

205 R.I.R.

206 R.I.R.

CONFIDENTIAL

ENEMY DISPOSITION MAP.

November 11th, 1917.

C   D   E   F

10 R.I.R.

11th RES. DIV.

11th BAY. DIV.
(7-8th NOV.)   (RELIEVED 7-8th NOV.)

156 I.R.

22 I.R.

5 R.I.R.

Dates of entry into line of Divisions shown in brackets.

61 R.I.R.

36th RES. DIV.
(22 OCT.)

15th DIV.   YPRES GROUP.

WYTSCHAETE GROUP.

34 I.R.

26 I.R.

165 I.R.

7th DIV.

393 I.R.

10th BAY. DIV.

I   J   K   L

86 R.I.R.

84 R.I.R.

18th RES. DIV. (9-10th OCT.)

49th RES. DIV.

RELIEVED
(9-10th NOV.)

31 R.I.R.

3 BAV. R.I.R.

2 BAV. R.I.R.

1st BAV. RES. DIV. (19th OCT.)

1 BAV. R.I.R.

153 I.R.

93 I.R.

MENIN

O   P   Q   R

8th DIV. (9th OCT.)

HALLUIN

72 I.R.

CONTINUATION SOUTHWARD.

177 I.R.
103 I.R.

32nd DIV.
WERVICQ

21 BAV. I.R.

5th BAV. DIV.

102 I.R.

32nd DIV.
(19th SEPT.)

7 BAV. I.R.

19 BAV. I.R.
(4th SEPT.)

SCALE 1:40.000

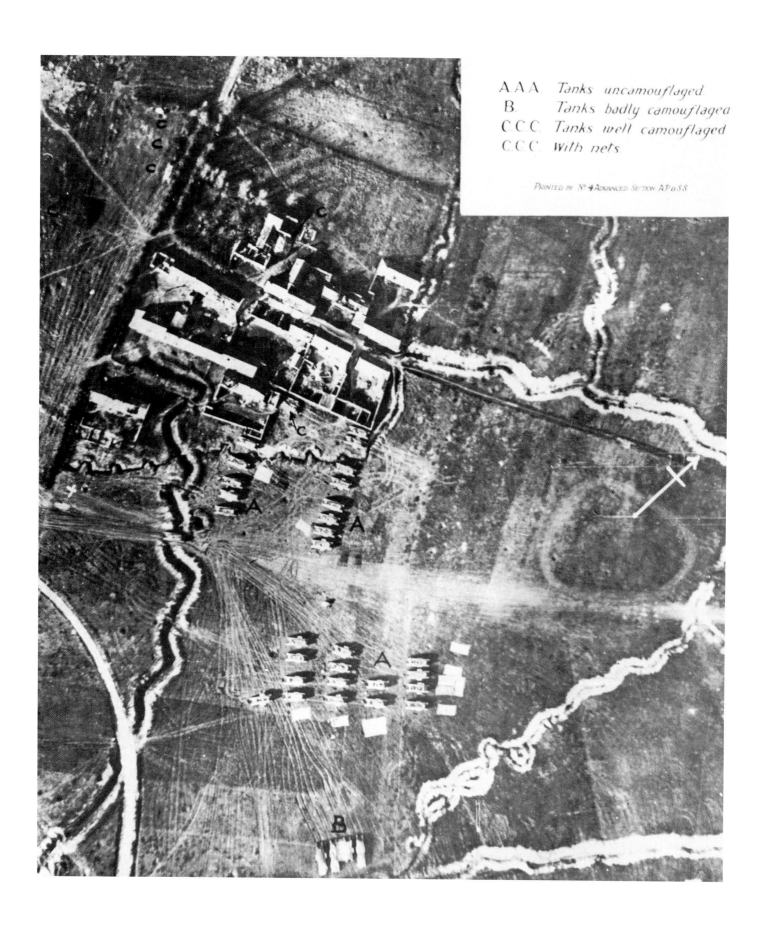

A.A.A. Tanks uncamouflaged
B. Tanks badly camouflaged
C.C.C. Tanks well camouflaged
C.C.C. With nets

PRINTED BY Nº 4 ADVANCED SECTION A.P.&S.S.

promising sectors, and identified the dry chalk downland around Cambrai, east of the old Somme battlefield. New artillery ranges were opened so that guns could be calibrated to shoot 'to the map' (i.e. their fire could be predicted), thus enabling the barrage to be as accurate as possible without prior registration. Third Army's field survey company undertook an immense amount of survey work for the artillery. This enabled a fully predicted barrage, and counter-battery fire that neutralized the German infantry and artillery. When the tanks and infantry went forward, the field survey company's flash-spotting and sound-ranging detachments advanced just behind the attacking troops to locate German guns.

Much of the credit for the Cambrai success belonged to Tudor, commanding the 9th Divisional Artillery. He was quick to realize the significance of survey methods, and had used them on the

Somme in 1916 and at Arras in April. The groundwork had already been laid by the Royal Engineers officers of the topographical sections and field survey companies in 1915 and 1916; the key survey element was not just the accurate fixing of guns and targets to the survey grid but the provision of accurate line to the gunners by the use of bearing pickets.

The devastating effect of semi-predicted fire had already been achieved in British and French offensives, and also by the Germans at Verdun in 1916 and in Bruchmüller's bombardment at Riga in September 1917, but this achievement had taken all armies years to develop. Before the war much had already been done in the way of calibration and ballistic and meteorological experiments, but little had filtered through to the field artillery. Survey was called in early in the war, but efficient calibration depended upon the development of the Bull-Weiss sound-ranging apparatus and the Tucker microphone, and this process took over a year. By the autumn of 1917, armies had permanent calibration ranges, and daily 'meteor' telegrams from GHQ supplied the necessary data on wind, temperature and barometric pressure. The location of enemy guns had, in most cases, been determined by sound-

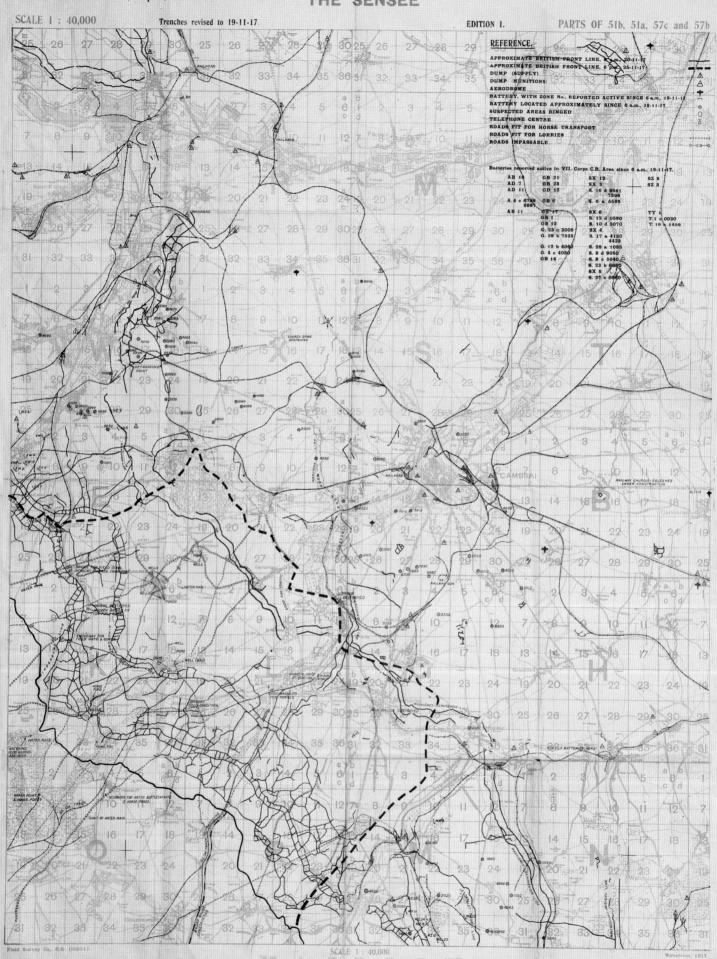

REFERENCE.

APPROXIMATE BRITISH FRONT LINE, 6 p.m. 20-11-17
APPROXIMATE BRITISH FRONT LINE, 6 p.m., 25-11-17.
DUMP (SUPPLY)
DUMP (MUNITIONS)
AERODROME
BATTERY, WITH ZONE No., REPORTED ACTIVE SINCE 6 a.m., 19-11-17
BATTERY LOCATED APPROXIMATELY SINCE 6 a.m., 19-11-17
SUSPECTED AREAS RINGED
TELEPHONE CENTRE
ROADS FIT FOR HORSE TRANSPORT
ROADS FIT FOR LORRIES
ROADS IMPASSABLE

Batteries reported active in VII. Corps C.B. Area since 6 a.m., 19-11-17.

AB 16	GB 21	SX 12	SZ 9
AD 7	GB 23	SX 3	SZ 3
AD 11	GD 12	S. 16 d 9581 7898	
A. 4 c 6789 6987	GB 6	S. 6 a 5549	
AB 11	GB 17	SX 6	TY 4
	GB 1	S. 13 d 0590	T. 1 c 0020
	GB 12	S. 10 d 5070	T. 19 b 1455
	G. 23 c 2005	SX 4	
	G. 29 b 7525	S. 17 a 4130 4429	
	G. 12 b 4060	S. 28 a 1085	
	G. 4 c 4050	S. 8 d 9050	
	GB 14	S. 8 c 5040	
		S. 22 b 8080	
		SX 5	
		S. 27 c 0520	

CAMBRAI

ranging and flash-spotting, both of which had become highly efficient. Many artillery officers were untrained in survey techniques, and field survey company officers had the task of educating the gunners to use their own weapons effectively.

A vast change had occurred in the way that artillery was used to open an attack. Before the Arras battle, Allenby's artillery commander suggested a two-day bombardment based on survey techniques. At Messines and Third Ypres, although the long bombardment prevailed, it was recognized that this was ineffective against the new German deep dispositions, and that it created an obstacle for the advancing troops. In the later stages at Ypres, Plumer experimented with shorter and more intense bombardments. Gunner officers and men of the many new batteries which arrived in France during 1917 had gained experience in the use of artillery boards and trigonometrically fixed bearing pickets, and applying the knowledge gained from calibration, meteorological data, etc. An 'Experimental & Wind Section' of 3rd Field Survey Company played an important part in providing crucial meteorological data to the sound-ranging sections prior to the attack.

Tudor, responsible for the field artillery of his Division's sector of 4th Corps front astride the Bapaume–Cambrai road, developed the idea of a diversionary surprise attack early in the Third Ypres battle. The Tank Corps had prepared a similar plan by the beginning of August, the key to which was the use of survey methods of gun-laying to achieve surprise. He envisaged that tanks should flatten the wire, creating lanes for the attacking infantry. This would obviate the normal wire-cutting by the artillery, so there would be no artillery fire before zero. Tudor's corps commander, Woollcombe, approved a plan for, at first, a large-scale 'raid', along these lines. Third Army's artillery commander, Lecky, did not support a surprise bombardment at zero using only predicted fire, but obeyed Byng (who had taken over Third Army from Allenby early in June) wholeheartedly when Byng approved the plan.

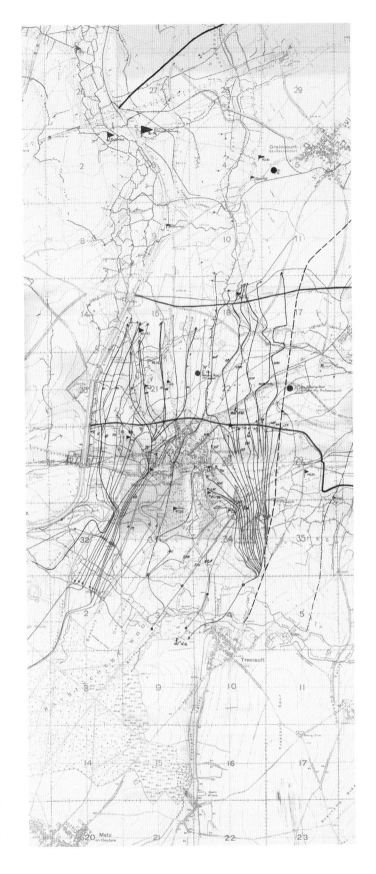

LEFT: *The Sensée. Edition 1. Overprinted Battle Situation Map, 6 p.m., 25-11-17*, prepared by [3rd] Field Survey Company 10204. The pecked black line shows the front line at 6 p.m. on 25 November 1917, during the Battle of Cambrai. German trenches in red (corrected to 19 November), German batteries and railways in black. Scale of original: 1:40,000.

RIGHT: Battle of Cambrai. Tank routes map of the Havrincourt area for 20 November 1917, drawn in many colours onto a composite of Third Army trench map sheets for the world's first tank attack.

On 23 August, Woollcombe sent the scheme to Byng, and soon Elles of the Tank Corps arrived to reconnoitre the front. Elles suggested a larger-scale attack, and Byng agreed. Haig was in favour, and encouraged Byng to proceed with secret detailed planning (Scheme 'GY'). No extra troops were available because of the Ypres operations, and it was a case of 'hanging fire' until the Flanders fighting was over. On 13 October, Haig accelerated preparations, providing four divisions and three brigades of tanks for combined training, but the Caporetto disaster of 24 October (see chapter 3) threatened the venture, men and guns being sent to Italy. On 13 November, Haig closed down the Passchendaele offensive, but went ahead with the Cambrai attack to keep the initiative and take pressure off the Italian front.

The ending of the Ypres offensive enabled large numbers of field and heavy batteries to be sent to Third Army; 1,003 guns and howitzers were in position on 20 November, of which 3rd Corps had 536 (including eight heavy artillery groups) and 4th Corps had 437 (including 7 heavy artillery groups). This array of guns involved a massive amount of rapid survey work. Byng, insisting on surprise, would not permit any gun to fire before zero, and Keeling, commanding 3rd Field Survey Company, supported him by promising that the survey would be done in time. All heavy batteries were fixed and given bearing by 3rd Field Survey Company, while field batteries had their pivot-gun positions surveyed and marked by a peg, so that they could lay out bearing by compass and director. Artillery boards were supplied to all batteries.

Keeling's trigonometrical officers covered 3rd and 4th Corps battery zones, working through the night fixing bearing pickets and running traverses through the fog, protecting their instruments from rain with umbrellas. In 3rd Corps zone, which was larger and had more batteries to fix, Captain Salmon didn't finish until 2 a.m., four hours before zero, when he carried the bearing, using torches and lamps from neighbouring trig points, to the sights of a 9.2-inch railway gun. As its task was to enfilade a road, accurate line was imperative. Survey also enabled batteries to be pushed far forward to 'silent' positions just behind the front line, from where

RIGHT: Battle of Cambrai. *Gouzeaucourt*, detail and trenches to 24 October 1917, overprinted with 3rd Corps' *Secret Objective and Barrage Map*, with smoke barrages overprinted hatched in black, barrage lines in green; corps boundary (brown chain-dotted), *First Objective* or 'Blue Line' (blue), *Second Objective* (brown). This sheet overlapped with the *Niergnies* and *Moeuvres* sheets, which also carried *Secret Objective and Barrage Map* overprints for 3rd and 4th Corps in the Cambrai tank attack.

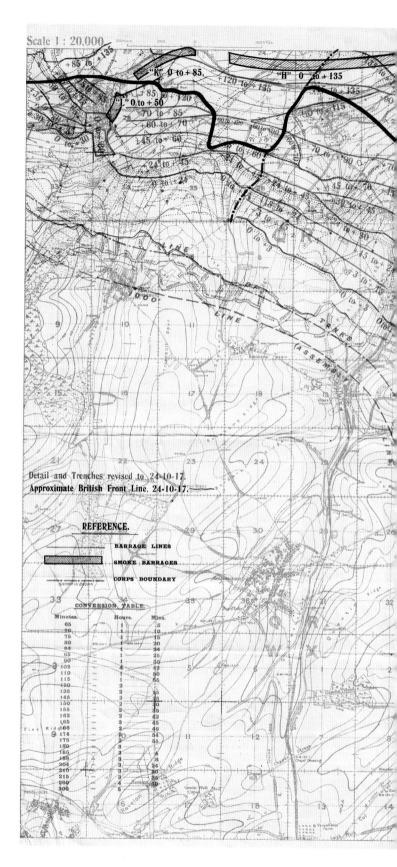

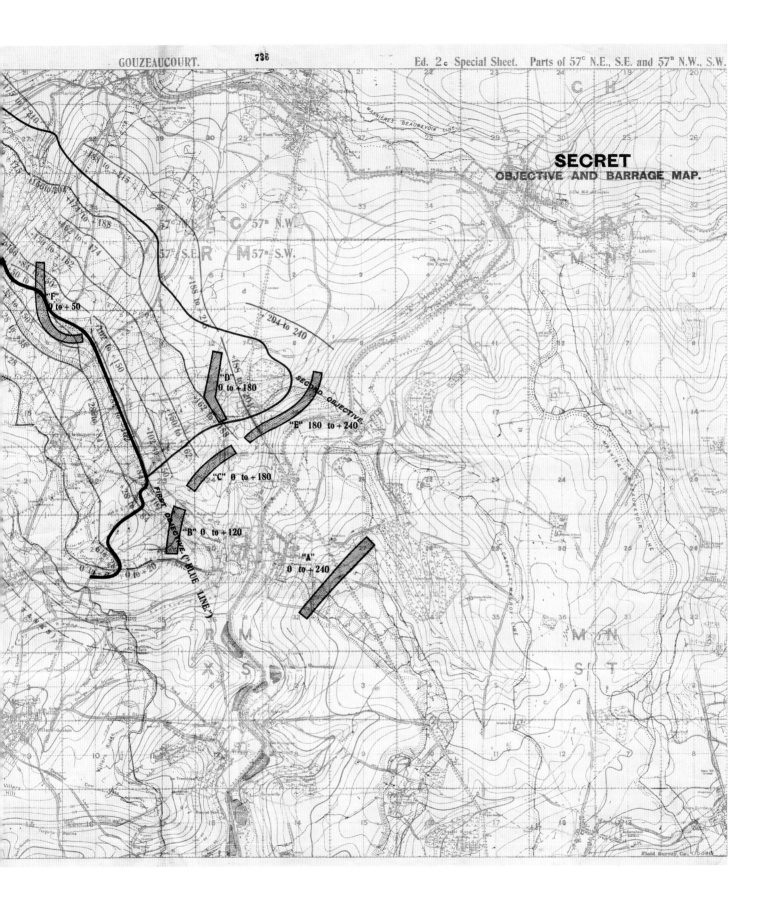

SECRET
OBJECTIVE AND BARRAGE MAP.

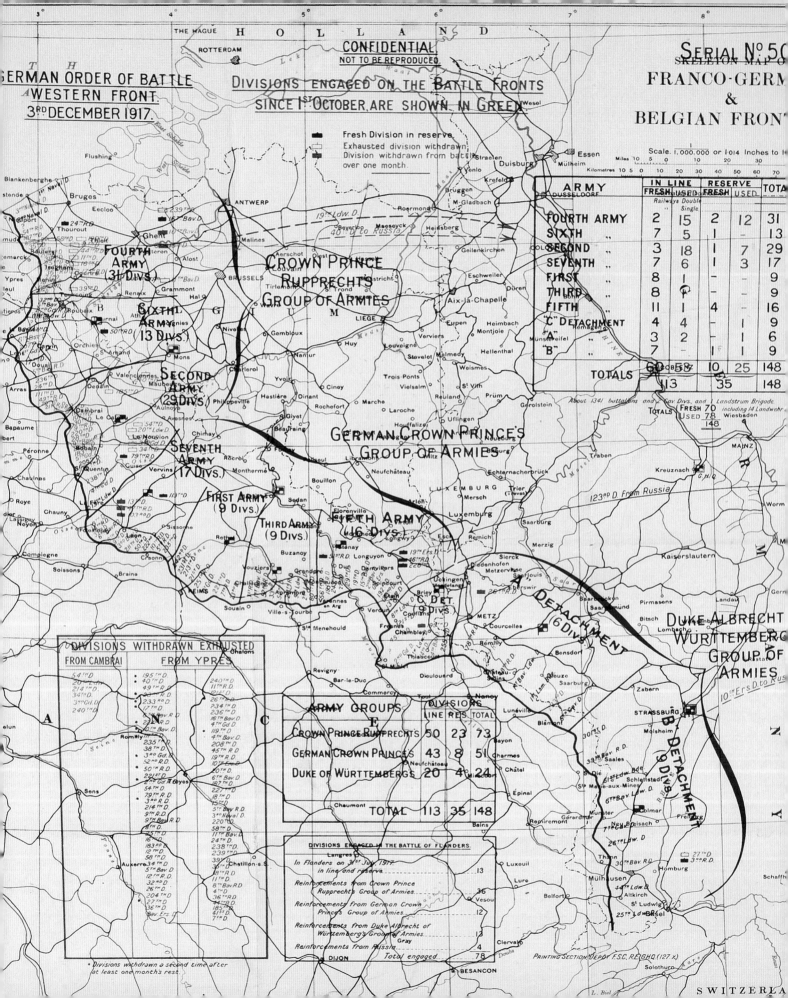

GERMAN ORDER OF BATTLE
WESTERN FRONT.
3RD DECEMBER 1917.

CONFIDENTIAL
NOT TO BE REPRODUCED

DIVISIONS ENGAGED ON THE BATTLE FRONTS
SINCE 1ST OCTOBER, ARE SHOWN IN GREEN.

SERIAL No 50
SKELETON MAP OF
FRANCO-GERMAN
&
BELGIAN FRONT

Fresh Division in reserve
Exhausted division withdrawn
Division withdrawn from battle
over one month.

Scale 1,000,000 or 1·014 Inches to 1

ARMY DUSSELDORF	IN LINE		RESERVE		TOTAL
	FRESH	USED	FRESH	USED	
	Railways Double	Single			
FOURTH ARMY	2	15	2	12	31
SIXTH "	7	5	1	—	13
SECOND "	3	18	1	7	29
SEVENTH "	7	6	1	3	17
FIRST "	8	1	—	—	9
THIRD "	8	1	—	—	9
FIFTH "	11	1	4	—	16
"C" DETACHMENT	4	4	—	1	9
"A"	3	2	—	1	6
"B"	7	—	1	1	9
TOTALS	60	53	10	25	148
	113		35		148

About 1341 battalions and 5 Cav. Divs., and 1 Landsturm Brigade including 14 Landwehr

TOTALS FRESH 70
USED 78
148

123RD D. from Russia

FOURTH
ARMY
(31 Divs.)

CROWN PRINCE
RUPPRECHT'S
GROUP OF ARMIES

SIXTH
ARMY
13 Divs.

SECOND
ARMY
(29 Divs.)

SEVENTH
ARMY
(17 Divs.)

GERMAN CROWN PRINCE'S
GROUP OF ARMIES

FIRST ARMY
(9 Divs.)

THIRD ARMY
(9 Divs.)

FIFTH ARMY
(16 Divs.)

C DET.
(9 Divs.)

DETACHMENT
(6 Divs.)

DUKE ALBRECHT
WÜRTTEMBERG'S
GROUP OF
ARMIES

B DETACHMENT
(9 Divs.)

DIVISIONS WITHDRAWN EXHAUSTED		
FROM CAMBRAI	FROM YPRES	
54TH D.	195TH D.	240TH D.
20TH Lw.D.	40TH D.	11TH R.D.
214TH D.	49TH R.D.	12TH D.
34TH D.	233RD D.	26TH D.
3RD Gd.D.	17TH D.	234TH D.
240TH D.	2ND R.D.	236TH D.
	16TH Bav.D.	16TH Bav.D.
	3RD Bav.D.	4TH Gd D.
	119TH D.	119TH D.
	4TH Bav.D.	4TH Bav.D.
	235TH D.	208TH D.
	38TH D.	45TH R.D.
	3RD Gd.D.	19TH R.D.
	52ND R.D.	10TH Ers.D.
	50TH R.D.	6TH D.
	221ST D.	6TH Bav.D.
	2ND Gd R Div.	187TH D.
	54TH D.	22ND D.
	79TH R.D.	18TH D.
	3RD R.D.	15TH D.
	214TH D.	5TH Bav.R.D.
	9TH R.D.	3RD Naval D.
	9TH Bav R.D.	220TH D.
	8TH D.	58TH D.
	16TH D.	11TH Bav.D.
	183RD D.	24TH D.
	12TH D.	238TH D.
	58TH D.	239TH D.
	49TH D.	39TH D.
	16TH D.	36TH D.
	5TH Bav D.	19TH R.D.
	32ND D.	8TH Bav.R.D.
	26TH D.	4TH D.
	204TH D.	36TH R.D.
	27TH D.	185TH D.
	36TH D.	71ST D.
	Bav. Ers.D.	

* Divisions withdrawn a second time after
at least one month's rest.

ARMY GROUPS	DIVISIONS		
	LINE	RES.	TOTAL
CROWN PRINCE RUPPRECHT'S	50	23	73
GERMAN CROWN PRINCE'S	43	8	51
DUKE OF WÜRTTEMBERG'S	20	4	24
TOTAL	113	35	148

DIVISIONS ENGAGED IN THE BATTLE OF FLANDERS.	
In Flanders on 31st July 1917, in line and reserve	13
Reinforcements from Crown Prince Rupprecht's Group of Armies	36
Reinforcements from German Crown Prince's Group of Armies	12
Reinforcements from Duke Albrecht of Württemberg's Group of Armies	13
Reinforcements from Russia	4
Total engaged	78

Printing Section Depot F.S.C. R.E. GHQ (127 X)

SWITZERLAND

they could support an advance to their maximum range, while other batteries leapfrogged through them to maintain momentum.

There was to be a lifting barrage, as used by some corps on the Somme on 1 July 1916, rather than the well-established 'creeper', because it was feared that the sudden opening of unregistered fire would be insufficiently accurate for a creeping barrage. Objective and barrage overprints were made on existing trench maps, which were issued in large numbers to gunners, infantry and tanks. Arrangements were made by 3rd Field Survey Company to carry the triangulation forward rapidly after the advance. This was

ABOVE: Battle of Cambrai, November 1917. A British tank destroyed by shellfire.
LEFT: *German Order of Battle. Western Front. 3 December 1917*, showing German formations in red, 'Divisions Engaged on the Battle Fronts Since 1 October' in green, and 'Divisions Withdrawn Exhausted From Cambrai, From Ypres' also in green. The situation after the Third Ypres and Cambrai battles shows a great density of German divisions in those sectors.

important not only for artillery work but also for the rapid fixing of points for flash-spotting and sound-ranging bases for enemy-battery-location. In the air, the RFC used the usual range of maps, in particular the 'positions maps' showing known German battery positions, with woods overprinted, and villages also outlined, in green. Pilots on ground-strafing tasks used strip-maps of their route pasted to a wing strut; these indicated landmarks and approximate times on a set compass course at 100 m.p.h.

Its initial success was astounding and surprised the Germans. The combination of predicted fire, infantry and 381 tanks that crushed the wire and then dropped bundles of brushwood into the deep trenches of the Hindenburg Line facilitated a swift advance of four miles. However, the battle then proved to be an anti-climax. Cambrai and the commanding position of Bourlon Wood were not captured. A rectangular salient was created, and a powerful surprise German counter-attack ten days later retook much of the terrain. It had been a brilliant but half-baked scheme. Its real importance was that it determined the all-arms surprise tactics pursued by the British army in its successful offensives in the second half of 1918.

Chapter 9

The 1918 Campaign in the East and the West

In 1917 the great sausage machine of the Western Front ground away at Arras, the Aisne and Ypres as remorselessly as it had done in 1916 at Verdun and the Somme. But in November the Battle of Cambrai had shown the Allies the key that was to open the deadlock: the return of the element of surprise.

Operations now included crash-predicted bombardments and creeping barrages opening at zero, with tanks advancing en masse to crush the barbed-wire entanglements, subdue the enemy's machine guns and then fight through the position with the infantry. An increasing proportion of the guns firing would be on counter-battery tasks, to neutralize the enemy's artillery. The Germans had evolved similar methods, without tanks, and usually including a brief predicted preliminary bombardment mixing gas with high-explosive. The Riga battle in September 1917 was a blueprint for this type of attack.

The Caporetto debacle in October 1917 forced the Allies to rethink their overall command arrangements. A unified command would have to wait until April 1918. But at least the Allied leaders who met on 5 November 1917 at Rapallo agreed to form a Supreme War Council. Though this was only a body for discussion among statesmen, it was served by an Executive Committee of military advisers, under Foch as chairman. This was an important first step to a more formal structure of cooperation.

The year 1918 saw the last, desperate, attempt by the Germans to win the war by a huge series of offensives on the Western Front. While these attacks caused a huge crisis for the Allies, only surmounted by the creation of a unitary command at the crucial moment, they did not succeed in breaking through. They were too late. The Yanks were coming; by mid-1918 a vast American Expeditionary Force was already 'over there'. Their effect on morale was incalculable – positive for the Allies and all-too-negative for the Germans, and also for their allies who could see that the arithmetic of attrition only worked in one direction.

THE EASTERN FRONT

Following the Bolshevik Revolution on 7 November, an armistice was signed at Brest-Litovsk on 16 December. This effectively took the Russians out of the war. Negotiations dragged on, and on

ABOVE: A German poster-map, *Der Schwerpunkt im Weltkrieg 1918*, showing all Europe, including Eastern Front, Greece, Rumania, etc.

RIGHT: *The Dismemberment of Western Russia, Supplement to The National Review*, April 1918. Even though engaged in a critical series of offensives on the Western Front, the Germans at this time had large numbers of troops on the Eastern Front with which they were obsessed.

9 February 1918 the Germans concluded a separate peace with the Ukraine. They summarily informed the Bolshevik delegation that if they did not immediately accept the peace terms, the armistice of 7 November would be invalid and the Central Powers would occupy the non-Russian lands at Brest-Litovsk.

THE DISMEMBERMENT OF WESTERN RUSSIA.

Scale 72 miles = 1 inch (1:4,500,000)

Statute Miles

Kilometres

REFERENCE

International boundaries in 1914

Approximate boundaries of proposed
States dependent on Germany

Poles

Great Russians

White Russians

Ukranians (Ruthenians and Little Russians)

Lithuanians and Letts

Finns and Esthonians

Rumanians

Limit of German Advance
to 23rd March, 1918

Principal Railways

GEORGE PHILIP & SON. LTD.

The London Geographical Insti

REFERENCE.

Broad Gauge Railway (Double Track)	Water Points for Lorries and Water Carts
" (Single Track)	(No. of Gallons available per
" (Under Construction)	day shown against each)
" (Proposed Construction)	Horse Troughs (Maximum No. of Horses
Light Railway (Constructed)	that can be watered per day
" (Under Construction)	shown against each)
" (Proposed Construction)	Water Points for Dixies (No. of Gallons
Metre Gauge Railway (Constructed)	available per day shown
Ammunition Railheads	against each)
Supply Railheads	Casualty Clearing Stations (No. in Centre)
Stone Railheads	Corps Main Dressing Stations
Roads (Maintained by Army)	Advanced Dressing Stations
Lorry Parks (No. of Lorries shown against each)	Rest Stations
Corps R.E. Dumps	Baths
Supply Refilling Points	Ordnance Workshops (Heavy)
Ammunition Refilling Points	(Medium)
Water Points for Water Carts (No. of Gallons	(Light)
available per day shown against each)	

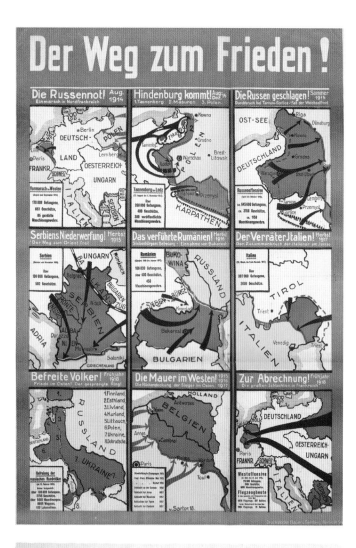

Der Weg zum Frieden!

PREVIOUS PAGES: *Passchendaele Ridge. Secret. Army Administrative Situation Map 1 March 1918, 1:40,000.* Overprint by 4th Field Survey Company RE showing ground forms; railways (standard gauge, howitzer spurs, light, metre gauge); roads and tracks; lorry parks; dumps; casualty clearing stations, corps main dressing stations and advanced dressing stations; ordnance workshops; ammunition, supply and water points; etc. In short, the immense logistical infrastructure required for a modern battle.

ABOVE: *Der Weg zum Frieden!* (The Road to Peace!), nine map images in one poster covering key campaigns between 1914 and 1918. The bottom row left shows territories gained by Germany at Brest-Litovsk, 1918 and, bottom right, the German spring offensives of 1918.

RIGHT: Western Front, 1914–18, from *Harmsworth's New Atlas of the World,* c.1920.

They carried out this threat in an eleven-day war, operation *Faustschlag* (meaning a punch or knockout blow), between 10 and 21 February. The Germans attacked and defeated the weak

Bolshevik forces in White Russia (present-day Belarus), in the Crimea and western Ukraine, and in the industrial area of the Donetz Basin in eastern Ukraine. This was the final major operation on the Eastern front, and succeeded in its aim of forcing the Russians to sign the punitive peace treaty. This was done at Brest-Litovsk on 3 March 1918, but did not stop the German advance. Not content with occupying great areas in the Ukraine and Crimea, they pushed on in operation *Donnerschlag* (Thunderbolt), establishing themselves on the river Don on 8 May, and moving into the Caucasus towards Baku and its oilfields. To the north, they were active around the eastern Baltic and Finland.

This obsession with the Eastern Front and its territories meant that huge numbers of German troops were not available for the crucial offensives in the West. During these offensives, exhausted German divisions were transferred to the East, in exchange for relatively fresh ones, but the drain on resources was heavy.

THE WESTERN FRONT
The German Offensives

The collapse of Russia in 1917, the armistice, and the peace negotiations at Brest-Litovsk, made possible a revised German strategy for 1918. This was to use forces and resources released from the Russian front to deliver a knock-out blow, or series of blows, in the west, before American troops arrived in sufficient numbers to make this impossible.

Germany's internal condition also called for speedy action. Food riots resulting from the Allied blockade, and the spread of revolutionary sentiment following the Russian revolution, threatened the whole war effort and the survival of the Hohenzollern regime. Germany's allies were all in a weak position, so at least she did not now have to support Austria against Russia. Although occupation forces remained in the east, over a million men and 3,000 guns were transferred to the Western Front, where the number of German divisions rose from 152 to 190.

The obvious German move in the west was a dividing strike against the junction of the British and French armies. Faulty intelligence reported that the British were in a critical state, verging on starvation, because of the U-boat blockade. If the British were hit hard enough, the German high command believed they would collapse, whereas France had far greater food resources and was thought to be more capable of conducting a mobile defence. The Germans also believed that the British, better at attacking strong positions than the French, would launch a formidable counter-offensive that would draw forces away from the attack on the French. So the initial thrusts were directed solely against the British.

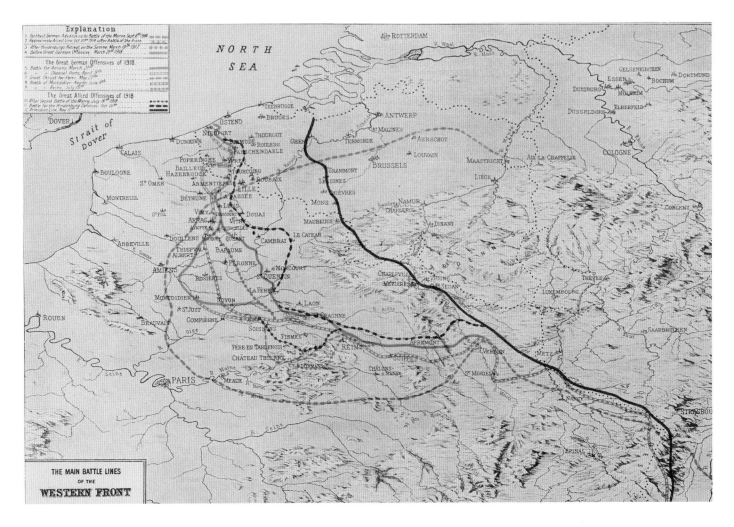

While Ludendorff preferred an attack in Flanders, its wet ground conditions in the early months of the year led to him to choose a broad front on the dry chalk terrain around St Quentin, east of the old Somme battlefield. A successful offensive on a southwesterly axis towards Roye and Montdidier would divide the British and French armies. Preparations were also made for attacks on other parts of the front, which naturally confused the Allies as to the direction of the main thrust. Pétain believed the attack would come on his Champagne front, while Haig expected it somewhere along his. British Intelligence eventually correctly identified the exact location and date, aided by careful analysis of aerial photographs, which clearly showed 'lice', or small ammunition dumps, near intended German battery positions.

The Germans gave codenames to their successive offensives, the first blow struck being the *Michael* attack, for which Bruchmüller (he was becoming known as *Durchbruchmüller*, or 'breakthrough-müller' by the Germans) had been transferred to the Western Front. A stupendous predicted five-hour bombardment by 6,000 guns and mortars, mixing gas and high explosive opened on the morning of 21 March. The assault, against Gough's Fifth Army and the right of Byng's Third, was made by specially selected, trained and equipped *Stosstruppen*, or storm-troops, carrying with them their own field guns and mortars.

The British defence scheme had been based on the German defence-in-depth concept developed in 1917, with some significant differences. The British plan emphasized scattered, wired strong-points, or 'birdcages', rather than continuous trench lines. Such strong-points had been a key factor in preventing a German breakthrough in 1914 during the First Battle of Ypres. Haig calculated that the British needed to be strongest further north to defend the Channel ports and the coalfield area. He had left the southern armies deliberately weaker in men and artillery, so that they could afford to give ground and conduct a more elastic defence. Not only was Gough's extended army very thinly spread along a front only recently taken over from the French, but labour had not been forthcoming to complete the defences. Many of

CONFIDENTIAL
NOT TO BE REPRODUCED

SERIAL No 66.

GERMAN ORDER OF BATTLE
WESTERN FRONT
23 . 3 . 18.

ARMY GROUPS	DIVISIONS				
	IN LINE FRESH	IN LINE ENGAGED	IN RESERVE FRESH	IN RESERVE TIRED	TOTAL
CROWN PRINCE RUPPRECHT'S	30	31	18	4	83
GERMAN CROWN PRINCE'S	28	19	11	2	60
GEN. v. GALLWITZ'S	21	—	5	—	26
DUKE OF WÜRTTEMBERG'S	14	—	9	—	23
TOTAL	93	50	43*	6	192
	143		49		192

* A considerable number of these were probably engaged on the 22nd and 23rd March, and at least 2 are not Fighting Divisions.

◼ Fresh Division in Reserve.
▭ Tired Division withdrawn recently.

HOLLAND

I unidentified Div. from the East ←

CROWN PRINCE RUPPRECHT'S GROUP OF ARMIES

FOURTH ARMY (25 DIVS)
(SIXT V. ARNIM)

SIXTH ARMY (12 DIVS.)
(V. QUAST)

(?) FOURTEENTH ARMY (21 DIVS)
(OTTO V. BELOW)

SECOND ARMY (25 DIVS.)
(V. DER MARWITZ)

EIGHTH ARMY (25 DIVS.)
(V. HUTIER)

SEVENTH ARMY (9 DIVS.)
(? V. BOEHN)

FIRST ARMY (13 DIVS)
(FRITZ V. BELOW)

THIRD ARMY (13 DIVS)
(V. EINEM)

FIFTH ARMY (16 DIVS.)

GERMAN CROWN PRINCE'S GROUP OF ARMIES

v. GALLWITZ'S GROUP OF ARMIES

SPA GHQ

GHQ WEST

237TH D. from Russia

DUKE ALBRECHT OF WÜRTTEMBERG'S GROUP OF ARMIES

"C" DET. (10 DIVS.) (FUCHS)

"A" DET. (9 DIVS.) (V. MUDRA)

"B" DET. (14 DIVS.) (V. GÜNDELL)

200TH from Italy

117TH D. from Italy

22ND Ldw. D. from Russia

3 Divisions from Flanders
8 Divisions from LILLE area
Attack of 21 Divs.
Attack of 35 Divs.
7 Divisions from Laon area
8 Divisions from Champagne
I Division from Verdun area
I Division from Woevre

SWITZERLAND

ARMY	IN LINE FRESH	IN LINE ENGAGED	RESERVE FRESH	RESERVE TIRED	TOTAL
FOURTH ARMY	16	—	9	—	25
SIXTH "	9	—	3	—	12
FOURTEENTH "	5	10	4	2	21
SECOND "	—	21	2	2	25
EIGHTH "	1	19	3	2	25
SEVENTH "	9	—	—	—	9
FIRST "	9	—	4	—	13
THIRD "	9	—	4	—	13
FIFTH "	12	—	4	—	16
"C" DETACHMENT	9	—	1	—	10
"A" "	6	—	3	—	9
"B" "	8	—	6	—	14
	93	50	43	6	
TOTALS	143		49		192

TOTAL FRESH DIVS. 136
TOTAL ENGAGED DIVS. 56

TOTAL DIVS. 192
About 1762 battalions and 2 Cav. Divs. including 15 Landwehr Divs.

Printing Section Depôt SC RE GHQ (13371)

Scale 1:1,500,000 or 1.015 Inches to 16 Miles
International Boundaries
Railways Double
Single

these were only sketchily 'spit-locked', or indicated on the ground by turned turf, rather than properly dug and wired.

Moreover, while German defensive thinking emphasized powerful counter-attack formations, the British had not even sufficient reserve troops to hold these lines in the event of a German attack breaking through the forward or outpost zone.

Fog on the morning of the attack meant that the British machine gunners could not see the oncoming enemy. As a result the storm-troops, specially trained to use ground for infiltration (valleys were specially coloured green on their operations maps) and to flow around centres of resistance, were soon through into the battle zone and pressing on. All German reserve echelons started moving forward at zero to maintain the attack's momentum. The Germans were soon well ahead on their forty-mile advance, crossing the Somme and the old battlefield to its west within a few days, and pressing on.

Further north, on the Arras front, the German *Mars* attack of 28 March was anticipated. Preparations had been clamant and

ABOVE: German field artillery firing in the March 1918 offensive against the British Third and Fifth Armies on the Somme – the *Kaiserschlacht*. In this offensive the Germans also used special light 'infantry guns', manhandled forward by their crew, for close-support.

LEFT: *German Order of Battle, Western Front, 23.3.18,* showing German formations and front line in red; 'Divisions moved' and 'Divisions on the Somme front' in black. The situation shows a key stage during the German Offensive which started on 21 March. Scale of original: 1:1 million.

Below, the army commander, scorned the use of predicted fire and the surprise it could bring; his artillery registered its targets beforehand, indicating exactly where the attack would fall. Moreover, the British troops were here thicker on the ground, the defences were well-established, and there was no fog. Rather than breaking through, the assault troops were mown down.

The attack at Arras failed, but to its south the German advance was now threatening Amiens and its important railway junctions. Ludendorff had opportunistically changed the axis of advance to due west, appreciating that the capture of Amiens would prevent the British and French from supporting each other, and also that a drive through Amiens to the Somme estuary would decisively split them apart. Pétain was already potentially helping Ludendorff in this by preparing to withdraw the French armies southwards to cover Paris. Pétain told an anxious Haig that defending Paris took priority over maintaining contact with the British. Haig, at an Allied conference at Doullens on 26 March, offered to place himself under French command in order to maintain a continuous front and, importantly, a flow of French reserve divisions to support the British armies. It was agreed that, to maintain Allied unity, Foch would coordinate all Allied forces in France and Belgium, and on 14 April Foch was appointed Commander-in-Chief of the Allied Armies in France. This move by Haig brought French troops to reinforce the Somme front, which had meanwhile stabilized at Villers-Bretonneux, east of Amiens. The German advance had lost momentum because of exhaustion, extended communications and transport difficulties over the wasteland of the old Somme battlefield. The storm-troops and follow-up divisions had also suffered very heavy losses.

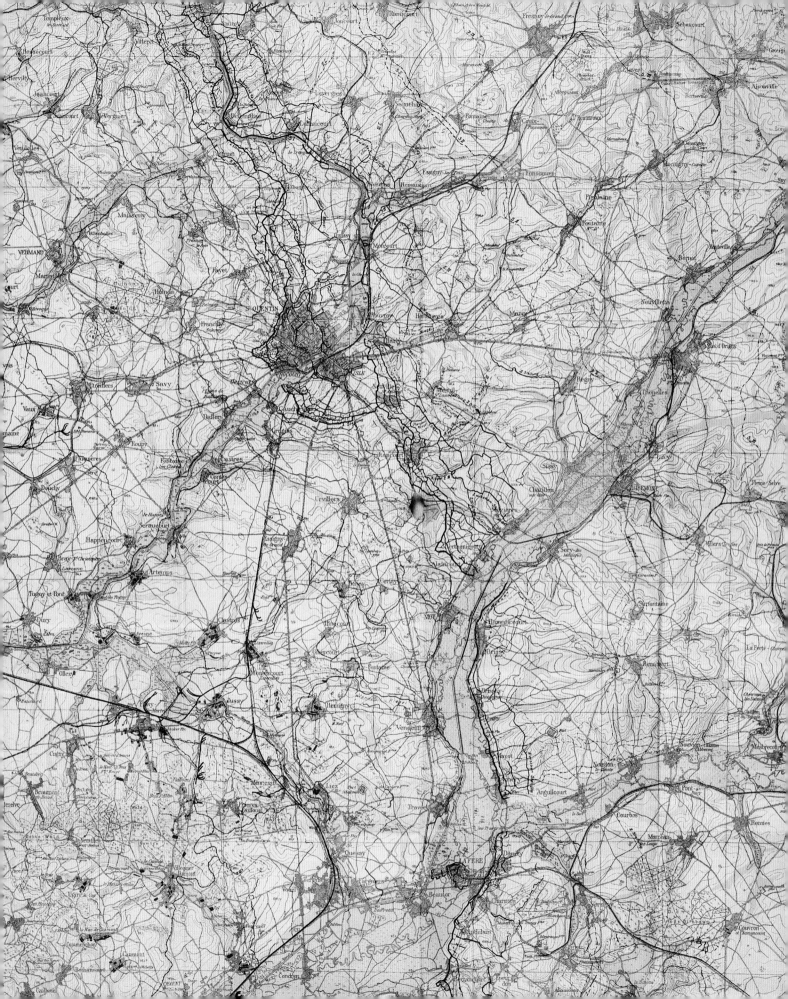

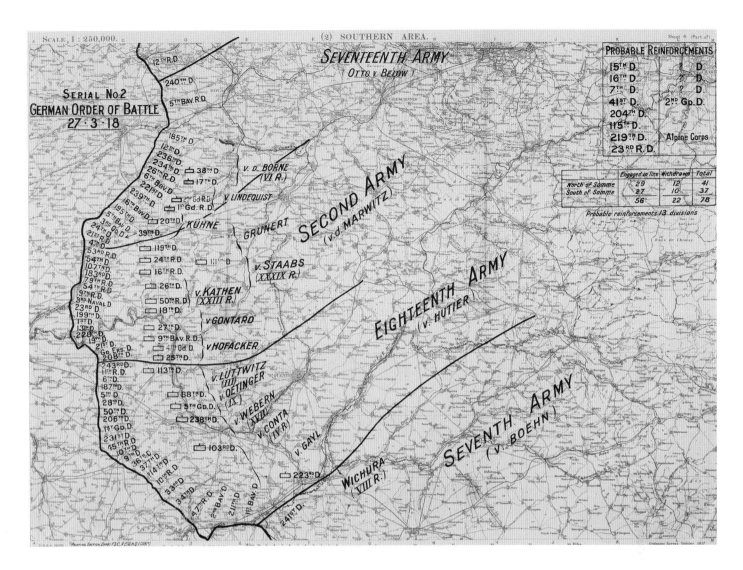

ABOVE: *German Order of Battle, Western Front, 27.3.18*, showing a further key stage during the German Offensive which started on 21 March. Scale of original: 1:1 million.

LEFT: *Übersichtskarte für die 18.Armee (St Quentin)*, 1:50,000, situation on 9 March 1918. Allied trenches in red, German in blue. Valleys shown in green, for infiltration. On maps of this medium scale the trench systems were slightly simplified.

On 9 April another German offensive, *Georgette*, was launched in the Lys valley between Béthune and Armentières, and soon extended north to Ypres. The Béthune–Armentières front was weakly held, as divisions sent south to reinforce the Somme front had been replaced by tired and battle-thinned divisions, and an important six-mile sector was held by a division of the Portuguese Corps, which lacked battle experience. This was to have been relieved by two British divisions on 10 April, but the Germans struck first. Another Bruchmüller bombardment pulverized the flimsy breastwork defences on a wide front, and the Germans, hitting the single Portuguese division with seven of their own, and aided by morning mist, cut through to create a nine-mile gap in the front. The British divisions on either side swung back to hold defensive flanks. The following day a new German attack north of Armentières, with a four-to-one superiority and again helped by mist, broke through the British defences and forced the abandonment of the Messines–Wytschaete ridge, captured the previous June. The Fourth Battle of Ypres had begun.

The Germans followed up rapidly with desperate attacks south of Ypres, but were held in front of Hazebrouck and in the Lys valley, having advanced eleven miles. The British evacuated most of the bleak, drying swamp of the now-untenable Ypres Salient, territory gained at such terrible cost the previous year. The crisis

led Haig to issue his 'Backs to the Wall' order-of-the day to his troops, calling on them to fight to the end. It was imperative for the British that the Channel ports be held. More rear defence lines were being hurriedly prepared, much digging being done by men of Chinese and African labour corps, and the port of Calais prepared for demolition. However, as so often, the defence stiffened as the attackers lost momentum. German losses had again been severe, and they made their last attack in this sector on 29 April, having captured the commanding Kemmel hill from the French on the twenty-fifth but making no further progress westward along the Flanders hills. The Germans, left holding a vulnerable, rectangular salient, now focused on attacks

against the French further south. But Ludendorff still planned to reopen the Flanders offensive when sufficient Allied reserves had been drawn south.

Meanwhile American troops were being convoyed across the Atlantic in increasing numbers. Fifty thousand were arriving every week and being given extra training for battlefield conditions. Time was running out for Ludendorff, who was all too conscious that he had to strike again quickly. His new focus of attack was the French front on the Aisne, between Soissons and Reims, the axis being south towards the river Marne. The intention was initially to draw reserves from the north, to enable a further attack in Flanders against the British in June. However Ludendorff, surprised by the success of the Aisne attack, opportunistically diverted his own reserves to exploit it.

The defending troops of Duchêne's Sixth Army, including five weak British divisions recuperating in this 'quiet sector' from earlier fighting, were crammed too densely into the narrow frontal area along the Chemin-des-Dames ridge north of the Aisne. On 27 May they found themselves pounded by 3,719 guns and mortars for three and a half hours, in yet another murderous Bruchmüller bombardment. On that day the Germans stormed through twelve

miles on a forty-mile front, advancing over the Aisne and Vesle rivers to the Marne in three days, reaching a point only forty miles from Paris. American troops, part of the one-and-a-half-million-strong American Expeditionary Force already in France, helped to hold the Germans on the Marne. French troops on both flanks held fast, Reims on the east acting like an anchor as Verdun had done during the First Battle of the Marne in 1914, and again the result was a huge German salient, against the west flank of which Pétain immediately launched counter-attacks. The contents of the wine cellars of the Champagne region, as well as the temptations of other forms of looting, contributed to the loss of impetus of the German attacks. Officers, as elsewhere during their 1918 offensives, found it difficult to get their men moving again.

From 31 May the Germans tried to drive out of the western part of the bulge created by the breakthrough to the Marne, aiming to push down towards Paris between the Ourcq and the Marne. On 9 June the Germans attacked at Compiègne between the two salients created by their Montdidier and Aisne attacks. This attack also was intended to draw Allied reserves from Flanders, as also was the later attack (15 July) astride Reims. Pétain was painfully aware of the disaster caused on the Chemin-des-Dames by a too-rigid defence. So he tried to destroy the impetus of the Compiègne attack by insisting on an elastic defence, but was to some extent foiled by the inflexibility of the local commanders. However the attacks met with little success.

Ludendorff's chief railway staff officer now insisted on the capture of Reims to ensure communications to the Marne salient; if this was not achieved, he claimed, the salient would have to be abandoned. On 15 July, the Germans used forty nine divisions in an attempt to pinch out the French salient at Reims by attacking on either side. They succeeded in crossing the Marne but were prevented from pushing their artillery over the river in support, and soon had to withdraw from this exposed position. To the east of Reims the French artillery, forewarned by Intelligence, smashed the German assault waves in their jumping-off positions by opening counter-preparation fire ten minutes before the assault. The defeat of these German attacks and the waxing Allied defence signalled that the tide had turned. Ludendorff had diverted his reserves from the Flanders attack, planned for June but cancelled, and his gamble had failed.

The German advances had enabled them to install their 'Paris guns', hitherto secret long-range guns firing 8-inch calibre shells. By careful survey, calibration and meteorological corrections these could place their shells in the centre of the French capital. Like the 'strategic bombing' that developed during the war, these pinpricks of terror had little real effect on the course of operations.

ALLIED COUNTER-OFFENSIVES
Battle of Château-Thierry

French counter-attacks developed rapidly. On 18 July, the Battle of Château-Thierry opened when the French Tenth and Sixth Armies and American infantry were launched out of the Villers-Cotterêts Forest on a twenty-five-mile front between Fontenoy and Château-Thierry. Their objective was to hack into the flank of the Marne salient, and they were supported by predicted artillery fire and 750 Renault light tanks and protected by smoke. The Germans were forced to withdraw, and by 7 August had pulled out of the salient, back to the river Aisne. The Allies were now strengthened in numbers and morale by the infusion of American blood. German morale was correspondingly lowered.

Ludendorff cancelled his intended Flanders operation, and German soldiers, and those of their allies, were only too aware that the war was now lost. The French were now exhausted, and most of their tanks were destroyed, damaged or unserviceable. So Foch insisted that the task of carrying out the next blow should fall to the British, who had recovered from their setbacks earlier in the year and were benefiting from a massive increase in their war production.

Battle of Hamel

On the British sector of the front, counter-offensives were in any case being organized. On 4 July the Australians, supported by an American infantry company, captured Hamel and Vaire Wood, east of Amiens, in an imaginative and spirited set-piece attack involving the cooperation of predicted artillery fire, infantry, tanks and air support.

To minimize casualties, Monash, the Australian Corps Commander, insisted that his men should be well covered by the artillery. There was a massive concentration of British and French batteries for this small operation, amounting to about 600 guns and howitzers, with an emphasis on counter-battery fire as well as bombardments in the days before the attack. For the attack itself, surprise was achieved by the barrage opening with a crash. This successful little attack became the model for a much larger offensive, the Battle of Amiens. This in turn opened a series of Allied offensives, in which the British, French and Americans all played a major part, known as the Battles of the Hundred Days.

RIGHT: *German Order of Battle, Western Front, 6.7.18*, showing front line and German formations in red, Divisions in green; Divisions of poor quality in red outlined in green. The situation at the turning point of the war, as the Allied counter-offensives were beginning. Scale of original: 1:1 million.

SERIAL Nº 92.

GERMAN ORDER OF BATTLE
WESTERN FRONT
6. 7. 18.

ARMY GROUPS	DIVISIONS				TOTAL
	IN LINE		IN RESERVE		
	FRESH	ENGAGED	FRESH	ENGAGED	
CROWN PRINCE RUPPRECHT'S	6	41	4	40	91
GERMAN CROWN PRINCE'S	8	40	-	33	81
GEN. V. GALLWITZ'S	4	10	1	2	17
DUKE OF WÜRTTEMBERG'S	13	1	-	2	16
UNLOCATED	-	-	-	-	-
TOTAL	31	92	5	77	205
	123		82		

* 1 Landwehr and 3 Fresh Divisions

CROWN PRINCE RUPPRECHT'S GROUP OF ARMIES

GERMAN CROWN PRINCE'S GROUP OF ARMIES

V. GALLWITZ'S GROUP OF ARMIES

DUKE ALBRECHT OF WÜRTTEMBERG'S GROUP OF ARMIES

UNLOCATED

SPA G.H.Q.

Legend:
- Fresh Division in reserve
- 38ᵀᴴ Ldw D. Division of poor quality.
- Engaged Div. rested for over one month.
- Engaged Div. rested for 14 days or over.
- Engaged Division, withdrawn recently.

FOURTH ARMY (27 DIVS.) (SIXT v. ARMIN)

SIXTH ARMY (22 DIVS.) (v. QUAST)

SEVENTEENTH ARMY (20 DIVS.)

SECOND ARMY (22 DIVS.) (v. DER MARWITZ)

EIGHTEENTH ARMY (23 DIVS.) (v. HUTIER)

SEVENTH ARMY (35 DIVS.) (v. BOEHN)

FIRST ARMY (14 DIVS.) (FRITZ v. BELOW)

THIRD ARMY (9 DIVS.) (v. EINEM)

FIFTH ARMY (9 DIVS.) (v. FRANÇOIS)

"C" DET. (8 DIVS.) (FUCHS)

NINETEENTH ARMY (6 DIVS.) (v. BOTHMER)

"A" DET. (4 DIVS.) (v. MUDRA)

"B" DET. (6 DIVS.) (v. GÜNDELL)

G.H.Q. West

ARMY		IN LINE		RESERVE		TOTAL
		FRESH	ENGAGED	FRESH	ENGAGED	
Prince Rupprecht	FOURTH ARMY	4	10	2	11	27
	SIXTH "	-	12	1	10	22
	SEVENTEENTH "	-	11	1	8	20
	SECOND "	2	8	1	11	22
German Crown Prince	EIGHTEENTH "	-	15	-	8	23
	SEVENTH "	3	13	-	19	35
	FIRST "	3	8	-	3	14
	THIRD "	2	4	-	3	9
v. Gallwitz	FIFTH "	2	4	1	2	9
	"C" DETACHMENT	2	6	-	-	8
Duke Albrecht	NINETEENTH ARMY	3	1	-	2	6
	"A" DETACHMENT	4	-	-	-	4
	"B" DETACHMENT	6	-	-	-	6
	UNLOCATED	-	-	-	-	-
		31	92	5	77	205
	TOTALS	123		82		205

TOTAL FRESH DIVS. 36
TOTAL ENGAGED DIVS. 169
TOTAL DIVS. 205

About 1891 battalions, 4 dismounted Cav divs including
18 Landwehr divs and 3 others of poor quality.

Scale 1.000.000 or 1.014 Inches to 16 Miles
Miles 10 5 0 10 20 30 40 50 Miles

HOLLAND

FRANCE

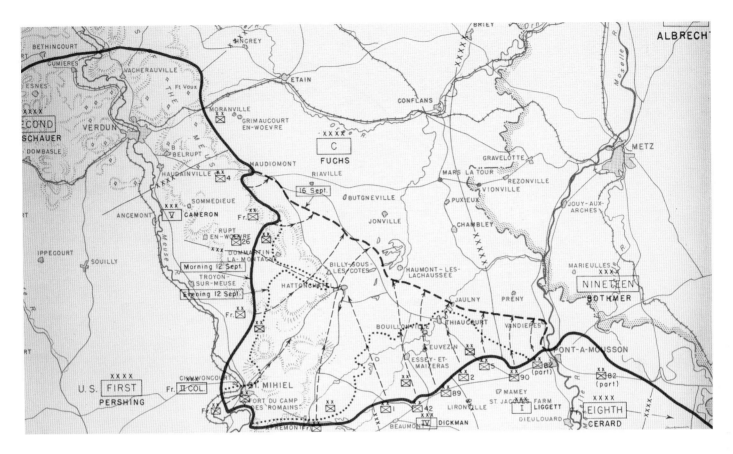

This succession of offensives only ended with the Armistice on 11 November.

Battles of Amiens and Montdidier

Benefitting from the experience of the Hamel attack, the Amiens offensive, launched on 8 August on a fourteen-mile front, was made by Rawlinson's Fourth Army, and spearheaded by the Canadian Corps. The aim was to disengage Amiens, which until now was within the range of German guns, and to free the Paris–Amiens railway. A deception plan was put into operation, involving a Canadian wireless station, two casualty clearing stations and two infantry battallions, to make it appear that the Canadian Corps was now in the Kemmel area in Flanders. The operations on the French sector of the attack frontage were known as the Battle of Montdidier.

ABOVE: St Mihiel Offensive, 1918. The Germans were withdrawing from the St Mihiel Salient in any case, so, for the Allies, it was more a question of following up.

LEFT: German column marching over a shattered battlefield, Marne 1918. The German Marne offensive in July was the last of a series beginning in March, and was soon pushed back by Allied counter-offensives.

Rawlinson's Fourth Army pushed forward rapidly on a nine-mile front, supported by the French on the right, and then the Canadians and Australians, with the British 3rd Corps on the left. They were under accurate predicted bombardment and creeping barrage fired by over 2,000 guns and howitzers, and supported by 456 tanks, including many of the new Mark V models. Following the precedent set by the Germans in March, all supports and reserves began to move forward simultaneously at zero. The artillery had done very well at counter-battery work, aided in particular by the sound-rangers who could locate moving German batteries in haze and mist, unlike the flash-spotters and the air force.

British offensive tactics, after the slogging of 1915–18, were now more mobile and efficient. An advance of eight miles was made on the first day, but many tanks, still slow and vulnerable to mechanical breakdown, were lost to direct artillery fire. On the second day of the battle, the British only had 145 tanks still ready for action. Armoured cars and relatively fast Whippet tanks exploited in the rear areas, and cavalry helped to gain and hold some positions until the infantry arrived.

German resistance stiffened, the attack soon lost impetus, and there were no new reserves to feed the battle. But a new attack doctrine had by now evolved. As soon as one attack lost momentum,

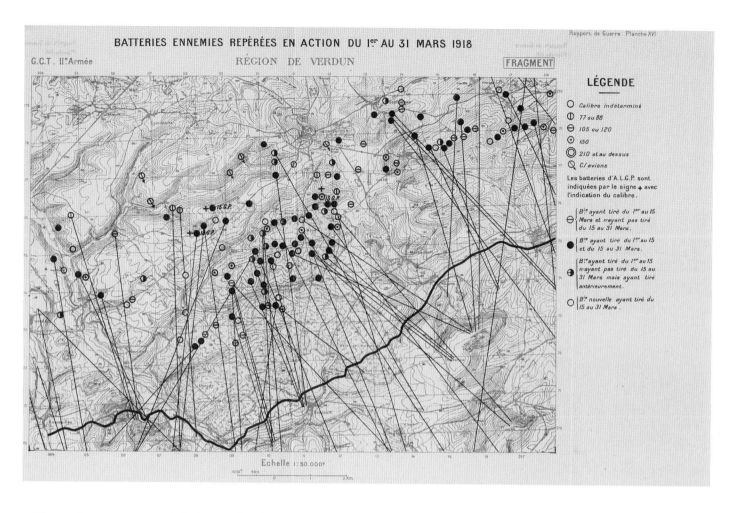

BATTERIES ENNEMIES REPÉRÉES EN ACTION DU 1er AU 31 MARS 1918

G.C.T. IIᵉ Armée   RÉGION DE VERDUN   FRAGMENT

Rapport de Guerre. Planche XVI

LÉGENDE

○   Calibre indéterminé
◐   77 ou 88
⊖   105 ou 120
◉   150
◎   210 et au dessus
⊙   C/ avions

Les batteries d'A.L.G.P. sont indiquées par le signe + avec l'indication du calibre.

⊖   B⁵ᵉ ayant tiré du 1ᵉʳ au 15 Mars et n'ayant pas tiré du 15 au 31 Mars.

●   B⁵ᵉ ayant tiré du 1ᵉʳ au 15 et du 15 au 31 Mars.

◑   B⁵ᵉ ayant tiré du 1ᵉʳ au 15 n'ayant pas tiré du 15 au 31 Mars mais ayant tiré antérieurement.

○   B⁵ᵉ nouvelle ayant tiré du 15 au 31 Mars.

Echelle 1:50.000ᵉ

artillery and reserves were switched to another front and the blow repeated. Predicted fire, based on accurate survey and mapping, maintained the element of surprise, keeping the Germans off-balance. Wherever possible, tanks were also used to strengthen the attack. Rawlinson's Army captured 400 guns and inflicted 27,000 casualties on the Germans, including 12,000 prisoners, for the loss of 9,000 men.

Battles of Albert, Bapaume and the Drocourt–Quéant Line

Following the Amiens operations, which lasted until 12 August, the weight of the British offensive was switched, at Haig's insistence, to the northern sector of the Somme battlefield. Foch's preference had been for a continuation of the Amiens battle. The Battles of Albert and Bapaume, from 21–31 August, turned the flank of the German position on the Somme and forced the Germans to pull back to the east bank. This series of blows continued when the new German position was then turned from the north from 26 August to 3 September in the Battles of Arras and the Drocourt–Quéant Line. That position being ruptured in an attack in which the

Canadians and Americans took a major role, the Germans were forced to fall back to the outer defences of the Hindenburg Line. As the direct result of these battles, the Lys Salient further north was evacuated by the Germans, and the British captured Lens, and recaptured Merville, Bailleul and Mount Kemmel, and freed Hazebrouck and its vital railway junctions, which had been under German artillery bombardment.

Battle of St Mihiel

It had always been the aim of General Pershing, the Commander-in-Chief of the American Expeditionary Force, to concentrate American forces in a field army under his command, rather than see them scattered piecemeal to reinforce other Allied armies. At St Mihiel, and then more particularly in the Meuse–Argonne battle, he achieved this. Between 12–16 September the Americans, led by Pershing, with a French corps and 267 light tanks also under his command, fought the Battle of St Mihiel to eliminate the German-held St Mihiel Salient, south of Verdun. Pershing planned to break through the German lines and capture the fortress of

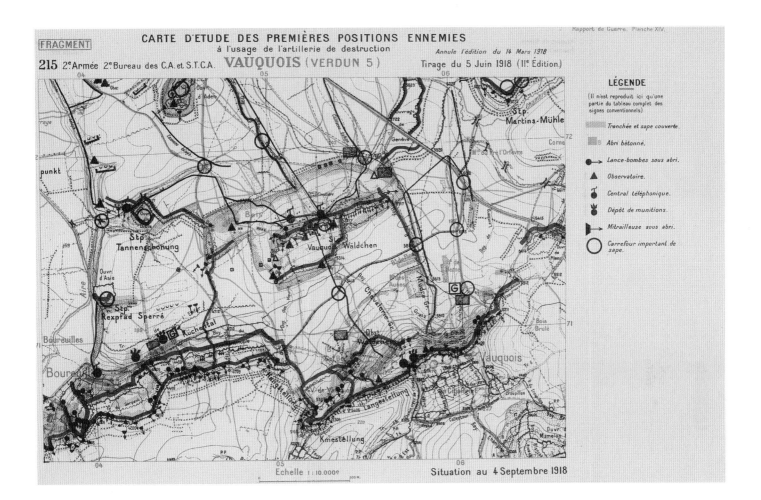

Metz, and as his attack caught the enemy withdrawing from the Salient, with their artillery also pulling back and most batteries therefore out of action, it proved more successful than expected. In a day and a half Pershing's army, at the cost of 7,000 casualties, captured 15,000 prisoners and 450 guns.

While the success of the American attack impressed the French and British, the operations demonstrated the difficulty of supplying large armies in a war of movement. The attack ground to a halt as artillery and ration trucks bogged down on the muddy roads. The US air service played a significant part in this battle,

ABOVE: *Vauquois, Carte d'Etude des Premières Positions Ennemies, 5 Juin 1918/4 Sept 1918*, showing trenches and mine craters, etc. The Butte de Vauquois was the site of savage mine warfare throughout the war.

LEFT: *Région de Verdun. Batteries Ennemies Repérées en Action du 1er au 31 Mars 1918. 1:50,000.* A French artillery intelligence map, showing batteries located (by sound-ranging, flash spotting, air observation, etc.), with type of gun and calibre, and their targets.

although American fliers had been serving with the *Escadrille Lafayette* since 1916. The intended attack on Metz did not in the end take place, as the Germans took up a strong rear position and the Americans turned their efforts further north, to the Verdun and Argonne Forest regions.

Battle of Epéhy and the Meuse–Argonne Offensive

In the Battle of Epéhy on 18 and 19 September, British forces broke through the outer Hindenburg defences and established jumping-off positions for the attack on the main Hindenburg position. Foch's grand offensive now gathered pace along the whole Allied front. On 26 September, Pershing's American First and Gouraud's French Fourth Armies began the Meuse–Argonne offensive, on the front from Verdun to the Argonne Forest, with Pershing's right flank on the river Meuse and the French attacking on his left. Twenty-two French and fifteen American divisions were involved. This, the largest American operation of the war, lasted from 26 September to the Armistice on 11 November. In the difficult Argonne Forest terrain of tangled woods, gullies and

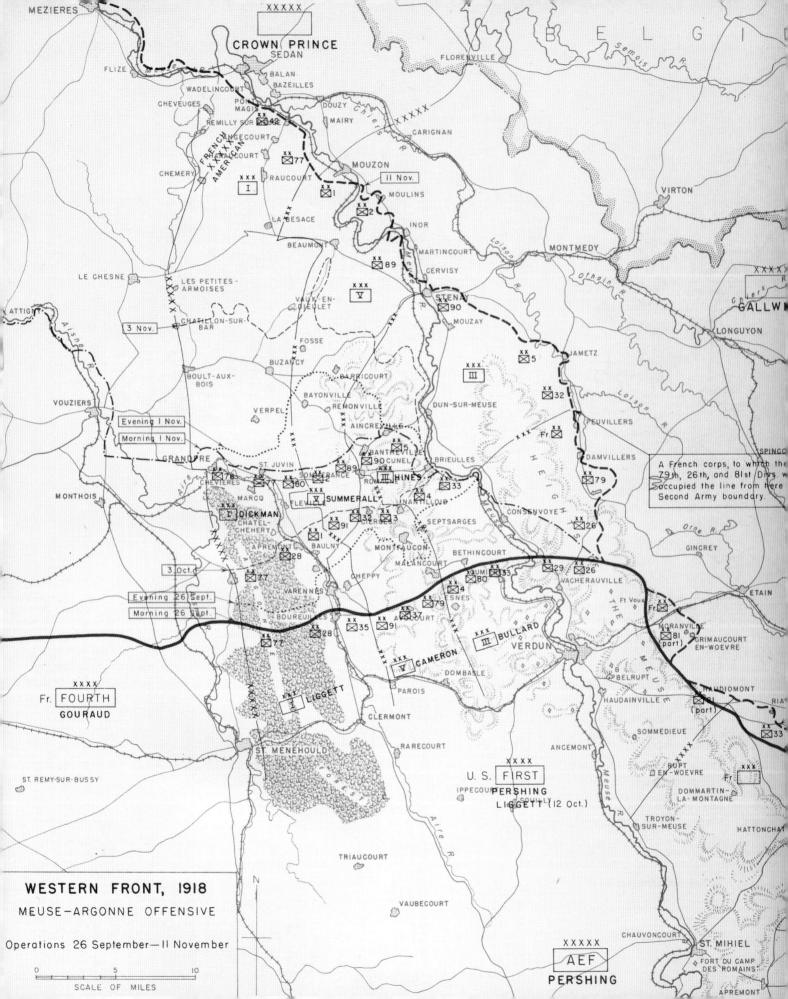

WESTERN FRONT, 1918
MEUSE-ARGONNE OFFENSIVE

Operations 26 September – 11 November

SCALE OF MILES
0   5   10

ridges, it was almost impossible for tanks to operate, and the Americans found themselves engaging in a bloody slog through a succession of strongly held German positions.

By 1 October the French and Americans had advanced some ten miles and taken 18,000 prisoners, and in a few more miles came up against the strong defensive position of the Kriemhild Line. While their advance was painfully slow, they were at least holding down thirty-six German divisions.

ABOVE: American soldiers, manning French Renault light tanks, advance to the Argonne Forest, 26 September 1918.

LEFT: *Meuse–Argonne Offensive, 1918*. The French were fortunate to have, in Pershing and the American Expeditionary Force, an ally who was happy to attack a determined enemy in the difficult terrain of the Argonne.

BELOW: British long-range, Mark V, 12-inch howitzer 'Peeping Tom' on railway mounting, firing near Quéant during the final advance, 27 September 1918. Not seen is the sophisticated system of survey, carrying the line-of-fire to its dial sight, so that its indirect fire hit its target.

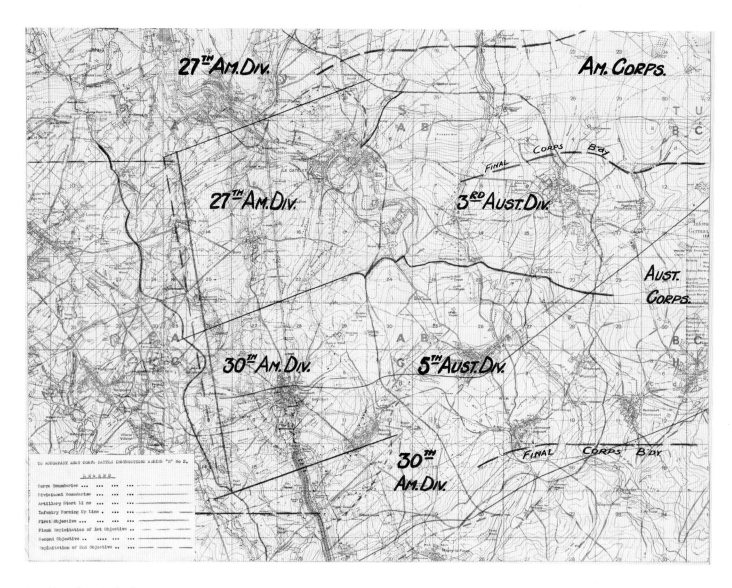

Within the map:
27ᵀᴴ AM. DIV.
AM. CORPS.
27ᵀᴴ AM. DIV.
3ᴿᴰ AUST. DIV.
CORPS B'DY
FINAL
AUST. CORPS.
30ᵀᴴ AM. DIV.
5ᵀᴴ AUST. DIV.
30ᵀᴴ AM. DIV.
FINAL CORPS B'DY

Legend box:
TO ACCOMPANY AMT CORPS BATTLE INSTRUCTIONS SERIES "R" No 2.
LEGEND
Corps Boundaries ...
Divisional Boundaries ...
Artillery Start Line ...
Infantry Forming Up Line ...
First Objective ...
Flank Exploitation of 1st Objective ..
Second Objective ..
Exploitation of 2nd Objective ..

Breaking the Hindenburg Line

In their operations from 8 August to 26 September (the eve of the great attack on the main Hindenburg Position), the BEF suffered 190,000 casualties. Between 26–29 September, one Belgian, five British, and two French armies attacked the Hindenburg Line and German positions extending north to beyond Ypres. Attacks were made by fifty British and twelve Belgian divisions, as well as the French and Americans further south. On the whole of the Western Front, 217 Allied divisions faced 197 German.

The attack on the Hindenburg Position, whose defences were up to three miles in depth and included the St Quentin Canal which made a superb anti-tank ditch, was made in the Battles of Cambrai and St Quentin, from 27 September until 10 October. The French First Army attacked on the right of the British Fourth Army (Rawlinson). In view of the strength of this well-sited and long-prepared position, Rawlinson and his artillery commander Budworth decided on an intense fifty-six hour preliminary bombardment in addition to the now-usual predicted crash and creeping barrage starting at zero hour on 29 September. Over 1,630 guns were used on a 10,000-yard front, firing an extremely

ABOVE: Breaking the Hindenburg Line, 29 September 1918. Operations map, using the *Wiancourt 1:20,000* sheet (trenches at 19 September), showing the attack of the Australian Corps (3rd and 5th Divisions) and the American 2nd Corps (27th and 30th Divisions) in the crucial St Quentin Canal Tunnel sector. After mid-1918, all the Allies adopted the French practice of printing the German trenches in blue.

RIGHT AND OVERLEAF: *The British Empire at Bay on the Western Front.* Produced at the end of 1918, this Stanford map shows the various stages of the final year's offensives and counter-offensives.

effective counter-battery and destructive programme beforehand, with a high proportion of high-explosive shell, and neutralizing fire during the attack. Operational and artillery planning was helped by a set of captured enemy defence maps, showing all the trenches, pill-boxes, dugouts, machine gun emplacements, battery positions, etc. The German defenders were stunned by the artillery, and overwhelmed by the attack.

In ten days of heavy fighting in the crucial sector from St Quentin to Epéhy, and especially north of this on a four-mile frontage between Bellicourt and Vendhuille, where the St Quentin Canal ran in a tunnel, the British and Americans eventually broke through the last and strongest of the Germans' fully prepared positions. A critical situation initially developed in the tunnel sector when the American 2nd Corps' two divisions (27th and 30th), supported by three Australian divisions, were delayed by the strength of the German defences and lost the barrage. Tanks became ditched in the deep trenches, and as the inexperienced Americans neglected the vital task of 'mopping up' German pockets as they went forward, the Australians had to fight through this ground again as they in turn moved up. Further south, at Bellenglise, the British 46th Division managed to cross the canal, using rafts and lifebelts, protected by a pulverizing barrage, punching a three-mile gap in the German defence and turning the enemy flank to the north in the sector facing the Australians and Americans. Advances were also made further north, on 27 September, between Péronne and Lens, on the fronts of the British Third and First Armies, and by 5 October the attacking Allied armies had broken through the whole Hindenburg Position. This opened the way for a war of movement and an advance towards the vital main German communications routes.

This group of assaults was undertaken in three phases. First came the storming of the Canal-du-Nord position on the left in

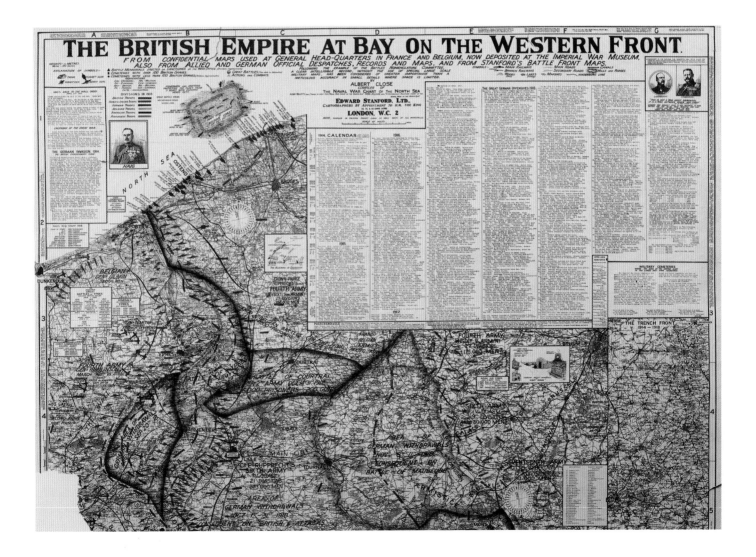

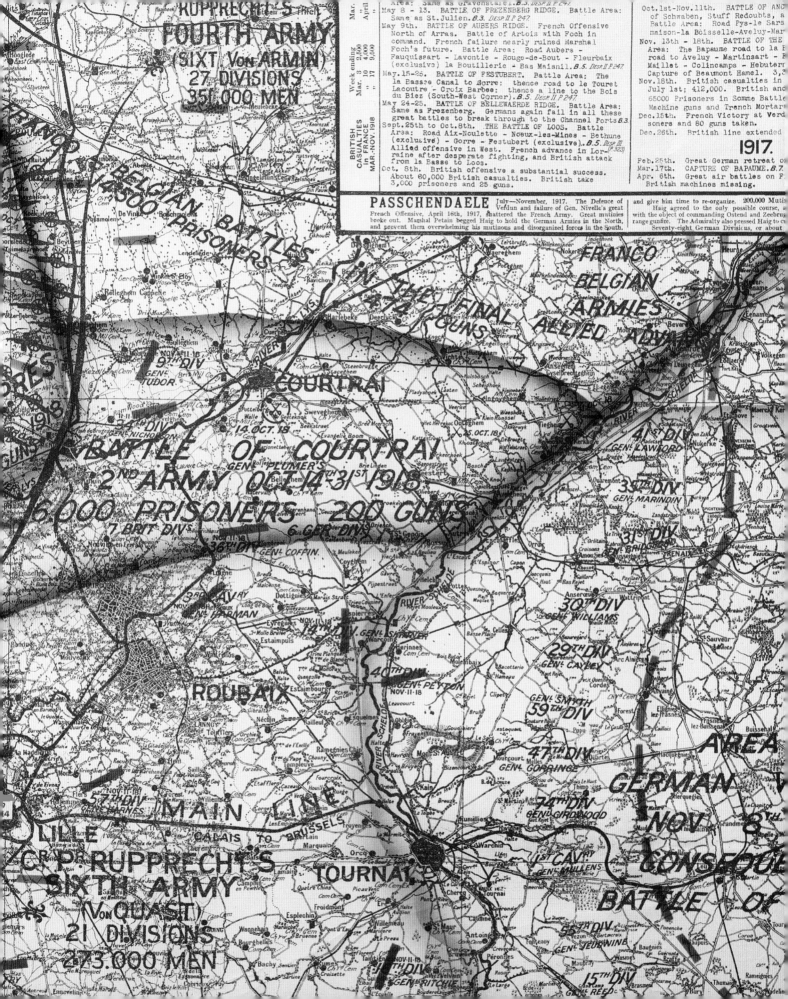

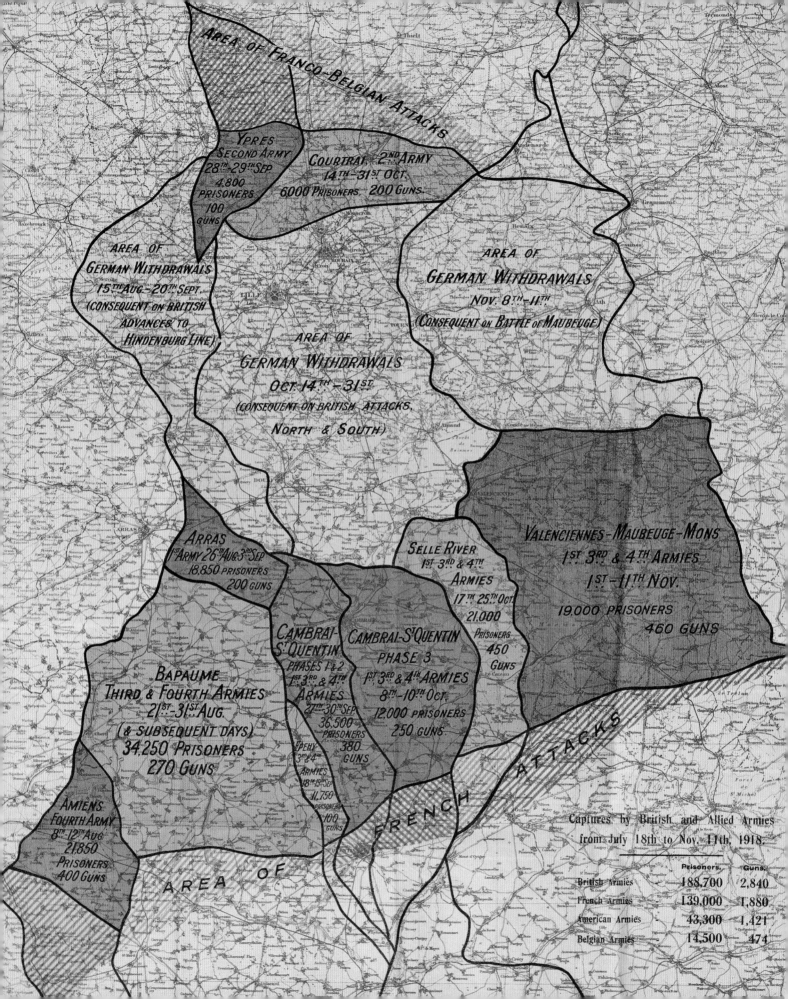

AREA OF FRANCO-BELGIAN ATTACKS

YPRES
SECOND ARMY
28TH-29TH SEP.
4,800
PRISONERS
100
GUNS

COURTRAI. 2ND ARMY
14TH-31ST OCT.
6,000 PRISONERS. 200 GUNS.

AREA OF
GERMAN WITHDRAWALS
15TH AUG.-20TH SEPT.
(CONSEQUENT ON BRITISH
ADVANCES TO
HINDENBURG LINE)

AREA OF
GERMAN WITHDRAWALS
OCT. 14TH-31ST
(CONSEQUENT ON BRITISH ATTACKS,
NORTH & SOUTH)

AREA OF
GERMAN WITHDRAWALS
NOV. 8TH-11TH
(CONSEQUENT ON BATTLE OF MAUBEUGE)

VALENCIENNES-MAUBEUGE-MONS
1ST 3RD & 4TH ARMIES
1ST-11TH NOV.
19,000 PRISONERS
460 GUNS

ARRAS
1ST ARMY 26TH AUG-3RD SEP.
18,850 PRISONERS
200 GUNS

SELLE RIVER
1ST 3RD & 4TH
ARMIES
17TH 25TH OCT.
21,000
PRISONERS
450
GUNS

CAMBRAI-
ST QUENTIN
PHASES 1 & 2
1ST 3RD & 4TH
ARMIES
27TH 30TH SEP.
36,500
PRISONERS
380
GUNS

EPEHY
3RD & 4TH
ARMIES
18TH-19TH SEP.
11,750
PRISONERS
100
GUNS

CAMBRAI-ST QUENTIN
PHASE 3
1ST 3RD & 4TH ARMIES
8TH-10TH OCT.
12,000 PRISONERS
250 GUNS

BAPAUME
THIRD & FOURTH ARMIES
21ST-31ST AUG.
(& SUBSEQUENT DAYS)
34,250 PRISONERS
270 GUNS

AMIENS
FOURTH ARMY
8TH-12TH AUG.
21,850
PRISONERS
400 GUNS

AREA OF FRENCH ATTACKS

Captures by British and Allied Armies
from July 18th to Nov. 11th, 1918.

	Prisoners.	Guns.
British Armies	188,700	2,840
French Armies	139,000	1,880
American Armies	43,300	1,421
Belgian Armies	14,500	474

the Battle of the St Quentin Canal, and the advance on Cambrai. Following this came the shattering blow which, after a stupendous artillery bombardment and with the help of hundred of tanks, broke through the Hindenburg Line and turned the defences of St Quentin. Lastly came the exploitation of these successes by a general attack on the whole front which broke through the last of the enemy defences and captured the Beaurevoir Line, to the rear of the Hindenburg Line, and the high ground above it, by 10 October. The Germans were forced to evacuate Cambrai and St Quentin and pull back to the river Selle. These three battles created a huge salient in the German position.

Fifth Battle of Ypres and Battles of Courtrai, Selle and Maubeuge

Meanwhile, further north, in the Fifth Battle of Ypres on 28 and 29 September, King Albert of Belgium's Army Group of twelve Belgian divisions, Plumer's Second Army (ten British divisions), and Degoutte's Sixth Army (six French divisions) forced the Germans back from Ypres and drove yet another salient into their lines, endangering the German position on the Belgian coast. In one day these armies swept over the ground that had taken two British armies, assisted by a French army, three months to capture the previous year.

Meanwhile Ludendorff, receiving news on 28 September of the Bulgarian request for an armistice, and after the Allied attack in Flanders had begun, suffered a temporary mental and physical collapse, a crisis of nerve in which he crashed to the floor and even foamed at the mouth. The succession of gloomy reports from the Western Front can hardly have helped. At 6 p.m. he told Hindenburg that an armistice was imperative. On the twenty-ninth, an armistice on the Macedonian front was signed with the defeated Bulgarians and the way was now open for an Allied attack from the south into Austria. Hindenburg, at a war council meeting, told the German leaders that, to prevent a catastrophe (this was the day the Hindenburg Line was broken), peace must be sought using Wilson's 'fourteen points' as a basis. Ludendorff now realized the game was up and, while he found six divisions to putty up the Serbian front, started to prepare the ground for peace proposals. On 3 October the Germans asked President Wilson for an immediate armistice.

Meanwhile the success at Ypres was extended by the Battle of Courtrai, from 14–31 October, which widened and deepened this wedge and resulted in the capture of Halluin, Menin and Courtrai. This series of great battles had, as their immediate result, in the south the evacuation of Laon and the German retirement to the river Aisne; in the centre the withdrawal to the river Scheldt, which

PREVIOUS PAGES
LEFT: *British Battles (8 Aug. to 11 Nov. 1918).* Widely distributed in the BEF this map, showing the battles of 'the Hundred Days', was printed in France after the Armistice by the 'Western Overseas Base' Printing Company, and was a record, a celebration and a souvenir.
RIGHT: 1:20,000 Barrage Map of the Le Cateau area, one of the last British actions of the war, on 17–19 October 1918, showing the attack of 13th Corps, with 5th Corps to the north and 2nd American Corps to the south. One of the war's many ironies was that, for the British, the fighting finished where it had started – in the Mons–Le Cateau area. Even in the last, mobile, phase of the war, it was possible to organize rapid and sophisticated artillery fireplans.
RIGHT: *German Order of Battle, Western Front, 11.11.18. 11.00,* at the moment of the Armistice. Scale: 1:1 million.

liberated Lille and the great industrial district of northern France around Roubaix and Tourcoing; and in the north the clearing of the Belgian coast, including the submarine bases of Ostend, Zeebrugge and Bruges. The Germans were now back on the line of the Scheldt and Selle rivers. The Battle of the Selle, from 17–25 October, forced the Germans from the latter and drove yet another wedge into their defences. Germany's remaining allies were now falling away; Turkey signed an armistice on 30 October, and Austria–Hungary did the same on 4 November, after which Germany was isolated.

The Battle of the Selle was followed by the final blow, the Battle of Maubeuge, from 1–11 November, which struck at and broke the Germans' last important lateral communications, turned their positions on the Scheldt and forced them to retreat rapidly from Courtrai. At the same time, the Americans attacked again, the French armies were cautiously moving forward (Foch was naturally unwilling for too much French blood to be spilled at this stage), and the British had not halted in their series of successful operations. This victory completed the achievement of the great strategic aim of the whole series of battles, by effectively dividing the German forces into two, one part on each side of the natural barrier of the Ardennes forest. The German fleet had mutinied on 29 October, while the German army, while it had been experiencing increasing indiscipline and desertion in the latter part of 1918, had been comprehensively defeated in the field. Revolution broke out in Berlin. The pursuit of the beaten enemy all along the line was only halted by the Armistice at 11 a.m. on 11 November. The Kaiser abdicated on 9 November, and the following day the desperate German authorities told their armistice delegation to accept any terms put in front of them. Fittingly, the Canadians entered Mons, where the BEF had fought its first battle in 1914, on the morning of the eleventh.

0419

SERIAL Nº 122

ENEMY ORDER OF BATTLE
WESTERN FRONT.
11. 11. 18.
11·00.

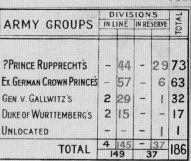

ARMY GROUPS	DIVISIONS				TOTAL
	IN LINE		IN RESERVE		
? PRINCE RUPPRECHT'S	–	44	–	29	73
EX. GERMAN CROWN PRINCE'S	–	57	–	6	63
GEN. V. GALLWITZ'S	2	29	–	1	32
DUKE OF WURTTEMBERG'S	2	15	–	–	17
UNLOCATED	–	1	–	–	1
TOTAL	4	145	–	37	186
	149		37		

German inf. divs. 182   1691 bns
German dism. cav. divs.   4   36

Total Enemy divs.   186   1727 bns

.... Line 21·3·18.
------- Limit of German advance.

1ˢᵗ Guard D. Fit division in line. } FIT
           Fresh division.

1ˢᵗ Ldw. D. Unfit Division in Line.
           Refitting Division.   UNFIT
           Tired Division, or of poor quality.

UNLOCATED
? 197ᵗʰ D.

HOLLAND

FOURTH (27)
(SIXT V. ARMIN)

? PRINCE
RUPPRECHT.

SIXTH (9)
(V. QUAST)

SEVENTEENTH (17)
(OTTO V. BELOW.)

SECOND (20)
(V. CARLOWITZ)

GHQ / SPA

EIGHTEENTH (23)
(V. HUTIER)

EX. GERMAN CROWN PRINCE.

SEVENTH (16)
(V. EBERHARDT)

FIRST (7)
(FRITZ V. BELOW)

THIRD (17)
(V. EINEM)

FIFTH (24)
(V. d MARWITZ)

v. GALLWITZ

C (8)
(FUCHS)

NINETEENTH (6)
(V. BOTHMER)

DUKE ALBRECHT OF
WURTTEMBERG.

'A' (4)
(V. MUDRA)

'B' (7)
(V. UNDELL)

	ARMY	IN LINE		RESERVE		TOTAL
? Prince Rupprecht	FOURTH ARMY	–	13	–	14	27
	SIXTH "	–	8	–	1	9
	SEVENTEENTH "	–	11	–	6	17
	SECOND "	–	12	–	8	20
Ex. German Crown Prince	EIGHTEENTH "	–	19	–	4	23
	SEVENTH "	–	16	–	–	16
	FIRST "	–	7	–	–	7
	THIRD "	–	15	–	2	17
Duke Albrecht V. Gallwitz	FIFTH "	1	22	–	1	24
	'C' DETACHMENT	1	7	–	–	8
	NINETEENTH ARMY	2	4	–	–	6
	'A' DETACHMENT	–	4	–	–	4
	'B' DETACHMENT	–	7	–	–	7
	UNLOCATED	–	–	–	1	1
		4	145	–	37	
	TOTALS	149		37		186

TOTAL FIT DIVS.   4
TOTAL UNFIT DIVS.   182
TOTAL DIVS.   186

There are 16 Landwehr divisions and 11 other German divisions of poor quality
in the Western Theatre.

Printing Cᵒ R.E. W.O.B. 2393.

Scale 1:1,000,000 or 1·014 Inches to 16 Miles
Miles 10 5 0   10   20   30   40   50 Miles
Kilometres 10 5 0 10 20 30 40 50 60 70 80 90 100 Kilometres

International Boundaries
Railways Double
Single

Chapter 10

The Peace Treaties and their Aftermath

The Collapse of Empires and the Armistices

The end had come with dramatic suddenness, as empires collapsed under internal and external pressures. It took most of the Allied military leaders by surprise. Foch was preparing for a 1919 campaign, but the ever-optimistic Haig had perceived that Germany could be defeated in 1918, and so it proved. As far as the German, Austria–Hungary and Ottoman Empires were

BELOW: *The New Europe.* Supplement to *The National Review, December 1918*, prepared by George Philip & Son, the London Geographical Institute, which records the major boundary changes in Eastern Europe.

RIGHT: *The Allies' Occupation of the Rhineland.* Supplement to *The National Review, January 1919*, showing the Armistice Line and the three Rhine Bridgeheads, from north to south, British (Cologne), American (Coblenz) and French (Mainz).

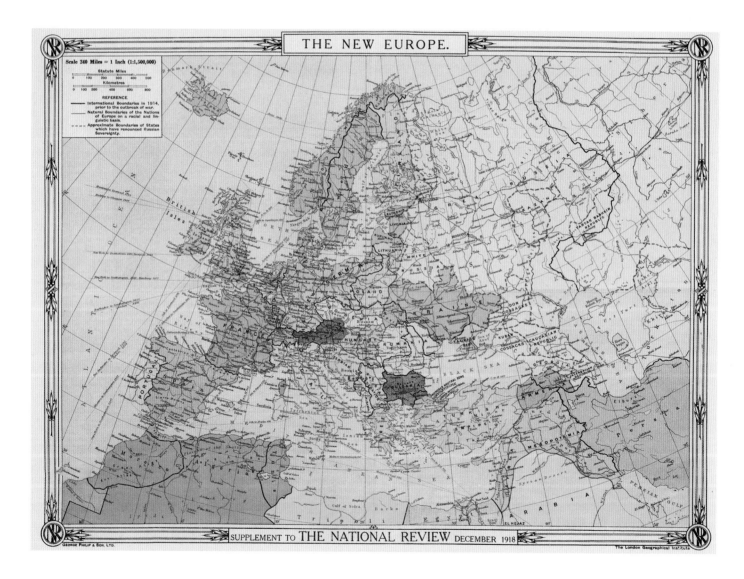

THE NEW EUROPE.

SUPPLEMENT TO THE NATIONAL REVIEW DECEMBER 1918

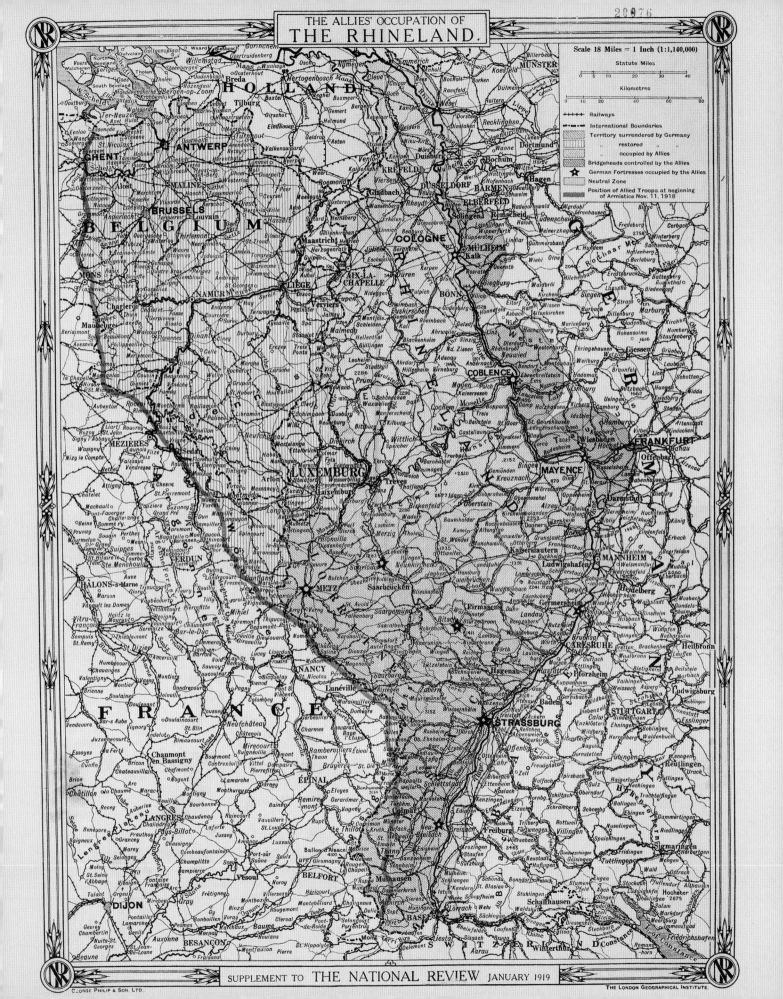

THE ALLIES' OCCUPATION OF
THE RHINELAND.

20076

Scale 18 Miles = 1 Inch (1:1,140,000)

Statute Miles

Kilometres

+++++ Railways

International Boundaries

Territory surrendered by Germany
restored
occupied by Allies

Bridgeheads controlled by the Allies

★ German Fortresses occupied by the Allies

Neutral Zone

Position of Allied Troops at beginning
of Armistice Nov. 11, 1918

GEORGE PHILIP & SON, Ltd.

THE LONDON GEOGRAPHICAL INSTITUTE.

BALKAN STATES illustrating the PEACE TERMS

65

REFERENCE (legend)

- ‑‑‑‑ Obsolete International Boundaries of 1914
- Territorial Acquisitions effected by the New Peace Treaties
  - By Rumania from Austria-Hungary
  - " " " Russia
  - Greece from Turkey
  - " " Bulgaria
  - Jugo-Slavia from Aust.-Hungary
  - " " " Bulgaria
- Internationalized Waterway

The Danube, internationalized below Ulm

Scale bar: Statute Miles / Kilometres — Railways — Steamer Routes — Canals — Heights in feet

DISTANCES AND TIMES BY TRAIN

From	Stat. Miles	Hrs. min
Athens to Salonica	322	19.30
" Patras	138	7.10
Belgrade to Constantinople	658	29.27
" Salonica	407	20.12
" Sofia	251	10.0
Bucharest to Galatz	158	5.15
" Kustenje	141	4.12
" Sofia	284	12.40
Constantinople to Philippopolis	310	13.43
" Salonica	498	25.28
" Sofia	407	18.25
Salonica to Adrianople	342	18.10
Sofia to Adrianople	208	9.30
" Varna	335	13.52

STEAMSHIP LINES TO BALKAN STATES.

To	From	Transit in days
Athens	Alexandria	2
	Brindisi	2½
	Genoa	4
	Liverpool	9
	Marseilles	4
	Naples	2½
	Venice	4
Constantinople	Alexandria	2½
	Batum	2½
	Brindisi	4
	Galatz	2
	Genoa	7
	Kustenje	1
	Liverpool	10½
	Marseilles	6
	Naples	4½
	Odessa	1½
	Sebastopol	1¼
	Trieste	7
Kustenje	Odessa	¾
Patras	Trieste	2½
Salonica	Marseilles	7
	Trieste	10
Syra	Liverpool	11
	Marseilles	5½

CRETE (CANDIA)

On same scale as General Map

George Philip & Son, Ltd., The London Geographical Institute

concerned it was a true *Götterdämmerung*, a twilight of the gods, or in this case of the imperial demigods which headed these empires: Kaiser Wilhelm II, the Emperor Karl and the Sultan, and their whole, aristocratic and undemocratic systems. The age of populist nationalism and totalitarian dictatorship was about to begin.

The Armistice on 11 November ended the fighting between the Allies and Germany, the other 'Central Powers' having capitulated earlier: Bulgaria on 29 September, the Ottoman Empire on 30 October and Austria–Hungary on 3 November. The Armistice terms were designed to prevent the Germans from restarting the war. They were given two weeks to evacuate the occupied territories of Belgium and France, Luxemburg and Alsace-Lorraine, and a month to withdraw from all Germany west of the Rhine, as well as from five large bridgeheads on the east bank. All prisoners of war were to be released, and the Germans were to hand over 5,000 guns and howitzers, 25,000 machine guns, 1,700 aeroplanes, 5,000 motor lorries, 5,000 railway locomotives and 150,000 railway wagons. In addition, all Germany's submarines and capital ships, and most of the rest of her navy, were to be surrendered. Despite the volatile situation in the East, all German troops were to withdraw from the occupied territories from the Baltic to the Caucasus, giving the Allies free access to those areas. Clearly the Allies had in mind the continuation of support for anti-Bolshevik forces. The Russian Civil War, between the Whites and the Reds, had already begun, as had Allied intervention (operation *Syren* – the Murmansk task force) on 2 August. Now the Allies had to hold a peace conference, to arrive at a Peace Treaty that would, like the Armistice terms, effectively be forced on Germany and her allies.

Urgent action was imperative. Europe was being ravaged by the influenza epidemic, with chaos and hunger resulting from the collapse of the Habsburg and Romanov Empires and the Allied blockade, and in other places disorder, revolution or civil war. Meanwhile the blockade continued.

British and French politicians and statesmen, aided and abetted by sections of the press, had whipped up popular enthusiasm for punitive reparations, calling for Germany to be 'squeezed until the pips squeak', to pay for the cost of the war (however that might be calculated). But the USA's President Wilson was an austere and idealistic liberal far detached from European realities. His country had only entered the war in April 1917,

and had only seriously been engaged in land operations in the last six months. Not unreasonably, his main preoccupation was with creating a global organization, the League of Nations, to prevent future wars.

At Versailles, outside Paris, representatives of all the victorious powers were present, including those, such as various South American states, that had only declared war at a late stage in the hope of picking up some crumbs. The actual hammering out of the peace terms, however, was left to the Great Powers on whom the brunt had fallen. As Japan was only concerned with the Far East, and Italy had withdrawn in a sulk because the three main powers – France, Britain and the USA – refused to support her rapacious demands, it was these powers, in the persons of the Prime Ministers Clemenceau and Lloyd George, and President Wilson, who shouldered the responsibility of framing the terms. This evoked angry and bitter disagreements, particularly between Clemenceau and Lloyd George on the one hand and Wilson on the other. Inevitably the result was a compromise.

As the Austro-Hungarian Empire had disintegrated, one of the jobs of the peacemakers was to determine the frontiers of the new states covering her former territories. Here Wilson's eminently reasonable principle of national 'self-determination' ran up against the harsh realities of centuries of European ethnic rivalries, conflicts and claims. In areas where there were multi-ethnic populations, often with different languages and religions, and where old and defensible frontiers refused to correspond to language boundaries, the task was almost impossible, particularly in the Balkans. As a result, the number of separate states rose from twenty-one to twenty-six. There were fewer great powers but more, smaller and weaker states, which soon began to form defensive alliances against Soviet Russia and Germany. This did not augur well for the future success of Wilson's League of Nations. Under Hitler, Germany would disingenuously use Wilson's principle of nationality to absorb Austria in the *Anschluss* and rebuild her empire, creating the Third Reich.

The Germans were treated in such a punitive way that their resentments sowed the seeds of the next war. Her military, naval and air power were minimized, and France made sure that the Rhineland, a thirty-mile wide band of territory east of the Rhine, was demilitarized, thus leaving Germany's western frontier open to any French intervention. Similar disarming was forced on the other defeated states.

Bolshevik Russia, even though engaged in a savage civil war, appeared as an incalculable but potentially powerful threat to the West's capitalist system and its business interests, and as a pariah outside the European system of diplomacy. States

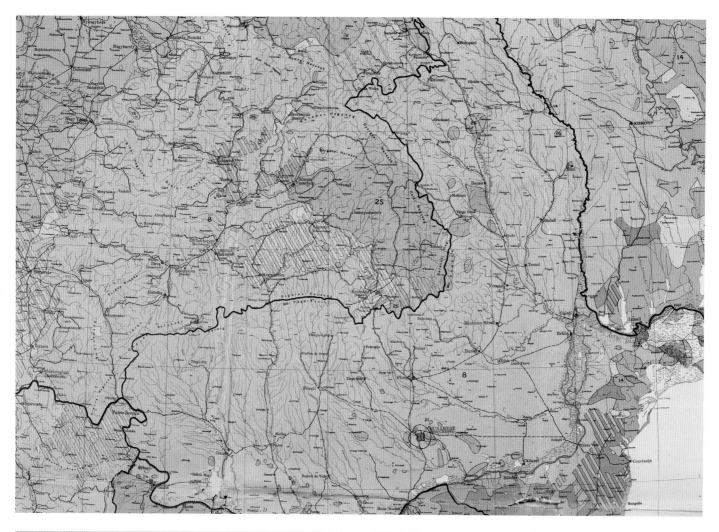

ABOVE AND RIGHT: Details from the *South East Europe Ethnographical Map*, drawn up by the Geographical Section General Staff, War Office, December 1918.

LEFT: On the back of the map is a manuscript annotation to the effect that this was one of several maps relating to the 'nationalities' question, used by British Military Intelligence, while preparing for the peace conference at Versailles.

who shared borders with her naturally felt threatened by this Red incubus, and built up strong armies that their neighbours in turn felt they had to match. While Germany lost territory, Wilson ensured that these losses were less than demanded by certain of the Allies. In the west, Alsace-Lorraine went to France, while in the east parts of Posnania (Posen) and Prussia went to the newly recreated Poland, which was formed from territory previously under the rule of Russia, Austria–Hungary and Germany.

The most destructive and portentous aspect of the peace settlement was the demand for reparations from Germany. As the brilliant economist John Maynard Keynes pointed out in his contemporary book *The Economic Consequences of the Peace*, which appeared in 1919, attempts to impose a 'Carthaginian peace' were self-defeating. Destroying Germany's capacity to wage a future war by confiscating German capital equipment (ships, machine tools, railway locomotives and rolling stock, etc.) or other resources such as coal or cattle, or to force Germany to pay gold,

which she did not have (and could only gain by exporting which required capital equipment), or to pay in goods, which would undermine the producers of the receiving countries, would be counter-productive and destroy Germany's ability to pay reparations in any case. A modern equivalent is the futile attempt to correct huge public-sector deficits by cutting public spending, which has the effect of deflating economies, reducing tax revenues, and making the situation worse. Keynes, who represented the British Treasury at the Peace Conference, was not able to prevent huge reparations sums being demanded, but in actuality the sums were continually renegotiated and reduced over the next decade, and eventually written off.

Plebiscites, or referendums, were held in some areas to assess the feeling of those populations where it was uncertain, while in other disputed areas, such as Danzig and the Saar Basin, the League of Nations was given the role of administering certain German-speaking districts. The Saar, north of Lorraine, was a coal-

mining area claimed by France, while Danzig represented Poland's access to the Baltic and therefore to world trade. A 'Polish corridor' was created linking Danzig with Poland, to provide a communications route. The Germans lost Eupen and Malmédy to Belgium, and North Schleswig to Denmark.

Although the peace treaties are generally collectively known as the Treaty of Versailles, there were actually several treaties reflecting the fact that the Allies had to make peace with several different enemies. The Treaty of Versailles, with Germany, was signed on 28 June 1919, of St Germain with Austria on 10 September and of Neuilly with Bulgaria on 27 November. Two more treaties followed in 1920: Trianon with Hungary on 4 June, and Sèvres with Turkey on 10 August.

A new state of Czechoslovakia was formed for the Czechs and Slovaks from parts of the former Austro-Hungarian Empire; Bohemia and Moravia had, under Austrian rule, been Czech-speaking industrial areas, while rural Slovakia had been part of

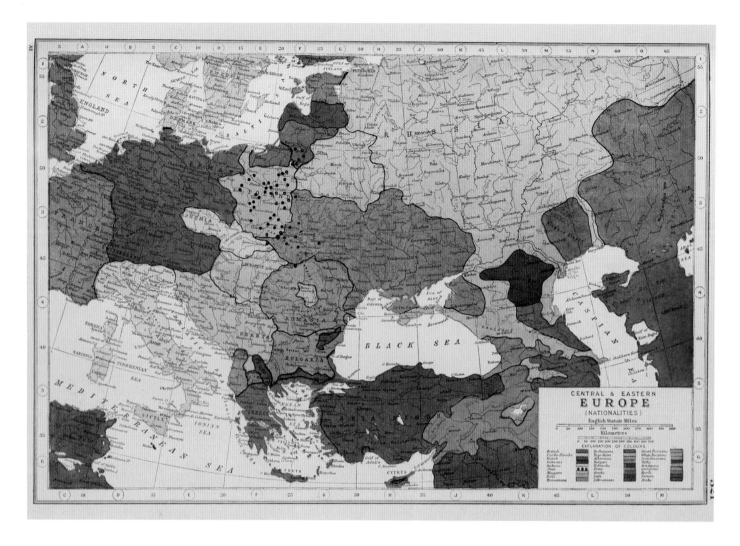

Hungary. In the Balkans, the new southern Slav state of Jugoslavia was created from Serb, Croat and Slovene areas of former Austro-Hungarian territory, and the former Serbia and Montenegro. Rumania gained Transylvania and the Bukovina from the former Austria–Hungary, and Bessarabia from Russia. Italy gained South Tyrol and Istria from Austria. In the north, the former Russian territories of Finland, Estonia, Latvia and Lithuania were made independent states. The pariah, Bolshevik Russia, was not represented at the Peace Conference and, fighting a bitter civil war, was in no position to argue when large chunks of former Russian territory were disposed of by the Allies.

The peace treaty with the Ottoman Empire (the Treaty of Sèvres signed on 10 August 1920) was made with the Sultan's government. This was soon replaced by a Turkish nationalist government under Mustafa Kemal (later restyled as Kemal Atatürk), and the treaty became a dead letter. However, the Arabian territories that had

gained their freedom from the Ottomans, either as independent states (Arabia) or as British or French 'mandates' under League of Nations supervision, retained their new status. These were Palestine, Transjordan, Mesopotamia (Iraq) in the case of Britain, and Syria and Lebanon in the case of France. The intention of the mandate system was that former colonies should be run in trust for their inhabitants, rather than as an extension of the colonial system or merely as military bases.

Further north, however, the original Allied intention to expel Turkey from Europe altogether and leave tracts of Asia

ABOVE: *Central & Eastern Europe – Nationalities*, from *Harmsworth's New Atlas of the World*, c.1920.

RIGHT: *Germany, Illustrating Peace Terms*, from *Harmsworth's New Atlas of the World*, c.1920.

Minor under Greek, French or Italian administration, proved impossible. Greece claimed former Ottoman territory in Thrace, and also an area of Asia Minor around Smyrna (Izmir) where there was a significant Greek population. A war ensued between Turkey and Greece. The Turks, who had amply demonstrated their fighting qualities at Gallipoli and in other theatres, would not stand for it. They defeated a Greek army in Asia Minor, and forced its evacuation, and the former Allies were too war-weary to attempt to enforce their will. Turkey, therefore, was able to create a modern state that included the whole of Asia Minor and also Eastern Thrace. A prohibition on the fortification of the Straits (the Dardanelles), however, continued until 1936. The

example of Turkey was not an encouraging demonstration of the effectiveness of the new international settlement.

Germany lost all her overseas Empire, the territories of which were awarded to victorious states as mandates. They covered the former German colonies in Africa, which became British and French Togoland, British Cameroons and French Cameroun, Ruanda-Urundi (Belgian mandate; part of German East Africa), Tanganyika (British mandate; part of German East Africa) and South-West Africa (South African mandate). In East Africa it took time for the news of the Armistice of 11 November to reach Lettow-Vorbeck who, with his 150 German soldiers and 1,200 native askaris, were still eluding British attempts to trap them.

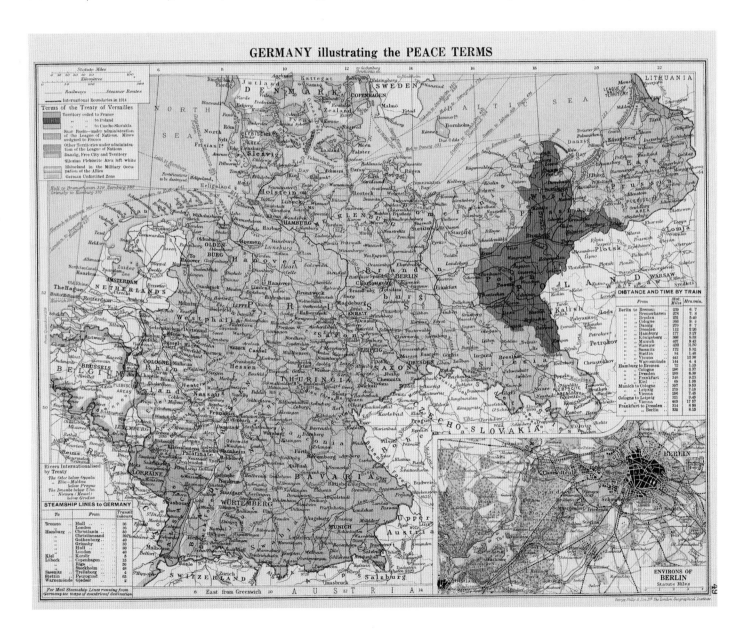

GERMANY illustrating the PEACE TERMS

Former German colonies in the Pacific were also covered by League of Nations mandates. The South Pacific Mandate was given to Japan, and covered several island groups whose modern names are Palau, the Northern Mariana Islands, the Federated States of Micronesia and the Marshall Islands. The Territory of New Guinea mandate was given to Australia, and covered the northeastern part of New Guinea and some outlying islands. The Nauru mandate was administered by Australia, New Zealand and the United Kingdom, while Western Samoa was a New Zealand mandate.

The peace negotiations and subsequent treaties considerably exercised the cartographers, and a special detachment of the Geographical Section of the British General Staff, and a Printing

RIGHT: Middle East Mandates awarded by the League of Nations after the war, showing Palestine and Mesopotamia (to Britain), Lebanon and Syria (to France), and also Smyrna and its hinterland to Greece, from *Harmsworth's New Atlas of the World*, c.1920.

BELOW: *The Danube Lands, illustrating Peace Terms*, from *Harmsworth's New Atlas of the World*, c.1920.

Section from the War Office, were sent to service the peace conference. New maps showing ethic and national divisions had to be drawn up to illustrate the various claims and counter-claims.

The peace treaties did not end the fighting in Europe. The Civil War in Russia continued, with alternating Red and White

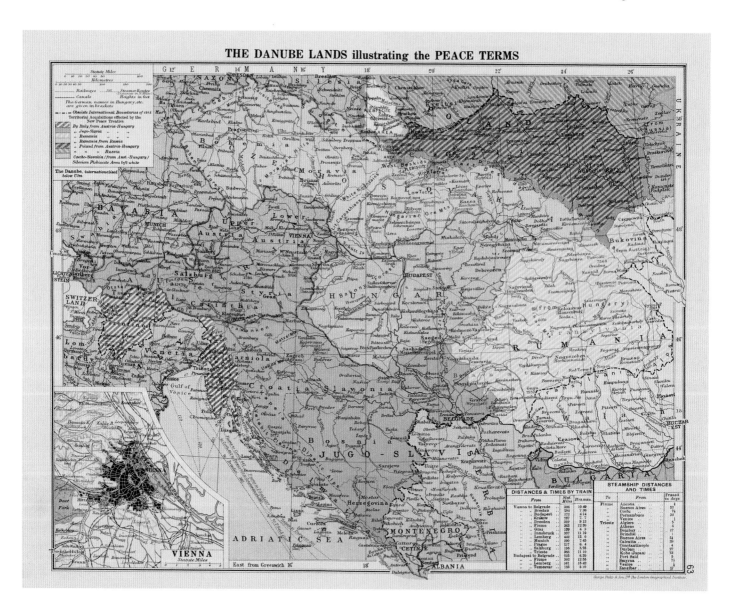

THE DANUBE LANDS illustrating the PEACE TERMS

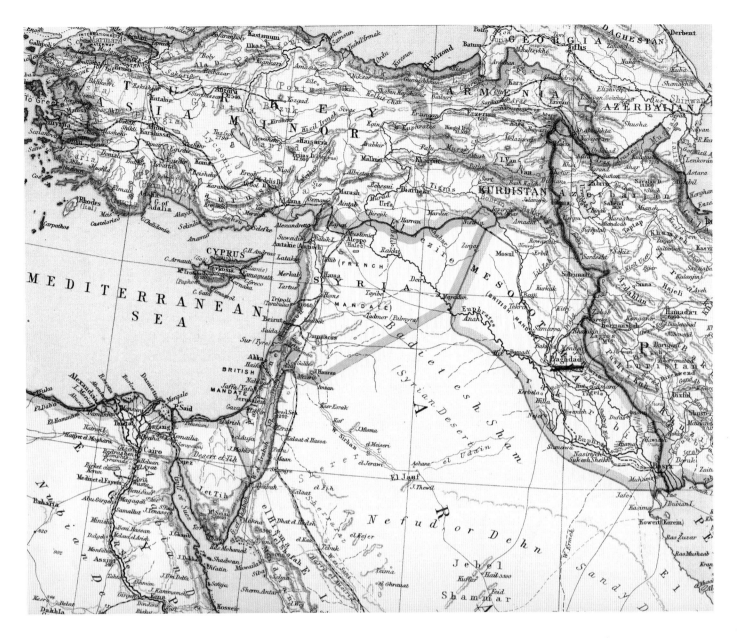

terrors in some localities. Allied intervention continued in Russia, but not on a large enough scale or with sufficient will for the Whites to defeat the Reds. Its legacy was to perpetuate anti-Western antagonism in Soviet Russia, and to confirm the Russian paranoid attitude to the West. Russia fought wars with Poland and Finland, and these again reinforced anti-Western bitterness and suspicion. A Bolshevik regime in Hungary was put down by Rumanian troops. A communist uprising in Germany was suppressed by ex-soldiers who enrolled in volunteer units, the *Freikorps*, who murdered the communist leaders Karl Liebknecht and Rosa Luxemburg on 15 January 1919.

Casualties

It had already become clear in conflicts in the nineteenth and early twentieth centuries that the combination of mass armies and modern firepower would involve horrendous casualties. That said, modern medicine and improved care reduced the proportion of casualties due to disease, and also the proportion of dead to wounded. In First World War battles, there were three or four wounded for every man killed. Gangrene, however, was still a terrible scourge, and it was not uncommon for even a minor wound to prove lethal. While the precise figures will never be known, total military and civilian casualties numbered over thirty-seven million. Perhaps seventeen million of these (ten million

AFRICA—HISTORICAL

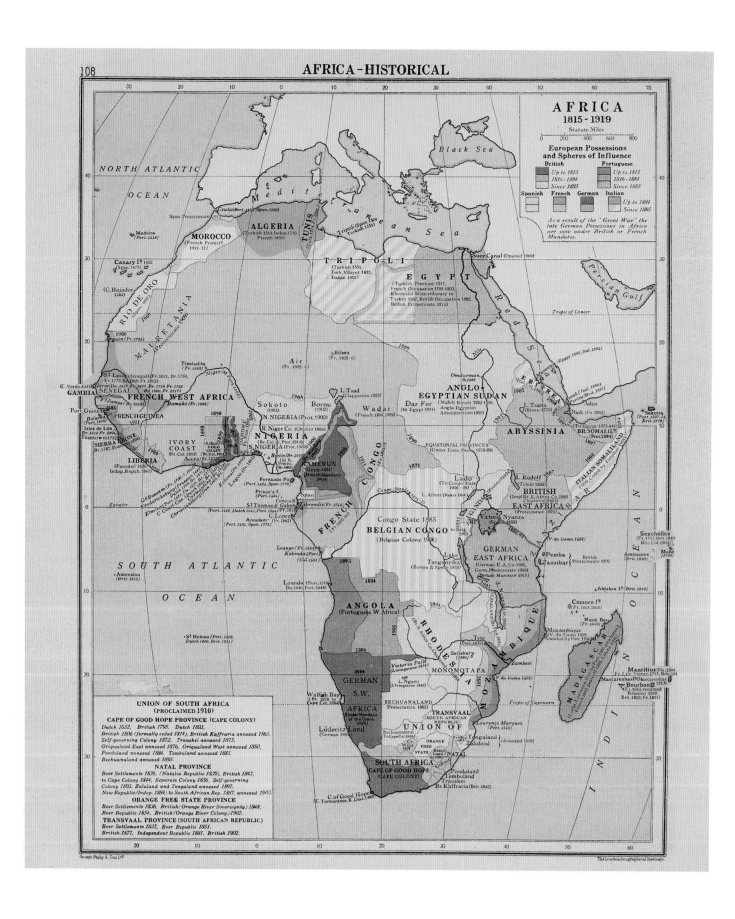

AFRICA
1815-1919

Statute Miles
0 200 400 600 800

European Possessions
and Spheres of Influence

British   Portuguese
Up to 1815   Up to 1815
1816 - 1884   1816 - 1884
Since 1885   Since 1885

Spanish   French   German   Italian
                                       Up to 1884
                                       Since 1885

As a result of the "Great War" the
late German Possessions in Africa
are now under British or French
Mandates.

UNION OF SOUTH AFRICA
(PROCLAIMED 1910)
CAPE OF GOOD HOPE PROVINCE (CAPE COLONY)
Dutch 1652, British 1795, Dutch 1803,
British 1806 (formally ceded 1814), British Kaffraria annexed 1865,
Self-governing Colony 1872, Transkei annexed 1875,
Griqualand East annexed 1876, Griqualand West annexed 1880,
Pondoland annexed 1884, Tembuland annexed 1885,
Bechuanaland annexed 1895.
NATAL PROVINCE
Boer Settlements 1836, (Natalia Republic 1839), British 1843,
to Cape Colony 1844, Separate Colony 1856, Self-governing
Colony 1893, Zululand and Tongaland annexed 1897,
New Republic/Indep. 1884/ to South African Rep. 1887, annexed 1903.
ORANGE FREE STATE PROVINCE
Boer Settlements 1836, British/ Orange River Sovereignty/ 1848,
Boer Republic 1854, British/Orange River Colony/1902.
TRANSVAAL PROVINCE (SOUTH AFRICAN REPUBLIC)
Boer Settlements 1837, Boer Republic 1851,
British 1877, Independent Republic 1881, British 1902.

George Philip & Son Ltd.

The London Geographical Institute.

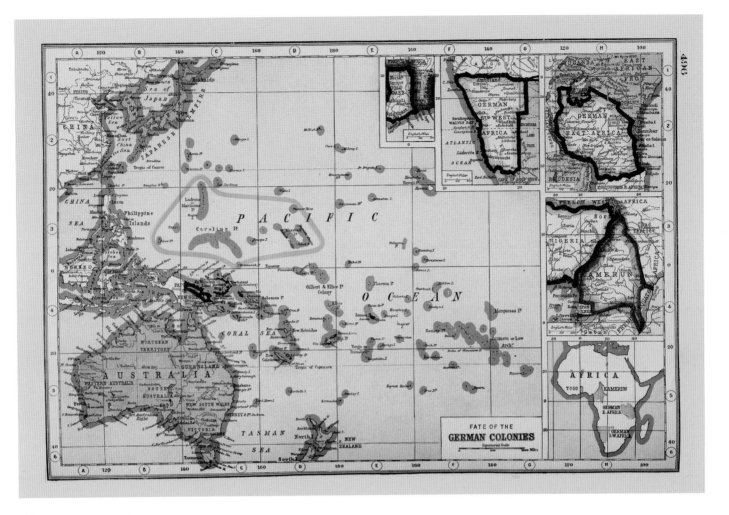

FATE OF THE
GERMAN COLONIES

military and seven million civilians) died and twenty million wounded. By contrast, the Second World War, which lasted longer (six years as opposed to four) proved far more lethal, with more than sixty million killed.

In the years 1914 to 1918, the Allies lost some six million dead (of which the British Empire total was over one million, with another two million wounded) and the Central Powers four million. Disease claimed another two million lives, while the 'missing' totalled six million. Most of the latter were, of course, battlefield deaths that were not witnessed, and for which the bodies were never identified among the countless corpses and

ABOVE: *The Fate of the German Colonies*, from *Harmsworth's New Atlas of the World*, c.1920.
LEFT: *Africa – Historical*, showing colonies, from *Harmsworth's New Atlas of the World*, c.1920.

mangled remains ploughed into the battlefield. They are still turning up, as the author has several times witnessed and, very occasionally, can be identified. During and after the war, the Graves Registration units and the Imperial War Graves Commission searched the battlefields and created 'body count' maps of the battlefields. Many temporary wartime cemeteries and marked burials had been destroyed by shellfire and lost, while many other men had been killed or wounded and sunk into the mud. Others had been hurriedly tipped into a shell hole, and their remains eventually melted into the landscape. Yet more were simply blown to pieces. The fighting areas were searched and, if found, bodies were transferred to military cemeteries.

The epidemic of Spanish influenza, which raged in and after the last year of the war, claimed three million soldiers, sailors and airmen of all belligerents. It has been estimated that worldwide 500 million people caught influenza, of whom some seventy-five million died, perhaps four per cent of global population at the time. This made it a bigger killer than the war, and one of the most lethal catastrophes in history.

The idea that 'The Great War' was 'the war to end all wars' soon turned out to be a hollow conceit. The Peace Treaties that ended the First World War contained within them, as Keynes had hinted, the seeds of the Second. These were in the form of anger and resentments at the 'Carthaginian Peace', at the scale of reparations, and of territorial, resource and population losses. To many historians, the Second World War was a continuation of the First – a matter of 'unfinished business'. Not only were a large proportion of the territories covered by the operations of 1914–18 also theatres of war in 1939–45 but, because the second conflict began only twenty years after Versailles, a remarkable number of statesmen, commanders and combatants in the Second had also served in the First. Adolf Hitler had been a corporal in a Bavarian infantry regiment on the Western Front in the First War. Junior and staff officers of the First War were the generals of the Second. There were also remarkable cases like Winston Churchill, a cabinet minister in the First War and a national leader in the Second. Or, in France, Pétain, who had commanded Second Army at Verdun, and later become French Commander-in-Chief in the First War and was 'Chief of State' of Vichy France in the Second.

Looking at the Middle East today, one might be forgiven for concluding that the legacy of Sykes–Picot, the Balfour Declaration and the taking-over, under the mandate system, of large parts of the Ottoman Empire, by Britain and France has not been entirely benign. Post-colonialism has continued in various forms, and the European powers, particularly Britain, seem reluctant to relinquish their former involvement in this part of the world. New forms of imperialism have also replaced the old. The USA extends its reach to this part of the world, as to others, and China has replaced European powers as a contender for Africa. Globally, economic imperialism and exploitation continues apace, with multi-national and trans-national corporations becoming the new imperialists, and resource wars appearing on the horizon. As the centenary of the First World War approaches, and the United Nations appears to be as unsuccessful in conflict-resolution as the League of Nations, we have avoided another major war since 1945, but mankind seems to love war so much that it lives in a Hobbesian state of continual conflict.

RIGHT: British 1:40,000 sheet *28 Ypres*, showing the number of bodies collected after the war from each 500-yard map square, in this case in the Zonnebeke–Passchendaele area.

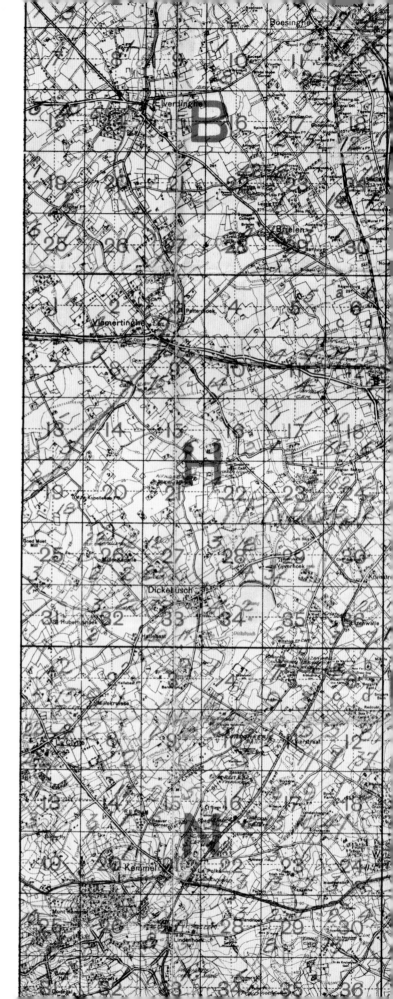

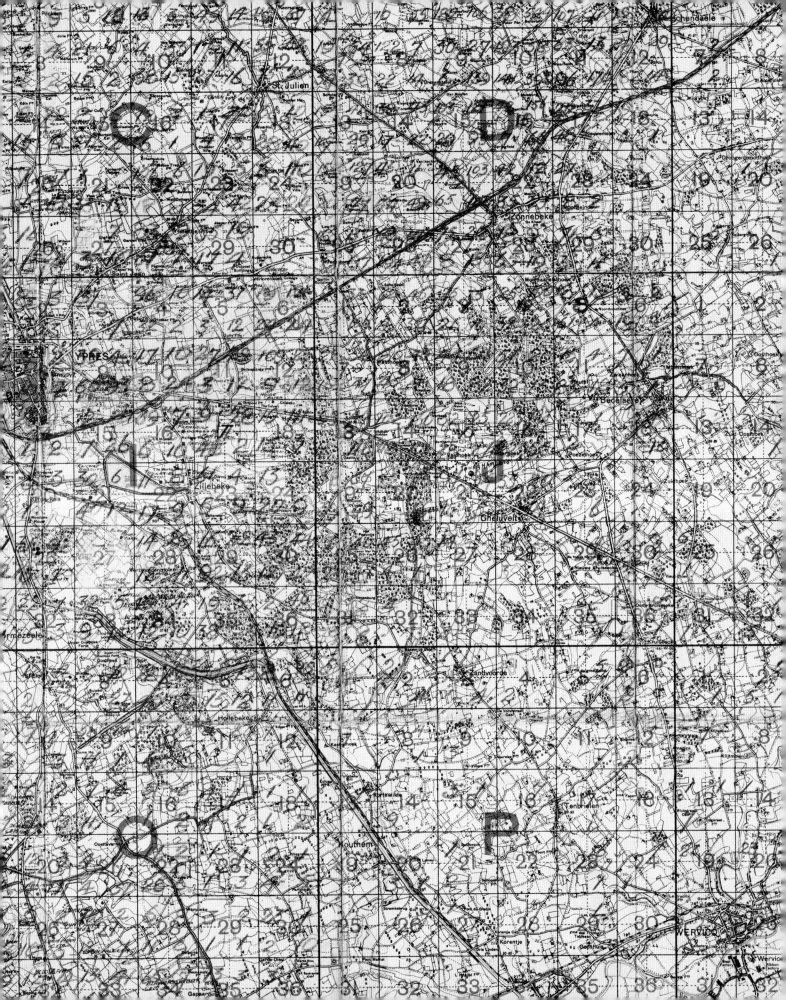

ABOVE: Cloth Hall, Ypres, Belgium just before the first bombardment by the Germans during the First Battle of Ypres, October 1914.
BELOW: The immediate aftermath of the first bombardment.
TOP RIGHT: Cloth Hall at the end of the war.
BOTTOM RIGHT: Cloth Hall today. Between 1920 and 1962, the hall was meticulously reconstructed to its pre-war condition.

Glossary

ANZAC Australia & New Zealand Army Corps.

Army Formation of two or more corps.

Army Group Formation of two or more armies.

Attrition Wearing down the enemy by inflicting casualties he can ill-afford.

Barrage Literally barrier, of shells. Types were standing, lifting, rolling, creeping, protective, etc.

Battery Artillery unit, of four to eight guns (field), or one to four guns (heavy).

Bearing picket Trigonometrically fixed point from which line-of-fire can be taken to the dial sight of a gun.

Bombardment Artillery preparation or counter-preparation.

Brigade Tactical formation of three or four battalions in the British service.

Casualties A total which includes killed, wounded and missing (including prisoners).

CIGS Chief of the Imperial General Staff (in London).

Citadel Old, castle-like, fortification.

Control point Trigonometrically fixed or other fixed point to which detail can be fitted.

Corps Formation of two or more divisions.

Counter-battery Neutralizing or destructive artillery fire directed against the enemy's battery positions.

Creeping barrage Artillery barrage starting in no man's land and moving slowly in front of advancing infantry, according to principle of fire and movement.

Defence-in-depth Organizing defensive positions in successive mutually supporting lines or checkerboard patterns to prevent an easy breakthrough.

Defilade Position hidden from view and fire, and therefore protected.

Dial sight Theodolite-like attachment to a gun which enables direction to be set.

Division Smallest all-arm tactical formation, 10,000–20,000 men, plus artillery, etc.

Enfilade Position which can be fired along, thus maximizing casualties and damage.

Flash-spotting Locating an enemy gun position by taking intersecting bearings onto the flash from surveyed points; also called cross-observation.

Formation Group of units or formations under a common command.

Fort Permanent fortification of masonry, concrete, etc., armed with guns.

Fortress System of interrelated forts, usually around a city and citadel.

FSC/FSB British Field Survey Company/Battalion.

GCT/GCTA *Groupe de canevas de tir/ Groupe de canevas de tir de l'armée* (survey and mapping unit).

GHQ British General Headquarters.

GQG *Grand Quartier Général* (French General Headquarters).

GSGS Geographical Section, General Staff, War Office.

Hachures Lines of hatching indicating ground forms on a map.

Howitzer High-angle, low velocity gun, suitable for bombarding forts, trenches, etc.

Lifting barrage Barrage which lifts directly from one trench mine to another.

MG Machine gun.

Mills bomb British hand grenade introduced in the autumn of 1915.

NCO Non-commissioned officer.

No man's land Contested space between the opposing front lines.

Oberost/OberOst *Oberbefehlshaber der gesamten Deutschen Streitkräfte im Osten* (German Eastern Front Headquarters).

OHL *Oberste Heeresleitung* (German Army Supreme Command).

OBOS Overseas Branch of the Ordnance Survey.

OS Ordnance Survey (Southampton).

Photogrammetry Measuring and plotting detail from photographs.

Plane-table A tripod-mounted horizontal board for graphic plotting of map detail, using an alidade (sight rule) and pencil.

Predicted fire Firing without prior registration of targets; enabled by precise survey of gun and target positions, and calculated sight adjustments for muzzle velocity, meteorological conditions and variations in projectile and propellant.

RAF Royal Air Force.

RE Royal Engineers.

Regiment Tactical formation of three battalions in continental armies.

RFA Royal Field Artillery.

RFC Royal Flying Corps (Royal Air Force from 1 April 1918).

RGA Royal Garrison Artillery (i.e. heavy and siege batteries).

RHA Royal Horse Artillery (light, to accompany cavalry).

Sap Short and/or shallow trench or tunnel.

Sheet (Map) Part of a map series covering a theatre, or even the whole world.

Shrapnel Shell filled with steel or lead balls, and a bursting charge.

Sound-ranging Locating an enemy gun by measuring the time intervals between the arrival of the sound wave at several carefully surveyed microphone positions.

Splinter Fragments of the casing of a high explosive shell.

Standing barrage A static barrage used to protect consolidating troops after an enemy position has been captured, or for any other reason.

Stavka Russian Supreme Command.

Stokes mortar British 'drainpipe' mortar, with firing pin at the base which the bomb/shell strikes when it is dropped down the tube.

T.C. The map series designation for Tigris Corps.

TM Trench mortar.

Unit Single-arm part of a formation, e.g., an infantry battalion.

Verm. Abtl. *Vermessungs Abteilung* (survey and mapping unit).

W.O. War Office (London).

Further Reading : List of Maps and Aerial Photographs

Further Reading

Chasseaud, Peter, *Topography of Armageddon, A British Trench Map Atlas of the Western Front 1914–1918*, Lewes: Mapbooks, 1991 and 1998.

Chasseaud, Peter, *Artillery's Astrologers – A History of British Survey and Mapping on the Western Front, 1914–1918*, Lewes: Mapbooks, 1999.

Chasseaud, Peter, 'German Maps and Survey on the Western Front, 1914–18,' *The Cartographic Journal*, 38(2): 119–134, 2001.

Chasseaud, Peter, 'British, French and German Mapping and Survey on the Western Front in the First World War', in Peter Doyle and Matthew R. Bennett (eds), *Fields of Battle – Terrain in Military History*, 171–204, Dordrecht, Netherlands: Kluwer Academic Publishers, 2002.

Chasseaud, Peter and Doyle, Peter, *Grasping Gallipoli – Terrain, Maps and Failure at the Dardanelles*, Staplehurst: Spellmount, 2005.

Collier, Peter, and Inkpen, Robert, 'Mapping Palestine and Mesopotamia in the First World War.' *The Cartographic Journal*, 38(2), 143–54, 2001.

Finnegan, Terrence J., *Shooting the Front: Allied Air Reconnaissance in the First World War*, Stroud: The History Press, 2011.

Gavish, Dov, *The Survey of Palestine Under the British Mandate, 1920–1948* (Routledge Studies in Middle Eastern History), London: Routledge, 2010.

Nolan, Col. M. A., 'Gallipoli – The Maps,' *The Gallipolian* (Journal of The Gallipoli Association), Part 1 Spring 1993 (71): 15–19, Part 2 Autumn 1993 (72): 1–24, Part 3 Winter 1993 (73): 6–20, Part 4 Spring 1994 (74): 10–24, Part 5 Winter 1994 (76): 11–25, Part 6 Spring 1995 (77): 17–31.

Services Historiques des Armées, *Du Paysage à la Carte – Trois siècles de cartographie militaire de la France*, Ministère de la Défense, Services Historiques des Armées: Vincennes (catalogue of an exhibition prepared under the direction of Marie-Anne de Villèle, Agnès Beylot and Alain Morgat), 2002.

Seymour, W. A. (ed.), *A History of the Ordnance Survey*, Folkestone: Dawson, 1980.

CD ROMs and DVDs

Various CD ROMs and DVDs of trench maps and maps from the British Official Histories have been produced by Naval & Military Press in association with the Imperial War Museum and the National Archives. The Western Front Association has also produced a series of DVDs of trench maps (including Gallipoli) in association with the Imperial War Museum.

List of Maps and Aerial Photographs

Key to references

BOV	Tank Museum, Bovington
IWM	Imperial War Museums
IWM/WFA	Imperial War Museum and Western Front Association*
NLS	National Library of Scotland
PHLC	Peter Chasseaud

*These maps are available on IWM/WFA DVDs

This list contains details of all the maps (and aerial photographs) that are reproduced in this book. Maps and photographs © as referenced. Words in italic indicate text taken directly from the map being described.

Index

Acknowledgements

The preparation of this book, including the selection of most of the maps and photographs, coincided with the closure for redevelopment of the Imperial War Museum. The Museum's reopening, with new exhibit space and special exhibitions, was planned to coincide with the First World War centenary commemorations. This closure, with its concomitant dislocations and restrictions of access for researchers, placed the museum's staff under a great deal of pressure, and I should like to record here my great appreciation of the gracious and friendly way in which they responded to my requests for access to the collections. In particular I should like to thank Jane Rosen, Mary Wilkinson and Fergus Read, and also Peter Taylor of the Publications Department and the staff of the Department of Photographs for dealing promptly with requests for large numbers of images.

With thanks also to the staff at HarperCollins Publishers; Mark Steward of Pixo Creative Services (www.pixocreative.com): project manager and map photographer; Christopher Riches (www.riches-edit.co.uk): managing editor; Richard Happer: editor; Michael Grossman (www.mg-grafik.com): designer;

Chris Fleet: map curator, National Library of Scotland; Stuart Wheeler: Librarian, Tank Museum, Bovington.

In addition I must pay tribute to those who have, over the years of my research into military survey and mapping, been so helpful and encouraging: Peter K. Clark, Dr Ian Mumford, Dr Yolande Hodson, Dr Roger Hellyer, Dr Dov Gavish, Dr Peter Collier, Francis Herbert, Dr Peter Doyle, Peter Barton, George Clout, David Nash, Colin Bruce, Col. (retd.) Mike Nolan RE, the late Col. Roderick MacLeod RA, Rose Mitchell, Tony Campbell, Peter Barber, Bob MacIntosh, Nick Millea, Georges Rachaine, Michel Bacchus, Claude Ponnou, Marie-Anne de Villèle, Bernd Nogli, Zdenek Krejci, the late Alan Sillitoe, Major-General David T. Zabecki, US Army (Retd.), Col. Terry Finnegan, USAF (Retd.) and many others whom lack of space precludes me from naming.

Dr Peter Chasseaud
July 2013

Photograph credits

Photographs © Imperial War Museums unless otherwise stated. The IWM reference number is given for each IWM photograph.

T/B picture located at the top/bottom half of the page
p10 Q 5817; **p13** PHLC; **p14** Peter Chasseaud; **p15** Peter Chasseaud; **p30** BFTM3G© The Art Archive / Alamy **p32** D9EAWX© War Archive / Alamy **p44** Q 83053; **p46** Q 53422; **p48T** Q 56307; **p49** Q 69527; **p50** Q 60744; **p52** Q 50719; **p61** Q 115126; **p64T** Q 45260/10549; **p64B** Q 65049; **p65** Q 07465; **p73T** Q 50468; **p77** Q 13828; **p79T** Q 13502; **p79B** Q 13428; **p81** Q 13340; **p85** Q 32634; **p86T** Q 52287; **p89** Q 31595; **p90** 15112; **p100** Q 45339; **p103** Q 13213c; **p105** Q 50855; **p106T** Q 12669/12760; **p106B** Q 19222; **p110B** Q 27574/12707; **p113** Q 107237; **p120** Q 59001; **p122T** Q 45777; **p122B** Q 45758; **p124** Q 49104; **p128T** Q 86849; **p129** Q 55044; **p131** Q 86781; **p132** HU 90418; **p133** 23532; **p134** Q 86702; **p140** Q 58509/14534; **p141** 11872; **p142** Q 50690; **p143** Q 60546; **p149** Q 69617; **p150** Q 69616; **p153** Q 17390; **p158** Q 23855; **p161** Q 86801; **p167** Q 78038; **p169** 20844;

p171 Q 23760; **p173** Q 754; **p177B** Q 3990; **p179** Q 49271/18500; **p180** Q 84; **p181** Q 3995; **p183B** Q 5576; **p186** Q 2041; **p189T** Q 22687; **p189B** Q 69359; **p193** Q 50992; **p195** Q 20220; **p197** Q 18121; **p199** Q 70605; **p203** Q 27459/12708; **p204** E(AUS)1178; **p205** Q 69650; **p209** Q 27468/14524; **p210** Q 58456; **p213** Q 61156; **p214B** Q 122033; **p216** Q 52228; **p219** Q 69408; **p222** Q 27481/14523; **p223** Q 3580; **p224** Q 69623; **p232** IWM E(AUS) 1220; **p235** Q 5935; **p237T** E(AUS) 1409; **p237B** E(AUS) 1318; **p238** IWM 13735; **p239** IWM E(AUS) 4677; **p241** IWM E(AUS) 4644; **p244** Q 17757/12702; **p245** B5MRE4© akg-images / Alamy **p251** B5MRDW© akg-images / Alamy **p259** Q 56489; **p263** Q 69550; **p266** Q 50595/13418; **p271T** Q 72560; **p271B** Q 64697; **p294T** BFTKKT © The Art Archive / Alamy; **p294B** BFNMYT © The Art Archive / Alamy; **p295T** © Bartholomew Archive held by National Library of Scotland: shelfmark: Acc.10222/Business Record/79; **p295B** AKG6HF © BRIAN HARRIS / Alamy

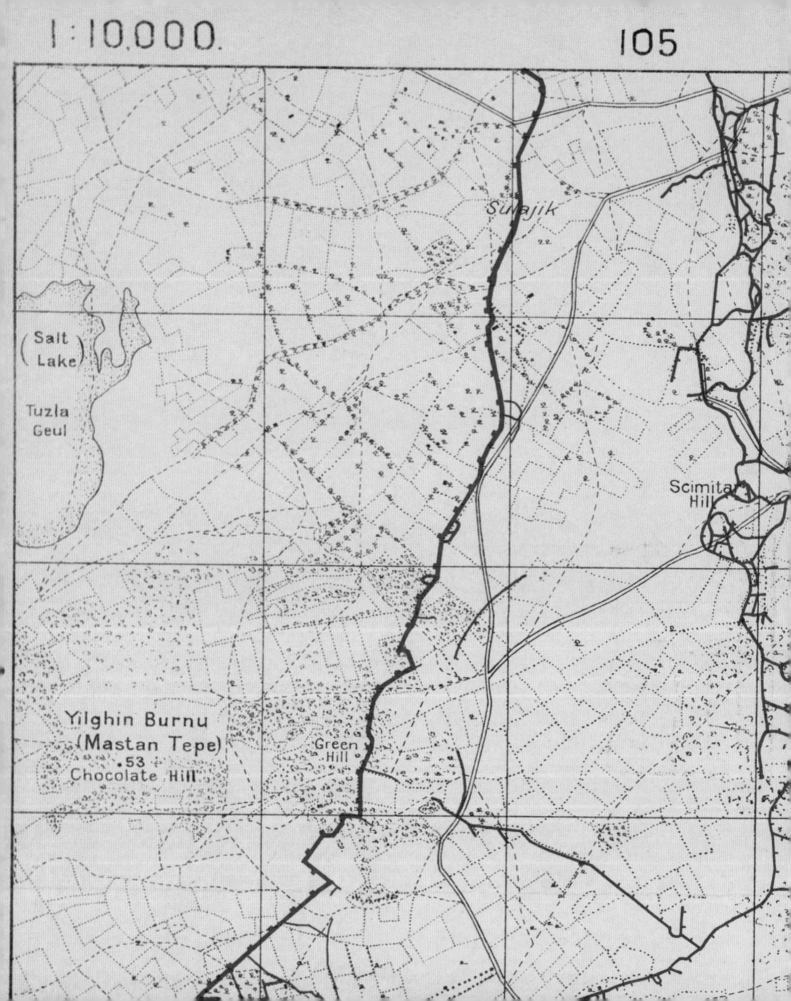

1:10,000.

105

Sulajik

Salt Lake

Tuzla Geul

Scimitar Hill

Yilghin Burnu
(Mastan Tepe)
.53
Chocolate Hill

Green Hill